The Defense of Moscow

The Defense of
of
Moscow

The Northern Flank

Jack Radey and Charles Sharp

Foreword by David M. Glantz

Pen & Sword
MILITARY

First published in Great Britain in 2012 by
Pen & Sword Military
an imprint of
Pen & Sword Books Ltd
47 Church Street
Barnsley
South Yorkshire
S70 2AS

ISBN 978 1 78159 070 6

Typeset in Ehrhardt by Phoenix Typesetting, Auldgirth, Dumfriesshire

Printed and bound in England by the MPG Books Group

Pen & Sword Books Ltd incorporates the Imprints of Pen & Sword Aviation,
Pen & Sword Family History, Pen & Sword Maritime, Pen & Sword Military,
Pen & Sword Discovery, Wharncliffe Local History, Wharncliffe True Crime,
Wharncliffe Transport, Pen & Sword Select, Pen & Sword Military Classics,
Leo Cooper, The Praetorian Press, Remember When, Seaforth Publishing and
Frontline Publishing

For a complete list of Pen & Sword titles please contact
PEN & SWORD BOOKS LIMITED
47 Church Street, Barnsley, South Yorkshire, S70 2AS, England
E-mail: enquiries@pen-and-sword.co.uk
Website: www.pen-and-sword.co.uk

Contents

Foreword

By David M. Glantz

The Soviet–German War (1941–1945), known in the West as Hitler's War on Germany's Eastern Front during World War II, and to Russians as 'The Great Patriotic War,' stands like a colossus astride the history of the twentieth century. The vast scale of the war, coupled with its unmatched ferocity and the human and material carnage it produced, has challenged the descriptive power of historians who have written about it and tested the imagination of readers who have attempted to comprehend it. Many past histories of the war have added to this confusion because they were marred by Cold War biases, the self-serving recollections of participants in the war, or, as was the case with many of the hundreds of histories written in the Soviet Union, appreciations designed to bolster the superiority of a political, economic and social system. Whatever the cause, these histories are replete with myth, legend, and outright inaccuracies, which have not only obscured or utterly concealed large segments of the war from the reader's view but have also perverted accounts of those portions of the wartime narrative relatively well known to contemporary readers.

Thankfully, however, the fading of the Cold War fears and animosities, coupled with the death of most participants in the war and the waning of ideological struggles characterizing the postwar years, has been accompanied by unprecedented releases of documentary materials from the once-locked archives of the Soviet Union. Today, by exploiting these new materials and re-examining documents from archives long-open but poorly exploited, a new generation of historians is slowly lifting the veil of inaccuracy and misunderstanding that has cloaked and obscured our understanding of the war. This new book by Jack Radey and Charles Sharp stands at the forefront of this vitally important process.

The Defense of Moscow: the Northern Flank is revisionist history at its best. It describes but a single aspect of the famous battle for Moscow, which, together with Stalingrad, Kursk and Berlin, is familiar to even the most casual readers of the histories of the war. This book demolishes myths and legends, replacing them with fresh and accurate insights as to how this battle, long famous as the first defeat suffered by Hitler's vaunted *Wehrmacht,* was actually fought and won by the soldiers and commanders of Stalin's Red Army. Without 'stealing the thunder' of Radey's and Sharp's book, by unearthing, exploiting, and studying newly released archival materials, the two historians clearly demonstrate why and how the battle for Kalinin was fought. In the process, their study has shown how this fight, which historians have long treated as a mere 'side-show' to the culminating stage of Operation Barbarossa, was, in reality, an important element in the German High Command's strategy for defeating the Red Army, capturing Moscow, and, ultimately, winning the war.

By skillfully exploiting newly released and long-neglected archival materials, the authors of this clear, concise, and well-written book have provided not only fresh insights as to how and why the battle for Moscow was fought, but also the necessary context for understanding why Germany ultimately lost the war. It is a 'must read' for historian and layman alike. I hope this is but the first of many books penned by these historians.

David M. Glantz, Carlisle, PA

Authors' Notes

Two issues confront a historian in any exploration of the 'Great Patriotic War,' as the Soviets referred to it. The first is finding appropriate maps, and the second is language. We'll take them in order.

Maps

The Germans went to war not only without a good intelligence picture of their opponents (they underestimated the Red Army by a factor of three, and totally misunderstood the Soviet ability to mobilize resources), but also without adequate maps of the country they were to invade. Using outdated 1:300,000 scale maps, they found themselves operating with great difficulty and being regularly surprised by the terrain. While maps were captured in small batches during 1941, it was not until the capture of the headquarters of 2nd Shock Army in 1942 that the Germans acquired a full, up-to-date map set of the western USSR. The Soviets, who by doctrine had assumed they would be fighting on their opponents' soil, lacked much in the way of good maps for the territory they had acquired in 1939, and were only 'on the map' once they were pushed back into the pre-war USSR territory.

A modern historian has to deal with trying to find maps that roughly date from the period to be studied. The best complete set of maps available to most readers is the US Army set of 1:250,000 maps issued in 1954. Fortunately these can be accessed online at http://www.lib.utexas.edu/maps/ams/eastern_europe/ thanks to the University of Texas. The maps are not complete; some villages are not named, and some have different names than were used at the time. Other villages were destroyed during the war, and there is some new construction shown on the maps that was not there during the war. Nonetheless, these are the most useful. Other sources that can supplement them include a collection of aerial photographs taken by the *Luftwaffe* during the war. They can be found at http://www.wwii-photos-maps.com/ under the heading 'target dossiers.' Some libraries have collections of maps at other scales that were captured from the Soviets by the Germans, and then captured by the American or British Armies during the war.

Language

Translating German presents relatively few challenges. At least the alphabet is pretty much the same. Russian, on the other hand, is written in Cyrillic. There are at least four different ways to transliterate Cyrillic into English. Is it Tsar Alexander or Czar Aleksander? General Rokossovsky or General Rokossovskii? Josef Stalin or Iosef Stalin? The system that is most familiar to the principal author of this work is the old-fashioned one used by Progress Publishers, the Soviet outlet for English translations of works in Russian. Consequently this one was used pretty much throughout the book. The principal researcher, on the other hand, learned a method used by the US Army in the early 1950s, which has since been superceded by yet another one. The Germans, naturally, transliterated Cyrillic names into German, producing yet another set of spellings, similar to the previous three, but different. The authors have made every attempt to be consistent throughout, but inconsistencies may remain.

Prologue

The staff of German Panzer Group 3's 1st Panzer Division were in a jubilant mood. Operation Typhoon, the climactic final German advance on Moscow during Adolf Hitler's invasion of the Soviet Union, had begun ten days before on October 2nd, 1941. Only five days after it began, the twin panzer pincers of German Army Group Center had snapped shut around the bulk of the Red Army's Western and Reserve Fronts in the Vyazma region, encircling the better part of five Soviet armies. 1st Panzer Division was part of XXXXI Motorized Corps, operating on Panzer Group 3's left (northern) flank.

By October 9th, 1941, the division had cut its way eastward from the Vyazma region to sever the Gzhatsk–Rzhev road and then had wheeled toward the north and northeast. The division had fought its way into Sychevka on the 10th and headed for Zubtsov, east of Rzhev, driving the remnants of the Soviet 247th Rifle Division before them. Brushing this obstacle aside, the panzers picked up speed, taking Zubtsov on October 11th and Staritsa on the Volga by the afternoon of the 12th. They had reached operational space and it was like the heady days of late June all over again.

As usual, Major Dr. J. Eckinger was leading the way. He commanded an advanced detachment (*vorausabteilung*), an ad hoc combat group built around his own 1st Battalion, 113th Motorized Infantry Regiment (I/113 Motorized Infantry Regiment), mounted in armored halftracks, reinforced with 3rd Tank Company of 1st Panzer Regiment, 2nd Engineer Company of 37th Panzer Engineer Battalion riding in halftracks, and two artillery batteries. Against no opposition, the column pulled out just after sundown at 1700 hours on October 12th and headed up the road to Kalinin. It soon began overtaking and destroying columns of Soviet transport and supply units retreating up the same road towards Kalinin.

The panzer division staff, tongue-in-cheek, radioed back to Colonel Hans Röttiger, Chief of Staff of XXXXI Motorized Corps that, 'Russian units, although not included in our march tables, are attempting continuously to share our road space, and thus are partly responsible for the delay in our advance on Kalinin. Please advise what to do.' Corps, in the same giddy mood, answered, 'As usual, 1st Panzer Division has priority along the route of advance. Reinforce traffic control!'[1]

It all seemed like a joke. It appeared that the Red Army was done and there was nothing to stop the *Wehrmacht*. Moscow would soon be theirs, and the war would be over. Less than a week later, by October 18th, Major Eckinger would be dead and the division would be fighting for its life.

1

Chapter 1

Background

Barbarossa

When Germany invaded the Soviet Union in June of 1941, the cutting edge of its attack comprised four panzer groups, numbered 1, 2, 3, and 4. These were army-sized organizations made up of motorized corps (often referred to as panzer corps, but this designation did not come into official use until 1942), each consisting of one or two panzer divisions and one or two motorized infantry divisions plus supporting artillery, engineers, antiaircraft and other elements. Army Group South deployed Panzer Group 1 in southern Poland and would attack south of the Pripet Marshes towards Kiev.

Army Group Center contained two of the panzer groups: Panzer Group 2 under General Heinz Guderian that attacked just north of the Pripet Marshes, and Panzer Group 3 led by General Hermann Hoth that struck north of and parallel to Guderian's group, acting as the northern pincer to Guderian's southern one. Jointly the two groups pinched off first the Soviet salient in the Bialystok area, then a larger bag at Minsk, and subsequently attempted to do the same at Smolensk in mid-July of 1941. This latter effort was only partly successful, being brought to a halt by stubborn Soviet resistance and ferocious counterattacks and large-scale counterstrokes. It also proved impossible to continue offensive operations after a 450 mile advance without adequate logistical support.

The northernmost panzer group, General Hoepner's Panzer Group 4, was the smallest of the four. It was deployed in East Prussia to strike through the Baltic States and Pskov towards Leningrad. Like the other groups it overcame initial Soviet resistance near the border, smashed up the counterattacking Soviet mechanized corps, and exploited at speed until roughly mid-July. It then ran into the same counterattacks and logistics trouble that slowed and stopped the rest of the German advance.

With Army Group Center fought to a standstill around Smolensk, Guderian's Panzer Group 2 was ordered south, where it and von Kleist's Panzer Group 1 successfully encircled the Soviet Southwest Front in the Kiev area in September. At the same time, part of Hoth's Panzer Group 3 was diverted north, along with General von Richthofen's VIII Air Corps, to reinforce Army Group North's drive on Leningrad. This reinforcement allowed Army Group North to break through to Lake Ladoga, cutting off Leningrad, and to reach the Volkhov River.

In September the Germans shuffled their panzer 'deck' preparing for the drive on Moscow called Operation Typhoon. Hoepner's Panzer Group 4's head-quarters was transferred from Army Group North to Army Group Center, and put into the line south of Smolensk, taking command of XXXXVI, LVII and the newly formed XXXX Motorized Corps. Panzer Group 3 now controlled the XXXXI and LVI Motorized Corps that had previously been under Panzer Group 4. Hoepner now had five panzer divisions (two of them fresh from Germany), while Hoth would have only three: the powerful 1st, and the 6th and 7th which were armed primarily with Czech tanks.

Operation Typhoon

The Battle of Kalinin took place in the context of Operation Typhoon, the offensive the *Wehrmacht* launched in late September and early October of 1941. The operation is usually understood to be a plan for seizing Moscow, but in fact its actual wording only went as far as directing an encirclement of the Soviet forces in front of Moscow, and their destruction. It was intended that further efforts towards Moscow would be directed once the initial objective was achieved. Three German panzer groups (Guderian's Panzer Group 2 had been dubbed 2nd Panzer Army) were to strike towards Moscow. Panzer Group 3 and Panzer Group 4 were to strike out from the northwest and west, respectively, on October 2nd, and Panzer Army Guderian was to strike from the southwest a few days earlier. Within days of unleashing their assaults, all three groups broke cleanly through the Soviet front line. By October 7th Panzer Groups 3 and 4 had surrounded most of the Soviet Western and Reserve Fronts' forces in a pocket west of Vyazma, while Guderian's forces cut up and partially surrounded those of the Bryansk Front further to the south.

Worse yet, it was days before the Soviet command even became fully aware of the penetrations. It was not until October 5th that the full magnitude of the disaster dawned on Moscow. At that point, not only were the overwhelming bulk of the Soviet forces defending Moscow nearly surrounded, but long German motorized columns had been spotted heading east. And there were no reserve armies available to stop them – only a small handful of divisions.

The most dramatic moment in the Second World War had arrived. Speculation and 'what if' scenarios are useless; as the famed historian S. L. A. Marshall put it, 'There is no telling what would have happened if what happened hadn't happened.' However, if one assumes that the Axis powers *ever* had an opportunity to win the war, it was in the middle of October 1941. *If* Hitler was to win the war, he had to knock out his most dangerous opponent on the continent of Europe, the USSR. It is not a given that the seizure of Moscow would have produced this result, but *if* there was any chance of defeating the Soviets, it could hardly be done without taking Moscow. There were only a few Red Army divisions standing between the surging Germans and Moscow, there were no reserve armies in place behind them (yet), and neither the rains and mud of late October nor the snow and bitter cold of winter had arrived yet. That the Germans never reached Moscow was due to a variety of factors, but one that must be recognized is the heroic stand of those units that were called upon to hold the roads to Moscow in mid October. 316th and 18th Rifle Divisions at Volokolamsk, 32nd Rifle Division at Borodino and Mozhaisk, Podolsk Officers' Schools at Maloyaroslavets, and others gave heroic evidence that the Red Army was far from finished. They succeeded in slowing the German advance until reinforcements could arrive from the far corners of the USSR and the fall rains coming at the end of the month could bring the German drive to a halt.

The Hitler Directive (Number 35) issued on September 6th, 1941, and the Army Group Center 'implementing orders' issued on September 16th for Operation *Taifun* (Typhoon, the attack on Moscow) do not even mention Kalinin.[2] According to the Operational Order, Panzer Group 3 was subordinated to 9th Army, and was supposed to break through north of the Smolensk–Vyazma–Moscow highway and, in cooperation with Panzer Group 4 to the south, to surround the enemy in the Vyazma area.[3] Although 9th Army was to 'use every opportunity to break through . . . and advance troops in the direction of Rzhev,' Torzhok (specifically) and all points north of Kalinin were north of the Army Group's area of operations.[4]

Therefore, the German troops that would become involved in the Battle of Kalinin initially attacked as part of the main Army Group Center assault to the east. These forces were commanded by the XXXXI Motorized Corps of Panzer Group 3, which initially consisted of 1st Panzer Division, 36th Motorized Division, 6th Infantry Division and 900th '*Lehr*' [Training] Brigade (Motorized). The corps had been given the assignment of protecting the northern flank of Panzer Group 3's drive. The initial German blow had torn through the Soviet 30th Army of Western Front, smashing its units and driving its headquarters, which had lost track of its troops, back to the Moscow Sea. This left two of Western Front's armies, the 22nd and 29th, north of the break-in and as a result they had not been surrounded in the Vyazma pocket.

On October 7th, the same day that the Soviet forces in and around Vyazma were encircled, the German Army's commander in chief, von Brauchitsch, met with the commander of Army Group Center (von Bock) and discussed changing the original plans. Specifically, while the Army Group advanced on Moscow with everything that could be spared from holding the encirclement ring, he proposed also advancing 9th Army and Hoth's Panzer Group 3 'in a northwestern direction' to clear the northern flank of Army Group Center.[5] The very next day the headquarters of the German Army, OKH, made it official with a directive to send Panzer Group 3 'in a general northern direction in order to destroy the enemy in the area between Belyi and Ostashkov.'[6] They were now directed against the flank and rear of the Soviet forces facing Army Group North's 16th Army, far outside the original direction of the attack on Moscow. Army Group Center's own directive to 9th Army followed on October 10th, sending Panzer Group 3 towards Kalinin and Staritsa.[7]

In other words, while Panzer Group 3 and 9th Army started Operation Typhoon as part of the advance on Moscow, by the second week of October both formations were directed in an entirely new operation, to strike to the north and then northwest, into the area of Army Group North's operations south of the Valdai Hills and almost directly away from Moscow!

Nor was this operation confined to Army Group Center. Army Group North had been preparing an attack with its one remaining mobile formation, XXXIX Motorized Corps (8th, 12th Panzer, 18th, 20th Motorized Divisions) in the direction of Tikhvin since the beginning of October.[8] After the first week in October, this attack was split in two: 8th Panzer and 18th Motorized Divisions were now to be directed southeast, not northeast, to cooperate with Army Group Center forces. This attack would not start before 16 October, however.[9]

On the same day that 1st Panzer Division would be fighting for Kalinin, October 14th, Army Group Center completed the chain of directives that would send 1st Panzer Division, and indeed most of Panzer Group 3, away from the Battle of Moscow. On that day the army group issued an order which started with the words, 'The enemy in front of the Army Group is defeated,' and went on to direct both 9th Army and Panzer Group 3 to the north. This move was intended to prevent the withdrawal of enemy forces facing 16th Army to the north by having Panzer Group 3 'reach the Torzhok area as soon as possible and advance without delay to Vyshniy Volochek.' This aimed to put 9th Army and Panzer Group 3 into the rear of Northwestern Front and of the 22nd and 29th Armies.[10]

It was in response to these orders and directives, representing a concept originating at OKH and OKW and therefore with the approval of the Fuhrer, that Panzer Group 3 and elements of Army Group North were sent plunging northwest and southwest, in an attempt to destroy the last intact Soviet Front between Lake Ladoga and Rostov. The objective was nothing less than the encirclement and destruction of seven armies; 22nd and 29th Armies of Western Front and the Northwestern Front's 11th, 27th, 34th Armies and Novgorod Army Group, and the *Stavka's* independent 52nd Army. The result would have been another gaping hole in the Soviet front, stretching over 300 kilometers (200 miles) from Kalinin on the Volga River to south of Chudovo on the Volkhov River. In space, it would have been larger than either the Smolensk or Vyazma encirclement battles, although it would have contained fewer Soviet troops, approximately 200,000 men.

The operation failed within a week, and so has been forgotten. As a result, the Battle of Kalinin is not seen, as it should be, as the defeat of a major German operation aimed at Northwestern Front, but instead as part of the initial phase of the Battle of Moscow. At the time the Soviet command regarded it as part of the Battle of Moscow, and was always very aware of the potential threat to the capital from an attack into the northern flank of Western Front from the Kalinin area. When Kalinin Front was established on 17 October, its mission included the task to 'liquidate . . . the enemy threat to encircle Moscow from the north.'[11] Thus, although German aims were actually in a different direction, the Soviet High Command at Kalinin was primarily concerned with the defense of Moscow.

Many aspects of the battle for Kalinin reflected common features of combat during the defensive phase of the Battle of Moscow; in particular, the Red Army's desperate improvisation, the lack of adequate resources on both sides of the line, the initial German euphoria turning to frustration, and the heavy fighting. But it also was unique in some ways. At Volokolamsk, Mozhaisk, Maloyaroslavets, Kaluga and Tula, for example, the German thrusts encountered stubborn Soviet defenses, and combat became basically frontal in nature. Kalinin, on the other hand, was a wide-open battle, with hanging flanks, surprise attacks, and sudden reversals of fortune. Here the Soviets counterattacked and in fact put together a serious and partly successful counterstroke, unlike everywhere else in the desperate battles of mid October. The results should have told the Germans something they needed to know, but the evidence was discounted, and the scales would not fall from their eyes until early December, by which time it would be far too late.

The Battlefield

Red Army General Staff studies of the war provide us with the following detailed assessment of the 'Characteristics of the Region of Military Operations:'

> The military operation along the Kalinin 'Direction' [axis] in 1941 took place in a region bounded by:
> – to the north: the Rybinsk, Bzhetsk, Akademicheskaya Station, and the northern shore of Lake Seliger line;
> – to the west: the western shore of Lake Seliger, Olenino, and Sychevka;
> – to the south: Sychevka and Dmitrov;
> – to the east; the Dmitrov, Rybinsk line.
>
> The region of military operations is part of the central Russian highlands, where most of the surface area is rugged and wooded. Of greatest operational-tactical significance is the Volga River and its tributaries – the Bolshoi Kosha and Malyi Kosha Rivers, the T'ma and the Tvertsa Rivers, and the basin of the Moscow Sea (south of Kalinin) into which discharges the Shosha and Lama Rivers.
>
> The Volga River is un-navigable between the cities of Selizharovo and Rzhev and, therefore, requires bridging to cross. In the sector from Rzhev to Kalinin, the river's width varies from 60 to 200 meters [196–656 feet],

with depths of up to two meters [6.5 feet]. There are permanent bridges at Staritsa and Kalinin. The railroad bridge at Rzhev was blown up on 11 October by retreating units of 31st Army.

The maximum width of the Bolshoi Kosha River is 40 meters [131 feet] and the Malyi Kosha, no more than 15 meters [49 feet]. Although most of the T'ma River is 10–30 meters [33–100 feet] wide, from the village of Strenovo to its mouth it is 60–80 meters [196–262 feet] wide and 1–2 meters [3.3–6.5 feet] deep. The banks of the Shosha, Lob' and Lama Rivers are characterized by marsh ridden valleys and present serious tactical obstacles.[12]

The most important terrain feature in the region is the Volga River, which describes an inverted broad, open U or V shape, flowing northeast from the Rzhev area, turning lazily east to pass through Kalinin, and then running southeast to the Moscow Sea and off to its long descent to Astrakhan on the Caspian Sea. Many smaller tributaries emptied into the Volga in the area, and there were many marshes and some peat bogs on both sides of the river.

The city of Kalinin stood at the apex of the Volga's northward curve. Named after the then President of the USSR, what had once been the Tsarist city of Tver was now a city of some 200,000 people in 1941.[13] It sat astride the rail line from Moscow to Leningrad and contained a number of factories and the Higher Pedagogical Institute. It was also a road hub, with major roads running southeast and southwest along the Volga to Rzhev and Klin, respectively, south to Volokolamsk, and across the Volga to the northwest to Torzhok and Vyshniy Volochek and north to Bzhetsk. The Volga flowed through Kalinin from west to east, and the Tvertsa River flowed from the northwest before taking a sharp turn to the south to empty into the Volga in the northeast part of the city.

There were three airfields serving the Kalinin area in 1941. The largest, featuring two hard surfaced runways, was just west of Migalovo, five kilometers [3 miles] west of Kalinin. Besides its all-weather runways, it boasted large fuel stocks, and a number of hangars and shelters for aircraft. There were two other smaller airstrips, with grass landing fields. One lay a kilometer south of the city, just west of the rail line, and the other was six kilometers north of the city, between the Tvertsa River and the town of Sofino (which served during the battle as Konev's advanced headquarters).

German Forces

9th Army, commanded by Colonel General Adolph Strauss, was deployed on the extreme northern wing of Army Group Center. On October 2nd, the day 9th Army began its advance, Strauss's army consisted of four army (infantry) corps (XXVII, V, VIII and XXIII) with fifteen infantry divisions, including one (the very weak 161st Infantry) in army reserve. Also loosely subordinate to 9th Army was Colonel General Hermann Hoth's Panzer Group 3, with two motorized corps (XXXXI and LVI) and, the strong VI Army Corps, with a total of three panzer divisions, two motorized infantry divisions, and three infantry divisions. Depending on the situation, the panzer group could be subordinate to 9th Army, or directly under the control of Army Group Center. Each corps had its own artillery, antiaircraft, and engineer battalions and other supporting elements. In addition, Army Group Center had 900th *Lehr* Brigade (Motorized) in reserve, which was soon committed to XXXXI Motorized Corps.

   Soon after Operation Typhoon began, on October 5th the German Army High Command (AOK) relieved General Hoth of command of Panzer Group 3 and sent him to command 17th Army in the Ukraine, replacing him with General of Panzer Troops Georg-Hans Reinhardt, the former commander of XXXXI Motorized Corps. Lieutenant General Otto Ottenbacher, the commander of 36th Infantry Division (Motorized), temporarily took over the corps (his division in turn was placed under the command of Major General Gollnick), only to be replaced by Lieutenant General Friedrich Kirchner on October 14th, when Ottenbacher's plane was forced down by Soviet fighters south of Kalinin and he was badly burned and evacuated to Germany.[14]

Most of the fighting in and around Kalinin was conducted by Ottenbacher's and Kirchner's XXXXI Motorized Corps, which was composed of the following units by the beginning of the battle (see Table 1):

Table 1:   The Composition of XXXXI Motorized Corps on October 2nd, 1941

1st Panzer, 36th Motorized, and 6th Infantry Divisions
900th *Lehr* Brigade
101st Panzer Battalion (*Panzer Abtielung 101*) (with flamethrower tanks)[15]
ARKO 30, a regimental-level artillery headquarters controlling:
   • 611th Heavy Artillery Battalion (with 10cm guns)
   • 620th Heavy Artillery Battalion (with 15cm guns)
   • II Battalion, 59th Artillery Regiment (*II/59 AR*) (with 15cm howitzers)
   • I Battalion, 51st *Nebelwerfer* Regiment (*I/51 Nebel*) (six-barreled 15cm rocket launchers)
10th Flak (*Flugabwehrkannon* – antiaircraft artillery) Regiment (command only) controlling:
   • 605th Flak Battalion (with 2cm self-propelled guns)
   • I Battalion, 29th Flak Regiment (I/29th Flak) (mixture of 8.8cm and 2cm antiaircraft guns)
616th Antitank Battalion (*Panzerjaeger I* self-propelled 47mm guns)*
52nd Pioneer (Engineer) Battalion
506th Bicycle Road Construction Battalion

Bridge Columns 36, 37 and 52
Communications elements and other assets[16]
*This unit was subsequently transferred to Panzer Group 4, and did not take part in the fight for Kalinin.

1st Panzer Division

1st Panzer Division, commanded by Major General Paul Krüger, had an unusual organization, but, in fact, variety was the rule among German panzer divisions. The division had begun Operation Barbarossa on June 22nd with 145 tanks, including 43 Pz II light tanks, 71 Pz III and 28 Pz IV medium tanks, and 11 command [*Panzerbefehlswagen*] tanks. In addition, there were 11–15 Pz I machinegun-armed light tanks assigned to the division's engineer battalion.[17] These combat vehicles were organized into a single panzer regiment (the 1st) with two battalions, each battalion having three panzer companies and a staff company.

Although it had fewer tanks than many of its sister divisions, 1st Panzer Division was blessed with more armored SdKfz 251 halftracks than any other division, enough to outfit two battalions, one in each *schutzen* (motorized infantry) regiment, and enough left over for its engineer battalion to have a company so equipped. Most panzer divisions only had a single *schutzen* company mounted in halftracks; a few had one battalion, but only 1st Panzer had two such battalions. In practice both of these battalions were used together during the battle. In addition to the halftracks, there were other extras, including a battery of self-propelled 150mm infantry guns, and 83rd *Luftwaffe* light flak battalion (reinforced with four 8.8cm AA guns) that functioned as part of the division.

The panzer division's infantry consisted of four battalions of *schutzen* organized into two regiments (1st and 113th *Schutzen*; later in the war these would be redesignated Panzer Grenadier [*panzergrenadier*]), with the first battalion of each regiment being mounted in halftracks and the second in trucks. In addition the division had a *kradschutzen* or motorcycle battalion. These *schutzen* battalions were so designated to distinguish them from ordinary infantry or motorized infantry which had only one light machinegun per squad, while the *schutzen* boasted two, effectively doubling their squad firepower. (I suspect this accounts for the common Soviet description of the infantry accompanying armored attacks in 1941 as 'submachine gunners.' The Germans had not issued large numbers of MP 38 submachine guns to their infantry in 1941, but the quantity of machineguns made a big impression on their opponents.) The division's artillery was the standard for a panzer division, one regiment (the 73rd) with two light battalions of 10.5cm howitzers and one medium battalion with two batteries of 15cm howitzers and one battery of 10cm guns. All were towed by unarmored halftracks.

1st Panzer Division had fought under XXXXI Motorized Corps' control since the beginning of Operation Barbarossa as part of Panzer Group 4, with Army

Group North during its drive to seize Leningrad. Its original commander, Lieutenant General Friedrich Kirchner, had been badly wounded in the fighting in the Luga River bridgehead in July, but was back with the division by October 10th, possibly as a supernumerary officer. Months of intense and costly fighting had taken a toll of the division's soldiers and its equipment. In fact, it had suffered such losses that well before the fighting around Kalinin and the Torzhok road produced heavy casualties for the division, it was already weighing plans to combine and consolidate its subunits. The losses it suffered during the fighting only accelerated this process. By the beginning of Operation Typhoon on October 2nd, the division could muster only 99 operable tanks. Although precise figures for personnel strength are hard to come by, Army Group Center's infantry divisions had suffered an average of roughly 40–50% losses of their *Gefecht Starke* or combat strength and the panzer and motorized divisions, leading the way, had doubtless suffered at least equivalent losses if not worse.

1st Panzer had gone into Operation Barbarossa with about 5,000 men in its front line units (*schutzen*, motorcycle, reconnaissance, and panzer battalions) and it would be surprising if the division had any more than 3,000–3,500 men in these by October. Besides tanks, its other vehicles likewise had had a very hard war so far. This was compounded by the fact that its tracked elements, which had been scheduled to move from south of Leningrad to their jump-off positions north of Yartsevo by rail had been forced instead to redeploy by road, which did nothing to improve their mechanical endurance. The troops themselves had been involved in some very hard fighting between the Luga River and Leningrad, and – while generally successful – they had seen Leningrad remain enticingly just beyond their reach. They had also, from the very beginning of the fighting, been rudely shaken out of their assumption that the Red Army was going to be a pushover. They were confident, tired, and warily optimistic. Once they broke through cleanly west of Vyazma, their morale again briefly soared.

36th Motorized Division
36th Motorized Division, commanded by Lieutenant General Otto Ottenbacher and composed primarily of Bavarians, had been a 'stable mate' of 1st Panzer during the drive through the Baltic Soviet Republics and the intense fighting across the Luga River up to the gates of Leningrad. Unlike the panzer divisions, whose composition varied widely, the motorized divisions were mostly built identically; essentially infantry divisions, but with only two infantry regiments rather than three, mounted on trucks. Later in the war they would be styled '*panzer-grenadier*' divisions, assigned tank battalions, and given other reinforcement; however, in 1941, this was all in the future. The division's trucks allowed its soldiers to keep up with the panzer divisions, operationally, and also provided much needed infantry power for both assaults and to defend the long corridors that the panzer spearheads carved. This meant that they often found themselves

in the way of desperate Soviet counterattacks and breakout attempts, and suffered accordingly.

The division was composed of two regiments of infantry (the 87th and 118th), and one of artillery (the 36th), with battalions each of motorcycle, antitank, engineer, reconnaissance, signals and other elements, all motorized. The motorcycle battalion, and the motorcycle company that was part of the reconnaissance battalion, each had two light machineguns per squad; the rest of the infantry only had one each. The infantry regiments each had three battalions of infantry, each with three infantry companies and a machinegun company with twelve medium machineguns and six 8cm mortars. The artillery regiment had two light battalions (I, II) of 10.5cm howitzers and a medium battalion (III) of 15cm howitzers, all towed. (See '*Lexikon der Wehrmacht*' and the *niehorster 'orbat wwII'* websites.) In November 1940 one light artillery battalion went to 111th Infantry Division, but another battalion was assigned to it from 72nd Infantry Division, so the division ended up with three battalions: two light and one medium. By October III Battalion was no longer with the division, although whether by detachment or for lack of prime movers is not clear. The antitank battalion had three companies, each with three 50mm AT guns and eight 37mm guns, and in theory was supposed to have a battery of two quad-20mm and eight single 20mm AA guns, all on unarmored halftracks, but the division had never received these AA guns.[18]

Like 1st Panzer, 36th Motorized Division had been through the mill on the way to Leningrad, and was considerably understrength, with many of its trucks missing or ready to break down.

900th 'Lehr' Brigade (Motorized)

Formed from the school and demonstration battalions and companies of the motorized training establishment, this unit, under Colonel Walther Krause (future commander of 1st Panzer Division), was a strange and unique one. Unlike Soviet school battalions which were thrown into the line when nothing else was available, this unit seems to have been organized deliberately to give the training establishment combat experience; subsequently, in the vastness of Russia it found itself called on because any mobile unit was badly needed.

The brigade consisted of five battalions; a *schutzen* battalion, a truck-borne infantry battalion, an antitank battalion, an artillery battalion, and a very well equipped signals battalion. The *schutzen* battalion had two companies mounted in halftracks and a company of motorcyclists; all of them with two machineguns per squad, and a *schwer* ['heavy'] company with two 7.5cm infantry guns and three 3.7cm AT guns, an engineer platoon, and six 8cm mortars. The AT battalion had two batteries, each with three 5cm AT guns and eight 3.7cm AT guns, and a third battery which had nine *Panzerjaeger I's* [*Pz.Jgr.Is* or Tank Hunter Is]. These had Pz I tank chassis with Czech 47mm AT guns mounted on them. The artillery battalion, in addition to twelve 10.5cm howitzers in three batteries of four guns each, also had seven *Sturmgeschutze* armored assault guns. In addition, the brigade had a large and well equipped signals battalion. For a pocket-sized force, the brigade was loaded for bear.

The brigade had been committed first in pocket closing efforts in the early summer of 1941, and then put into the line north of Smolensk where it held for August and part of September, being subject to repeated Soviet assaults. It had suffered significant losses in the process.

Corps Attachments

Other units and subunits were attached and detached from the XXXXI Corps during the course of the battle. For example, 6th Infantry Division was repeatedly shuffled back and forth between VI Army Corps and XXXXI Motorized Corps. Elements of other divisions, including *vorausabteilungen* ['advance detachments'] of 6th Panzer Division (of LVI Motorized Corps), 86th, 162nd Infantry Divisions (of XXVII Corps), the reconnaissance and motorcycle battalions of 14th Motorized Division (of LVI Motorized Corps), and, eventually, 129th (of V Corps) and 161st Infantry Divisions (from 9th Army's reserve) were scheduled to be or actually were subordinated to the corps. The corps also received two battalions of 38th Flak Regiment and the 600th Assault Gun Battalion with two batteries of StuG III (*Sturmgeschutze*) assault guns.

6th Panzer Division under Major General Franz Landgraf was formally assigned to XXXXI Corps, but except for its motorcycle battalion, with an attached battery of self-propelled light flak guns, it never received the fuel necessary to bring it to Kalinin before the battle ended. The division was equipped with Pz 35 (t) Czech tanks as its medium tank, all of which were on their last legs mechanically at this stage of the campaign.

The artillery allocated to XXXXI Corps consisted of three artillery battalions (II/59th Artillery Battalion with 15cm howitzers, 611th Artillery Battalion with 10.5cm guns, and 620th Artillery Battalion with 15cm cannon) and I/51st Nebelwerfer Battalion. These units, mostly due to loss of prime movers from breakdowns, were all under strength to one degree or another.[19]

Infantry Divisions

Several infantry divisions played a role in the battle for Kalinin. 6th Infantry Division, commanded by Lieutenant General Helge Auleb, had fought as part of 9th Army and at the beginning of Operation Typhoon was under the control of General of Engineers Otto-Wilhelm Förster's VI Corps. During the battle it would be transferred back and forth between XXXXI Motorized Corps, LVI Motorized Corps, and back to VI Corps again. 129th Infantry Division, commanded by Major General Stephan Rittau, went into Typhoon as part of General of Infantry Richard Ruoff's V Corps. It had taken a heavy battering during the Soviet attacks north of Smolensk in mid-August, 1941, and was understrength and weak in supporting weapons. Finally, 161st Infantry Division began Operation Typhoon as the reserve of 9th Army. Commanded by Major General Heinrich Recke, the division was a sad remnant by October, 1941. It had been nearly destroyed by General Konev's 19th Army, which had hit Recke's division in August with four rifle divisions and a tank division, and forced it back in rout, killing, wounding or capturing over two-thirds of its soldiers, and capturing a regimental headquarters and most of the division's artillery. That it was committed to support XXXXI Corps in Kalinin was a sign both of the Germans' desperate lack of reserves, and perhaps of 9th Army's reluctance to divert one of its more capable divisions from its own objectives to support Panzer Group 3.

German Strengths and Weaknesses

XXXXI Motorized Corps had some significant advantages going into combat against the northern flank of the Red Army's Western Front. First, it had the initiative, and this, coupled with the advantage in mobility it enjoyed at the beginning of the battle, permitted it to strike where it chose and pre-empt any Soviet attempts to establish a stable defense. Second, in most cases its soldiers were better trained, equipped, and far more experienced than their opponents. Third, its communications were far superior and, despite some command turbulence, its units were mostly part of a coherent team used to working together. Additionally, even though its strength had been significantly worn down by the fighting since June, the *Luftwaffe* devoted a surprisingly generous amount of combat power to support the attack of the left wing of Panzer Group 3. It very aggressively forward-based significant amounts of aircraft into the airfields around Kalinin early in the battle, which allowed for rapid response and quick turn-around time. Aerial resupply was available when the weather permitted.

Conversely, the Germans also suffered from some serious disadvantages, a few of which were already readily apparent either to their commanders or to their opponents at the beginning of the battle. First, most of their units were well under-strength and their equipment worn. Second, their supply bases were a considerable distance away from the fighting, over roads that were both bad and crowded, meaning that a round trip by supply trucks to the dumps in the Smolensk area required up to nine days.[20] This, exacerbated by delays in construction of railroads to the forward area, a shortage of vehicles in the supply chain, and the insufficient quantities of supplies reaching the Army Group Center's forward dumps near Smolensk, had dire effects on both the corps' mobility and combat power. Particularly irksome were recurring fuel and ammunition shortages.

Like the Soviets, the attention and priorities of the German high command were focused on Moscow, and Panzer Group 3's actions were peripheral to the primary objective of Army Group Center. Consequently, with supplies woefully tight for all German units, Reinhardt's group had a lower priority for fuel, ammunition, and other supplies than Panzer Group 4 and 2nd Panzer Army striking directly at Moscow.

The weather also began causing the Germans problems in October, although these affected the Soviets as well. Even though the worst of the fall mud season had not yet arrived, with temperatures around freezing and some precipitation, the roads were not in good shape, and cross-country mobility in the marshy and wooded countryside was limited. There were numerous reports of culverts breaking, either from heavy traffic or enemy action, and the combination of critical fuel shortages and poor traffic conditions eventually slowed and disorganized the German advance. By the last week in October, the rains would come in earnest, and movement became nearly impossible until the arrival of the hard frosts of mid-November. Nonetheless, the common German excuse that 'General Mud' kept them out of Moscow in mid-October does not stand up well to examination, given the road marches that were performed by both sides when fuel was available.

Both sides had a near equivalence of strength in armor and artillery (roughly 100+ tanks were involved on each side), with the latter hampered for both sides by shortages of ammunition. In infantry numbers, the Soviets eventually would amass a comfortable margin of superiority, but at the beginning of the battle the Germans had the advantage of overall strength where it mattered. The Germans, however, had one serious disadvantage, which replicated on a small scale a misconception that the whole planning of *Fall Barbarossa* labored under, and would indeed be the downfall of Hitler's and his generals' ambitions in the East. They underestimated their opponents' willingness and ability to fight, and their ability to mobilize reserves. This, combined with limited intelligence and hopelessly optimistic interpretations of the information that they had, would set them up for a stinging reverse.

Soviet Forces

When Operation Typhoon swept away the center and left wing of Western Front and the entirety of Reserve Front, as well as crumpling the defenses of Bryansk Front to the south, a gaping hole appeared in the Soviet defensive lines directly in front of Moscow. It was a moment of supreme crisis; the Soviet *Stavka* (Headquarters of the Supreme High Command) had no reserve armies at its disposal, and had to scramble to find a few divisions, tank brigades, and antitank regiments to cover the key roads leading to the capital. Consequently, on October 7th *Stavka* ordered the forces on the right (northern) wing of Western Front – 22nd, 29th, and 30th Armies – to detach certain divisions to help man the Mozhaisk Line being formed as the defensive position in front of Moscow.[21] But the drive north by XXXXI Motorized Corps from Sychevka forced a change in plans, and about half of these divisions were diverted to defend Staritsa on the Volga and Kalinin itself. Although Zhukov on October 12th requested *Stavka* to send one rifle division and one tank brigade to bolster the front at Kalinin if the

Germans took the city, all that was sent was one tank brigade; it was all that was available.

Northwestern Front was also ordered to send a force to move down through Vyshniy Volochek, through Torzhok, to strike at Kalinin by October 15th. This group of two rifle divisions, two cavalry divisions, a tank brigade and a motorcycle regiment was put under the command of Lieutenant General Nikolai Feodorovich Vatutin, chief of staff of Northwestern Front. Vatutin was already standing out as the most aggressive commander among the Soviet generals, a reputation he would continue to build until his death in the Ukraine in early 1944.

The Red Army forces that took part in the Battle of Kalinin consisted of 22nd, 29th and 30th Armies originally from Western Front, 31st Army (initially headquarters only) from its second echelon, Operational Group Vatutin from Northwestern Front, and 21st Tank Brigade from the *Stavka* reserve. Colonel General Ivan Konev had been commander of Western Front when the Germans launched their drive on Moscow on October 2nd, 1941. He failed to cope with the situation and was replaced on October 10th by General of the Army Georgi Konstantinovich Zhukov, who had been commanding the Leningrad Front. Zhukov retained Konev as his deputy and dispatched him to Kalinin to control the northern flank of Western Front. On October 17th, *Stavka* organized the forces defending the Kalinin area into Kalinin Front, and appointed Konev as its commander.

22nd Army was only peripherally involved in the fighting for Kalinin, being occupied on the line Ostashkov–Rzhev–Baumutovo west of Kalinin, fighting a defensive battle against the bulk of the forces of the German 9th Army, which was pressing against it from the southwest and south. On October 1st it consisted of six rifle divisions and five artillery regiments, commanded by Major General Vasily Aleksandrovich Yushkevich, the former commander of 44th Rifle Corps during the heavy fighting for Yartsevo in late July and August.[22]

This study will focus on those units that were more closely involved in the fighting for Kalinin itself.

29th Army

Lieutenant General Ivan Ivanovich Maslennikov commanded 29th Army. Maslennikov had joined the Red Guard in 1917 and fought in the Red Army through the Civil War, ending up as a cavalry brigade commander. He continued in the army until 1928, when he was transferred to the OGPU, predecessor of the NKVD, and was active in fighting the *Basmachi* bands in Central Asia. He graduated from the Frunze Academy in 1935, and by the beginning of the war commanded all NKVD border and internal security troops.

When Hitler invaded the USSR, a group of fifteen rifle divisions was raised, with 1,500 NKVD men, mostly border guards, assigned to each as officers and cadres.[23] Maslennikov, while retaining his post as a deputy director of the NKVD, was assigned to command 29th Army, which was in part made up of some of these divisions.

29th Army, as of October 10th
- 119th Rifle Division
- 174th Rifle Division
- 178th Rifle Division
- 220th Rifle Division
- 243rd Rifle Division
- 246th Rifle Division
- 250th Rifle Division
- 252nd Rifle Division
- Separate Motorized Rifle Brigade
- 29th Cavalry Regiment
- 644th Corps Artillery Regiment (122mm howitzers)
- 432nd Howitzer Regiment (until September 14th, this was the howitzer regiment of 178th Rifle Division, armed with 122mm and 152mm howitzers)
- 213th Antitank Battalion (similarly detached from 178th Rifle Division, armed with 45mm antitank guns)
- three engineer battalions and a pontoon battalion

On October 10th, 29th Army was deployed west and southwest of Rzhev, falling back under pressure from the German 9th Army's 26th, 110th, and 206th Infantry Divisions and 6th Infantry Division of Panzer Group 3's XXXXI Motorized Corps. The army's headquarters was in Rzhev. The initial attack of Panzer Group 3 had smashed 30th Army, which had been south of 29th Army. Maslennikov's left flank was wide open and was attempting to pull back as XXXXI Motorized Corps began cutting behind them.

29th Army's right wing, composed initially of 174th, 178th, 220th and 250th Rifle Divisions (all of which were eventually transferred to the control of 22nd Army), spent the battle fending off the advance by German VI Army Corps through Rzhev towards Torzhok to the north. This fighting was essentially linear, and although the Germans gradually forced back 22nd Army and the right wing of 29th Army, no breakthrough was achieved and the offensive ran out of steam before reaching its objectives. In fact, the Germans got no further on this front, leaving substantial Soviet forces overhanging the northern flank of Army Group Center. This would come back to haunt them during the winter of 1941/42. Our attention will focus on the efforts of the army's left wing, composed of 243rd, 252nd, 246th and 119th Rifle Divisions and the Separate Motorized Rifle Brigade.

Maslennikov's army had the support of 644th Corps Artillery Regiment, 432nd Howitzer Regiment and 213th Antitank Battalion (both of the latter taken from

178th Rifle Division), 71st, 72nd, and 267th Engineer Battalions and 63rd Pontoon Battalion. It was later reinforced by taking 510th Howitzer Regiment from 119th Rifle Division, and by the addition of 873rd Antitank Regiment, armed with twenty 45mm antitank guns (from 31st Army).

119th Rifle Division

Although German accounts of the Battle of Moscow are replete with descriptions of masses of 'fresh Siberian' troops (which for the Germans seemed to mean anyone in a fur hat), 119th Rifle Division, formed in 1939 at Krasnoyarsk, actually was a Siberian division. During the summer it had been assigned to 24th and then 31st Army, in Reserve Front. On October 6th, the division lost its 365th Rifle Regiment, which was transferred to 18th Rifle Division, which had made its way out of encirclement. To replace it, the 119th received 920th Rifle Regiment, transferred from 247th Rifle Division (made up of NKVD cadre and reservists). Transferred to 29th Army in early October, the division ended up assigned to 31st Army by the end of the battle. Subsequently it performed well during the counterattack at Moscow and in March of 1942 became 17th Guards Rifle Division. The division commander during the battle, Major General Aleksandr Dmitrievich Berezin, had commanded the division ever since it was formed in 1939.

The division was far stronger than the average Red Army rifle division at this stage of the war. It was still organized on the pre-war *shtat* (table of organization and equipment), and had all of its subunits still intact. On September 20th, before Operation Typhoon began, it was in fact overstrength, with 1,142 officers, 14,804 noncommissioned officers and enlisted men, 13 tankettes, 4 armored cars, 166 machineguns, 408 light machineguns, 54 45mm antitank guns, 85 artillery pieces, 109 mortars, and 4 antiaircraft guns. It was involved in heavy fighting in the defense of Rzhev in the first week in October, but was still a large unit going into the battle for Kalinin.[24]

243rd Rifle Division

This division was formed between June 26th and July 10th, with 500 officers and 1,000 men from the NKVD assigned as cadre. Although formed on the July 1941 *shtat*, the division nonetheless was organized with an antitank battalion of its own. Initially assigned to 30th Army, the division fought in July as part of 29th Army, along the Western Dvina River north of Smolensk. It remained part of Western Front through the end of 1941, but was then assigned to the *Stavka* reserve and, from there, was sent to the Ukraine. Subsequently, it fought through Romania, Hungary, and towards the end of the Great Patriotic War into Czechoslovakia, and was then sent east by rail to participate in the offensive into Manchuria. During the Battle of Kalinin, 243rd Rifle Division fought under the command of Colonel Yakov Gavrilovich Tsarkoz.

246th Rifle Division

This division was yet another formed in July in the Moscow Military District from NKVD cadre. Commanded by Major General Ivan Ivanovich Melnikov, the division was initially assigned to 31st Army, and then 29th Army. During the counterattack at Moscow in early December, the division reported having 6,800 men, an exceptionally large unit for the time. It fought in 29th and 31st Armies until January, 1943, when it briefly went into reserve. It was then sent south, first to Central Front and then, in December, 1943, to 1st Ukrainian Front's 60th Army, where it fought for most of the remainder of the war.

250th Rifle Division

Like 243rd Rifle Division, the 250th was formed at the same time with another 1,500 NKVD troops as cadre. Initially, it joined the fighting in July as part of 30th Army, receiving a tank battalion from the disbanded 110th Tank Division. The first division commander, Major General Ivan Sergeyevich Gorbachev, was killed in the fighting around Smolensk in late July. By August 1st, the division's three decimated regiments numbered 727, 1,195, and 526 men, respectively. In August the 250th still had eight T-34s, one T-26, two BT-7 and six BT-5 tanks on its books but all of this armor had been lost by the time the division was transferred to 29th Army in early October. By October 10th the division had been reduced to 500 men, fighting at Olenino, west of Rzhev.[25] Subsequently it was reinforced with 500 stragglers rounded up from the Soviet rear – survivors of 247th Rifle Division and men who had come loose from rear echelon units of 30th and 31st Armies during the retreats in the first half of October. This did not, of course, make for a cohesive fighting unit, and the division was not considered effective by the command of 29th Army. The division, commanded by Colonel Pavel Afinogenovich Stepanenko, fought most of the war subordinate to Western Front and then Byelorussian Front, and ended the war in Berlin.

252nd Rifle Division

Yet another NKVD-cadre division, the 252nd was assigned to 29th Army from the beginning in July. Like 243rd Division, it also had its own antitank battalion. Colonel Aleksandr Alekseyevich Zabaluev commanded the division in the Battle of Kalinin and throughout the winter fighting. After the spring of 1942, the division was pulled into reserve, then sent south to Don Front and fought the rest of the war in the Ukraine, Hungary, and Austria.

Separate Motorized Rifle Brigade

This was a very unusual unit, even for the latter part of 1941. The brigade was formed from the 'Separate Mixed Division' which never made the army rolls and had been formed in the latter half of August from the 'Composite [Mixed] Brigade', which consisted of 29th Cavalry Regiment and 1st Motorized Rifle Regiment.

29th Cavalry Regiment had 940 men and a little over 1,000 horses in July, when it was supposed to be assigned to 19th Cavalry Division; however, that unit was never formed. This regiment was replaced in the brigade by 2nd Motorized Rifle Regiment, and became an independent unit in 29th Army.

1st Motorized Rifle Regiment was a different unit from the regiment with the same name that was assigned to 1st Tank Division at the beginning of the war. It appeared in 29th Army in mid-July, and may have been formed from school units in the Moscow area.

There is no information available on the organization of 2nd Motorized Rifle Regiment, but it is likely that its story is similar to that of the 1st.

The brigade was also assigned 2nd Artillery Regiment, which had originally been the 'Separate Mixed Battalion of 29th Army'. In addition, when the new Motorized Rifle Brigade *shtat 010/200* was issued on October 9th, the brigade was assigned a hastily organized tank battalion with twelve T–34s and twenty light tanks, which were supposed to be T–40s or T–60s but were probably BT–7s.

The commander of the Separate Motorized Rifle Brigade was *Kombrig* A.N. Ryzhkov. (*Kombrig* is short for Brigade Commander, a prewar rank equivalent to colonel, abolished in 1939, and often an indication that the officer was one of those imprisoned during the purges of 1937–41 and had been returned to service with his old rank.) The brigade was nearly destroyed in the fighting at Staritsa, counting only 300 men by October 19th, and in December it was combined with the remnants of 247th Rifle Division to form a new rifle division of the same number. Colonel Sergey Pavlovich Tarasov, the 247th's previous commander, was put in command of the new unit.

29th Cavalry Regiment

Little is known about 29th Cavalry Regiment. Formed after the beginning of the war, it would have had little more than a thousand 'sabers' and a machinegun squadron at full strength. During September, it had been part of 29th Army, performing screening duties as part of the army's reserve. It was essentially a lightly armed overstrength mounted battalion by the time of the Battle of Kalinin.

30th Army

30th Army, commanded by Major General Vasily Afanaseyevich Khomenko, had been directly facing Panzer Group 3 when the Typhoon offensive began on October 2nd. Losing communications with its troops, the army's headquarters retreated to the vicinity of the Moscow Sea, southeast of Kalinin. When the battle began, such units of the army that had survived were either leaderless and scattered, or withdrawing as fast as they could to get out of the path of the oncoming panzers. 30th Army was assigned forces stripped out of 22nd and 29th Armies.

30th Army
- 5th Rifle Division
- 133rd Rifle Division (operated at first as an independent division under Front control)
- 256th Rifle Division (less one regiment detached to reinforce 22nd Army)
- Special Reserve Rifle Regiment
- 20th Reserve Rifle Regiment
- 2nd Motorcycle Regiment
- 11th Motorcycle Regiment
- 16th NKVD Regiment
- 84th NKVD Regiment
- 392nd, 542nd Corps Artillery Regiments (the 392nd was assigned to 31st Army during part of October; the 542nd was armed with 122mm guns and 152mm howitzers)
- 12th Mortar Battalion (with 120mm mortars)
- 871st Antitank Regiment (formed from Moscow's antiaircraft defenses on July 16th, 1941, with twenty 85mm AA guns)
- 263rd Sapper Battalion

As the Germans approached Kalinin, 30th Army was reinforced with the militia of the Higher Pedagogical Institute, 16th and 86th NKVD Regiments, and the Junior Officer's Course (a company-sized unit) of Northwestern Front that was stationed in the city. During the battle the army was further reinforced with 21st Tank Brigade, 2nd and 11th Motorcycle Regiments, Special Reserve Rifle Regiment, and 185th Rifle Division. Three rifle divisions, the 162nd, 242nd and 251st, which had been part of 30th Army but lost contact with Khomenko's headquarters when he retreated to the Moscow Sea, were surrounded by the German 110th and 6th Infantry Divisions and fought in encirclement west of the Rzhev–Vyazma north–south road on October 10th. They broke out successfully at the end of October and were assigned to 31st Army, though by that time the three divisions totaled fewer than 1,500 men, and two were disbanded soon thereafter.

Khomenko had been the head of the NKVD Border Guards in the Ukraine before the war began, and, like Maslennikov, was given a military command largely composed of divisions that had initially been formed with NKVD cadres. He continued after the Battle of Kalinin as an army commander, and died in combat in the early part of 1944 near Nikopol, when he accidentally drove his staff car into German lines while on a personal reconnaissance.

5th Rifle Division
5th Rifle Division had been formed in 1918 at Kurgan in the Volga Military District and was in the Baltic Special Military District when the war broke out,

camped near the border. The division was pushed back to the area south of Lake Ilmen as part of 27th Army and within a month had been reduced to 3,500 men. In September it was transferred to Reserve Front's 31st Army and was to some extent rebuilt. However, when it was pulled from 31st Army by a *Stavka* order on October 5th and sent south to man the Mozhaisk Line in front of Moscow, it had only 1,964 men, with 1,549 rifles, seven medium machineguns, eleven light machineguns, eight 76.2mm guns and four 122mm howitzers, and six 45mm anti-tank guns. Its regiments averaged 430 men each. Commanded by Lieutenant Colonel Petr Sergeyevich Telkov, the division was ordered detrained in Kalinin to provide a defense of the city against the oncoming German tanks. Despite its depleted state, according to Colonel General Ivan Konev, 'the division had not yet lost its combat effectiveness.'[26]

After the fighting at Kalinin, the division was rebuilt, and fought well in the fruitless offensives Western Front conducted from July through September of 1942, and was rewarded by being redesignated 44th Guards Rifle Division in October of 1942.

256th Rifle Division

This division, commanded at Kalinin by Major General Sergei Georgievich Goryachev, was yet another of those divisions formed with NKVD cadres. It also had its own antitank battalion, which came in handy during the fighting for Kalinin. However, only two of the division's rifle regiments, the 934th and 937th, were with it at Kalinin. 930th Regiment was detached before the battle and fought during this period under the control of 178th Rifle Division with 22nd Army. When the Germans stormed Kalinin, the division was split in half, with 934th Rifle Regiment retreating over the rail bridge and fighting the rest of the battle northwest of Kalinin, while 937th Regiment, with the division's artillery, HQ, and other subunits, fought first to hold the northeast quarter of Kalinin and then around the northeast edge of the city. After the battle the division was transferred to 39th Army when Maslennikov was transferred to command that unit. It subsequently moved north to Volkhov Front, and fought the latter part of the war in the Baltic Republics.

Special Reserve Rifle Regiment

The regiment was formed in October from schools units and administrative personnel in the Moscow Military District. It had fewer than 1,000 men, and no heavy weapons. It was first used to cover the southern flank of 5th Rifle Division, and then added to the division and used to reinforce its depleted ranks.

20th Reserve Rifle Regiment

This regiment was also raised in October in the Moscow area, and consisted of about 400 'bayonets' and no heavy weapons.

16th NKVD Regiment

16th Border Guards Regiment was formed from 16th '*Dzherzhinsk*' Border Guards Unit in July, 1941. The original Border Guards unit had been on the Western Special Military District border in the area of Radoshkovichy, Negoreloye, Zaslavl, Timkovichy, and Krasny Sloboda under Major A.A. Alekseyev. It was hit by panzers on 27 June, forced back with losses, and reformed as a rear area security unit for 19th Army in July. The regiment was officially in the rear of Western Front with three battalions totaling 798 men on October 5th, still under the command of Alekseyev, who had been promoted to lieutenant colonel by then. It retreated to the Kalinin area by October 14th, and was cited for its participation in the fighting in the city. It was directly in the path of 1st Panzer Division's advance just south of the Torzhok road and was overrun, but enough of its soldiers survived for the regiment to avoid being disbanded, and it was restored to its border guard status in 1944 and assigned to the borders of Byelorussia.

84th NKVD Railroad Regiment

This regimental headquarters was assigned to the Kalinin area in early October. It was ordered to take charge of all internal security and other forces it could find in the area. It included a 300-man battalion of NKVD internal security and railroad troops, a workers' militia battalion of 600 men, and four regional militia battalions of 200 men each. Each militiaman was armed with a Canadian Enfield rifle, two grenades, and 120 rounds of ammunition. This probably represented all the .303 rifle ammunition available in Kalinin. The NKVD men's weapons are not known, but likely included Soviet rifles, light machineguns, and possibly a few submachine guns. It is highly unlikely that the regiment had any other automatic weapons, or any mortars, antitank guns, or light artillery. Unlike in Odessa, Mogilev, Tula and other places where there was time to prepare for the enemy's arrival, the Germans arrived in Kalinin so suddenly that there had been no time to produce 'bottles of flammable mixture' (known as Molotov cocktails to the rest of the world) to equip the defenders.

21st Tank Brigade

One important reinforcement Moscow assigned to 30th Army was 21st Tank Brigade, temporarily commanded by Lieutenant Colonel Andrei Levovich Lesovoi. This brigade had started forming at Vladimir in the Moscow Military District in late September and was ordered to Kalinin just five days later. While the brigade had barely a week to organize, it had many officers and men in its ranks with experience as 'tankists' from fighting the Japanese in the Far East in 1939, from the war with Finland in 1940, and from the summer's fighting against the Germans.

The brigade was organized with a tank regiment (the 21st) of two battalions.

1st Battalion had twenty-nine T-34s, but instead of a company of KV heavy tanks as authorized, it included the only ten T-34s built in 1941 mounting the ZIS-4 57mm cannon. This gun had an extremely high muzzle velocity and better armor-piercing capability than the 76mm gun usually mounted. Six of the ten T-34-57s also had radios, so the regimental and battalion commanders were mounted in them. 2nd Battalion had seven elderly BT-2s, six BT-5s, seven BT-7s, two T-34 flamethrower tanks with experimental ATO-41 flamethrowers installed (or possibly T-26 flamethrower tanks) and ten brand-new T-60 light tanks from the Gorky factory, the first to go into action with any tank unit. This motley collection is a good indication that the brigade had been thrown together hurriedly with whatever was to hand. By October 20th there remained eight T-34s, four BT-2s, five BT-5s, six BT-7s, two T-26 or T-34 flamethrower tanks, nine T-60s and three ZIS-30s.

The brigade also included a motorized rifle battalion of 700 officers and men that included a mortar company of twelve 82mm mortars, three rifle companies, reconnaissance and sapper (combat engineer) platoons, a battery of antiaircraft guns, a company of antitank riflemen, and a battery of four ZIS-30s – more 57mm guns, these mounted on Komsomolets tractors as self-propelled antitank guns. The motorized riflemen had had no opportunity to practice working with tanks unfortunately.

2nd and 11th Motorcycle Regiments
Later in the battle for Kalinin, two motorcycle regiments (the 2nd and 11th) were added to 30th Army from Moscow's reserves. Both of these units had seen action with various mechanized corps since June and July, and while relatively well equipped with light machineguns, they had little else in the way of heavy weapons or hitting power.

Both of these formations were left over from disbanded tank divisions, and like 46th Motorcycle Regiment, were made up of lightly armed motorcyclists. When they arrived from Moscow late in the battle they were used to screen the flank of 30th Army.[27]

Operational Group Vatutin
Even in 1941, Lieutenant General Nikolai Feodorovich Vatutin was recognized as one of the most offensive-minded of the Red Army's senior generals. He had organized a large-scale counterstroke by the Northwestern Front in the Soltsy region in July of 1941 that had rocked General Erich von Manstein's LVI Motorized Corps. In August he orchestrated another counterstroke, this time at Staraya Russa which, although it ended up as a very costly defeat for the Red Army, seriously disrupted Army Group North's drive on Leningrad. In October of 1941 Vatutin was serving as Northwestern Front's chief of staff, and, in an example of Soviet flexibility, was assigned to take personal command of the

Front's forces that were dispatched to help rescue the city of Kalinin. To do so, he was assigned a tank brigade, a motorcycle regiment, two rifle divisions and two cavalry divisions. Characteristically, he wasted no time and did not pause to allow his infantry and cavalry to catch up with the speeding tank brigade before committing it to combat. Vatutin went on to command *fronts* for the Red Army later in the war, becoming one of the most important *front* commanders in 1943, leading the Voronezh and then 1st Ukrainian Front until he was mortally wounded by right wing Ukrainian Nationalist partisans in the spring of 1944.

Vatutin's Operational Group:
- 183rd Rifle Division
- 185th Rifle Division
- 46th Cavalry Division
- 54th Cavalry Division
- 8th Tank Brigade
- 46th Motorcycle Regiment
- an unnumbered Guards Mortar battalion (with M-13 132mm rocket launchers on trucks)

At the end of October 17th the forces of the group were transferred to the control of 31st Army and Vatutin returned to the Northwestern Front to resume his duties as chief of staff.

8th Tank Brigade
8th Tank Brigade was formed in the Urals in August of 1941 from elements of the disbanded 4th Mechanized Corps' 32nd Tank Division. It was equipped with factory fresh KVs, T-34s and T-40s and many of its tank crews and commanders had been seasoned in combat during the fighting against the Germans in the summer of 1941. Its commander was Colonel Pavel Alekseyevich Rotmistrov, who would later go on to command tank corps, then tank armies, and would finish the war in charge of all of the Red Army's armored and mechanized forces. Scholarly looking, with horn-rimmed glasses, a high forehead and a walrus mustache, Rotmistrov had the heart of a cavalryman. His operations were notable for his ability to conduct long road marches rapidly without excessive mechanical attrition to his vehicles, and for his aggressive high-speed style of attacking. Major Yegorov, the commander of 8th Brigade's 8th Tank Regiment, would rise to command 18th Tank Corps and serve as deputy commander of 1st Guards Mechanized Corps by the war's end.

Since Rotmistrov's brigade had missed most of the fighting during the Staraya Russa counterstroke, it was in fact overstrength, according to the commander of its tank regiment, Major Aleksandr Vasilevich Yegorov, with seventy tanks when the order came to go south. Some of the tanks were left as a reserve for Northwestern

Front in the area of Lychkovo, since that Front had lost almost all of its tanks in the bitter fighting around Staraya Russa, leaving forty-nine tanks to go to Kalinin, including ten T-34s in its 1st Battalion, thirty-two heavy machinegun armed tankettes in its 2nd Battalion, and seven KV-1s in its heavy tank company.[28] The motorized rifle battalion of the brigade had 449 men, 337 automatic weapons, and eighteen mortars, while the brigade's antitank battery had six 45mm antitank guns. In addition, the brigade had two batteries totaling eight 76.2 mm guns.

46th Motorcycle Regiment

Like the other motorcycle regiments that turned up in many places during the battle for Moscow, this regiment was formed from a disbanded mechanized corps. Each regiment in theory consisted of four companies of motorcyclists, which were to have eighty-three motorcycles, with three motorcycle platoons, a machinegun platoon, and a mortar platoon. The whole unit by *shtat* would have 1,417 men, forty-six officers, forty-six junior officers, 148 NCOs, 1,177 soldiers, six radios, seventeen armored cars, six 45mm antitank guns, twenty-four 50mm mortars, sixteen DS medium machineguns, 192 DP light machineguns, twenty flamethrowers, 434 motorcycles (most with sidecars), sixty-one trucks, two cars, six light tractors, 406 rifles, fifty-five carbines, and 504 submachine guns. On October 10th, the regiment had only seventeen mortars, five antitank guns, and eleven armored cars running (another three were under repair); unfortunately no other details of its strength are available for this date. Intended as light and mobile scouting and screening forces, motorcycle regiments lacked both staying power and punch. When put into the line as infantry, they had trouble surviving. The regiment was commanded by Major V.M. Fedorchenko.

183rd Rifle Division

Major General Konstantin Vasileyevich Komissarov commanded this division throughout the Battle of Kalinin. The 183rd had been formed from two divisions of the Latvian army in 1940, with only 6,000 men and a mixture of foreign and Soviet weapons. Engaged in the first weeks of the war, the division had been reduced to 2,000 men by July 10th. It was then rebuilt and became part of the Northwestern Front at the beginning of October, entering the battle at Kalinin with 7,898 men, 232 automatic weapons (including heavy and light machineguns and submachine guns), twelve mortars and fifteen artillery pieces, but no antitank guns. After the winter of 1941, the division was again decimated during attacks on Rzhev in the summer of 1942. Rebuilt in the *Stavka* reserve, it was sent to 69th Army, fought around Kharkov, and later operated subordinate to 1st and 4th Ukrainian Fronts.

185th Rifle Division

Formed from the remnants of the disbanded 21st Mechanized Corps' 185th

Mechanized Division in late August, 1941, the division, commanded by Lieutenant Colonel Konstantin Nikolayevich Vindushev, was shifted from the Northwestern Front's 27th Army to Operational Group Vatutin. Heavily reinforced, it entered battle with 12,046 men, 196 automatic weapons, seventeen mortars, one antitank gun, and thirty-two artillery pieces. A division this size was very unusual, but despite its size, its performance at Kalinin can only be termed lackluster. It seems very likely that it had lost a large number of its experienced officers and NCOs when it was converted from a mechanized to a rifle division and had been subsequently rebuilt with conscripts without time for adequate training. After the Battle of Kalinin it stayed in Kalinin Front, then fought in 2nd Baltic Front and, finally, in 1st Byelorussian Front's 47th Army to the war's end, participating in Operation Bagration (in Byelorussia) and the Vistula-Oder and Berlin operations.

46th Cavalry Division
The division was formed in the Volga Military District in the summer of 1941 and was dispatched to the Northwestern Front in September. There is some question as to whether the division actually had enough horses and tack to function as genuine cavalry that fall. In the second week of October it had 1,859 men, seventy-seven automatic weapons, and six mortars. After the fighting at Kalinin was over, the division fought as part of 29th Army, and was then assigned to 39th Army during the counteroffensive at Moscow. When 39th Army was surrounded and destroyed in June 1942, the division was disbanded.

54th Cavalry Division
Formed in July in the Moscow Military District, 54th Cavalry Division was sent to Northwestern Front and took part in the Staraya Russa offensive in early August as part of that Front's 34th Army. It then went into Northwest Front reserves to be rebuilt and was sent to Kalinin as part of Operational Group Vatutin. The rebuilding process was far from complete, and the division had only 1,308 men, 230 automatic weapons, and twenty-four mortars when it was committed. After the battle its combat path was similar to that of 46th Cavalry, taking part in the offensive by 39th Army, and perishing with it in the summer of 1942.

The Soviet units that fought at Kalinin varied widely from badly understrength to nearly full strength. The *Stavka*, in its order establishing Kalinin Front on October 17th, noted that 'Military composition of many of the divisions was less than 50% of *shtat* and short of artillery, mortar and machineguns.'[29] The divisions initially assigned to Operational Group Vatutin, and those of the left wing of 29th Army, all seem to have been above average in strength. The quality of the divisions, as evidenced by their performance during the battle, was quite varied, reflecting differences in leadership, training, and experience.

Kalinin Front

One division was under the direct control of Kalinin Front when it went into action. Subsequently it was assigned to 31st Army. It played a key role in the defeat of German efforts to drive up the road to Torzhok and beyond.

133rd Rifle Division

133rd Rifle Division was another Siberian division, formed in September of 1939 in Novosibirsk. From the time of its formation, it was commanded by *Kombrig* (promoted to Major General when the *Kombrig* rank was abolished) Vasily Ivanovich Shvetsov, who had been senior instructor in division-level tactics at the Red Army's Frunze Academy, the Soviet's premier military academy, since 1931. The division then had two years of intense training under the same commander, uninterrupted by deployment to the Finnish War or elsewhere. Like 119th Rifle Division, it was still on the pre-war *shtat* with two artillery regiments and a number of subunits that were not present in divisions formed according to the July, 1941 *shtat*. It was assigned to 24th Army when the war began and then to 22nd Army in September. It was one of the divisions pulled out by the *Stavka* to try to fill the huge hole in front of Moscow, only to be redirected to the north-west side of Kalinin to try to contain the German attack. The division fought very well in the battle and later, as part of Western Front's 1st Shock and 49th Armies, in the counterattacks at Moscow. In March of 1942 it became 18th Guards Rifle Division. General Shvetsov went on to command 29th Army in December, and held various army commands for the rest of the war, being wounded once.

Soviet Strengths and Weaknesses

At first glance, Soviet weaknesses were more apparent than their strengths. Many of the units involved were understrength, and several were at less than half strength. The rifle divisions were lacking everything: officers, riflemen, machine-guns, mortars, antitank guns, artillery, transport, communications gear and all other sorts of equipment. Similarly, their artillery units were mostly well below strength in guns, prime movers, and technical equipment. When Kalinin Front was created during the middle of the battle, it lacked staff, communications equipment, all rear services establishment, and supporting air and antiaircraft units. The former were to be supplied by using the headquarters of 10th Army, from the *Stavka* reserve, while Northwestern Front was to supply the air support, but unfortunately it had little enough to share. It was only after the end of the battle, on October 28th, that 10th Army's HQ actually arrived. This was also true of the rear services units, and only towards the end of the battle was *Stavka* able to assign several air regiments to Konev.

The Soviets began the battle at a time when the initiative was firmly in enemy hands; their commanders were reacting to events and desperately short of reserve units to fill in the great hole torn in the front. Since both intelligence and communications were weak, throughout much of the fighting confusion reigned regarding organization, lines of authority, and command and control. This would not be sorted out until near the end of the battle.

The weather, of course, was neutral, and while the Soviets were able to make use of their rail system to move some units into position, in general, they were dependent on the same muddy roads that inhibited German maneuverability. In addition, their supply lines were subject to German air interdiction. This only added to their logistical woes, which were primarily due to the fact that weapons, ammunition fuel and supplies of all kinds, and transport to move them, were in short supply, and the forces directly in front of Moscow had a greater priority for what was available. For example, antitank rifles were just being issued to the Red Army, and one of the first units well supplied with such was 316th Rifle Division of Rokossovsky's 16th Army, which was south of 30th Army, defending the Volokolamsk area. The only significant numbers of PTRD 14.5mm AT rifles that appeared at Kalinin were in an AT rifle company attached to 21st Tank Brigade.

However, the Soviets had several assets that only became apparent during the battle. Rather than being discouraged by the Germans' operational triumphs at Vyazma and Bryansk, the fact that Moscow was near and the Soviet state was in grave danger inspired the Red Army to put up an exceptionally dogged defense in the middle of October. The phrase 'mass heroism' used by Soviet historians seems to some like bombast and hyperbole. However, careful examination suggests that it is not entirely an empty phrase. Many examples can be seen in the battle around Kalinin.

The Soviets also had some very talented officers involved in the fight for Kalinin. Ivan Konev, as he demonstrated commanding 19th Army during the fighting in the Smolensk region, was a competent, reliable commander, confident and energetic, if somewhat competitive with his comrades and tough on his subordinates. Although he bore a fair amount of the blame for Western Front's disastrous initial defeat in Operation Typhoon, he was eager to redeem his name after he was demoted to Zhukov's deputy when the latter was brought down from Leningrad to take charge of Western Front on October 10th. Konev's aim in the battle for Kalinin was nothing short of the total annihilation of XXXXI Motorized Corps. The fact that this goal was somewhat beyond his reach is not a reflection on his thinking, but rather on the paucity of the resources at his command, and the German Command's response of diverting badly needed resources to hold the city.

Operational Group Vatutin had Nikolai Vatutin in command, a protégé of both Shaposhnikov and Zhukov, both an exceptional staff officer and the most offensive-minded general in the Red Army. Under him was Colonel Pavel Rotmistrov, destined to become one of the most prominent Soviet tank commanders of the war. Like Vatutin, he thought offensively, and had already developed some techniques that he would use, on a larger and larger scale, in the future as he rose to command corps and finally 5th Guards Tank Army. Rotmistrov had also been born and raised just to the northwest of Kalinin, and was fighting on familiar ground.

In Vasily Ivanovich Shvetsov Kalinin Front could boast one of the most qualified division commanders in the Red Army, with an outstanding background as an instructor on tactics who had had two years to train his division. Although suffering from fatigue, cold, and widespread upper respiratory infections, his division would perform superbly under its aggressive commander.

One more important advantage enjoyed by the Soviets derived from congenital German arrogance. Advancing on a narrow front deep into enemy territory after a penetration is fine, assuming the enemy forces will obligingly roll over and play dead. However, if they do not, and if they are able to put together enough reserves to counterattack, an overextended and rapidly weakening pursuit force can find the tables turned in short order. When the blow fell, the Germans were taken completely off guard, and found themselves in the position their foes had been in only a week before, desperately scrambling to deal with threats appearing suddenly from unexpected quarters and struggling hard for their very survival. In addition, the Germans had launched Operation Typhoon on a completely inadequate logistics base, without enough supplies to continue the battle for more than two weeks, and without sufficient transport, roads, or fuel and ammunition in the pipeline to sustain their momentum. As the battle went on, the increasing gap between German ambitions and the means to realize them, is striking, as we will see.

The Battle for Kalinin: An Overview
The Battle of Kalinin, which lasted from October 10th to October 24th, can be divided into four distinct stages, as follows:
• **October 10th–14th: The German Pursuit and Capture of Kalinin**
XXXXI Motorized Corps' advance from Zubtsov to Staritsa and its seizure of Kalinin.
• **October 15th–18th: The German Advance on Torzhok**
1st Panzer Division's and 900th *Lehr* Brigade's attack up the Torzhok road northwest of Kalinin, and the counterattack by Rotmistrov's 8th Tank Brigade, the surprise tank raid by Lesovoi's 21st Tank Brigade from the southeast, the cutting off of the German spearhead on the Torzhok road, and 29th Army's attempted crossing of the Volga.
• **October 18th–21st: The Battle Along the Torzhok Road**
Soviet attempts to annihilate the German grouping by attacks by 29th, 31st, and 30th Armies.
• **October 22nd–24th: The Battle for Kalinin City**
The Soviet attempt to take the city, the German defense, and the shift in weight to the west by Kalinin Front to resist the advance of the German 9th Army.

Histories of this period of the Soviet–German War have generally overlooked the Battle for Kalinin. This has been largely because the high drama taking place in front of and south of Moscow attracted most of the attention. In addition, the German Army Group North's attempt to take Tikhvin, thus completing the intention to cut off supplies to Leningrad, and, to a much lesser extent, the attempts by Army Group South to take Rostov, have taken whatever attention was left after looking at Operation Typhoon and the fight for Moscow. When German authors or those whose material is primarily drawn from German sources depict the battle for Kalinin, it is primarily in terms of the dramatic stab by Eckinger's small force to take the city. Thereafter, all discussions regarding the battle become vague, dwelling on mud, fuel shortages, and the successful German defense of Kalinin against Soviet attempts to retake it.

Conversely, Soviet accounts of the action tend to mention it only in passing, emphasizing that the Germans got no further than the city, but, once again, focusing on the dramatic events taking shape around Moscow. Therefore, this battle has been viewed primarily as a German operational exploitation of a breakthrough intended to widen the breach in Soviet lines and provide flank protection for Army Group Center's drive on Moscow. A study of the German Army High Command's *Lage Ost* (Situation East) daily situation maps for the period seems to indicate a German intent to envelop and destroy the Soviet 22nd and 29th Armies on the northern wing of Western Front with Panzer Group 3 in cooperation with 9th Army. However, since this never happened, largely due to the vigorous if poorly coordinated Soviet counterstroke at Kalinin, historians have largely ignored the entire battle.

However, closer examination of previously known and newly released German and Soviet archival records now demonstrates that German offensive intentions in the Kalinin region were far more ambitious than previously understood. These records indicate that the Germans planned to employ two operational pincers to form yet another pocket rivaling those formed at Vyazma and Bryansk. This pocket was designed to encircle and destroy Western Front's 22nd and 29th Armies, Northwestern Front's 27th, 34th, and 11th Armies, as well as 52nd Army and Novgorod Operational Group, which were under the *Stavka's* direct control. The northern pincer of this offensive, half of Army Group North's XXXIX Motorized Corps, was to advance to the southeast to link up with XXXXI Motorized Corps striking northwestward from the Kalinin region. Specifically, the forces under Army Group North's XXXIX Motorized Corps began their attack on October 16th by conducting an assault crossing over the Volkhov River with 126th Infantry Division, and followed the river-crossing operation with an attempted exploitation with 8th Panzer and 18th Motorized Divisions toward Bolshaya Vishera, Malaya Vishera, and Bologoye.

The ultimate failure of this ambitious offensive clearly demonstrated the German failure to assess the situation accurately and to correctly evaluate the capabilities of their own forces and those of their enemy. Detailed examination of the ebb and flow of the fighting around Kalinin will make this abundantly apparent. The fighting at Kalinin smashed this ambitious German plan and shattered the XXXXI Motorized Corps, leaving Panzer Group 3 very weak as it went into the final stages of the Battle of Moscow.

Chapter 2

Preliminaries, October 7th–9th

On October 7th, Panzer Group 3's 7th Panzer Division (LVI Motorized Corps) reached Vyazma and linked up with 10th Panzer Division from Panzer Group 4's XXXX Motorized Corps, striking up from the south. Encircled west of Vyazma were Western Front's 16th, 19th, and 20th Armies, together with Operational Group Boldin and Reserve Front's 32nd Army. The 24th and 30th Armies, which had stood in the path of the twin panzer drives, were mostly smashed or scattered. Little stood between Moscow and the German spearheads. The troops in the pocket put up what resistance they could until their ammunition was exhausted, but, while some small groups and a few formations did manage to make their way out to the east, and others evaded capture and later became the nucleus of a number of partisan formations, most of General Ivan Konev's Western Front and all of Marshal Semyon Budyenny's Reserve Front were swept from the board by October 14th.

Three days into the Typhoon offensive, on October 5th, Colonel General Hermann Hoth was relieved of command of Panzer Group 3 and sent south to command 17th Army, then advancing on Kharkov. General of Panzer Troops Georg-Hans Reinhardt, who had previously commanded XXXXI Motorized Corps, replaced Hoth. Command of XXXXI Motorized Corps went temporarily to Lieutenant General Otto Ottenbacher, who had commanded 36th Motorized Division, and in turn he was replaced as division commander by Major General Hans Gollnick.

Reinhardt's panzer group received new orders on October 7th, the day the pocket at Vyazma slammed shut. His panzer group was to move northward towards Kalinin. Reinhardt objected, expressing his preference for an advance to the east, towards Klin, 75 kilometers (49 miles) northwest of Moscow, but he was overruled by orders from the German High Command.[30] The group's LVI Motorized Corps, under General of Panzer Troops Ferdinand Schaal, was still tied down holding the eastern and northeastern shoulders of the closed Vyazma pocket. Ottenbacher received orders to push his XXXXI Corps eastward to the road running north from Vyazma to Rzhev, and then to wheel north. When it did so, his corps advanced with 1st Panzer Division on the left (north) and 36th Motorized Division on the right, the latter moving south of and somewhat behind Kruger's 1st Panzer. 6th Infantry Division followed 1st Panzer, and it in turn was followed by Colonel Walther Krause's 900th *Lehr* Brigade. 1st Panzer reached the

Vyazma–Rzhev road on October 8th, where it encountered strong resistance from two regiments of the Soviet 247th Rifle Division, defending just south of Sychevka. The forward detachment of Gollnick's 36th Motorized Division also reached the road. To the south, SS '*Das Reich*' Motorized Division, part of XXXX Motorized Corps of Hoepner's Panzer Group 4, was moving northeast towards Gzhatsk.

The next day, 1st Panzer Division fought its way through a line of bunkers manned by two regiments of 247th Rifle Division defending Sychevka and began sending forces eastward around the town to outflank the Soviet defenses. Simultaneously, a strong advance guard of 36th Motorized Division swung further eastward, heading for Karmanovo, north of Gzhatsk. XXXXI Corps was now in position to move north, with 1st Panzer on its left and elements of 36th Motorized on the right. The corps issued orders for the next day at 2230 hours on October 9th to 'strike north and smash the enemy between Byeloye and Ostashkov in cooperation with the northern wing of 9th Army and the southern flank of 16th Army,'[31] as well as keeping the enemy from breaking out of the pocket along the main Minsk–Moscow highway at Vyazma. (Ostashkov is 154 kilometers (96 miles) west of Kalinin on the south shore of Lake Seliger; Byeloye is 149 kilometers (90 miles) south of Ostashkov.)

1st Panzer, supported by 900th *Lehr* Brigade, was to strike rapidly northward along the road to seize Zubtsov, Staritsa, and Kalinin, while 36th Motorized was to move parallel to and east of the panzers to capture Karmanovo, bypass Pogoreloye-Gorodishche (38 kilometers – 23 miles – east of Rzhev), and reach the woods east of Staritsa. Both divisions were instructed to conduct their advance with strong leading detachments because the fuel situation ruled out moving entire divisions at this time. Their orders read, 'Exploit all improvisations!'[32] The supporting 6th Infantry Division was to clear enemy forces from the Sychevka region, thus opening the road for 1st Panzer, if necessary. Corps reported that the roads were 'strongly choked by mud with numerous routes torn up, strongly handicapping movement and supply.' On the other hand, enemy air activity during the day was 'weak,' though it picked up with several bombing raids during the evening.[33]

On the Soviet side of the lines, all was confusion. Like 31st and 30th Armies, which had lost all communications with their subordinate divisions, Western Front was similarly out of contact with its forces, and was naturally far more concerned about the enemy armored columns pushing rapidly towards Moscow than about the situation on the approaches to Kalinin. Things seemed to be sliding inexorably towards the abyss. Focused on cobbling together a force that could keep the Germans out of Moscow, at 0200 hours on October 10th, the *Stavka* ordered seven rifle divisions pulled out of Western Front's right wing, specifically, 5th and 110th Rifle Divisions from 31st Army, 126th, 133rd, and 256th Rifle Divisions from 22nd Army, and 243rd and 246th Rifle Divisions from 29th Army.

126th and 256th Rifle Divisions were to move by truck, the rest by railroad or by marching on foot.[34] Other divisions were being railed to Moscow from as far away as Vladivostok on the Pacific coast, but it would take time for them to arrive. Officers' schools, newly formed tank brigades that combined survivors of the tank divisions and mechanized corps of the summer with new trainees and whatever tanks could be found, and antitank regiments armed with sixteen guns each of any kind of gun with a chance of killing a tank, were being pushed to the front as quickly as they could be formed. There was little enough, and there was nearly nothing to spare for secondary fronts such as Kalinin to the north.

Chapter 3

The German Pursuit and Capture of Kalinin, October 10th–14th

The German Pursuit, October 10th–12th

October 10th

For two days 1st Panzer Division had been fighting its way through disorganized elements of the Soviet 30th and 31st Armies as it pushed eastward. Kruger's panzers then conducted a stiff fight to overcome the defenses of 247th Rifle Division, whose riflemen were deployed in bunkers and trenches astride the road south of Sychevka. Desperately trying to hold off the Germans, Colonel Tarasov's 247th had only two rifle regiments (the other was in Rzhev fighting with 119th Rifle Division) and a light artillery regiment under its control at this point. Nonetheless it had been only slightly understrength in late September, and like a number of NKVD-based divisions was overstrength in officers, small arms, machineguns, trucks, radios, and, surprisingly, 76mm field guns.[35] With a backbone of NKVD cadres, it gave the panzers a tough fight.

At 1300 hours on October 10th, in cold and clear weather, the panzer division stormed Sychevka with help from one regiment of 6th Infantry Division while most of 36th Motorized Division was still sitting halfway between Gzhatsk and Karmanovo. The 900th *Lehr* Brigade reached Sychevka late that day, following Kruger's panzers.

Without waiting for reinforcements, 1st Panzer pushed through and around Sychevka to the east and then advanced northward along the road to Zubtsov, fighting its way through 247th Division's rearguards that were falling back before it. Briefly delayed by lack of fuel, by 1700 hours it reported it had taken 2,000 prisoners and forty artillery pieces (the division had reported it had 12,031 men, thirty-three 76mm guns and eighteen 45mm AT guns on September 20th). 247th Rifle Division had been smashed. One prisoner informed his captors that there were no reserves behind the division.[36]

XXXXI Motorized Corps recorded in its evening order at 2245 hours that the tough Soviet resistance had been broken, and the enemy was being overrun by the pursuing armored spearheads. 'In front of the northern flank of 9th Army and in front of the 16th Army in the Valdai region and west of Rzhev is an enemy group with a combat strength of seven divisions, and three cavalry divisions. Most are tied down on the front. Additional forces must be reckoned with.'[37] 36th

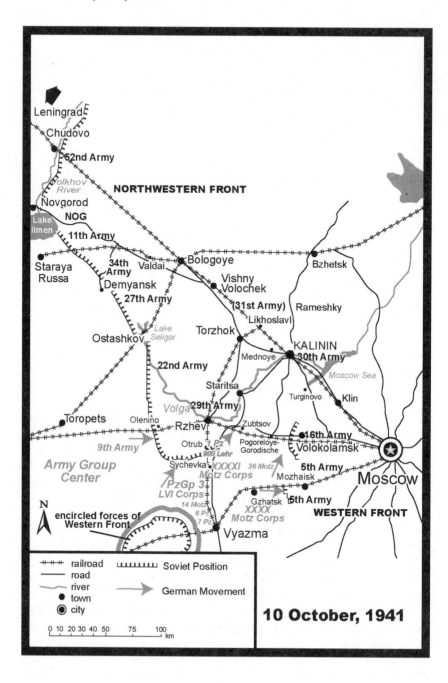

10 October, 1941

Motorized Infantry Division, advancing well to the east of the rest of the corps, took Gzhatsk in the late afternoon, capturing sufficient fuel, it believed, to supply the entire corps for a day.

Meanwhile, General of the Army Georgi Konstantinovich Zhukov, having finished his inspection of the shambles of Western and Reserve Fronts, spoke to Stalin from Western Front's headquarters at Krasnovidovo, 25 kilometers (15 miles) northwest of Moscow. Stalin told him, 'General Headquarters has decided to appoint you Commander of the Western Front. Konev will be your deputy. Any objections?' Zhukov replied, 'No, what objections can there be? I think Konev should be put in command of the forces in the Kalinin sector of the Front. That sector is too far removed, and we've got to make it a secondary division of the Front.' 'Very well,' Stalin replied.[38] Konev had commanded Western Front when Operation Typhoon had commenced, but had badly lost touch with the situation, failing to notify the *Stavka* in a timely manner or to maneuver his troops to either block the breakthroughs or evade the encirclement of most of his forces.

The situation was desperate, and Zhukov and the *Stavka's* first priority was to find something, anything, to throw into the way of the oncoming panzers and keep them out of Moscow. A new defensive position was to be established, called the Mozhaisk Defense Line. For the moment, building and manning this position was the most important priority. Kalinin would have to wait until Konev got there and found out what the situation was.

Over the Vyazma region, the *Luftwaffe* had taken advantage of the good weather to fly 537 sorties against Soviet units in the pocket attempting to break out. On the other hand, while the Germans had sent two fighter groups [*gruppen*], II and III of 53rd Fighter Squadron [*Jagdgeschwader* 53, or JG 53], to the rear for a rest, and another, II of JG 3, had been sent to reinforce the German effort in the Crimea, the Soviet Air Force (VVS) had flown four bomber regiments from Central Asia into Moscow, and from October 11th through the 18th conducted an all-out air offensive, striking primarily at the threatening German panzer spearheads.[39]

October 11th

The day dawned cold and dry, and partly cloudy. In the morning all three divisions of XXXXI Motorized Corps continued their advance, with 6th Infantry on the left, pushing enemy rearguards from 162nd and 242nd Rifle Divisions towards Rzhev. 1st Panzer in the center moved northeast, taking the road from Sychevka towards Zubtsov, followed by 900th *Lehr* Brigade, and leaving the Sychevka–Rzhev road to the 6th Infantry to mop up. 36th Motorized Infantry's leading elements (two battalions and the reconnaissance battalion) were pushing north, well out to the east of the rest of the corps. At 1745 hours, after sundown, they took the town of Pogoreloye-Gorodishche, and the bridge there over a small tributary that flowed west into the Volga River. Most of the division, however, remained stuck south of Sychevka for lack of fuel.

Beset by fuel problems, the corps ordered all of its divisions to form strong advanced detachments to push the advance with active *Luftwaffe* support.[40] The *Luftwaffe* informed Panzer Group 3 at 1535 hours that a 'Gigant' transport glider would be sent to fly in fuel for LVI Corps. By noon the panzers reached Zubtsov and entered on the heels of the fleeing Soviets, capturing 600 cubic meters of fuel. They also seized the bridge there, reporting triumphantly that they had an intact bridge over the Volga in their hands.[41]

At 1500 hours the XXXXI Corps' combat journal (*kriegstagebuch*, or KTB) reported that air reconnaissance had spotted 'strong enemy columns on the road and railroad Rzhev–Staritsa . . . . On the ground these reports give 1st Panzer Division the opportunity to strike the enemy northeast of Rzhev, near Koljedino and destroy him.' Panzer Group 3 described 5–600 vehicles retreating from Rzhev towards Staritsa. Koledino is on the west side of the Volga River, 17 kilometers (10.5 miles) northeast of Rzhev, at a crossroads where the Rzhev–Staritsa road is joined by the road from Zubtsov to the south. The plan was based on the understanding that the bridge at Zubtsov actually crossed the Volga River. However, it did not; only a tributary of the Volga passed through Zubtsov.[42]

The next entry in the corps' KTB states, 'Report from 1st Panzer Division indicates that the attempt to capture a Volga bridge in Subtsow [Zubtsov] was a mistake, and therefore it is not possible for the division to advance on Koljedino. The reported bridge in Subtsow does not cross the Volga.' The entry also noted orders from Panzer Group 3 that, due to the serious fuel shortages, the divisions of the corps were to establish 'strongpoints' for all the vehicles that did not have full fuel tanks, and that officers and men should remain in these strongpoints to fill up the vehicles as gasoline became available. 'Once this is done, the divisions to take elements of the divisions, make them as mobile and well-supplied as possible, and give them all possible support.' Fuel supply was noted as being 'in only restricted amounts and the 36th Motorized Division's captured supply cannot be concentrated [for distribution].' Presumably this meant that there were no containers to ship the fuel in, nor vehicles to carry it.

There was more than a little confusion detectable in the German intentions at this point. Panzer Group 3 concluded that not only had enemy resistance been broken, but the enemy had no reserves left. It was time for advancing boldly, even if fuel was in very short supply. But where should they go, and by what route? Compounding the problem was the lack of good maps, which meant they had to feel their way forward. 1st Panzer Division, having smashed through 247th Rifle Division at Sychevka and taken Zubtsov, thought it could advance across the Volga on the bridge they captured, only to find the bridge crossed a minor tributary. At 1425 hours Reinhardt informed Ottenbacher that he wanted him to advance on Rzhev, 'He could take it as a license to go and loot, especially fuel. He should get there, but not get involved in a fight (such as in front of Sychevka).' Five hours later, however, Reinhardt learned from *Luftwaffe* reconnaissance flights that 'the spearhead of 1st Panzer is not marching towards Staritsa, but rather towards Rzhev.' The record of the Panzer Group expresses displeasure with this, feeling it would have been better 'if the division had moved to the east.' [The emphasis is in the original.] Reinhardt wanted the enemy retreating from Rzhev to the northeast to be cut off, not pushed back. At 2120 hours Panzer Group 3 issued an order to Ottenbacher, telling him that the *Schwerpunkt* (point of concentration) was Staritsa, and it should be reached 'from the east,' which is to say from the east side of the Volga, not the west. 1st Panzer was to turn 180°, push east to Pogoreloye-Gorodishche, then, taking control of the advanced force of 36th Motorized, turn sharply north and push on to take Staritsa.[43]

The forward detachment of 36th Motorized Division had captured Pogoreloye-Gorodishche, while after a sharp fight 6th Infantry Division had taken Otrub, 10 kilometers (6 miles) south of Rzhev, and was setting up a series of strongpoints to defend the corps' left flank against the concentration of enemy forces around Rzhev.[44]

At 1800 hours, the commander in chief of Army Group Center telephoned General Reinhardt at Panzer Group 3 to inform him that 'the Panzer Group will probably be directed from Kalinin to the northwest (Torzhok, Wyschnij Wolotschek [Vyshniy Volochek].)' The shape of the battle was coming into focus. While LVI Motorized Corps was still largely immobile due to lack of fuel, with just a few battalion-sized groups following well behind Ottenbacher's corps, he was to strike through Staritsa to Kalinin, take the city, and wheel to the northwest, to encircle the Soviet armies hanging over the flank of Army Group Center.

At this time, Konev had not yet reached Kalinin, and Soviet defenses in front of the advancing XXXXI Motorized Corps were nearly nonexistent. There was little the Soviets could yet do to parry this ambitious German thrust.

October 12th

On October 12th, the *Stavka* signaled Zhukov to retain the 5th, 133rd, 243rd, 246th and 256th Rifle Divisions for the defense of the Kalinin region. The 110th and three battalions of the 133rd had already passed through Kalinin, but the 5th, the rest of the 133rd, and 256th were all moving on the city, and the 243rd and 246th were waiting to detrain in Rzhev and march on Staritsa. 5th Rifle Division detrained in Kalinin station in the early afternoon of the 12th. General Konev, who had just arrived with a small group of officers, ordered the division to establish defensive positions south of the city.[45]

In his memoirs, Konev reported he arrived in Kalinin from Moscow during the evening of October 12th, where he found the city under attack by German bombers, fires burning, a single battalion of militia without arms, civilians demanding evacuation, and panicky reports of German paratroopers.[46] He issued his first order to 30th Army at 1620 hours:

1. An enemy group of up to forty tanks took Zubtsov on 11 October and smaller groups of tanks have moved to the northeast.
2. Major General Khomenko [30th Army's commander] is to collect the scattered elements of 30th and 31st Armies and organize the defense in the area Turginovo–right flank of the Volokolamsk fortified area.
3. Unload 5th Rifle Division, which is tasked with organizing defenses along the Ivanishchi–Moscow Sea line to securely cover Kalinin from the south and southwest.
4. Subordinate 5th Rifle Division and all scattered elements of 30th and 31st Armies, collect and organize into fighting units, and move them to defend the specified line.
5. Establish order and decisive actions against cowards, panic-mongers and deserters fleeing the front, and shoot [them] on the spot.
6. Create blocking detachments to arrest fugitives from the front.[47]

Interestingly, Konev describes Lieutenant Colonel Telkov's 5th Rifle Division as a division that 'had suffered losses in previous battles, but had not yet lost its combat effectiveness. It had artillery units and a small number of tanks.' No other Soviet records indicate 5th Rifle Division had any tanks and one can only conclude that by 'effectiveness' he meant the division was still cohesive. When it arrived in Kalinin, the division's strength amounted to 1,964 men, 1,549 rifles, seven medium machineguns, eleven light machineguns, six 45mm antitank guns, ten 76.2mm guns, and four 122mm howitzers. Its rifle regiments averaged 430 men each. Its 'combat effectiveness', therefore, was that of an understrength rifle regiment with some artillery rather than a rifle division.

Once it reached Kalinin, 30th Army ordered the division to man defensive positions along an extended front from the Volga River to the Moscow Sea; its 142nd Rifle Regiment deployed with its right flank anchored on the Volga River west of Kalinin, and its left on the T'maka River, straddling the road from Staritsa, with 336th Rifle Regiment on its left, covering the road up from Volokolamsk, and 190th Rifle Regiment in reserve in the southern portion of Kalinin. To cover the southeast approaches to Kalinin, there was only the company-sized junior lieutenants' training course from the Northwestern Front, which was in Kalinin. With no prepared defensive positions, there was little chance of this division holding back the oncoming 1st Panzer Division.[48]

Zhukov at Western Front reported to the *Stavka* that two tank [panzer] divisions, one motorized division, and at least three infantry divisions were attacking towards Kalinin from the Sychevka and Zubtsov region. [The Soviets consistently identify 6th Panzer Division as part of XXXXI Motorized Corps. While this division *was* assigned to the corps, and was desperately wanted, it never arrived during the battle; only its motorcycle battalion reinforced with an antiaircraft battery reached Kalinin before the last week of October.] The 1st Panzer Division was reported to be in the region 25 kilometers (15 miles) southeast of Staritsa as of 0935 hours on October 12th. A regiment of antitank guns was to be sent from 22nd and 29th Armies [it is unclear if this meant a regiment from each] by truck to the Staritsa area to cover the approaches to Kalinin. 174th Rifle Division was ordered to Staritsa to cover it from the direction of Rzhev, and the chief of the Kalinin garrison was to assemble such troops as he had to protect the Borisovka and Pokrovskoye sector, 13 kilometers (8 miles) southwest of Kalinin. If the enemy succeeded in breaking through to Kalinin, Zhukov requested the *Stavka* release one rifle division and one tank brigade to his control from its strategic reserves.[49]

In fact, however, the *Stavka* had no rifle divisions available, but Lieutenant General Yakov Nikolayevich Fedorenko, chief of the Red Army's Armored Forces, sent orders to 21st Tank Brigade in Vladimir to entrain and head for Kalinin, by way of Moscow.[50]

The Soviet High Command was stirring, becoming aware of the threat XXXXI Motorized Corps' drive to the northeast was posing to Western Front's right wing and potentially to Northwestern Front's flank and rear, and was beginning to move forces to the Kalinin region. The next few days would indicate whether or not these forces would arrive in time.

The Germans, of course, had not been standing idly by. Kruger's 1st Panzer Division took to the roads east at 0500 hours, heading from Zubtsov through Pogoreloye-Gorodishche, turning north and passing through 36th Motorized Division's advance detachment there by 0830, and continuing on to Staritsa and Kalinin. Meanwhile, 6th Infantry Division fended off a weak Soviet counterattack in the Otrub area, and by 1245 hours 36th Motorized Division also began attacking toward the north. At the same time, General Gollnick 'demanded' that 118th Regiment be returned to his division, but the corps refused. There was little Soviet resistance during the corps' northward advance; most of the problems the Germans had to overcome were bad roads and, especially, acute shortages of fuel.

The German advance was plagued by a dearth of good roads, and what with the weather, scattered retreating groups of Red Army men from time to time cutting them, deterioration resulting from continuous traffic by heavy vehicles, delayed action Soviet mines, and damage to culverts and the like, competition between German units for the use of the few roads to Kalinin is a motif that recurs repeatedly during the battle. In the early hours of October 12th, 9th Army issued an order restricting motorized traffic to the hours of 0500–1800 hours, and foot and horse-drawn traffic to the hours of 1800 to 0500. The infantry were to sleep by day, while the motorized units could sleep and do maintenance by night.[51]

1st Panzer Division's vanguard rolled into the town of Staritsa at 1500 hours.[52] They captured a battery of what they described as 210mm guns (more likely 203mm gun/howitzers) on the outskirts of town and, more importantly, captured the bridge across the Volga.

Or not, depending on which account you believe. There is more confusion about the Staritsa bridge situation than most other questions concerning the battle of Kalinin. At 0900 hours on October 12th Panzer Group 3 reported in its diary that, 'The Flieger Corps will attack the northern part of Staritsa and the Volga bridge there by (later this) morning.' By 1530 hours the same day it recorded that, 'The Volga bridge in Staritsa was destroyed by its own (the enemy) air force.' Stoves, who was in the battle, says that the Soviets destroyed the bridge before Eckinger's detachment rolled in. In contrast, the Soviet Western Front reported that the bridge fell intact to German paratroopers. While German paratroopers *were* used to seize a number of bridges and airfields early in the invasion, there is no mention of any paratroop drop during the battle for Kalinin, and this almost certainly refers to the sudden and unexpected arrival of German troops, by motorcycle not parachute, in Staritsa. The Russian word *desant* (literally 'descent') can be used to describe troops who arrive by parachute, or boat, or even from the back decks of tanks. In its daily report on October 12th, XXXXI Corps reported that the bridges at Staritsa were 'broken'. The next day's report indicated that the broken bridge was repairable within 36 hours, with a carrying capacity of eight tons. By October 14th Panzer Group 3 was ordering LVI Motorized Corps' engineers to 'undertake the restoration of the Russian 16 ton expedient (temporary) bridge over the Volga at "Sztaritza" . . .' The best description seems to come from Panzer Group 3, which on October 13th at 0600 hours recorded that 'On the road Staritsa–Torzhok there is no bridge over the Volga, only a 'catwalk' [*Laufsteg* – which would indicate a footbridge]. The high banks there are not suitable for a bridge. But 1–1.5 kilometers west of Staritsa there is a damaged Russian temporary bridge (16 ton) and a captured 6–8 ton capacity ferry. Repairing the temporary bridge seems possible.' In other words, there were actually three different crossing means in or near Staritsa with varying capacities, and even professional German military observers on the spot confused them (and the people they were reporting to).

Kruger then ordered his division to send Major Eckinger's advance detachment ahead (*Vorausabteilung Eckinger*). The rest of the division was to drain fuel from all of its tanks and trucks, 'top off' Eckinger's vehicles, and form a strongpoint in Staritsa to await future gasoline deliveries. Major Eckinger had led advanced detachments for the division before, usually leading from the front, and he was perceived as very heroic by the whole of 1st Panzer (he was the first man in the division to win the Knight's Cross). His detachment was formed around the nucleus of his own 1st Battalion, 113th Motorized Regiment (I/113) of armored halftrack-mounted *schutzen*. To this was attached 3rd Panzer Company from I Battalion, 1st Panzer Regiment (3.I/1 Pz). It also had one or two batteries of divisional artillery and two antiaircraft platoons. By 1700 hours Eckinger reported his group had been 'cutting through flying enemy columns, and has captured an immense amount of material and destroyed motor vehicles and equipment of all kinds.'[53] These 'enemy columns' were the rear elements of 30th and 31st Armies, fleeing up the highway from Rzhev to Kalinin. Meanwhile, the panzer division's 1st Motorized Regiment remained in Zubtsov providing security and awaiting fuel.

Many historical accounts of the battle of Kalinin place great emphasis on Eckinger's detachment, and more than a few give it credit for taking the city by itself in a brilliant display of superior German daring and skill.[54] The true story is a bit more complex.

36th Motorized Division began its advance from Pogoreloye-Gorodishche after most of 1st Panzer Division had already passed through the town. Half of the motorized division, 118th Motorized Infantry Regiment, was diverted to help 1st Panzer hold Staritsa, over the heated objections of General Gollnick. It appears that the rest of the division made very little progress to the north from Pogoreloye-Gorodishche, but not due to enemy opposition, for at 1700 hours the division reported it could not continue the attack north until it received more fuel. In its response, the corps noted that it was taking eight to ten days for a truck to make the round trip to the supply dumps and even then they could not get enough gasoline.[55]

At 1800 hours, General Reinhardt from Panzer Group 3's headquarters ordered XXXXI Motorized Corps to seize all roads leading north or west, and be prepared to attack in either direction. General Ottenbacher replied that the corps estimated an attack northward promised the greatest victory, but also insisted that, once captured, the city of Kalinin would have to be defended with 'stationary' (infantry) forces or it would be impossible for his corps to attack towards Torzhok-Bologoye or Bezhetsk at all.

One hour later, now well after dark, XXXXI Motorized Corps' chief of staff Colonel Röttiger expressed his concern that the 'enemy collection south of Rzhev' might attempt a breakout in the direction of Zubtsov, 16 kilometers (10 miles) west-southwest of Rzhev, and Otrub. Therefore, he ordered one battalion of 36th Motorized to concentrate in the Zubtsov region and prepare to counterattack any Russian penetration. By 2200 hours the bulk of the motorized division had found enough gas to close up on Pogoreloye-Gorodishche.

Meanwhile Eckinger continued his pursuit in the dark, finally reporting before midnight to Kruger that his group was 15 kilometers (9 miles) southwest of Kalinin and going into defensive *laager* for the rest of the night.

The corps set its objectives for October 13th as seizing the line extending from the Volga River southward through Kalinin and Staritsa to Zubtsov, and taking the Otrub and Sychevka line against enemy forces who were believed to be retreating to the north and west. Another road to Kalinin further east was to be seized so that motorized elements could advance on Kalinin from the south and southeast through Nikulino-Gorodishche. 'Lively hostile low-flying aircraft and isolated bombing attacks,' were noted.[56]

The Initial Fight for Kalinin City, October 13th–14th

October 13th

The Soviet Air Force (VVS) in the Moscow area had been reinforced by four bomber regiments flown in from Central Asia on October 10th.[57] As the *Stavka* and Western Front began to react to the increased threat to Kalinin, on the night of October 12th/13th, some of these aircraft were active over the extended XXXXI Motorized Corps. Although they failed to inflict much damage on the Germans, their presence was a portent of things to come.

The Soviet 133rd Air Division's 42nd Long Range Bomber Regiment flew its first sortie on October 13th. Led by Deputy Regimental Commander Captain V.V. Ulyushkin, a dozen DB-3Fs (later renamed the Il-4) came in just under the cloud layer at 500 meters (roughly 1,700ft), hunting German columns on the roads south of Kalinin. The enemy was spotted in a forest just southwest of the village of Boriskovo, 20 kilometers (12 miles) southwest of Kalinin on the Staritsa road. Fifteen bombs were dropped, four of which hit among the vehicles on the road. As their flight continued, Lieutenant Nekhay's aircraft fell behind and was intercepted by two German fighters. Forced to attack from below due to the cloud cover, one of the fighters closed in for what looked like an easy kill, only to be shot down by two bursts from the DB-3F's belly gunner. Reaching the Lotoshino–Kalinin road, the Soviet bombers dropped five more bombs on a German column, claiming hits, but Nekhay's plane was hit by a 2cm antiaircraft shell that started a fire. The pilot put out the fire by drastic maneuvering and diving to 150 meters altitude. There it was attacked by another pair of German fighters but Nekhay was able to bring his damaged plane home, flying just over the tree tops.[58]

The day dawned to cloudy skies that soon produced snow flurries, an ominous sign for the Germans, but by afternoon the sky was clearing. Besides the snow, there were other worrisome indications. As Major Eckinger's detachment began moving towards Kalinin, at 0915 hours they encountered reconnaissance elements of the Soviet 5th Rifle Division's 142nd Regiment. 1st Panzer reported to corps that it was encountering 'stiffening enemy defenses' and 'strong air attacks.'[59] The very weak 5th Rifle Division had been ordered to erect defenses along a 30-kilometer-wide front extending from the Volga River southwest of Kalinin all the way to the Moscow Sea to the southeast. It had established a more sensible position, with its 142nd Regiment straddling the Staritsa–Kalinin road at Boriskovo, 336th Regiment to its left at Ryazanovo, 16 kilometers (10 miles) south of Kalinin, and 190th Regiment, together with Northwestern Front's junior lieutenants' course, deployed further to the east to protect the road from Volokolamsk and the rail line from Moscow. With only six 45mm antitank guns in the division, even with effective air support there was no way it could hope to halt the German advance. Nevertheless, it tried.

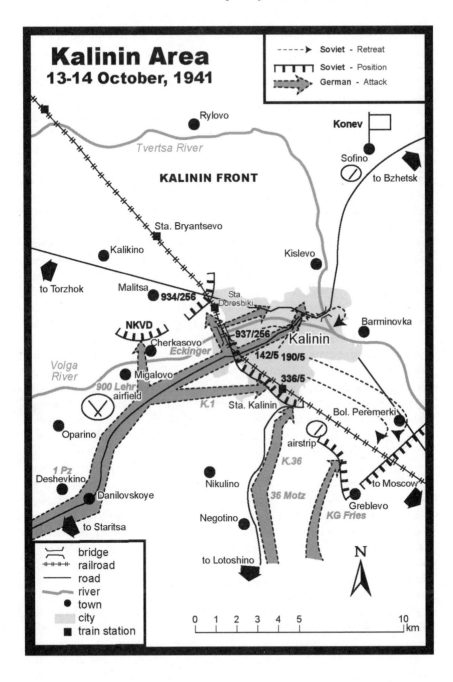

Kalinin Area
13-14 October, 1941

Soviet - Retreat
Soviet - Position
German - Attack

Rylovo

Tvertsa River

KALININ FRONT

Konev

Sofino
to Bzhetsk

Sta. Bryantsevo

Kalikino

Kislevo

to Torzhok   Malitsa
934/256

Sta. Doroshiki

Barminovka

NKVD

Cherkasovo
Eckinger

937/256   **Kalinin**

Volga River

Migalovo

142/5 190/5

900 Lehr
airfield

336/5

K.1   Sta. Kalinin

Bol. Peremerki

Oparino

airstrip

K.36

1 Pz
Deshevkino

Danilovskoye

Nikulino

36 Motz

to Moscow

Greblevo
KG Fries

to Staritsa

Negotino

N

to Lotoshino

⌣ bridge
┼┼┼┼ railroad
── road
～ river
● town
   city
■ train station

0   1   2   3   4   5   10
                     km

By 0900 hours 142nd Rifle Regiment reported enemy tanks attacking in the area west of Danilovskoye. Eckinger's group pushed up the highway and its left wing swung around the Soviets, attacking the village of Oparino, just southwest of Kalinin, and the large airfield at Migalovo situated next to the village. One group of Germans, identified by the Soviets as a battalion (but probably less), forded the Volga west of Kalinin and seized the village of Cherkasovo on the river's northern bank. 142nd Regiment then fell back to the southwestern edge of Kalinin, where it was joined by local militia.[60]

The two battalions of 1st Panzer that had remained in Staritsa awaiting fuel supplies were not idle; they cleared Soviet troops from the western part of the town and by noon had seized the bridge spanning the Volga River. Corps noted that there was no noticeable enemy, and the bridge across the Volga was 'in hand.'

This situation, however, did not last long. Earlier General Maslennikov's 29th Army had dispatched some of its forces to Staritsa; not 174th Rifle Division as ordered, since it was busy fending off XXIII Corps' 226th Infantry Division west of Rzhev, but instead Brigade Commander A.N. Ryzhkov's Separate Motorized Rifle Brigade. This force arrived on the banks of the Volga opposite Staritsa in late afternoon. Attesting to its arrival, by 1700 hours XXXXI Corps reported, 'strong enemy attacks against the Staritsa bridgehead repulsed . . . it is already obvious that the Corps cannot hold the line taken with [its] weak strength, and also loss of vehicles from accidents, ammunition shortages, and terrain obstacles.' Therefore, corps directed Lieutenant General Auleb's 6th Infantry Division to 'send strong forces to secure the [flank of the] attack against Kalinin, so that the weak security line Otrub–Sychevka isn't driven in.'[61] Thereafter, the town of Staritsa would remain a serious distraction for XXXXI Motorized Corps for nearly a week, tying down quite a number of battalions that could have been better used in other places.

Meanwhile, Western Front, in a report signed by its chief of staff, as well as its chief of operations and military commissar, provided what can only be described as a wildly inaccurate and confused picture of the situation. This report described the Germans at the end of October 13th as having tank columns 15 kilometers (9 miles) northeast of Zubtsov and infantry 12 kilometers (7.5 miles) southwest of Zubtsov. It also claimed that German 'parachutists' had seized the bridge at Staritsa, and then, one sentence later, stated, 'Staritsa was taken by an enemy reconnaissance group on 13 October. A motorized rifle brigade has been sent to liquidate the enemy near Staritsa.'[62]

By this point, Soviet resistance in the Vyazma pocket was coming to an end, with the Germans claiming over 600,000 prisoners of war and a mountain of captured equipment, although a number of Red Army formations successfully fought their way out of the encirclement and many other individual soldiers hid in the forests and little villages. They would be heard from again, but for the moment this meant that increasing numbers of German divisions would become available to reinforce the panzer spearheads that had lunged eastward and north-eastward. To get these divisions forward, however, would take time.

At Rzhev, the Germans were closing in. Two Soviet I-16 fighters from 46th Mixed Air Division's 180th Fighter Regiment, based in Rzhev, flew an air recon-naissance sortie over Zubtsov and reported that German columns were crossing the river there; some headed for Staritsa to the north, some turning northwest towards Rzhev. The regiment was then ordered to scramble out and fly to Kalinin. The first squadron off, under Captain Timofeyev, landed at Kalinin, and the pilots were surprised to see no friendly aircraft on the ground. Taxiing up to the control tower to find out what was going on, they suddenly came under fire from a German soldier who stepped out from behind a tent. Timofeyev wheeled his I-16 around and led his squadron back into the air. One pilot, hesitating, was hit by machinegun fire that caused his engine to stall after take-off. He crash-landed near a wood; after a few days in hiding he managed to make his way back to Soviet lines and rejoin his regiment.

The regimental commander, Captain Sergeyev, flew out last with his adjutant, Lieutenant Khlusovich. On the way to Kalinin they flew over Staritsa, where they observed Junkers Ju-87 Stukas active, and shot down one, but themselves came under attack by German fighters which damaged Khlusovich's aircraft. Coming in to land at Kalinin in their MiG-3 fighters, they too were surprised to see no friendly aircraft around the runway. Instead, they noticed strange vehicles parked on one side of the airfield. Captain Sergeyev got out of his plane to investigate, despite Khlusovich's warnings. Suddenly a truck drove up, and German soldiers jumped down. The regimental commander had no chance, and was captured immediately. Attempting to take off again, the adjutant had to knock one German off his aircraft's wing with his pistol but got away, landing safely at Klin. In December the mutilated body of Captain A.P. Sergeyev was recovered when the airfield was retaken by Soviet troops. The technical staff and airfield service unit successfully evacuated Rzhev by driving north through Torzhok to Likhoslavl, where they entrained for Klin.[63] These would not be the last aircraft to encounter enemy ground forces on Migalovo airfield. The next encounter would come four days later, when 'the shoe would be on the other foot.'

While the Red airmen were having a bad day, they nonetheless made a number of attacks on the advancing German columns, and in the afternoon scored a major victory when two Soviet fighters pounced on a *Fieseler Storch* single-engined liaison plane south of Kalinin. The plane was flown by *Luftwaffe* Colonel Meister, chief of staff of VIII Air Corps, and he was carrying Lieutenant General Ottenbacher to visit the forward units of his corps. The plane was forced down in flames, and both Meister and Ottenbacher were severely burned, and subse-quently evacuated to Germany. Panzer Group 3 indicated that, 'Temporary command of the corps will remain with him [Ottenbacher] until the commander of 1st Panzer Division [General Kirchner] gets back from his visit with the troops and can take over the corps.' Interestingly, there is no mention at all of this incident in the KTB of XXXXI Motorized Corps![64]

At Kalinin, by 1900 hours Eckinger reported that his men had fought their way into the southwestern part of the city. Enemy resistance was reported as heavy, and the Red Air Force was 'especially active.' Elements of 36th Motorized Division were advancing slowly on Nikulino, just south of Kalinin, and, at the same time, attacks on Staritsa from the west continued. At Zubtsov Soviet artillery was reported as active.

Forty-five minutes later, according to XXXXI Corps' records, General Reinhardt changed his mind about Staritsa, and Röttiger recorded: 'The existence of the Volga bridge at Staritsa raises the possibility of an offensive to the north across the Volga. The commander of the Panzer Group has ordered an attack through Staritsa to the north with 36th Motorized Division, so the division has accordingly been given the order.'[65] But interestingly, there is no mention of 36th Motorized Division in the diary of Panzer Group 3 until 2100 hours that day, and then it attributes the idea of changing the axis of advance for the motorized division to XXXXI Corps, and states: 'XXXXI Corps is considering turning 36th Motorized Division because of the enemy situation on the road to Staritsa. That decision appears to no longer be necessary because the situation at Staritsa is improving.'[66]

The problem the Germans faced was that there were only four bridges that they were aware of crossing the Volga in the area. One was at Rzhev, and this placed it in the path of 9th Army. Two more were in Kalinin, but at this point there was no assurance that they could be captured intact. That made the footbridge and the damaged Soviet pontoon bridge in the Staritsa area a temptation. If they managed to take Kalinin, which they assumed would be no difficult task, and the bridges fell into their hands, all well and good. But if the Kalinin bridges were blown, then an alternate route across the Volga would be important. On the other hand, having 36th Motorized Division cut across the supply lines of 1st Panzer was bound to cause problems, and putting one division of the corps on each side of the Volga, with no way to effectively support each other could be a perilous decision if in fact the Soviets were in some strength on the other side of the river. The Germans were certain that their enemy was defeated and fleeing. But the thought of having Gollnick's 36th Motorized across the river with only a very rickety 'temporary' bridge connecting it to its supply line must have caused someone at Panzer Group or at Corps to think twice.

By this time, two battalions of 36th Motorized Division's 118th Motorized Regiment were arriving in Staritsa to relieve the elements of 1st Panzer that were fighting there, but the rest of the division remained south of Pogoreloye-Gorodishche, waiting for fuel. At the same time, the advance detachments [organization uncertain, but probably either a reinforced infantry battalion or a reconnaissance battalion] of 86th and 162nd Infantry Divisions were reported to have reached Sychevka, likewise headed for Staritsa to relieve the panzer and motorized troops there.

After sundown there were several more attacks on the Staritsa bridgehead, which XXXXI Corps reported included tanks from *Kombrig* A.N. Ryzhkov's Separate Motorized Rifle Brigade, as well as fighting by 6th Infantry Division in the Otrub area, some 16 kilometers (10 miles) south of Rzhev, and more Soviet artillery firing on Zubtsov. At 2300 hours 1st Panzer Division was able to report that it had taken the railroad bridge west of Kalinin against strong enemy defenses. Panzer Group 3, which overheard 1st Panzer Division's report to XXXXI Corps that the bridge had been taken, was dubious about whether 1st Panzer had actually penetrated into the city, since the bridge lies on the edge of it.[67]

Meanwhile, 250 kilometers (156 miles) northwest of Kalinin, Colonel Pavel Rotmistrov, commander of 8th Tank Brigade, had been summoned to the headquarters of General Pavel Kurochkin, commander of Northwestern Front. Kurochkin filled him in on the situation of their neighbor to the south, Western Front, and during the briefing they were joined by the Front's chief of staff, General Vatutin, and the chief of the Front's armored forces, Colonel Pavel Pavlovich Poluboyarov (who would go on later in the war to be a highly successful tank corps commander). Vatutin explained to Rotmistrov the creation of the special operational group and informed him that the two rifle and two cavalry divisions were to assemble in Vyshniy Volochek but that Rotmistrov was to precede them with his brigade and 46th Motorcycle Regiment, acting as the advance detachment of the group. His assignment, said Vatutin, was to reach Vyshniy Volochek by forced-march from his current concentration area in Valdai no later than the morning of October 15th. Once there, his force was to prevent enemy tanks from penetrating to Torzhok and Kalinin.

Kurochkin asked Poluboyarov what assistance the Front could give Rotmistrov, and was told that its maintenance shops were in Valdai, but at the moment there were no tanks available to reinforce the brigade. Although it is not stated in Rotmistrov's memoirs, it seems very likely that Poluboyarov provided 8th Tank Brigade with some repair and fuel trucks beyond its normal allotment. Most of the tanks available to Northwestern Front had been lost in the offensive it had launched against Staraya Russa in August and September, leaving it with maintenance units but with no tanks to maintain.

Even with this additional support, Rotmistrov had been given a tall order. Not only was he to make a forced march of 250 kilometers (156 miles) in 24 hours, but information about what was happening in the Kalinin area, and the strength and intentions of the enemy, was almost completely lacking. Due to Northwestern Front's weakness, Kurochkin hedged his bets, and ordered Rotmistrov to leave twenty-six of his tanks behind in the Lychkovo area near Demyansk to provide at least a small armored reserve. This left forty-nine tanks, which included a full company of seven KV-1 heavy tanks, a one-company battalion of ten T-34 mediums, and a full battalion of thirty-two T-40 light tanks.[68]

That night, the bulk of General Goryachev's 256th Rifle Division arrived in Kalinin by truck: two rifle regiments, the 934th and 937th, and 531st Light Artillery Regiment. The regiments averaged 700 men. The 934th was deployed to the north bank of the Volga west of Kalinin, where it forced the German group out of Cherkasovo, while the 937th took up positions in Kalinin itself in army reserve. After seeing to the defenses, General Konev drove to the headquarters of 29th Army and ordered General Maslennikov to prepare to attack over the Volga with part of his forces to destroy the enemy south of Kalinin and cut off those fighting on the city's edge.[69]

October 14th

October 14th dawned with heavy clouds and cold temperatures, and it was snowing by evening. When Kirchner took command, XXXXI Corps with two divisions and one brigade was deployed roughly in a line running south to north, from Sychevka in the south, northward through Zubtsov and Staritsa to the outskirts of Kalinin, a distance of 152 kilometers (95 miles). It was oriented north and west, attacking northward towards Kalinin with the bulk of 1st Panzer, all of 900th Lehr Motorized Brigade, and part of 36th Motorized Division. The rest of the 36th was strung out south of Pogoreloye-Gorodishche, with its reconnaissance and motorcycle battalions in the lead. 6th Infantry Division was stretched between Sychevka and Zubtsov to the south, fending off attacks from the west and attempting to encircle from the east the three Soviet rifle divisions located south of Rzhev. To the east, there seemed to be only a void. The other corps of Panzer Group 3, General Schaal's LVI Motorized Corps, was further south in the Vyazma–Gzhatsk area, where its 7th Panzer Division was still heavily engaged in containing breakout attempts from the Vyazma pocket, while its 6th Panzer and 14th Motorized Divisions had detached small groups that were probing to the northeast. All were severely short of fuel. Colonel General Adolph Strauss's 9th Army, with five infantry corps, was stretched out south of and mostly to the west of Rzhev, in a line running to the north and northwest to where it connected with 16th Army of Army Group North above Ostashkov and Lake Seliger.

At 0600 hours, just before sunrise, Röttiger recorded that 'It has been agreed that the advance of 36th Motorized Division in the old assault direction to the north be permitted to halt . . .' The reason was again concern for the corps' left flank. Röttiger also noted at this time that the security of Staritsa 'is in the hands of the advance units of 86th and 162nd Infantry Divisions, so the Reconnaissance Battalion of 14th Motorized Division is released.'[70] Interestingly, the corps' diary represents optimism, not facts. At the time, the infantry divisions' advanced detachments were more than a day's march to the south, and 14th Motorized Division's reconnaissance battalion, which was assigned to the corps' control at

1100 hours, was stuck far to the southeast as late as 2100 hours, waiting for gasoline resupply.[71]

The idea of a strike across the Volga with 36th Division had apparently been abandoned overnight, but communications within the division had partly broken down, and division was having difficulty controlling 87th Motorized Regiment as it had lost most of its radios. Consequently, the leading elements of 36th Motorized Division, *Kampfgruppe Fries* (two battalions of 87th Motorized Regiment) and the division's reconnaissance and motorcycle battalions, spent from 0545 to 0717 hours starting off towards Staritsa, then doubling back to go north to Kalinin. They finally got off in the right direction by 0850 hours, after patrols reported that things looked very promising ahead: 'low enemy activity, bridge and road conditions good.' The reconnaissance battalion led the way, followed by the motorcycle battalion, reaching the southern edge of the city just after noon, where they began pushing into the urban area against weak resistance, or at least so the motorcycle battalion reported. The reconnaissance battalion found the going much harder and urgently requested *KG Fries* come up in support. They had no contact with 1st Panzer Division, but the sound of fighting at 1430 hours led them to believe that Krüger's division had not yet taken the Volga bridges.

General Gollnick was not in a hurry to commit the two battalions of *KG Fries* because he was not clear exactly what his mission was at this point. Was he to push his forces into Kalinin to help 1st Panzer Division to clear the city, or was he to protect the corps' right flank? At 1600 word came from Corps that his primary duty was to protect the eastern flank. But communication problems delayed full implementation, as II Battalion, 118th Motorized Infantry Regiment, which had been assigned to support *KG Fries*, had subsequently received an earlier written order, to protect the same flank but from Lotoshino, 70 kilometers (45 miles) south of Kalinin, all the way down to Ostrog, some 80 kilometers (50 miles) further south! Thinking that this was the most recent order, their move north was delayed, and the battalion's southernmost subunits were 150 kilometers (95 miles) to the south and could not be expected until the next day at the earliest. As a result of the confusion surrounding the division's mission, by late afternoon *KG Fries*' two battalions were still 3–6 kilometers (2–4 miles) south of the city, and west of the rail line. This indecisiveness allowed 5th Rifle Division to pull two regiments out of Kalinin to the southeast, under the nose of Gollnick's division.[72] Had 36th Motorized Division brought up two or three battalions to block the southern edge of the city in a timely manner, it might have been possible, when 1st Panzer took the Gorbatov Bridge, to trap 5th Rifle Division against the Volga River. Its continued existence was to prove a sore trial for Gollnick's division in the following week.

The fighting for Staritsa and the German bridgehead over the Volga River was ongoing. Defending the town was a composite command under Colonel Franz

Westhofen of 1st Panzer Division, which consisted of the two truck-borne *schutzen* battalions (I/1, I/113), two battalions of 118th Motorized Infantry Regiment, an artillery battalion from 36th Motorized Division, and some corps artillery. The reconnaissance battalion of 1st Panzer was watching the bank of the Volga south of Staritsa, and beginning to move north.[73]

The XXXXI Corps headquarters, which had reached Pogoreloye-Gorodishche the previous evening, had its attention focused primarily on the situation in Kalinin. Overnight, Major Eckinger's detachment had been heavily reinforced when at 0200 hours 1st Motorcycle Battalion (*K.1* or *Kradschutzen.1*) arrived at the Migalovo airfield just west of the city, accompanied by another tank company. Before dawn more units rolled in, including the halftrack-borne battalion of 1st *Schutzen* Regiment (I/1), 101st Flame Tank Battalion, the rest of the division's 73rd Artillery Regiment, plus engineers, antitank guns, and 900th Lehr Motorized Brigade. The division set up its headquarters just south of Danilovskoye, on the Staritsa–Kalinin road, about 13 kilometers (8 miles) south-west of the city.

For the Soviets, Yushkevich's 22nd Army was resisting the push by 9th Army, giving ground slowly north towards Rzhev. Maslennikov's 29th Army was deployed in two groups: three divisions on 22nd Army's southern flank resisting the German advance on Rzhev, and four divisions moving to pressure the German bridgehead at Staritsa and to mass on the Volga River's western bank between Staritsa and Kalinin. Khomenko's 30th Army, which consisted at this point of only 5th Rifle Division and not much else, was trying to defend Kalinin, and had responsibility to the south, but no units to do anything about it. Finally, Goryachev's 256th Rifle Division was directly under Front control, which meant that Konev was at its headquarters, but it was participating in the defense of Kalinin along with 30th Army, to which it would soon be assigned. As for 31st Army, its headquarters had been withdrawn into Western Front reserve on October 12th, with no units assigned to it.[74] There were other Soviet units converging on Kalinin, amounting to three more rifle divisions, two cavalry divisions, two tank brigades and several motorcycle regiments, but none had yet arrived.

The Germans, however, were largely unaware of these approaching forces and thus perceived the Soviet concentration of forces in the Rzhev–Ostashkov area as a target rather than a possible threat. Although the resistance in Kalinin was serious, and the pressure on Staritsa and Zubtsov worrisome, the Germans were confident it represented the last gasp of a defeated foe and could soon be over-come.

Soviet accounts (whose clocks were set to Moscow time, two hours later than the Germans') report that the Germans assaulted Kalinin along both banks of the Volga at 1030 hours, while the first daily entry in XXXXI Corps' *Kriegstagebuch* speaks of the fighting there beginning at 0900 hours. On the other hand, the

German historian Werner Haupt describes the attack as starting at 0500.[75] At first, the attack involved only Dr. Eckinger's reinforced battalion, and Major *Freiherr* von Wolff's motorcycle battalion, but they were soon reinforced by several tank companies, the flame tank battalion, several engineer companies and all of 1st Panzer Division's three artillery battalions.[76] The 900th *Lehr* Brigade relieved the left flank units of 1st Panzer Division and fought on the north bank of the Volga to secure Doroshika Station and the rail–road intersection just north of it.

The initial assault, attacking from west to northeast, ran into trouble at the railroad underpass in northwestern Kalinin, just south of the Volga and the railroad bridge, where Red Army troops knocked out three German tanks. Subsequently, the motorcyclists were forced to work their way around to the southeast, penetrating the city from there, while Eckinger's battalion attacked the area around the underpass. 256th Rifle Division's 937th Regiment fiercely defended the northern part of the city, forcing the Germans to fight building by building. The Germans made good use of their flame-throwing tanks, and the assault engineers of 37th Engineer Battalion, but were hampered by the limited amount of infantry taking part in the assault.

Although the Germans were in the city center by 1230 hours, the fight continued on all day. 5th Rifle Division, which had been deployed facing 1st Panzer Division's drive, was forced back to the east. Either by order, or because they got cut off from the Gorbatov Bridge and had no choice with the Volga at their backs, 190th and 336th Rifle Regiments were forced to the southeast, slipping out of the city between the railroad line and the Volga east of the city. 142nd Rifle Regiment, the third regiment in 5th Rifle Division, and the division's artillery and support units managed to fall back over the Gorbatov Bridge, and then made their way to the east, taking up positions east of the Volga. The regiments that fell back to the southeast were successful at making their escape because the delay in getting 36th Motorized Division on the right road in the morning meant it was not until early afternoon (German time) that the reconnaissance and motorcycle battalions began tentatively probing the southern edge of the city towards the railroad station. 937th Rifle Regiment of 256th Rifle Division covered the retreat of 5th Rifle Division, and then was forced back across the bridge and then across the Tvertsa River into the northeast quarter of the city. 256th Rifle Division's 934th Rifle Regiment and 16th NKVD Regiment were defending the city's northwestern suburbs against pressure from Germans already across the Volga at the railroad bridge and from the ford at Cherkasovo, again in German hands. The division was split in half and would not be reunited until after the battle.

At 0900, 1100, 1330 and 1700 hours, XXXXI Corps reported that 1st Panzer Division was engaged in bitter and heavy fighting, noting that enemy civilians were also strongly supporting the fight.[77] 36th Division reported light to moderate resistance, but was making very little progress towards the city center, and had neither linked up with Krüger's panzers nor managed to reach the positions they had been ordered to reach on the Volga at Vlasyevo, 8 kilometers (5 miles) southeast of Kalinin. Instead the division's reconnaissance and motorcycle battalions had a foothold in the southern edge of the city, while two motorized infantry battalions were at the east of Mozharino, 7 kilometers (4 miles) south of Kalinin. The rest of the division was scattered: two battalions of 118th Motorized Infantry Regiment at Staritsa, one coming up from Otrub, and one, dismounted, at Pogoreloye-Gorodishche.

Finally, at 1800 hours 1st Panzer Division proudly reported, 'after hard and costly street fighting, [it] has the highway bridge over the Volga in the middle of Kalinin in hand.'[78] This had been accomplished by Eckinger's detachment, pushing from the west and then turning north towards the Gorbatov road bridge. It had a very hard fight against troops from 937th Regiment and 85th NKVD Regiment's militia before it reached the bridge over the Volga, and then had to force its way across a canal and clear a well defended position in a stadium. This was held by stubborn infantry and a number of Soviet artillery batteries emplaced on the river's southern bank.

The commander of Eckinger's 3rd Company, thinking he had a free run to the 250-meter (280-yard) long bridge before coming under heavy fire as he neared the canal and stadium, reported that his company had gone, 'Out of a dream, into the *sauerei!*', which could be translated as pigsty, pickle, or other less pleasant environments. After suppressing the Soviet positions with a smokescreen, his 3rd Company reached the stadium, only to discover the defenders were falling back over the bridge to the northern bank of the Volga. Lieutenant Feig and a *schutzen* platoon were the first over the bridge, quickly followed by others. Although the bridge had been rigged with explosives, either the wires had been cut by artillery fire or else in the confusion no one set them off, and the Germans were able to clear the bridge of all demolition devices and secure a bridgehead on the north bank of the Volga.[79]

937th Rifle Regiment, along with the division's headquarters and artillery, retreated across the bridge, crossed the Tvertsa River to the east, and took up positions in the northeastern part of the city, behind the Tvertsa River, establishing fortified positions in a brewery, several hospitals, and along the embankment of the Tvertsa. Major General Sergei Goryachev, commander of the 256th, was from Kalinin, and was fighting on his home ground. Once the fighting died down, he was able to replenish the division's ammunition and evacuate his wounded; food was found to be readily available in the city.

During the fighting, the Soviets reported that up to sixty aircraft had supported the German attack, bombing factories and other targets, while XXXXI Corps' records complain that in Kalinin, at 1100 hours, 'The air force of the enemy is battling the weak standing forces of the VIII Air Corps constantly.' Again, at 2200 hours, the corps' reported, 'for the greater part of the day, the enemy air force has been active and inflicted "marked" losses.'[80] Similarly 36th Motorized Division complained: 'During the approach to Kalinin [under] continuous bombing attacks. No sign of our own fighters. Bombers are armored.'[81] In response to these complaints, Richthofen's VIII Air Corps [*Fliegerkorps*] would move fighter and ground attack units into Kalinin's airfields two days later.

At the end of the 14th, XXXXI Corps reported that, if other units (1st *Schutzen* Regiment and the reconnaissance battalion from the Staritsa area) could be brought up by the next day, 1st Panzer Division would be prepared to attack northwestward toward Torzhok. 36th Motorized Division was expected to complete mopping-up operations in Kalinin proper. However, the timely arrival of other units remained an open question because of the 'wretched' roads, and by 2200 hours Corps felt that, due to shortages of fuel and ammunition, it would be necessary to 'put future combat operations on hold.'[82]

Kirchner's intentions for the next day required 1st Panzer to strike northwestward up the Torzhok highway with part of the division, while other parts of 1st Panzer and 36th Motorized Divisions would clear Kalinin of enemy forces, and elements of 6th Infantry and 36th Motorized would cover the Staritsa–Zubtsov line. Earlier plans were discussed to organize the defense of Staritsa incorporating the advance detachments of 86th and 162nd Infantry Divisions into a group to be led by the commander of ARKO 30. After defending Staritsa, these detachments would eventually be brought north to relieve 36th Division in Kalinin. However, by 1700 hours it was recorded that neither detachment would in fact reach Staritsa before noon, October 15th, due to 'wretched weather and snowfall soaking the roads.' Heavy enemy pressure was reported continuing at Staritsa, and 6th Infantry Division, which had reached Zubtsov with one regiment at 1500 hours, was still taking heavy artillery fire from the southwest.[83]

At the end of the day, as Germans were settling in to positions around the grain elevator in the southeast part of Kalinin, these men of 36th Motorized Division's 87th Regiment did not know they were being observed by two Red Army artillery lieutenants, I.E. Larinovich and V.I. Kirillov, from positions on the east side of the Volga. Soon after, an order was dispatched over the telephone line, and eight BM-13 launchers of 1st Battalion, 14th Guards Mortar (*'Katyusha'* rocket launchers), let fly their first salvo of the war. Quickly changing positions, the rocket launchers hurled another salvo of 128 132mm rockets at the Germans in Peremerki, a small village along the Volga just southeast of Kalinin.[84]

Other Soviet reinforcements were on their way. Rotmistrov's 8th Tank Brigade formed up into three groups. The first was composed of 46th Motorcycle Regiment, 2nd Tank Battalion (with thirty-two T-40 tanks) and most of the brigade's motorized rifle battalion. This group was followed by another consisting of 1st Tank Battalion, with ten T-34 tanks, and, finally, by the company of seven KV-1 tanks under Lieutenant Dotsenko. Each column was accompanied by a fuel truck and repair vans from Northwestern Front's repair depot in Valdai. Despite occasional enemy bombing, the columns made their best speed towards Vyshniy Volochek and Torzhok. A normal day's march for a tank brigade was considered 60 kilometers (37 miles), or 80 (50) for a forced march. Rotmistrov drove his forces 200–250 kilometers (125–155 miles) in 24 hours, stopping a few times for rest, maintenance, and refueling. With the extra maintenance support, he managed to bring his brigade to Torzhok largely intact. The rapid approach march to battle was to become part of Rotmistrov's characteristic style, whether commanding a brigade, a corps, or a tank army. (Other elements of his style, including an extremely aggressive tactical approach and the use of tractors without mufflers to simulate tank concentrations to mislead the enemy, would also be on display during the fight for Kalinin.)[85]

It is also interesting to contrast Rotmistrov's rate of advance and the regular references in XXXXI Motorized Corps' daily records regarding the 'wretched' state of the roads. It seems unlikely that the road from Valdai to Torzhok was any drier than those from Sychevka to Staritsa and Kalinin, and while Rotmistrov's T-34s were far better at moving through mud than most tanks, his columns could move no faster than their slowest vehicles, and Soviet trucks were not much better than German trucks in handling muddy roads.

The Torzhok road was patrolled by German aircraft during breaks in the cloud cover, both reconnaissance planes and Bf-110 twin-engined fighters of *ZG 26* (Destroyer – long-range fighter – *Geschwader 26*). On October 14th, Soviet fighters, probably from the *PVO* (air defense interceptor) units stationed at Moscow, fell on the Germans and shot down three of the big fighters for no losses.[86]

Just as Rotmistrov's brigade was approaching the battlefield from the northwest, 21st Tank Brigade was approaching from the opposite direction. Like Rotmistrov, Lieutenant Colonel Lesovoi was given no information as to what the situation was, or where the enemy was and in what strength. Ordered to move by rail through Moscow to Kalinin, the brigade's lead elements arrived in Moscow at dawn on October 14th. There the brigade chief of staff, Major D.Y. Klynfeld (who would later command the brigade) met Colonel Demidov from the General Staff, who confirmed General Fedorenko's order to proceed to Kalinin, but had no information about the situation in Kalinin itself. However, a liaison officer did provide the brigade with maps of the Kalinin area. Only later in the day, when the first train reached Zavidovo Station south of the Moscow Sea, 90 kilometers (60 miles) northwest of Moscow, did Klynfeld and Lesovoi learn from railroad workers that the Germans had occupied Kalinin. They decided to unload the brigade and proceed at once through Turginovo towards the city.

While 21st Tank Brigade had been provided with little useful information about the situation it was advancing into, it was not lacking for orders. In ordinary times, the transfer of a tank brigade to the front would be conducted in a normal military manner, with orders coming down from the top and subordination clearly defined. But these were far from ordinary times. The crisis that had begun at the end of September was coming to a head as the Vyazma pocket was dying, and the Mozhaisk Defense Line was coming under heavy pressure. Confusion reigned, communications were poor, and the 'chain of command' necessary for coordinated military operations was showing some serious weaknesses.

As a result, Lesovoi received orders from Lieutenant General Artemeyev, commandant of the Moscow Defensive Zone; from Army General Zhukov, commander of Western Front; from Lieutenant General Rokossovsky, who believed that the brigade had been assigned to his 16th Army; and from Lieutenant General Konev, deputy commander of Western Front, who had been placed in charge of the Kalinin sector. The only officer who does not seem to have tried to direct the brigade was Lieutenant General Khomenko, to whose 30th Army the brigade had been assigned that day. Each set of orders, except Artemeyev's, who wanted the brigade for his reserve, prescribed a blow at the enemy south of Kalinin, but by a slightly different route. By the end of the day, as the tanks detrained in Zavidovo and Reshetnikov, the snow was falling, grounding German air reconnaissance flights. This was a blessing, as the brigade's presence had not been detected by the enemy.[87]

Other Soviet units were in motion besides the tanks. The rest of Vatutin's group, 183rd and 185th Rifle Divisions and 46th and 54th Cavalry Divisions, were on the move, but far more slowly than the speeding tanks, heading down the road towards Vyshniy Volochek and Torzhok. 133rd Rifle Division was also marching on Kalinin from the north, and would arrive the next day, but with only two battalions in each of its regiments. Maslennikov's 29th Army was moving too, massing four divisions on the north bank of the Volga between Staritsa and Kalinin.

Chapter 4

New Operational Plans

Initial German planning for Operation Typhoon, the offensive against Moscow, had not spelled out exactly what the various armies and panzer groups of Army Group Center were to do after the encirclement and destruction of Western and Reserve Fronts and the penetration and smashing of Bryansk Front. Not unreasonably, the Germans could not predict the exact course of events after their initial attacks. Unfortunately for their further efforts to exploit their initial success, they had not stockpiled fuel or other supplies sufficient to take them much beyond Vyazma, their initial objective. Rail lines had been re-gauged up to the Smolensk–Yartsevo area, but the damage to rail yards, stations, water points, signals and switches severely restricted the tonnage that could be railed in from Germany to the dumps around Smolensk, and the limited number and quality of roads, along with the wear, tear, and attrition to the German truck assets, meant that bringing supplies forward was a nightmare. The paucity of roads also meant that there was severe competition for priority on them between the aggressive motorized corps, the plodding infantry armies, and the logistics units trying to supply both. The roads began deteriorating under the heavy traffic, a process accelerated by both the uncertain weather and by the efforts of Soviet sappers who had planted time-fused mines under the main roads as they retreated.

Panzer Group 3 had been the northern pincer that enveloped the Vyazma pocket. This put LVI Motorized Corps into the area north of Vyazma, helping to seal the pocket against repeated Soviet breakout attempts, while XXXXI Motorized Corps had pushed north of the LVI, taking Belyi and turning to the north and northeast to secure the northern flank of the operation. But bigger things were in the works, and they gradually coalesced into a concrete plan. On October 11th Army Group Center had notified General Reinhardt at Panzer Group 3 that his forces would 'probably' be expected to go to Vyshniy Volochek once they had taken Kalinin. During the evening of October 12th the 'probably' had hardened into an order from Army Group Center that Reinhardt's forces should, while holding the line Zubtsov–Staritsa–Kalinin with strong forces, strike up the road to Torzhok and from there to Vyshniy Volochek and also towards Ostashkov to encircle the inner flanks of the Soviet Northwestern and Western Fronts by getting to the east of them.

The next day the Panzer Group was freed from subordination to 9th Army and put directly under the direction of Army Group Center. General Strauss's 9th

Army informed the Panzer Group that the army would not be marching on Moscow, as expected, but towards Kalinin. Panzer Group was attempting to keep its options open, figuring that if the bridges in Kalinin were captured, all well and good, but if they were blown before capture the best way to get to Torzhok would be over the Volga near Staritsa, where the river was narrower. The staff of XXXXI Corps flirted with the idea of putting 36th Motorized Infantry Division over the river at Staritsa to be able to attack Torzhok from two directions, and briefly considered sending the two battalions of 1st *Schutzen* Regiment of 1st Panzer Division from Staritsa to Torzhok by themselves, but Panzer Group nixed both ideas as being a little too risky.

With XXXXI Corps in control of the Kalinin bridges, Panzer Group assigned Major General Franz Landgraf's 6th Panzer Division to Kirchner's XXXXI Corps and ordered it north to Kalinin. The advanced detachment of 14th Motorized Division, its reconnaissance battalion, was ordered to Staritsa, also to come under Kirchner when it got there.[88]

On the evening of October 14th, General Reinhardt issued Order #25, outlining the next tasks for his forces.

German Planning

Panzer Group 3's Order #25[89]

Order #25 makes it very clear that Army Group Center had two objectives: 'Army Group Center is finishing the battle near Vyazma, is beginning the advance on Moscow, *and destroying the enemy halted or retreating in the area of Valdai–Ostashkov–Rzhev*' [author's emphasis]. It noted that 9th Army was advancing towards Kalinin, and through Rzhev towards Torzhok, and would relieve Panzer Group 3 in stages. It also states, 'Army Group North has started an advance in a southeastern direction to destroy the enemy southeast of Leningrad . . .' It hadn't, but would begin its part of the operations in the next two days.

Army Group North's thrust, which involved half of XXXIX Motorized Corps, specifically, 8th Panzer and 18th Motorized Divisions, was to begin with 126th Infantry Division conducting an assault crossing over the Volkhov River north of Lake Ilmen, to be followed by the panzers and motorized infantry. The attacking forces were to advance across the Volkhov River towards Bolshaya and Malaya Vishera and ultimately southeastward toward Bologoye. This German force was opposed by Major General Nikolai Kuzmich Klykov's 52nd Army, two of whose rifle divisions (267th Rifle Division – 3,169 men and twenty-one guns; and 288th Rifle Division – 6,385 men and twenty-four guns) were facing the assault. The *Stavka*, which directly controlled Klykov's army, subsequently reinforced him with one additional division (259th Rifle Division from 34th Army, with 3,563 men and eleven guns, plus a battalion of *Katyusha* rocket launchers), and although

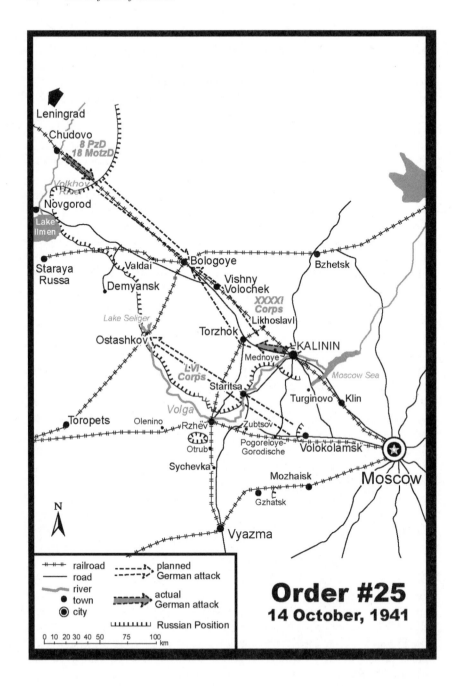

the Germans managed to advance 39 kilometers (24 miles) in eleven days, by October 27th they were halted after taking Bolshaya Vishera.

At this point Army Group North transferred 8th Panzer and 18th Motorized Divisions northward to reinforce XXXIX Motorized Corps, whose drive on Tikhvin was faltering. Its axis of advance was through some of the most dismal terrain imaginable, through swamps and forests, greatly simplifying the Soviets' defensive problems and allowing them to focus on the few roads over which the Germans were attempting to advance.[90]

The planned attack southeastward by half of XXXIX Motorized meant that the advance on Tikhvin was initially conducted with only one panzer division and one motorized division (12th Panzer and 20th Motorized). This makes sense only within the context of the general euphoria that had seized the German high command after the pocket at Vyazma was closed. Even so, the word 'sense' should be used in quotes, as more properly the entire concept of operations should be classified somewhere on the continuum between wildly optimistic and simply harebrained.

Fuel shortages throughout Panzer Group 3 were already so severe that its units were relying on captured gasoline and what the *Luftwaffe* could deliver by air. As a result an order had been issued that operations would have to be carried out by small units: 'It is not possible to fulfill the pursuit and blocking tasks with complete divisions. Frequent special pursuit operations [raids] in the front line with vehicles with small fuel consumption [trucks and motorcycles, not tracked vehicles] will be sufficient.'[91]

The encirclement line from Kalinin to Chudovo on the Volkhov River would be more than 360 kilometers (225 miles) long. The force expected to cover it would be four panzer divisions, three motorized divisions, and a brigade. Since in fact Panzer Group 3 was unable to provide enough fuel to move more than three battalions of LVI Corps during the entire battle of Kalinin, practically it would have meant 1st Panzer Division and 900th *Lehr* Brigade (because 36th Motorized Division was required to hold on to Kalinin) covering the 160 kilometers (100 miles) from Kalinin to Bologoye, and 8th Panzer and 18th Motorized Divisions from 16th Army covering the other 200 kilometers (125 miles). To supply these forces would be a Herculean task logistically, and that was assuming the Red Army simply lay still and waited to be surrounded.

The final paragraph listing the Group's objectives in Panzer Group 3's order #25 stated:

Hold Kalinin, 'Sztaritza' [Staritsa] and 'Subtsow' [Zubtsov] and, with strong forces, advance on Torzhok and prevent the enemy from moving to the north and east by blocking the roads and trails. The Panzer Group is to hold itself ready when relieved by infantry to advance through 'Wyschni Wolotschek' [Vyshniy Volochek] to the railroad junction at 'Bologoje'

[Bologoye] or eastward in the direction of Yaroslavl [245 kilometers (139 miles) northeast of Moscow, 200 kilometers (125 miles) east of Bzhetsk].[92]

A successful northwestward advance by XXXXI Corps to the Vyshniy Volochek and Bologoye regions would link up with the divisions of Army Group North's XXXIX Motorized Corps attacking southeastward and thus envelop the Soviet Western Front's 29th and 22nd Armies and Northwestern Front's 27th, 34th, 11th, and 52nd Armies and the Novgorod Operational Group, the latter two under direct control of the *Stavka*. Indeed, this 'bag' would be larger than the one being mopped up at Vyazma, even though the armies Western Front had lost at Vyazma had contained more rifle divisions and more tank brigades. If successful, this operation would encircle and presumably destroy the remnants of Western Front's entire right wing and much of the forces on Northwestern Front's left wing, putting the Valdai Hills in German hands, removing the threat to the northern flank of Army Group Center and tearing a hole between the reconstituting Western Front and Soviet forces defending Leningrad that could not be repaired.

The Germans could have contemplated this wildly ambitious operation only if they were sure the Red Army was on the verge of collapse. There was considerable evidence to support that conclusion, and the German command was not alone in believing it. Western embassies in Moscow were beginning to report that a collapse was imminent, and Muscovites were beginning to cast fearful eyes to the west. Even though official communiqués carefully avoided admitting the full scope of the approaching catastrophe, the rumor mill was full of reports of units smashed and towns taken, and the smell of panic was in the air.

But neither the German High Command, nor the scared Muscovites, nor the Allied governments, had a clear picture of what was actually happening with the Red Army. Reinforcements were speeding from all corners of the USSR, and there were, in fact, far more forces in the proposed encirclement area than the Germans dreamed. Their belief was that the Red Army now consisted of fleeing remnants, with only rearguards putting up stubborn resistance. Order #25 tasked the 2(F)/33 *Luftwaffe* reconnaissance squadron to fly over the areas of Volokolamsk, Klin, Kimry, Kaschin [to the southeast], Bzhetsk [north], Bologoye, Valdai [northwest] and Ostashkov [west], to find out 'What enemy remains in the area of Torzhok–'Wyschni Wolotschek'–'Waldaj' [Valdai]–'Szelisharowo' [Selizharovo]? What is on the line Torzhok–'Bologoje' to the north, east or southeast behind the Volga?'

The drive on Torzhok was to be conducted not only by Kirchner's XXXXI Motorized Corps, but by Schaal's LVI Motorized Corps as well, the entire Panzer Group 3. Schaal was to swing his forces to the west, passing south of Kirchner's troops, to 'undertake with part of its forces to secure and hold "Sztaritza" and "Subtzow". With the bulk of the Corps, move through Torzhok and block to the west and southwest. Reconnaissance in the direction of Ostashkov.' This meant that LVI Corps, which was to transfer its 6th Panzer Division to Kirchner's XXXXI Corps while taking control of 6th Infantry Division, was to cross the Volga at Staritsa, and drive northward toward Torzhok and would advance to the left of Kirchner's forces as they drove from Kalinin through Torzhok to Vyshniy Volochek and Bologoye. So instead of putting a single regiment or division over the Volga at Staritsa, it was proposed to push a whole motorized corps of two divisions over, despite the lack of a suitable bridge.

To facilitate Schaal's drive, LVI Corps' engineers were to stop repairing the Pogoreloye-Gorodishche– Staritsa road and instead 'urgently undertake the restoration of the Russian 16-ton expedient [temporary] bridge at "Sztaritza", build ramps, as well as establishment and repair of a road on the west bank of the Volga to the road "Sztaritza"–Torzhok.' The panzer group would, 'in the next several days,' send several B-type bridging columns to Pogoreloye-Gorodishche to be assigned in future where needed.

In fairness to Hoth and his successor Reinhardt, it should be pointed out that neither had any particular enthusiasm for this plan. On October 7th, as the Vyazma pocket was closed, the German high command reaffirmed its previous orders that 9th Army and Panzer Group 3 were to head north, away from Moscow. Reinhardt expressed his preference for advancing eastward towards Klin, instead of on Kalinin, but was overruled.[93] On October 14th, Reinhardt noted that his intentions were to:

> If possible, on 15 October to proceed with part of the forces from Kalinin to Torzhok. 1st Panzer Division has enough fuel for 70–100 kilometers. But whether a push by the Panzer Group to Torzhok without a simultaneous attack by 16th Army [of Army Group North] promises success remains questionable: the enemy can always escape to the north.[94]

It is unlikely that von Bock, at Army Group Center, who was as oriented on Moscow as his panzer generals were, would have been too happy with this diversion of strength away from his primary objective, but while many postwar German memoirs emphasize how little faith they had in the grand schemes of Hitler and the OKH, it must have seemed at this point, with Kalinin nearly cleared, that there was little chance of the Red Army being able to stop the victorious *Wehrmacht* from going anywhere it chose to go.

The plan had Hitler's fingerprints all over it, although the orders came down from Army Group Center to the Panzer Group. To emphasize this point, Hitler's adjutant, Colonel Rudolf Schmundt, arrived at Group headquarters at 1330 hours and briefed Reinhardt and his staff as to what was expected of them: 'He reported that XXXXI Corps did not expect the Panzer Group to head northwest. What matters to the Führer is that before the onset of winter as many enemy forces as possible would be destroyed. Gaining more ground is not so important.'[95]

Soviet Planning

The Soviets also had plans for the coming battle for Kalinin. On October 13th, General Konev ordered Yushkevich's 22nd Army to contain the advance by Strauss's 9th Army from Selizharovo to Baumutovo [southeast of Ostashkov to northwest of Rzhev]. The 29th Army of General Maslennikov was to screen the Volga from Baumutovo to Staritsa, while the army's main strength was to move out to the area of Staritsa. 'Other forces' of 29th Army were to force the Volga between Staritsa and Akishevo, halfway between Staritsa and Kalinin, and attack toward Pushkino, 32 kilometers (20 miles) south of Kalinin, and Ryazanovo, 14.5 kilometers (9 miles) south-southwest of Kalinin, in cooperation with the forces defending Kalinin, and smash the enemy's advancing group without giving them the opportunity to take Kalinin.[96] Konev, in his memoirs, claims that after driving to Maslennikov's headquarters he ordered 29th Army to 'Strike a blow across the Volga into the rear of the enemy attacking Kalinin.'[97] He makes no mention of Staritsa.

While, in theory, Konev was to control all forces on Western Front's right wing, he did not have adequate headquarters or communications means to keep track of, much less control, all the forces converging on Kalinin. Vatutin's operational group was streaming down the road from Northwestern Front, with Rotmistrov's reinforced tank brigade well out in front and the follow-on rifle and cavalry divisions far behind them. Rotmistrov lacked a clear picture of the situation in Kalinin, regarding both friendly and enemy forces. He had no

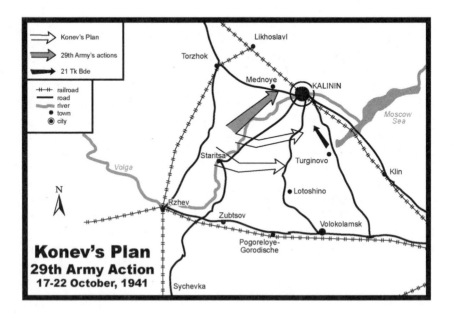

communications with Konev, or with 29th and 30th Armies. Vatutin had ordered Rotmistrov to take command of any friendly forces that he encountered north-west of Kalinin. Similarly, Lesovoi's 21st Tank Brigade, which was coming up from Moscow, neither knew what the situation was in the Kalinin area, nor was apparently aware of Konev's plan to send 29th Army across the Volga, aiming for the same area into which the tank brigade was ordered to attack.

Orders had gone out to Vatutin's group, to 29th Army, and to 21st Tank Brigade, all to attack towards Kalinin, or, in the case of 29th Army, to cross the Volga and strike the enemy south of Kalinin, but there was no information about enemy or friendly forces, or any attempt to coordinate the blows. The whole could not be dignified by the term 'plan,' but at least a substantial Soviet force was converging on the German spearhead with the intention of counterattacking it. While neither overwhelming in strength nor well coordinated, this action by the Red Army was something that no German headquarters had taken into consider-ation in their own ambitious plan. In fact, it would appear to have been the furthest thing from their minds. Therefore, as the pursuit phase of Operation Typhoon was about to end and some very hard fighting about to begin, the Soviets would go into this battle with the advantage of surprise.

Chapter 5

The German Advance on Torzhok, October 15th–16th

October 15th

As dawn broke on October 15th, the skies were gray and heavy with snow clouds scudding along with a brisk wind. The snow wasn't long in coming, and continued all day, with occasional breaks. The day began on a triumphant note for the Germans as Army Group Center announced that the Vyazma pocket had been 'finished', and all mobile units that had been helping seal and reduce the pocket were now released and available for further exploitation.[98] The only fly in the ointment was the lack of fuel needed to actually move these units. Panzer Group 3 recorded in its morning reports that it was prepared to execute its orders, sending XXXXI Corps up the Torzhok road from Kalinin, while LVI Corps was to first take over the security at Zubtsov–Staritsa, and then advance with the bulk of its forces across the Volga at Staritsa, to strike towards Torzhok and Ostashkov.

After spelling this out, the diary of Panzer Group 3 contains a note: 'Again, emphasis to not give extensive direction to the [subordinate] units.'[99] This apparent self-reminder makes for a striking contrast between the German and Soviet command styles. In Soviet orders, headquarters as high as Front commands would spell out exactly what each division in its subordinate armies was to do and in some cases would even give directions as to how many tanks, anti-tank guns, etc, were to be allotted to divisions. In general it was German practice to give orders in terms of objectives, leaving the subordinate corps, divisions, and battle groups free to figure out how to achieve these objectives. Increasingly as the war went on, Soviet micromanagement from the top decreased and German practice became more centralized, but at this point the two armies were directed very differently.

With no clear picture of exactly where the Germans were or how many to expect, Rotmistrov, fearing that enemy soldiers might already be in Torzhok, ordered 8th Tank Brigade and 46th Motorcycle Regiment to deploy and advance cautiously into that town. Finding no enemy, they continued on, reaching Kalikino (also spelled Kalikina and Novoye Kalikino, and now named Zavolzhskii), 10 kilometers (6 miles) west-northwest of Kalinin, by 1000 hours.

En route they were attacked through gaps in the clouds several times by German bombers but without serious losses. The tank brigade then paused in Kalikino for its slower elements to catch up while scouts went forward to find out exactly what the situation was ahead of them.

Reconnaissance revealed that the Germans were holding in the northwestern outskirts of Kalinin. Liaison officers found 256th Rifle Division's 934th Rifle Regiment deployed in the Malitsa region, between the rail line and the Torzhok highway, and 16th NKVD Regiment of border guards holding on to their right, down to the Volga by Cherkasovo. These forces had been engaging elements of 900th *Lehr* Brigade, which were now fighting to control the junction of the rail line and the Torzhok road just north of Doroshika Station.

Since Vatutin had ordered Rotmistrov to take charge of any Soviet forces he found to the northwest of Kalinin, the tank brigade commander took control of the rifle regiment and the NKVD forces. 8th Tank Brigade deployed with its motorized rifle battalion near Kalikino, north of the Torzhok road, and 46th Motorcycle Regiment on the motorized rifle battalion's left; 1st Tank Battalion, with its T-34s, was behind the motorized rifle battalion, and 2nd Tank Battalion, with its T-40s, behind the 934th Regiment. Lieutenant Dotsenko's company of heavy KV-1 tanks was still slowly coming up behind the rest of the brigade while the brigade's two batteries of artillery were still further back up the road. Rotmistrov, taking his time for the whole brigade to close up, rest, and refuel, and for coordination to be worked out with the infantry units he had taken under his command, decided to begin his attack towards Kalinin at 1500 hours.[100]

German records note that 1st Motorcycle Battalion and *I/113 Schutzen* Regiment were fighting to clear the northern part of Kalinin, while the 900th *Lehr* Brigade, reinforced by tanks, led the attack up the Torzhok road and for possession of the intersection of the Torzhok road and the rail line. General Gollnick's 36th Motorized Division was spread all over the XXXXI Corps area. Two battalions of 87th Regiment were clearing the area southeast of Kalinin, while the motorcycle and reconnaissance battalions were in southern Kalinin, trying to mop up scattered groups of Red Army men and militia who were still holding out in the southeastern part of the city. One battalion of 118th Regiment was to move up and join them, while one battalion of 87th Regiment was in Pogoreloye-Gorodishche, out of fuel and providing security for Corps HQ. Two other battalions of the 118th were over in Staritsa. General Gollnick was nervous. The interrogation of several Soviet prisoners had all pointed to heavy reinforcements heading towards the battlefield from the direction of Moscow. While it is very unlikely that any men of 30th Army had any notion of 21st Tank Brigade's approach, it seems possible that in attempts to raise the morale of the troops defending Kalinin commanders and commissars had spread the word that Moscow would send reinforcements.

At 1000 hours 36th Motorized Division recorded that an enemy motorized column, led by motorcyclists, had attempted to drive through the lines of III Battalion, 87th Motorized Regiment (III/87) along the Volga, threatening the fuel tanks between Bolshaya and Malyi Peremerki. The battalion was hastily reinforced, providing it with support from five antitank batteries, two batteries of *Nebelwerfers*, a 10.5cm howitzer battery and a 10cm gun battery from 611th Artillery Battalion. There is nothing in the Soviet records that suggests any motorized unit was just south of Kalinin on this day, but there is just a chance that, if this was real, it was an advanced group from 11th Motorcycle Regiment, which did come up from the southeast between October 17th and 20th.

By noon II/118 Motorized Battalion arrived at Kalinin, and took up positions in the southern part of the city to act as a reserve. To better organize the actions of the motorcycle and reconnaissance battalions, who were still trying to mop up the eastern part of the city, the latter was made subordinate to the former. Although the Soviet motorized column never materialized, the Germans remained jumpy, and for good reason. Beginning at 1400, a series of attacks, described as 'regimental sized', began to come in from the southeast, between the railroad line and the Volga River, all directed against the III/87 that stood there. These attacks were made by 30th Army's 5th Rifle Division, with its 190th and 336th Rifle Regiments. 142nd Rifle Regiment had apparently retreated over the Gorbatov Bridge, and then made its way across the Tvertsa and down the left bank of the Volga, from where it supported the other two regiments of its division across the river. Eventually it too would transfer across the Volga on rafts to join them.

937th Regiment of Goryachev's 256th Rifle Division continued to resist strongly behind the Tvertsa River in the northeast corner of Kalinin; even though the Germans brought tanks forward, they were repulsed trying to cross the Tvertsa Bridge.[101]

At 1030 hours, in keeping with Reinhardt's Order #25, XXXXI Corps' issued an order to its divisions to dismount the majority of their forces and fight on foot in the future, due to heavy losses in vehicles and the fuel situation. Corps HQ had advanced to Pogoreloye-Gorodishche, where corps troops established a strongpoint. At noon, the corps' staff recorded that 6th Panzer Division's advance detachment was to 'combine all the last fuel reserves in the area of "Lataschino" [Lotoshino, on the Volokolamsk road 25 kilometers (15 miles) south of Pogoreloye-Gorodishche], since the arrival of the division in Kalinin is expected in the next few days, and they will reach Lataschino without fuel.' 129th Infantry Division had received orders to march northward to Staritsa the following day. The corps' chief of staff, Röttiger, recorded in his evening report that in late afternoon, 'An enemy counterattack from the west in regimental strength was beaten off. The advance on Torzhok will resume on 16 October when 36th Motorized

Division reaches the northern part of Kalinin.' Panzer Group 3 similarly records opposition on the Torzhok road as an attack in 'regimental strength' that was beaten off by 1st Panzer Division. As of evening, elements of 1st Panzer Division and 900th *Lehr* Brigade were holding in the area of Malitsa and the rail/road junction just west of Kalinin.[102]

The Soviet General Staff study about the battle for Kalinin is similarly reticent about combat operations on the 15th, simply stating:

> Military operations on 15–16 October along the Kalinin axis did not bring about any significant change in the conditions . . . Advances by German XXIII and XXVII Army Corps against the forces of 22nd and 29th Armies reached the Selizharovo, Bolshoi Kosha, Mologino, Panino, and Staritsa line.[103]

However, in fact a significant fight took place towards late afternoon between Rotmistrov's forces and the vanguard of 1st Panzer Division. The German attack was spearheaded by 900th *Lehr* Brigade, reinforced with tanks from 1st Panzer Regiment.[104] Before Rotmistrov could assemble, refuel, rest, and coordinate all of his forces, the Germans began their own attack. Rotmistrov had intended to signal his troops to advance by firing three red flares. However, just before they were to be fired, German aircraft appeared overhead during a break in the snowstorm and bombed the Soviet positions. Immediately thereafter, Yegorov reported a battalion of enemy infantry, supported by fifteen panzers, attacking along the highway. While moving to Yegorov's command post, Rotmistrov ordered the attack to proceed anyway and the KV company be brought forward to support the infantry.

Responding to the brigade commander's attack order, 1st Tank Battalion's T-34s swung in from the north, striking the German flank just as Dotsenko's KVs attacked from the front. At least two German tanks and, according to both Rotmistrov and Yegorov, ten other German armored vehicles went up in flames. A second German airstrike, aimed at the Soviets' left flank, was then delivered, followed by thirty more German tanks attacking the Soviet right flank by the Volga. 8th Tank Brigade's 2nd Battalion, under Captain J.D. Baskakov, engaged this German force, and a very confused and swirling meeting engagement ensued, one that Yegorov described as a 'layer cake' of tanks between Kalikino, Bryantseva Station, and Dmitrovskoye on the Volga. During this fight, Brigade Commissar N.V. Shatalov's T-34 tank took a round in the turret, jamming it, but the tank made it back to headquarters. Catching the Germans in a fire pocket, the Soviet forces advanced all along the line, taking Cherkasovo on the right and Bryantseva Station on the left, and breaking through the German center to reach the Gorbatov Bridge over the Volga.

Soon after, however, a fresh German counterattack drove the motorized rifle battalion back and forced Rotmistrov's troops and tanks onto the defensive. Lieutenant Dotsenko's KV-1 was knocked out on the bridge. That evening it was successfully towed off under the protective cover of an attack by 46th Motorcycle Regiment, led personally by its commander, Major Fedorchenko. Dotsenko was wounded, but survived and was evacuated. It seems likely that Dotsenko's wasn't the only KV knocked out in this fighting. While the German panzers and antitank guns were virtually helpless against the heavy Soviet tanks, the Germans had brought up several batteries of antiaircraft guns, including deadly 88s, to protect the bridges from Soviet air strikes, and these guns had no difficulty dealing with the KV's thick armor.

When the fighting ebbed, the Soviets dug in along a line extending from Cherkasovo and Malitsa, 600 meters northwest of the Gorbatov Bridge, to Doroshika. During this sharp fight, Rotmistrov claimed the Germans lost a total of three tanks, five to ten armored vehicles (presumably SdKfz 251 armored half-tracks of Eckinger's battalion and 900th *Lehr* Brigade), and 600 casualties. Yegorov's account claims that twelve German tanks were knocked out.[105] Rotmistrov's figures, except for the infantry casualty numbers which appear to be too high, seem quite credible. One thing is certain: the appearance of Rotmistrov's brigade was an ugly surprise for the Germans.

1st Panzer Division, while simultaneously complaining that the cold and driving snow, and 'strong Soviet air superiority' were impeding their offensive, was fairly close-mouthed about this action, noting only that: 'On the evening of 15 October the division can report to have secured the front line up to the eastern edge of . . . Malitzy against multiple counterattacks by newly brought up enemy forces with tanks.'[106]

As 8th Tank Brigade was fighting it out with Kruger's panzers on the Torzhok road, 21st Tank Brigade was assigned to 30th Army and ordered to advance north-ward through Nikulino, 3 kilometers (2 miles) southwest of Kalinin, to destroy enemy reserves south of Kalinin and then to retake the city with the help of 5th Rifle Division. Having detrained south of the Moscow Sea, Lesovoi's tank brigade had a difficult march to Turginovo, 37 kilometers (23 miles) south-southwest of Kalinin, at the west end of the Moscow Sea, crossing first the Lama and then the Shosha Rivers. Since the brigade's movement south of the Moscow Sea was cross country through boggy terrain, it took the whole of October 15th. In fact, the brigade suffered its first losses during the move, losing a tank crossing the Shosha River just south of Turginovo. In this instance, the last T-34 to cross over the bridge veered to the right edge of the bridge, causing it to collapse, dumping the tank upside down into the river, on its turret. Unable to escape, the entire crew drowned.[107]

Brigade Chief of Staff Klynfeld later wrote in his unpublished memoirs that, in the afternoon on the 15th, he reached the village of Gologuzovo, 22 kilometers

(13 miles) southeast of Turginovo, where he encountered a staff car containing a tall officer dressed in a cloak. The officer introduced himself as Colonel Lev Mikhailovoich Dovator, the commander of a cavalry group. Klynfeld was delighted, as Dovator was the first representative of the Red Army the brigade had encountered since detraining. Dovator had already earned fame for himself and his cavalry during the August fighting around Smolensk, when he conducted a successful raid deep into Army Group Center's rear area. Thereafter, Dovator's cavalry group had evaded encirclement at Vyazma and had been attached to Rokossovsky's 16th Army. Dovator quickly set Klynfeld and Lesovoi straight, explaining that his 'cossack girls' were conducting a mobile defense on 16th Army's open right flank by covering the 60 kilometers (37 miles) of open territory between the Moscow Sea and Kalinin with two cavalry divisions (the 50th and 53rd – the latter with only 1,100 men, five 45mm antitank guns and forty-five machineguns).[108] After a short meeting, it was agreed to post one company of motorized infantry and one of BT-2 tanks to support Dovator and to cover 21st Tank Brigade's left flank as it headed north.[109]

In Staritsa the German defenders, who included one battalion of 1st Panzer Division and two battalions of 36th Motorized Division's 118th Regiment, with artillery support, were soon to be joined by the motorcycle battalion from 14th Infantry Division (Motorized), and by a battalion each from the 86th and 162nd Infantry Divisions. These six battalions were formed into *Kampfgruppe* [Combat Group] *Metz*, under the commander of 30th Artillery Command (ARKO 30). This group was under heavy pressure from the Separate Motorized Rifle Brigade.

29th Army, following Konev's direction, issued order #30 to its troops at 1130 hours. The order spelled out in detail what role the army was to play in the coming counterstroke. While 220th and 250th Rifle Divisions on the army's right flank were to 'stubbornly defend in accordance with . . . order number 29,' the main forces of the army were to concentrate on the Volga's bank in two groups. The northern group, with 246th, 252nd and 119th Rifle Divisions was to assemble in the Brody area, cross the Volga at Akishevo, and attack *en echelon* on a front of no more than 750–1000 meters towards Ryazanovo, 16 kilometers (10 miles) south of Kalinin, a distance of 29 kilometers. 246th Rifle Division was to lead, reinforced by 432nd Howitzer Regiment and a battery of 85mm antitank guns from 873rd Antitank Regiment, followed by 252nd Rifle Division with 644th Corps Artillery Regiment and a battery of 213th Antitank Battalion, and finally 119th Rifle Division, with three 122mm howitzer batteries attached, to develop the success of the other two divisions.

South of them the Right Group, consisting of 174th and 243rd Rifle Divisions, was to cross the Volga at Staritsa and attack towards Pushkino, 27 kilometers (17 miles) south of Kalinin, to destroy enemy formations on the way to Kalinin, and to provide protection to the south for the Left Group attacking Ryazanovo. 243rd Division was to lead, with 510th Howitzer Regiment and a battery of 873rd

Antitank Regiment, and was to destroy the enemy in the Staritsa area first, then it and 174th Rifle Division, with 360th Howitzer Regiment (minus one battery), and one battalion each of 56th and 336th Corps Artillery Regiments, would join 243rd Rifle Division in its drive on Pushkino.

The plan was detailed and ambitious, and the units were to be in their concentration areas by noon of the next day at the latest. The Separate Motorized Brigade was to go into army reserve as soon as 243rd Rifle Division arrived opposite Staritsa. Detailed orders were issued to the masses of artillery. They were expected to:

• Deny the enemy approaches to the south and southeast along the Volga on the line Staritsa, Ulitino, Gorky
• Mass fires to support the attack firing at enemy defensive systems on the south bank of the Volga and in the areas of Staritsa and Gorky
• Deny the approach of enemy reserves and counterattacks from the depth (of the defense)
• Prevent enemy tank attacks, by preparing the entire fire of the artillery on possible lines of advance of enemy tank attacks
• Suppress enemy artillery blocking the advance of the divisions

This was asking an awful lot of the Red Army's artillery in the fall of 1941. Whether this speaks to the good quality of the army's artillery, or to the unrealistic expectations of its command, is hard to determine. It is noteworthy that the order contains as its last instruction orders to report to the army headquarters when the divisions were each concentrated, when the offensive was begun, every two hours once the battle was under way, and when the objectives were reached. There were also orders for the chief of engineer forces for the army. The order was accompanied by a map, showing the routes the two groups were to take. This map is interesting in that it very clearly indicates the locations of Dovator's cavalry group on the far side of the Volga, and also indicates the planned operation of 21st Tank Brigade, but has no indication at all of the location of Operational Group Vatutin (29th Army's neighbor to the north), nor of General Khomenko's 30th Army, with which the attack would presumably link up. Order #30 has no discussion of the existence or activities of either of these groups, except a brief notation that 'On the left 30th Army is active in the area of Kalinin.'[110]

To the south, the German 26th Infantry Division had taken Rzhev and seized the bridge over the Volga intact. 174th, 250th and 178th Rifle Divisions on the right wing of Maslennikov's army and part of 22nd Army were being pushed northward by General of Infantry Albrecht Schubert's XXIII Army Corps of 9th Army. Three rifle divisions (the 251st, 162nd and 242nd) that had been part of 30th Army were encircled south of Rzhev, contained in a loose sack by 26th Infantry Division and elements of 6th Infantry of 9th Army's VI Army Corps.

161st Infantry Division was approaching Zubtsov from the south with 162nd Infantry following it. To the east, 129th Infantry Division was approaching the Rzhev–Volokolamsk road, heading north.

Panzer Group 3 recorded optimism for the next day. It looked like the weather would improve, the *Luftwaffe* was scheduled to fly in supplies directly to Kalinin, and there were hopes that the fuel situation would improve, 'now that Panzer Group 4, after repeated requests by Panzer Group 3, is ready to return about 500 cubic meters of fuel captured at Vyazma, which they had seized in the area of 7th Panzer Division. It is, however, only a partial refund.'[111]

October 16th

The snow and rain had stopped by morning, and the ground hardened again (though it got soft in places as the temperature rose during the middle of the day). There were still heavy clouds, but flying conditions were acceptable, and it looked like the new German plans could be implemented without interference from the weather.

The orders issued to XXXXI Motorized Corps for the morning of October 16th began by stating:

> The enemy in front of Panzer Group 3 and 9th Army has been defeated. The remainder is either conducting local counterattacks around Moscow and from the northeast, around Torzhok, or retreating. Panzer Group 3 in cooperation with 9th Army will prevent a retreat of enemy forces standing before the north flank of 9th Army and the south flank of 16th Army and destroy them. To do this the Panzer Group will take the zone around Torzhok and from there immediately move against 'Wyschni Wolotschek' in order to prevent the mass of the enemy units from retreating over the 'Twerza' [Tvertsa River] and the upper reaches of the 'Msta' to the east.[112]

The German intentions were clear: to surround and mop up a defeated enemy.

The idea that the Red Army had been defeated was not only current at German headquarters. As the word spread that the Germans had cut through to Kalinin and that the Mozhaisk Defense Line in front of Moscow was beginning to crumble, panic broke out in the capital. Mob scenes erupted at Moscow's many railroad stations as people fought for space on trains out of the city. There was looting, fires, and disorder in the streets. Government ministries were ordered to evacuate, along with the foreign embassies. The next day the announcement was made over the radio that Stalin was remaining in Moscow, and that the capital would be defended 'to the last drop of blood.'[113] Within a few days, the Soviet government declared martial law, and, thereafter, the situation calmed a bit. One cannot criticize the German command too much for their misguided perception, because it was widely shared on both sides of the lines.

With the weather improving, the *Luftwaffe* was able to step up its efforts substantially. Fuel was flown in to Kalinin's Migalovo airport, allowing 1st Panzer Division to refuel. Along with the Ju-52 transport aircraft, the *Luftwaffe's* VIII Flying Corps aggressively transferred *Bf-109* fighter aircraft of *II/JG 52*, Stuka *Ju-87* dive-bombers of *Stab*, *I/StG 2*, and ground-attack planes and *Hs-123* and *Bf-109E* fighter-bombers of *II(S)/LG 2* into the Migalovo and Peremki airfields, respectively southwest and southeast of Kalinin, where they could provide on-call air cover and support for Kirchner's troops. In his report at the end of the day Röttiger could report that, 'Our own air force [provides] cover over Kalinin, [only] isolated overflights by single enemy bombers and close support aircraft.'[114]

However, *Bf-109* fighters of the Luftwaffe's *JG 51* patrolling in the area of Kalinin reported losing three fighters in dogfights, against only two claims of downed Soviet aircraft.[115] On the 'other side of the hill,' Stalin, livid at the German capture of both Kalinin bridges despite preparations to blow them up, ordered the Gorbatov and rail bridges across the Volga destroyed by bombing. A plan was developed to use a remotely piloted TB-3 four-engined bomber loaded with explosives, controlled from a DB-ZB bomber, to crash into the Gorbatov Bridge. However, the Soviets liberated Kalinin before this materialized.[116]

According to Soviet accounts, 1st Panzer Division and 900th *Lehr* Brigade struck out up the Torzhok road at noon.[117] XXXXI Corps' records report that the attack by 1st Panzer was already under way at 0800 hours and, although mounted with 'weak forces', it made 'a good advance.'[118] While XXXXI Corps did not specify what a 'good advance' constituted, Panzer Group 3 recorded that by 1600 hours the 1st Panzer Division had taken Kalikino and was 'advancing further in the direction of Torzhok, parts [of the division] securing north of Kalinin.'[119] According to the Soviet accounts, Rotmistrov's defenses gave way under the attack. Attacking from the Doroshika Station area, the Germans struck at 934th Rifle Regiment, 46th Motorcycle Regiment, and Rotmistrov's tanks (by now numbering only eighteen, including one KV-1, five T-34s, six T-40s and six T-38s, according to Yegorov), capturing the villages of Malitsa, Kalikino, Poddubki, and, by the end of the day, Mednoye, 22 kilometers (14 miles) northwest of Kalinin, and its bridge over the Tvertsa River.

. In this fighting a German tank group penetrated Soviet lines and overran 8th Tank Brigade's headquarters, killing its chief of staff, Major M. Lyubetsky. What was left of Rotmistrov's tank regiment then took up positions in Polustovo, a small village just north of the Kalinin–Torzhok road, a little more than 5 kilometers (3 miles) northwest of Mednoye. By this time, the brigade's motorized rifle battalion and the survivors of 46th Motorcycle Regiment were in the woods and swamps north of the Bryantseva Station, above Kalinin. Thus, the Germans seemed to have achieved the breakthrough they sought.[120]

Konev's report about the situation in his memoirs is even more extreme, and not very credible. He asserted he dispatched Colonel Vorobyev, a liaison officer (actually Konev's chief of operations), to find out what was happening on the Torzhok road. After traveling along a road 'parallel to the Kalinin–Torzhok Road,' (presumably north of the Tvertsa River, although no such road appears on any map, neither Soviet staff maps, nor German *Lage Ost*, nor US Army maps made just after the war), Vorobyev failed to find Rotmistrov's brigade at all, and, instead, reported back that the Germans were in Torzhok unopposed.[121] No other source, Soviet or German, confirms this account.

General Konev, traveling northwest of Kalinin, presumably to find out what was happening in this area, encountered the headquarters of the newly arrived 133rd Rifle Division, commanded by Major General Vasily Ivanovich Shvetsov, at Likhoslavl on the rail line northwest of Kalinin. However, only six of the division's battalions were with Shvetsov, and these were exhausted after a forced march across wet roads from Andreapol, where they had been fighting as part of 22nd Army's right wing.

Lieutenant I. Shcheglov, chief of staff of 2nd Battalion, 418th Rifle Regiment, tells how the battalion was bound for the town of Rylov, on the north bank of the Tvertsa River north of Kalinin. It had been marching for twelve hours, many of the men suffering from colds and coughing. Plans were to bivouac in Rylov, rest and feed the men, and let them bathe in a local bath-house. They reached the village at nightfall, only to be greeted by an officer from division HQ, who summoned the battalion's commander and chief of staff. Following the officer to a farmhouse, they discovered Shvetsov and Konev bending over a map. Shvetsov ordered the battalion, which had just completed a 50-kilometer (31-mile) march, to attack the village of Kalikino and cut the Kalinin–Torzhok road behind the German spearhead. This put an end to the plans for the troops to enjoy a rest in heated buildings, a pot of hot soup, and a bath. Instead, they were marched down to the banks of the River Tvertsa.

Once on the bank of the river, the battalion commander, Captain Aleksandr Tchaikovsky, found that the bridge over the Tvertsa had been destroyed. Since there were no pontoons, inflatable rafts, or any kind of boats available, Tchaikovsky put the weary men to work tearing down barns and houses for lumber to build rafts. Meanwhile, mounted scouts crossed the cold river and headed for Bryantsevo. There civilians informed them that German motorcyclists had been through two days previously, but had moved on. It took until dawn to get the battalion and its heavy weapons across the river; the last to cross were two field kitchens. The tired troops managed a cheer for the hot food.[122]

At the same time that the weary men of 133rd Rifle Division were moving into position north of Kalinin, Maslennikov's 29th Army was assembling troops on the western bank of the Volga in preparation for an assault crossing toward the east to cut the roads leading into Kalinin from the south and sever the German spearhead's communications. 246th Rifle Division was bombed while assembling near the village of Akishevo, 41 kilometers (26 miles) southwest of Kalinin.[123]

The plan to thrust 29th Army across the Volga had first been enunciated by Zhukov on October 12th. His initial thinking had been for 5th Rifle Division to cover Kalinin, while a force of one tank brigade with a motorcycle regiment and a rifle regiment attacked from the southeast towards Salygin and Kalinin and four rifle divisions from 29th Army were to cross the Volga and attack towards Ryzhanov, with one cavalry division covering their southern flank. Simultaneously, Northwestern Front was to send a tank brigade and a rifle division to Mednoye to attack towards Kalinin from the northwest. Zhukov expected the operation to get under way by October 16th. However, both the *Stavka* and Konev had altered and added to the plan, and events had moved faster than Zhukov had anticipated.[124]

Konev had ordered Maslennikov to conduct his 29th Army's assault across the Volga with three rifle divisions, while another (the 119th) was to advance along the left bank of the Volga towards the bridges into Kalinin. For its part, the *Stavka* had insisted that Northwestern Front send three rifle divisions (subsequently reduced to two) and two cavalry divisions, as well as Rotmistrov's tank brigade and the motorcycle regiment, to Kalinin. At 2300 hours on October 16th, on behalf of the *Stavka*, General Vasilevsky ordered Vatutin not to disperse his group's forces from Kaschin on his right to Likhoslavl and Vyshniy Volochek, but instead to form the whole force 'in one group to the area of Likhoslavl–Torzhok, to act jointly to attack and destroy the enemy at Kalinin.' He also admonished Northwestern Front to provide water and supplies to Maslennikov's troops.[125] Three hours and fifteen minutes earlier, he had clarified the command situation, ordering again in the *Stavka's* name, 'Active forces operating against the enemy along the Kalinin axis will all be under the direction of the commander of the Western Front, General of the Army Zhukov.' This order would stand less than 24 hours before it too was altered.[126]

Meanwhile in Kalinin itself, 6th Panzer Division's advanced detachment (*vorausabteilung*) had finally arrived in the city. From the beginning of the war in June, 6th Panzer had used I Battalion of 114th *Schutzen* Regiment, which had the only halftrack-equipped company in the division, as its advance detachment. But the minimal amount of fuel available meant that there was only enough to move the fuel-efficient motorcycle battalion of the division. It was reinforced with one battery of self-propelled 2cm antiaircraft guns on unarmored halftracks and subordinated to 36th Motorized Division, whose own motorcycle battalion had attempted to cross the Tvertsa River on rafts, but was met by direct artillery fire from 937th Rifle Regiment, which sank a number of rafts and turned back the others. The motorcyclists from 6th Panzer arrived too late to take part in this attack, but the next day were scheduled to try to seize the bridge over the Tvertsa with tank and artillery support.[127]

36th Motorized Division had been reinforced, and also had received some supplies by air. It had reason to believe that it would have air support the next day, and it believed that it had successfully defeated the Soviet threat from the southeast. But its staff were unaware that 21st Tank Brigade had finally crossed the marshy Shosha and Lama Rivers, and reached the village of Selino, 4 kilometers (2.4 miles) south of Turginovo. There Brigade Commander Lesovoi issued his orders for the next day's action. He announced that German panzer and motorized divisions had seized Kalinin on the 14th, and were continuing to advance northwestward along the Leningrad highway. They should also expect to encounter strong columns of enemy tanks and motor vehicles on the Volokolamsk–Kalinin road. The brigade's mission was to disrupt the enemy's defenses southeast and south of Kalinin by conducting a deep raid on his rear to prevent him from attacking from Kalinin towards Moscow. 5th Rifle Division was to support the brigade during its raid and seize territory southeast and south of Kalinin. Unfortunately 5th Rifle Division was apparently not informed of the imminent arrival of the tankers.

The brigade formed two combat groups to accomplish these missions. The first, led by the tank regiment's commander, Hero of the Soviet Union Major M.A. Lukin, a veteran of the fighting against the Japanese at Khalkin Gol in Mongolia, was to take the tank regiment's 1st Battalion, which was equipped with T-34 tanks, reinforced with a company of 'tank riders' from the brigade's motorized rifle battalion, and strike westward before dawn. When this force reached the Volokolamsk highway south of Pushkino, it was to turn north, and attack through Pushkino (29 kilometers [18 miles] south of Kalinin), Ivantsevo, Troyanovo (11 kilometers [7 miles] south of Kalinin), Lebedevo and Inkulino into the southwestern edge of Kalinin. The second group, consisting of the remainder of the brigade, with BT tanks and motorized infantry, was to advance up the Turginovo road by moving parallel to but east of Lukin's group through Pokrovskoye (31 kilometers [19 miles] south of Kalinin, currently called Alekseyevskoye), Ogrishkino, and Salygin (not found on any of the maps consulted) to support Lukin's column. The attack was to begin at dawn. Nothing in the records of 36th Motorized Division, XXXXI Motorized Corps, or Panzer Group 3 indicates that German reconnaissance had detected the approach of the tank brigade, even though the *Luftwaffe* had been requested to pay attention to the Moscow direction.

36th Motorized Division had started the day with a large Soviet force within the security line of 87th Motorized Regiment just southeast of Kalinin. A counterattack with the support of a battery of *StG III* assault guns was launched from the west that penetrated to the Volga behind the troops of 5th Rifle Division, and by 0800 hours, the division claimed 400 POWs taken and the penetration wiped out.[128]

The only Soviet unit southeast of Kalinin was 5th Rifle Division, with a few small attachments (a militia battalion from the Higher Pedagogical Institute, the company-sized Junior Officers Course of Northwestern Front, and some NKVD

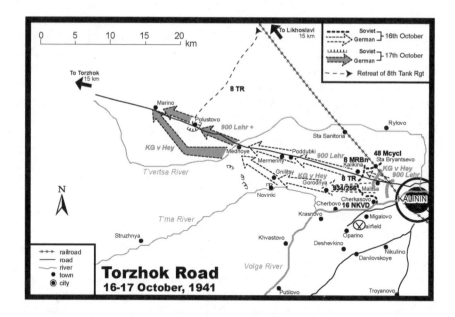

Torzhok Road
16-17 October, 1941

and militia elements). It had started the battle with less than 2,000 men, and then taken part in hard fighting for Kalinin, being squeezed out of the city and pushed away to the southeast by about 14 hours. It had launched several strong attacks against Kalinin from the southeast, which were successfully repulsed. The only way the division could have sustained the effort is that it received substantial replacements during this period. It also demonstrated considerable courage and resolve: even after losing 400 prisoners to the morning counterattack by 36th Motorized Division, it still launched what the Germans described as a strong attack in the same afternoon.

By the end of the day, Panzer Group 3 learned from air reconnaissance that an enemy force was building up north of Kalinin and it issued a warning to expect attacks from the north. Presumably this force was made up of elements of 133rd Division, making their weary way south.[129]

At Staritsa, repeated Soviet attacks against the bridgehead defenders were driven off, despite the fact that the German artillery defending Staritsa had run completely out of ammunition. These attacks were conducted by 243rd Rifle Division of Maslennikov's 29th Army. After dark the division began to move off to the northwest to support the intended crossing of the Volga. Panzer Group 3 interpreted the Soviet efforts as directionless, reluctant to continue attacking, and the movements it detected suggested that 'The overall impression of the enemy is: He is fighting and marching without a unified direction.' On the other hand the same report, which described Soviet losses at Staritsa as heavy, had to admit that the defenders had taken losses as well.[130] The enemy was in disarray, and the movement of divisions from Northwestern Front and from the right wing of Western Front towards Kalinin, as well as Soviet reconnaissance across the Volga, was interpreted as flight, instead of preparations for an offensive.

German efforts to move reinforcements forward to Staritsa and Kalinin were beginning to pay off, albeit slowly. However, due primarily to lack of fuel and traffic problems, reality was lagging far behind their ambitious plans. For example, 14th Motorized Division's 54th Motorcycle Battalion had reached Staritsa and the division's reconnaissance battalion had taken up positions along the Volga River south of the town. 6th Infantry Division was detached from XXXXI Corps and assigned to LVI Corps, while 129th Infantry Division, which was east of Pogoreloye-Gorodishche, was attached in its place to XXXXI Corps.

One puzzling anomaly in the German records is that 1st Panzer Division and its attached 900th *Lehr* Motorized Brigade are recorded as getting no further than Kalikino, while the Soviets report that the Germans took Mednoye on the 16th. Panzer Group records note that, 'The advance from Kalinin to Torzhok is delayed by tough fighting with enemy tanks.' For some reason, XXXXI Corps at no time in the battle makes any mention of Soviet tanks on the Torzhok road at all.[131]

From the perspective of the Panzer Group, the prospects for success during the remainder of October seemed excellent. The enemy seemed to be falling back in disorder, and, although acknowledging the problems with fuel and ammunition supply, and the fact that its spearhead was badly extended, Reinhardt felt that it was worth trying to reach Vyshniy Volochek and possibly Bzhetsk while the opportunity beckoned.[132] 1st Panzer Division was to attack towards Torzhok, while 'holding a supporting position at Mednoye.' The division was to hand over all responsibilities for helping clear enemy forces from Kalinin to 36th Motorized Division, and to bring forward the elements of *Kampfgruppe Westhofen* (the truck-borne battalions of *schutzen*, II/1 and II/113) which were still occupied in Staritsa, to join the rest of the division on the Torzhok road. At the same time, 36th Motorized Division was to clear the remainder of Kalinin (937th Rifle Regiment was still holding out northeast of the Tvertsa) and, after doing so, was to advance westward in the wake of Krüger's Panzers, to relieve its security elements, and especially to prevent the Soviets from 'pushing between the Volga and 1st Panzer Division' – in other words, to keep Maslennikov's army from moving northeastward along the north bank of the Volga and getting away, and across Krüger's communications. 1st Battalion, 118th Motorized Regiment (*I/118*), was to move out of the Staritsa bridgehead and join the rest of the motorized division during the day on October 17th.

At Staritsa, *Kampfgruppe Metz* would remain in control, but was to pass elements of the corps there on to Kalinin as soon as possible on the 17th, while replacing them with elements of LVI Motorized Corps. 6th Panzer Division, still officially under the control of XXXXI Corps, despite the fact that most of it was still stuck just north of Gzhatsk, was to hand over all its fuel to 1st Battalion, 114th *Schutzen* Regiment (*I/114*), to permit it to join the division's advance detachment in Kalinin. When it reached the city, 6th Panzer would resume control over both battalions (the motorcyclists had been functioning under the command of General Gollnick of 36th Motorized Division). Finally, 129th Infantry Division was to move from the area south of 'Uljanowskoje' [Ulyanovskoye] and march on Kalinin by way of Cholmyetz, Gnilitsy, and Negotino to relieve 36th Motorized Division by 0600 hours on October 21st, thus freeing up the motorized troops for the drive on Torzhok, Vyshniy Volochek, and Bologoye.

The corps was to focus its reconnaissance efforts to the north and the southeast, and also to watch for Soviet movements opposite the bridgehead at Staritsa. 2nd Battalion, 59th Artillery (*II/59*), was to switch from 1st Panzer Division's control to that of ARKO 30, 3rd Battery of 611th Artillery Battalion (*3./611*) was to return to its own battalion control (it had apparently been supporting the elements of 36th Motorized at Staritsa), while 620th Artillery Battalion's heavy guns would continue to support the advance by 1st Panzer Division. Finally, 665th Assault Gun Battery of 660th Assault Gun Battalion was to refuel at Pogoreloye-Gorodishche and move northward through Lataschino and Ulyanovskoye to reach Negotino, 10 kilometers (6 miles) south of Kalinin, where the battery commander was to report his arrival to the commander of 36th Motorized Infantry Division. 664th Battery of 660th Assault Gun Battalion was already in Kalinin, supporting 87th Motorized Regiment.

In support of this extensive regrouping, the corps' engineers were to work on the Staritsa–Kalinin road, as well as clearing barriers and mines in Kalinin itself. The engineers were ordered to 'make the broadest use of prisoners and the civilian population under supervision of German guards.' In addition, the corps' motorized engineer regimental staff was to explore the road from Pogoreloye-Gorodishche through Ulyanovskoye and Charpay to establish an alternate to the Rzhev–Staritsa–Kalinin route.

The corps' flak (antiaircraft) assets were to focus on protecting Kalinin against high- and low-level attacks, particularly the bridges across the Volga and the airfield at Peremki, 6 kilometers (3.7 miles) southeast of Kalinin. Some flak batteries were to move up to support 1st Panzer Division as well.[133]

On the corps' long left flank, 9th Army's forces had encircled three Soviet rifle divisions (the 251st, 162nd, and 242nd) southwest of Rzhev. XXIII Army Corps was pushing three other Soviet divisions of 29th Army slowly toward the northeast, 206th Infantry Division was occupying Rzhev, and XXVII Army Corps' 161st Infantry Division was moving northward through Zubtsov, followed by 162nd Infantry. 129th Infantry Division, which had just been attached to XXXXI Motorized Corps, was moving northward through Krasnyi Kholm, just east of Pogoreloye-Gorodishche, with parts of 6th Infantry and 14th Motorized

Divisions just to its west. To the east of Gzhatsk, the forces of Panzer Group 4's XXXX Motorized Corps were heavily engaged at Borodino, and, although they suffered serious casualties, their opponent, 32nd Rifle Division, was fast running out of reserves, and, in fact, the Soviet position covering the main highway to Moscow was about to crack. Two more divisions of that panzer group, 2nd and 11th Panzer, were just reaching the defensive positions of Rokossovsky's 16th Army covering Volokolamsk. In general, therefore, things seemed to be going fairly well for the Germans.

It didn't seem that way, however, at the headquarters of XXXXI Motorized Corps. At 1920 hours, just before the daily orders for October 17th were written up, XXXXI Corps' KTB records the following, based on a telephone conversation between General Kirchner, the corps' commander, and General Reinhardt at Panzer Group 3's headquarters:

> To date, the clearing and defense of this city of 200,000 people has taken all the forces of 1st Panzer Division and 36th Motorized Division such that the continued attack towards Torzhok is currently only possible with 900th *Lehr* Brigade. The enemy's defenses along both sides of the Kalinin–Torzhok road is, in most cases, so strong that a wide-ranging attack without the forces of 1st Panzer Division is pointless, since any territory taken can be held only with strongpoints and 900th *Lehr* Brigade already faces strong enemy pressure from three sides. The facts are that, at the present time, 36th Motorized Division has a strength of around 3 battalions left in Staritsa. The total strength, which 36th Motorized Division has in and around Kalinin, totals 4 battalions, plus 2 battalions in Staritsa and 1 battalion must remain in Pogoreloye-Gorodishche. Because of this description, the commander of the Panzer Group orders that the offensive against Torzhok should perhaps be halted until the daily reconnaissance yields information on the enemy to the north.[134]

This statement is remarkable. It correctly notes that the corps' units are scattered and overextended. However, while its estimate of potential dangers turned out to be all too real in the next few days, its assessment of Soviet strength *in contact* with the corps on October 16th is a gross overestimate. At this point, the 'defenders of Kalinin,' which were 'taking all the forces' of the two divisions to deal with, amounted to one significantly worn-down rifle regiment, specifically, 256th Rifle Division's 937th Regiment, which had joined battle on October 13th with no more than roughly 700 'bayonets' and had presumably suffered additional losses during the ensuing three days of intense city fighting. Similarly, 'the defenses on both sides of the Torzhok road,' whose strength rendered an attack without 1st Panzer Division (the bulk of which was already participating in the attack, and successfully) 'pointless,' were manned by one heavy and five medium tanks, a dozen tankettes (machinegun-armed light tanks), and three under-strength rifle units, specifically, 934th Rifle Regiment of 256th Rifle Division, 46th Motorcycle Regiment, and 8th Tank Brigade's already decimated motorized rifle battalion. After beginning their fight with fewer than 1,500 men, these infantry units too had certainly suffered significant losses in the three days of ensuing combat.

Interestingly enough, XXXXI Corps made no references whatsoever to the tenuous supply situation or to reconnaissance reports of enemy forces massing on the flanks of the penetration. In fact, although such forces were indeed massing, the Germans seem to have been only aware of 133rd Rifle Division, and possibly 183rd Rifle Division approaching from Torzhok, and had not detected Vatutin's other rifle division and two cavalry divisions, or 21st Tank Brigade approaching from the southeast. Although the Germans were aware of Maslennikov's group massing on the left bank of the Volga between Staritsa and Kalinin, their only point of concern on this flank seems to have been at Staritsa, due to the repeated shelling and attacks by 243rd Rifle Division.

So why did XXXXI Corps complain so loudly about the opposition it was facing? It is impossible to tell exactly. It is true that German intelligence had identified a number of Soviet units, including 361st Rifle Division and 151st Tank Brigade as being in Kalinin at this point, but while 361st Division was indeed committed to the Kalinin Front, this did not happen until December, 1941. 151st Tank Brigade was not formed until May of 1942, and in any event, there were no Soviet tanks in Kalinin at all.

It is definitely possible that Kirchner and Röttiger felt that they were rather far out on a thin branch. Their supply situation was poor, the fighting in Kalinin and at Staritsa had used up a lot of artillery ammunition, and the clash with Rotmistrov's brigade had burned up a lot of tank ammunition. Fuel was an ongoing problem with no solution in sight, and its lack was preventing much significant movement by LVI Corps to come join in the drive on Torzhok. They were aware that they had no units, except those battalions moving up to Kalinin from Group Metz, to defend the Volga River line between Staritsa and Kalinin, and their main road ran very close to the river in places. As operational maps indicated, there was also a yawning gap in the front lines off to their east, and southeast, towards Moscow, there was only the reconnaissance battalion of 6th Panzer Division around Lotoshino screening a very wide front in the direction of Volokolamsk. Although German air reconnaissance was active, between the weather and the massive forests, spotting approaching Soviet reserves was anything but a sure thing. Kirchner had, as it turned out, good reasons to be nervous. But on October 16th he had mostly instinct to warn him of his danger.

Panzer Group 3 had one corps largely immobilized between Vyazma and Gzhatsk, and the other corps dispersed between Pogoreloye-Gorodishche,

Staritsa, Kalinin and Kalikino, a distance of some 75 kilometers (45 miles). Its flanks were open, its supplies very limited, and its formations badly worn down. It would appear that the Panzer Group was not in a good position to push on at once to distant objectives. But that was exactly what Reinhardt decided. At 1240 hours, the KTB of the Panzer Group stated:

> Despite the doubts of the commander, XXXXI Corps, as to whether it is correct on 17 October to proceed even further on to Torzhok, the commander of Panzer Group 3 stresses to him the importance of a rapid advance. At least it must be tried, since air reconnaissance has the enemy in retreat everywhere to the north where he can be seen. At Torzhok LVI Corps also will come from the south to help.[135]

It didn't seem to matter to Reinhardt, or his superiors, that his units were unable to find enough fuel to operate in division strength, or that his spearhead, XXXXI Corps, was low on ammunition, nor that the units under his command were increasingly showing the effects of attrition. For example: 'The Panzer Group has only just learned that 7th Panzer Division in the defensive battles northwest of Vyazma suffered considerable losses. The division has lost 900 men since 2 October, including 700 in the defense. One company of the 7th *Schutzen* Regiment lost 105 out of 140 men.'[136] (Historians often overlook the fact that the German triumph against Western and Reserve Fronts at the beginning of October cost the Germans a serious butcher's bill as well as the Soviets.)

Meanwhile, far to the north, near Chudovo, 110 kilometers (68 miles) southeast of Leningrad, and 500 kilometers (312 miles) northwest of Kalinin on the Volkhov River, Army Group North unleashed its offensive that day. The main thrust was towards Tikhvin, and further to the Svir River to link up with the Finns and cut the rail line bringing supplies for Leningrad to Lake Ladoga, but half of Schmidt's XXXIX Motorized Corps, 8th Panzer and 18th Motorized Divisions followed 126th Infantry Division across the Volkhov River, and began slowly pushing two rifle divisions of General Klykov's 52nd Army southeastward towards Bolshaya Vishera, 40 kilometers (24 miles) southeast of Chudovo. Due to the swampy forested terrain, and the very poor quality of the roads, the German advance was limited to no more than 3 kilometers a day. The intention was to drive to Bologoye, 190 kilometers (118 miles) southeast of Chudovo, where, if Panzer Group 3's advance proved successful, Army Group North's forces might link up with XXXXI Corps' forces coming northwest through Torzhok and Vyshniy Volochek.[137] But it was a very long stretch for both.

The stage was now set for the tipping point of the battle for Kalinin and the planned encirclement operation to the northwest. The dawn would reveal that the German commanders at Panzer Group 3, Army Group Center, and *OKH* and *OKW*'s perception of the situation had been sorely in error, and that Kirchner had been right. Although they were becoming dimly aware of the presence of Soviet forces converging on Kalinin, the German command still seriously under-estimated their opponent's will to fight. As a result, for the Germans, things were suddenly about to take a sharp turn for the worse.

Chapter 6

The Soviet Counterstroke Begins, October 17th

Major Lukin's group from 21st Tank Brigade moved out of the Turginovo–Selino region, near the southwest tip of the Moscow Sea, before dawn. Concentrating in the edge of a wood, the commander of the brigade's tank regiment looked out through the murk. A German column was moving north on the Lotoshino–Kalinin road, the road leading to Kalinin from the south. He knew he could expect no air or artillery support, and, besides the four or five riflemen riding on the back decks of each of his tanks, he could expect no infantry support either. The brigade was so new that there had been no time to train and practice working with tank riders. Worse yet, only a few of the tanks were equipped with radios, so once into action in a high-speed advance, it would be hard to keep them together. The plan was for Captain Agibalov, commander of 1st Tank Battalion, to lead, with two T-34s, commanded by Lieutenant Kireeva and Sergeant

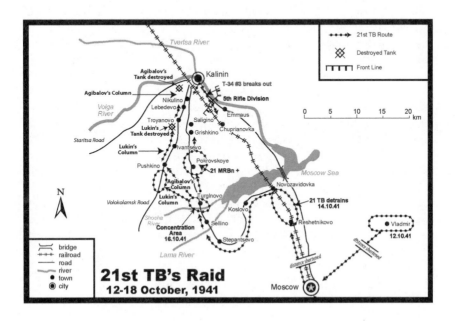

85

Gorobets, out in front as a reconnaissance element. Lukin himself would lead the second group of the same battalion. In all, Lukin's force consisted of twenty-seven T-34s, including ten of the 'tank-killer' T-34-57s, and possibly a few T-60s as well. Since there was no time to conduct a thorough reconnaissance towards their ultimate objective, Kalinin, the raid would be literally a stab in the dark.

Spotting a gap in the German column, Lukin keyed his microphone and broadcast to Captain Agibalov, 'Forward, my friends, for the Motherland! Death to the German occupiers!' Orders were not to open fire, but to fall in with the German column and get as close to the city as possible. A little south of the village of Pushkino, 32 kilometers (20 miles) south of Kalinin, a German antitank gun opened fire, and Lieutenant Kireeva's T-34 went into the ditch, smoking. Three red flares went up, and the Soviet tanks spurred forward, shooting up and crushing German trucks in their path with their treads. In Pushkino the brigade claimed to have shot up a German headquarters.

Agibalov then ordered his tanks to increase their speed. At some point cohesion must have been lost, and the tank riders desperately clinging to the charging T-34s either bailed out, fell off, or were shot off. But the tanks plunged ahead, destroying German transport, guns, tanks and personnel, mostly by simply running over them. By now, however, the Germans were aware that they had a tiger on their tail. At 1055 hours, German time, *Luftwaffe* reconnaissance spotted 21st Tank Brigade's advance, and soon bombs were raining down on Lukin's column, knocking out at least one tank.

As they approached the village of Troyanovo, 15 kilometers (9 miles) south of Kalinin, Lukin's speeding T-34s ran into a wall of fire as they crossed the small Kamenka River, just south of the village. Near the bridge, Lukin's tank was hit and immobilized in an exchange of fire with the 10.5cm guns of 611th Artillery. After using up its fairly ineffective 57mm HE rounds on the German guns, Lukin ordered the crew to bail out and tried to cover their retreat but he was cut down by machinegun fire. The Germans subsequently stripped his body of its insignia, medals, and boots, but several teenagers were able to get the body away three nights later and bury it by the river, from where it was retrieved for burial with honors after the liberation of the area in January, 1942.[138]

36th Motorized Division had two battalions of its 87th Motorized Infantry Regiment in Kalinin, along with its motorcycle and reconnaissance battalions and some supporting units. They had begun the morning at 0600 with an attack by their motorcycle battalion against 937th Rifle Regiment holding out in the northeast corner of the city, defending the eastern bank of the Tvertsa River. The attack seemed to be going well. At 0930, however, a report came in from the adjutant of 87th Regiment:

> . . . two Russian tanks rolled through 'Messharino' [Mozharino: 6.5 kilo-
> metres (4 miles) south of Kalinin] in the direction of Kalinin. Immediately

raised the alarm to all other units and the airfield (*Schlacht Gruppe* [this would be the *II(S)/LG 2* that was apparently stationed at Peremki airfield, just southeast of Kalinin]), then immediately the Antitank Battalion commander began strongly concentrating antitank and reconnaissance battalion guns [the reconnaissance battalion had one *schwer* or 'heavy' company, which on paper had a platoon of three 37mm antitank guns and two 75mm infantry guns, while the antitank battalion at full strength would have had three batteries, each with three 50mm and eight 37mm antitank guns; it is unlikely that any of these units were near full strength at this time] and other available antitank artillery, field artillery, and antiaircraft guns. By 0945 hours another report from 87th Regiment: enemy tanks in regimental strength are rolling through. Then the telephone connection terminated.[139]

Meanwhile, Agibalov continued to lead the remainder of the battalion forward through Nikulino, 4 kilometers (2.4 miles) south of Kalinin. He took ten T-34s toward Kalinin; the brigade's headquarters received the last radio transmission from him at around 1200 hours. His tank was hit and knocked out, and like his regimental commander, he tried to cover his crew's retreat. When his machinegun ran out of ammunition, he shot himself rather than be taken prisoner. His battalion commissar's tank reached the airfield at Migalovo, 10 kilometers (6 miles) west and slightly south of Kalinin, where he destroyed one aircraft attempting to take off with his cannon, and another by ramming. Commissar Gnyri's tank was badly damaged, but managed to make it back to the brigade. Separated from the rest of the battalion, Sergeant Rybakov's tank reached the airstrip near Peremki. He also ran his T-34 over several aircraft on the ground, but was knocked out by a German shell. Taken prisoner along with his crew, Rybakov strangled a guard the next day and escaped back to Soviet lines.[140]

36th Motorized Division reported that several tanks had reached the southern outskirts of the city; one of them was shooting up the airfield (the report maddeningly doesn't specify which of the airfields), while another was ramming vehicles from the division's rear services. The *Luftwaffe* reacted to being shot at by sending aircraft to bomb the T-34s, destroying one of them. Then another wave of Soviet tanks appeared, probably Agibalov's.

. . . the antitank defense was up, as was infantry security by the motorcycle squadron of the reconnaissance battalion. A large part of the tanks (four) were knocked out in front of the defensive positions of 87th Infantry Regiment (Motz), and 36th Artillery Regiment by antitank and infantry weapons, another five tanks ran full speed into mines set by the Pioneer Battalion (engineers) and the tanks that reached the edge of the city were finished by the antitank artillery. The *Sturmgeschutze* battery had been ordered earlier to assemble in the southern part of the city [and make itself] available to the division, it moved south behind the enemy tanks and destroyed another. All available antitank guns were also used, but had no effect.[141]

In a last desperate gasp, nine T-34s reached Kalinin itself, and tried to fight their way through the city. These are the tanks referred to by the German report above. However, with no infantry support, and with no way to communicate between the tanks, they were at a severe disadvantage: eight of them were destroyed, together with their crews, before the end of the day. Sergeant Gorobets' tank, number 03 (a regular T-34 armed with a 76.2mm gun), fought its way through the center of the city and out again to the southeast. Emerging with its turret jammed, its armor blackened, its main gun and one machinegun out of action, it came under fire from 5th Rifle Division, which at first didn't recognize it as a Soviet tank. It reached Soviet lines and rejoined the rest of the brigade.[142]

By 1100 hours 87th Motorized Infantry Regiment reported, by radio, that it believed the last attack had been fought off. It claimed a total of twelve tanks destroyed, apparently a very accurate count. The regiment's III Battalion was holding south of Peremki with one flank on the Volga by this time, with I Battalion pulling back its hanging right flank, trying to link up with 1st Panzer units in the southwest edge of Kalinin.[143]

The remnants of Agibalov's 1st Battalion, led by the commissar of the tank regiment, fell back under enemy air strikes to the Turginovo road, where they reunited with the rest of the brigade.[144] Soviet claims for the damage done in the raid amounted to 1,000 German soldiers, 210 trucks, thirty-four tanks, and thirty-one guns.[145]

The records of 36th Motorized Infantry Division give considerable detail about the raid, and the *KTB* of Panzer Group 3 reported at 1300 hours that: 'An enemy tank column from the south pushed onto the approach road of 36th Motorized Division and 6th Panzer Division to Kalinin. Five enemy tanks were destroyed by 36th Motorized Division, one drove through Kalinin.'[146]

XXXXI Corps' records on the other hand contain only the interim report that: 'Counterattacks with tank support against south and southeastern Kalinin were defeated.'[147] Panzer Group command noted at 1055 hours that air reconnaissance reported, 'strong enemy motorized columns are advancing on Kalinin along the road which 36th Motorized Division used, so that road is not available for supplies.' Then, a fresh report issued at 1700 hours read, 'New report of a 30-km long enemy column on the road Nikolino-Gorodische–Kalinin, possibly part of the enemy group attacking the eastern flank of 6th Panzer Division, and the elements attacking Kalinin from the south.'

By sundown on October 17th, Röttiger expressed further concerns, stating, 'On the front southeast of Kalinin the enemy has made a break-in with tanks, which has not been handled yet, and 36th Motorized Division has had marked losses, especially in vehicles.' As further indication of the losses suffered in the raid, an entry on October 20th states that 36th Motorized Division had lost eighty-four trucks, twenty-one cars, thirteen halftracks (unarmored prime movers), fifteen motorcycles, five field kitchens, one communications van, one light field howitzer, one heavy field howitzer, and eight antitank guns in defense against tanks.[148]

21st Tank Brigade's raid in some sense duplicates the developing Soviet stroke against XXXXI Corps, but in miniature. The attack was poorly coordinated and suffered heavy casualties and failed to achieve its objective. At the same time it was carried through very aggressively and very bravely, and it came as a complete surprise to the Germans, inflicting significant losses on 36th Motorized Division. It also severed one of two German supply lines – which given the very precarious state of German logistics had an important effect on the battle. The surprise caused by the appearance of enemy tanks in their rear also dealt the Germans a serious psychological blow. Specifically, it demonstrated to the Germans that the Red Army was not giving up, it was not running out of reserves, and its men were aggressive and highly motivated. All of this boded ill for the ambitious German plans formulated on the assumption that the Red Army was on the verge of utter collapse.

Despite the setback southeast and south of Kalinin, the day had actually begun well for the Germans on several other fronts in the Kalinin region. 1st Panzer Division and 900th *Lehr* Brigade jumped off at 0600, and made steady progress up the Torzhok–Kalinin road during the morning. At noon Röttiger recorded that there was a possibility of capturing the bridge over the Tvertsa River at Mednoye, 28 kilometers (17 miles) west-northwest of Kalinin and almost halfway to Torzhok. Soviet accounts indicate that this had already happened the previous day.[149]

In any event, by evening the Germans had secured not only the bridge at Mednoye, but also the bridge over the narrow Logovezh River at Marino, 42 kilometers (25 miles) from Kalinin and two-thirds of the way from Kalinin to Torzhok. The only force opposing them was the remnants of the tank regiment of Rotmistrov's 8th Tank Brigade, which had been forced out of the village of Polustovo northwest of Mednoye. The Germans had been attacking up the highway directly and flanking the Soviet defenders by attacks south of the highway.

It is not clear what Rotmistrov's thinking was, or if he had any real choice, but after being either driven or flanked out of Polustovo, instead of falling back on Torzhok he led his tanks northeastward toward Likhoslavl, roughly 40 kilometers (24 miles) northwest of Kalinin. According to his memoirs, the withdrawal was not executed until dusk, when he used tractors to simulate tank noise, providing *disinformatsiia* (disinformation) to the Germans that there was a group of tanks concentrating in the woods north of the Torzhok road. The Germans reportedly went for the bait, and bombed the woods later that night.

There were certain advantages to falling back on Likhoslavl. The brigade's workshops had been set up there, near the rail line. Many tanks had been recovered and were there under repair. But by this move, Rotmistrov uncovered the road to Torzhok, which he was supposed to be protecting, and with it the flank and rear of Northwestern Front. He was out of touch with Konev, and it seems likely he made the decision without consulting Vatutin either. When Konev heard of it, he 'hit the ceiling,' and ordered Vatutin to arrest Rotmistrov and try him for cowardice before a field tribunal. Under the circumstances, there was only one likely sentence – death. Fortunately for Rotmistrov, however, Vatutin was not as bloodthirsty as Konev, and instead sent Rotmistrov a blistering order, stating, 'Immediately, without losing a single hour, return from Likhoslavl, and with parts of 185th Rifle Division, rapidly strike at Mednoye to destroy the group of enemy that have broken through and seize Mednoye. It is time to finish with cowardice!'[150]

During the course of the morning, events were also going the Germans' way in Kalinin proper. There, 36th Motorized Division's 118th Regiment, supported by the flamethrower tanks of 101st Panzer Battalion and the motorcyclists of 6th Panzer Division's advanced detachment, attacked 937th Rifle Regiment in its positions in the northeastern part of Kalinin. Supported by direct fire artillery and tank guns, this time the Germans went right for the bridge over the Tvertsa River. Although Soviet troops had set demolition charges, the German artillery fire cut the wires leading to the bridge and the motorized infantrymen stormed across, followed by the flamethrower tanks. By the end of the day, only a few buildings in the city remained under Red Army control and these pockets were cut off as the Germans reached the city limits. Even though 256th Rifle Division's 937th Regiment repelled German attempts to probe northward up the road to Bzhetsk, 134 kilometers (83 miles) distant, the regiment had been badly damaged and its morale was sinking. In this instance, 21st Tank Brigade's 'stab' into 36th Motorized Division's rear must have diverted German attentions, for they mounted no major push up the Bzhetsk road.[151]

At 1600 hours Röttiger recorded a sad piece of news: Major Doctor Eckinger had been killed while leading his battalion in an attempt to outflank Rotmistrov's *tankists* [tankers]. Veteran of 1st Panzer Division, tank officer and historian Rolf Stoves notes,

> Attempts to push further north towards Torshok [Torzhok] were repulsed by counterattacks from fresh Siberian formations. Near Mednoye, north of Kalinin, Major Dr. Eckinger was killed in front of his battalion, while trying to pass packs of Soviet heavy tanks![152]

The death of the leader of 1st Panzer's advanced detachment was not without symbolic meaning, for the date of October 17th marked not only the end of Major Eckinger but also of any forward movement by the division. Rather than advance and pursuit, the next stage of the battle for Kalinin would be about survival and escape.

By the evening of October 17th, the forces that the *Stavka*, Zhukov, and Konev had envisioned to conduct the general counterstroke were finally moving into position. Vatutin's Operational Group was intended to play a vital role, striking at Kalinin from the northwest, meeting the German drive on Torzhok head on. Vatutin's group's 183rd Rifle Division had already passed through Torzhok, and its advanced guard was engaging the Germans around Marino, 42 kilometers west-northwest of Kalinin. 185th Rifle Division had arrived about 16 kilometers (10 miles) north of Mednoye, while 46th and 54th Cavalry Divisions were just reaching Torzhok. Major General Berezin's 119th Rifle Division was at Nesterovo, 31 kilometers (19 miles) southwest of Kalinin, heading toward the northeast. Finally, the group's Separate Motorized Rifle Brigade was south of Torzhok, 27 kilometers (16 miles) southwest of Marino.

At the same time, as we have already seen, 133rd Rifle Division was moving into position just northwest of Kalinin with two of its regiments. The division's lead battalion, under Captain Tchaikovsky, received his orders directly from General Shvetsov, his division commander, and General Konev himself. Shvetsov ordered the battalion to move through Bryantsevo, where Tchaikovsky was to assume command over 46th Motorcycle Regiment if it was still in the area, and then deploy secretly into jumping-off positions for a surprise attack on Kalikino. For his part, Konev added, 'The main task of your battalion is to dislodge the enemy from Kalikino, cut the Leningrad highway, and take up a perimeter defense.' The battalion spent the morning conducting reconnaissance, in the process discovering two soldiers from 46th Motorcycle Regiment, who reported their regiment had been hit the night before by a group of half a dozen German tanks and infantry in at least twenty armored halftracks, which had scattered the motorcyclists into the woods north of the Torzhok road.

Tchaikovsky reported to Shvetsov and division commissar V.G. Sorokin that he could not take Kalikino because it was too strongly held and he lacked weapons with which to engage the enemy tanks. Shvetsov was angry, and when the young captain, tongue in cheek, asked for a couple days' respite, threatened to have him court-martialed. Calming down, Shvetsov acknowledged the junior officer's point and reinforced him with antitank guns from the division's 249th Antitank Battalion.

The battalion then moved out and occupied the railroad station at Bryantsevo, 8 kilometers (5 miles) from Kalinin. The station master sent his teenage son and a friend off to reconnoiter German defenses at Novoye Kalikino, 3 kilometers (2 miles) to the southwest.[153]

Altogether, at least in theory, Vatutin controlled four rifle divisions (119th, 133rd, 183rd, and 185th), two cavalry divisions (46th and 54th), one tank brigade (8th), one motorized rifle brigade (Separate), one motorcycle regiment (46th) and one rifle regiment (934th of 256th Rifle Division). This force totaled about 20,000 men, 200 guns and mortars, and twenty operational tanks.[154] They were facing a German force that was greatly inferior in numbers, strung out along 54 kilometers (33 miles) of road, low on fuel and ammunition. The Soviet forces were converging from north, northwest, west, and southwest and were spoiling for a fight.

The German forces deployed along the Kalinin–Torzhok road consisted of 900th *Lehr* Brigade, with two battalions in Marino, and three battalions (I/1 and I/113 of *schutzen* in armored halftracks, and the division's *K.1* motorcycle battalion) of 1st Panzer Division, with the entire panzer and artillery regiments, operating between Marino and Mednoye.[155] The German force totaled roughly 5,000 men, three artillery battalions (but almost without ammunition), and forty to fifty tanks.

Vatutin ordered his forces to attack at dawn the following day. His plan called for 183rd Rifle Division to strike at Marino straight down the Torzhok road, while the Separate Motorized Rifle Brigade was to join the attack from the southwest. Simultaneously, 8th Tank Brigade and 185th Rifle Division would strike south towards Mednoye, while 119th Rifle Division would continue its march along the left bank of the Volga River, aiming for 1st Panzer Division's rear in the vicinity of Gorodnya, 14 kilometers (8 miles) due west of Kalinin. From there it was intended to seize the rail bridge on the western edge of Kalinin. 133rd Rifle Division was to employ one of its regiments to seize the Kalikino region, in cooperation with whatever was left of 46th Motorcycle Regiment and 256th Rifle Division's 934th Regiment. If the plan worked, the attacking forces could cut off 1st Panzer Division and 900th *Lehr* Brigade from Kalinin, and crush them in a converging attack.[156]

General Konev had a far more ambitious plan in the works. He had ordered Maslennikov to send five divisions of his 29th Army (174th, 246th, 252nd, 243rd and 119th Rifle Divisions) southward across the Volga River in the vicinity of Akishevo, Ryazanovo, 15 kilometers (9 miles) south-southwest of Kalinin, where they were to link up with the forces of 30th Army, which were supposed to be attacking toward Kalinin from the southeast. If successful, the double envelopment would cut off the German XXXXI Motorized Corps in Kalinin, severing both of the roads over which it was being supplied and reinforced. Maslennikov had developed a detail plan to implement this scheme, and was moving to carry it out.

Konev's plan went into effect well before dawn on October 17th. The first division of Maslennikov's 29th Army to cross was 246th Rifle Division, whose 914th Regiment, after spending the previous day under enemy bombing, marched down to Akishevo, 27 kilometers (16.5 miles) upriver from Kalinin – Akishevo does not show on many maps, but is opposite the town of Brody on the west bank of the Volga. Here, despite a lack of assault boats, it improvised rafts and got across the river without significant opposition. The regiment quickly emplaced two assault bridges, and 915th Regiment began to follow it across. At this point, however, the water suddenly began rising rapidly. While it had been 1 meter deep the night before, it now quickly rose to 2.2 meters. The men of the division speculated that the Germans had blown a dam upstream, though this seems unlikely given that the Germans were trying to maintain a bridgehead of their own upstream at Staritsa.[157] The rushing waters carried away 70 meters of the bridge the Germans had under construction at Staritsa and then washed out the two Soviet assault bridges by Akishevo; further crossings became nearly impossible. The division's 777th Artillery Regiment tried to build rafts but was unable to get their guns across the river.

Panzer Group 3 became aware of the crossing at 1030 hours when a light aircraft reported the Soviets were erecting two pontoon bridges over the Volga near 'Kutschkowa' (Kuchkovo), 47 kilometers (29 miles) southwest of Kalinin, close to Brody, and ordered XXXXI Corps to capture or destroy them. This turned out to be harder than anticipated, and while only one Soviet regiment had gotten across the river, it managed to tie down substantial German forces for the next two days, and briefly cut the Staritsa–Kalinin road.

Having crossed the river, 914th Regiment, under its commander, Major A.P. Krutikhin, struck southward to the Staritsa–Kalinin road, cutting it at Redkino, 48 kilometers (30 miles) south-southwest of Kalinin. Here, in the early afternoon, they came under attack by the reconnaissance and motorcycle battalions of 14th Motorized Division sent northward from Staritsa. Heavy Soviet artillery fire on Staritsa during the night had held the Germans' attention, and 'For this reason, orders were given to counterattack the enemy near Brod(y) in the course of the night with such weak forces to, at most, keep them from moving east.'[158]

Konev's most daunting problem on the 17th was that the Soviet command structure in the Kalinin region was a mess. Yushkevich's 22nd Army, having been pushed out of Rzhev, was facing west and south, slowly giving ground in the face of the German 9th Army's advance. To their left (east) was Maslennikov's 29th Army, with its right wing facing southwest against the German forces coming up from Rzhev, its center pressuring the Germans at Staritsa, and its left wing regrouping to the northeast in preparation for crossing the Volga. Both armies were part of Western Front, but to their left (north) was General Vatutin's Operational Group of Northwestern Front. The Germans operating along the Torzhok road had nearly severed Maslennikov's and Yushkevich's communications with the rest of the Front, and Northwestern Front had been ordered to provide 29th Army with supplies and water.

133rd Rifle Division and two regiments of the 256th, situated north and northeast of Kalinin respectively, were directly under the control of Konev, who, at this point, was still Deputy Commander of Western Front. (One of the 256th's regiments, the 930th, was supporting 178th Rifle Division northwest of Rzhev; the 934th was northwest of Kalinin under Rotmistrov's theoretical control and the 937th, with the division command and artillery, was holding on to the northeast edges of Kalinin.) South of these two divisions was 30th Army, with 5th Rifle Division, 21st Tank Brigade, and a few other separate regiments. Finally, northwest of Kalinin was the headquarters of the reforming 31st Army, which, as yet, had no troops (except possibly some artillery) under its command, and had played no role in the battle up to this point.

In theory, Konev was supposed to be controlling all of these forces, but in practice, without a real headquarters group, he seems to have had little control over or communication with his far-flung armies. Although the *Stavka* had emphasized on the evening of October 16th that Zhukov's Western Front was to control all of these forces, in fact, no one really had control over the whole picture. With Soviet defenses all along the Mozhaisk Defense Line, at Borodino, Naro-Fominsk and Maloyaroslavets, barely holding, Zhukov had more than enough trouble focusing his attention directly in front of Moscow.

By the evening of October 17th, at Stalin's direction, the *Stavka* sought to clarify command and control of its forces around Kalinin by establishing a new Kalinin Front to control them. This new Front was to include 22nd, 29th, and 30th Armies and Group Vatutin, and its commander was to be General Konev. The mission of Konev's forces was to clear the enemy from the Kalinin region and cooperate with Northwestern and Western Fronts' forces in liquidating the German threat to Moscow from the north. To do so, the new Front was given control of sixteen rifle and two cavalry divisions, two tank brigades, and one motorized rifle brigade.

This seemed an eminently rational plan, given adequate resources and the time to pull it all together. However, simply declaring this diverse and scattered group of forces to be a full-fledged Front, even under the command of such a forceful leader as Konev, was not the same as actually forming these forces into a coherent and effective unit. This was especially so since the new Front lacked a headquarters, any logistical support units and facilities, and any air assets of its own. It was to draw its supplies and other support from Western and Northwestern Fronts, and the latter was supposed to provide twenty aircraft to support the fighting around Kalinin.[159]

The *Stavka* understood that Konev lacked the resources he needed to pull his forces together. On October 17th it ordered the newly reformed 10th Army headquarters, which had begun supervising the formation of an army in the Donbas area far to the south, to hand its subordinate formations over to Southwest Front and to proceed to Bzhetsk and become the headquarters of the new Kalinin Front. However, it would not arrive until October 28th, far too late to have any influence on the battles around Kalinin. It would soon be demonstrated just how little control Konev actually had over some of his forces.

On the evening of October 17th, with the crossing over the Volga going very slowly, General Maslennikov and Division Commissar Kuzma Akhimovich Gurov (who would later serve as the commissar of Chuikov's famous 62nd Army at Stalingrad) visited the crossing site of 246th Rifle Division. Looking at the swollen river, and listening to the report of the division commander, Maslennikov ordered the operation halted. Instead, he ordered four rifle divisions (the 119th, 243rd, 246th and 252nd) to reorient their axis of attack radically by striking north-eastward along the western bank of the Volga to cut the road between Kalinin and Marino instead of crossing the river and striking to the east to cut the roads south of Kalinin.[160]

Soviet historians have not been kind about Maslennikov's decision. Konev himself was outraged. In his memoirs, quoted in *Na Pravom Flange Moskovskoye Bitvy* ('On the Right Flank of the Battle of Moscow'), he indicates that, in orders he issued to Maslennikov on October 13th, 29th Army was supposed to 'castle' its divisions southeastward across the Volga and then advance east, in collaboration with Vatutin's forces and 256th Rifle Division, to strike the enemy in the rear. But, Konev added, 'Maslennikov, apparently not understanding the situation, failed to carry out the task, and secretly appealed my decision to Beria [head of the NKVD]. I only learned about this after the war, during Beria's trial.' Konev indicates that Beria told Maslennikov to talk to Zhukov, who OK'ed the decision, but according to Konev neither Maslennikov nor Zhukov ever informed him of this change. Konev's charge that Maslennikov did not understand the situation or Konev's plan and intentions seems hard to justify in light of 29th Army's Order # 30 issued on October 15th. It demonstrated a very clear understanding of Konev's intentions, and spelled out how this was to be carried out in great detail.[161]

The study of the battle prepared by the General Staff after the war portrays an altogether different picture. It notes that, while the situation in the Kalinin region was indeed favorable for 29th Army to go over to an offensive across the Volga, the crossing went very slowly. Thus:

> On the night of 18 October, elements of the 243rd and one rifle regiment of 246th Rifle Division crossed to the right bank of the Volga. The slow rate of crossing was partly alleviated by fording until the abrupt rise of the Volga from the area of Ostashkov; the command of 29th Army apparently had no notion of the problem . . .

The General Staff study goes on to accuse 29th Army's command of underestimating the strength of the German 9th Army's forces pushing from the Rzhev area towards Torzhok, although it is hard to see just how much more effectively

Maslennikov's divisions could have resisted this drive from the far side of the Volga. It then concludes:

> On 17 October the commander of 29th Army appealed directly to (the) commander of Western Front with a request to cancel General Konev's order to force the Volga and allow the main forces of the army to remain on the left bank of the Volga and to strike north and northeast to Kalinin.
>
> Receiving approval for this maneuver, on the morning of October 18th, the commander of 29th Army, without informing General Konev, ordered a halt to the crossing and redirected the main forces of the army [119th, 252nd, 243rd and 246th Rifle Divisions] to the area of Shiryakovo, Gorodnya, Novinki and Mednoye. [The former three villages lie just south of the Torzhok road between Kalinin and Mednoye, which is on the road.] The troops were to start an offensive towards Kalinin to the north and northeast. Elements of 243rd Rifle Division, which had crossed to the right bank of the Volga, returned to the left bank. Most of 914th Rifle Regiment of 246th Rifle Division began an advance toward Kalinin along the right bank of the Volga ... The decision by the commander of 29th Army did not coincide with General Konev's desire to maneuver to destroy the enemy that had broken into the Kalinin region.

The staff study goes on to criticize Maslennikov's overestimation of the strength of enemy forces along the Torzhok road, while conceding that his change of direction had indeed 'promoted the liquidation of the Marino–Mednoye group of the enemy,' although it also infringed on Konev's plans to envelop and rout the larger enemy force in Kalinin.[162]

In reality, the picture is even more complicated than described in these passages. One key factor that the staff study fails to mention is that Maslennikov, while a lieutenant general in the Red Army, was also a general in the NKVD, having headed the NKVD's Border Guards Directorate controlling all border guard forces before the war. When the NKVD was ordered to provide cadres to form fifteen rifle divisions in the summer of 1941, many of these divisions were formed into armies commanded by high ranking NKVD officers, like Maslennikov, Kalinin, Dalmatov, and Khomenko. While these units and commanders were now part of the army, it appears that they maintained ties and communications to the NKVD headquarters in Moscow. Beria was no slouch as a bureaucratic infighter and wanted to keep some control over what had previously been his assets.

This does not mean that men like Maslennikov and Khomenko were policemen pretending to be soldiers. The NKVD border guards were high-quality light infantry, and usually gave a good account of themselves against the Germans. Their commanders were mostly men who had previously served in the Red Army before transferring to the '*Cheka*.' But there were rivalries and resentments stemming from the recent purges of the officer corps. Konev had many friends in the historical department of the Red Army, and scapegoating an NKVD officer was a safe choice after the de-Stalinization era led by Nikita Khrushchev.

There is, of course, no telling 'what would have happened if what happened hadn't happened,' as S.L.A. Marshall put it, but Maslennikov's actions do not seem to result from cowardice or incompetence. Instead, he was on the scene, and he made a decision. It is clear that he was not in communication with Konev, and, given Konev's very limited communications facilities and the fact that Maslennikov and his forces had most of 1st Panzer Division between them and Konev's combat HQ at Sofino, just northeast of Kalinin, his actions are not surprising. He did attempt to carry out Konev's order to cross the river, and when that seemed not to be working, he contacted the higher authority he was able to reach. Beria, if the account is accurate, also did the right thing, by not interfering in military decision-making, but directing Maslennikov to talk to Zhukov. Zhukov was no more fond of interference in his command than was Konev, and while Maslennikov's position as a very high ranking member of the NKVD would have probably shielded him from the fate that Colonel Rotmistrov nearly met, it is hard to see how Maslennikov would have kept his command if Zhukov saw him as someone who had dodged orders to attack.

It is worth noting that many NKVD generals who commanded corps and armies during the crisis of 1941 were fairly quickly transferred to more appropriate posts in the rear as soon as the Red Army regained its balance. General Dolmatov, who had commanded 31st Army, is an example. Maslennikov, on the other hand, was not relieved, censured or punished, but instead went on to command other armies and an entire *front* in 1942.

Another indication of the failures of Soviet communication and coordination is that 29th Army had received no specific orders to cooperate with 21st Tank Brigade, although its expected route of attack was clearly marked on 29th Army's planning maps. Similarly, Lesovoi's tankists had been given no information concerning friendly forces coming from the west to cut the same roads along which they were to travel. The failure to coordinate these as mutually supporting attacks, which had the potential for 'friendly fire' incidents, is striking.

Additionally, had the army made it across the Volga, it would have been in a very difficult position; its artillery and supplies on the western bank, XXXXI Motorized Corps to the north, and several German divisions (most of 6th, 129th and 161st Infantry Divisions, and a regiment of 14th Motorized Division) approaching from the south, and a swollen river behind them. Although they might have caused the Germans in Kalinin serious problems with their supplies, and might have been able, if pressed, to escape to the east, the gambit could also easily have resulted in the destruction of the four rifle divisions.[163]

Konev also made one other serious error that has been criticized by some Soviet historians. His first act as Front commander, the decision to disband Vatutin's

Operational Group and assign its forces to other armies, could hardly have been more badly timed. Thus:

> Simultaneously with the creation of Kalinin Front, it was decided to disband Operational Group Vatutin and put its forces under command of the control of 31st Army under Major General V.A. Yushkevich and to also include in it 119th and 133rd Rifle Divisions.

The critics noted, 'In this connection, it should be noted that Kalinin Front's command made a mistake.' Since Vatutin's group had been acting as a shock force of five formations:

> The transfer of these formations disrupted well-established control . . . In the most crucial days, 31st Army could not quickly establish contact with the troops of the operational group . . . Thus, the operational group of the troops of Northwestern Front was no more. The only shock forces in the Kalinin region were separated armies.[164]

The reasons for this decision looked good on paper: in essence, to send Vatutin back to Northwestern Front and reestablish clear and tidy lines of authority at the front in the Kalinin region. However, this decision showed a lack of understanding of the real command and communication capabilities of the Soviet forces at this early stage of the war. All of this does leave one question unanswered. Since 10th Army's headquarters, which was supposed to move to Bzhetsk to form a nucleus of the new Kalinin Front's headquarters, could not arrive quickly enough (and did not in fact arrive until October 28th), why wasn't 31st Army's headquarters used to form the Front headquarters instead? None of the existing sources provide a clear answer to this question.

However, while Konev seems to have lacked control over his forces at this point in the battle, the situation is nowhere near as bad as Soviet historians have painted it. General Vatutin, instead of obeying his orders and turning over the forces of his operational group, or, since there was really no one to turn them over to yet, just walking away from the battle, chose instead to remains, and to continue to control the battle on the Torzhok road for the next several days. Although he passed on Konev's orders to 31st Army headquarters, including instructions of how they could establish telephone communications with Kalinin Front, in fact Vatutin continued to issue concise and clear orders to all of his subordinate formations from October 18th through the 20th, only leaving the field when Yushkevich was finally able to take control.[165]

On the German side of the lines, the mood – except perhaps in 36th Motorized Division – was fairly upbeat. Reinhardt's Panzer Group 3 treated the attack of 21st Tank Brigade as a nuisance, recording that 36th Motorized Division had beaten off the attack, destroyed five Soviet tanks, and one tank had penetrated through Kalinin. Similarly the attack across the Volga was seen as yet another example of disorganized Soviet efforts to flee to the east, not as a serious attack. The panzer group *was* concerned about protecting its supply lines, but from the German 9th Army, not the Red Army. At 1600 hours, it was stated:

> When 9th Army, without a sharp separation of the route movement, and without timely marching scheme [what would be called 'March Tables' in the US Army] also follows the Panzer Group's march routes, forward movement on the supply routes will come to a standstill in a short time from the back up of traffic. In the view of the Panzer Group the movement of the infantry divisions, which follow the same routes as the Motorized Corps, should take place in sections, only in accordance with [the movement of] the fast divisions, or must be stopped. More convenient would be a wide withdrawal of the army to the west and give up the intention to follow with the 9th Army <u>behind</u> [emphasis in the original] the Panzer Group.[166]

Colonel General Adolf Strauss of 9th Army wasted no time and by 1800 hours had rejected Reinhardt's plan.

General Ferdinand Schaal's LVI Motorized Corps joined in the struggle for the roads at 1600 hours, demanding that the supply traffic of XXXXI Corps not be allowed through Staritsa. The engineer officer of the Panzer Group agreed that the Pogoreloye-Gorodishche–Lotoshino–Kalinin road be assigned to XXXXI Corps as its supply road. Panzer Group informed Kirchner that the engineer battalion of 129th Infantry Division would be assigned to work to improve that road.

Fuel for all of his units and ammunition for 1st Panzer Division were the main supply concerns for Reinhardt. The weather, the inadequate quality and quantity of the roads, and Soviet delayed-action mines all contributed to the problem. But a revealing passage in the KTB of the Panzer Group points to the fundamental root of the problem: 'The basis for the bad fuel situation is that the Panzer Group had been initially supplied and stockpiled for an advance to Vyazma and that further fuel in significant quantities can not now be brought forward.'[167]

This lets the cat out of the bag. The Germans had not stockpiled sufficient fuel, ammunition, food and other supplies to bring about the capture of Moscow, or the encirclement of the right flank of Western Front and the left flank of Northwestern Front, before launching Operation Typhoon. Further evidence can be found in the records of 6th Panzer Division, which reported as of October 10th that the division was out of fuel, and the corps supply point likewise had no fuel for it. The roads were described at the same time as being firm and cross country movement easy.[168] The problem was not mud, the problem was a complete failure to stockpile adequate resources to carry Operation Typhoon past its first objective at Vyazma.

It is not in the scope of this study to evaluate the different factors that led to the failure of the attack on Moscow in mid-October. In part it can be attributed to the inability of the German state to provide adequate support in supplies (and replacements) for the exceedingly ambitious project of invading and defeating the Soviet Union. Pre-war studies had pointed to the problem, and had predicted that continuous high-speed operations would not be possible; that the logistical 'leash' would force halts to build up supplies for the next bound. But these studies were essentially ignored in the *Fall Barbarossa* plan that had assumed that the Red Army could be rounded up on the frontier before it could retreat behind the Dnepr River. After the battles around Smolensk had exposed that the initial German planning was woefully optimistic, the German political and military command had continued to overestimate their abilities and underestimate the difficulties they faced. They also continued to underestimate the Red Army's ability and willingness to resist. This combination of weak logistic support and stronger than expected Soviet resistance doomed Operations Barbarossa and Typhoon to failure.

Despite a lot of missteps and confusion on the Soviet side of the lines, the operational initiative that the Germans had controlled since October 2nd was about to be torn from their grasp, although they did not yet realize it. The pursuit phase of Operation Typhoon, at least in the north, was over, and the next days would reveal that the battle had taken on an entirely unexpected character. A very painful lesson was about to be taught.

Chapter 7

The Battle Along the Torzhok Road, October 18th–21st

October 18th

Shortly before dawn, Lieutenant Tchaikovsky's 2nd Battalion, 418th Regiment of 133rd Rifle Division, was poised in its jumping-off positions for the attack along the edge of the woods just northeast of the village of Novoye Kalikino. An elderly Russian emerged from one of the houses and approached the woods, looking for firewood for the fire that his unwanted German guests had ordered him to build for them in the stove. To his surprise he came upon a concealed Red Army scout, who was observing the village. The old man pointed out the house next to his, where the German officers were billeted. Based on the scout's report, Tchaikovsky deployed his attached antitank guns to cover the road from Mednoye to the west, set up his mortars, and issued his battalion its orders, emphasizing the importance

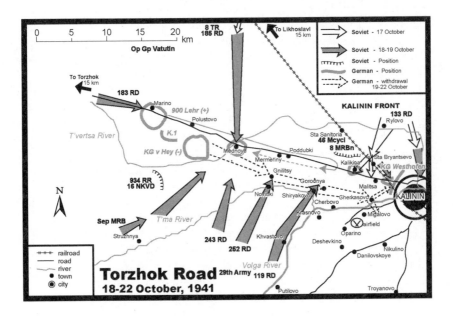

of keeping the attack a surprise. His engineers crawled to the highway and planted mines against the possible threat of Germans appearing from Mednoye.

When it began, the attack caught the Germans just as they were sitting down to breakfast. The elderly man had returned home with his firewood and had begun to make breakfast when he was interrupted by a German soldier suddenly bursting in crying, 'Rus!! Rus!!' Leaping up, the Germans ran into the street only to run into a hail of fire. One German tank, concealed under a haystack, emerged to drive off the attackers, but was itself set ablaze by fire from Tchaikovsky's antitank batteries. Another tank tried to withdraw up the highway, where it ran over a mine and was disabled. In short order, Tchaikovsky's men had Novoye Kalikino under their control and were digging in for an all-round defense. It appears that 418th Regiment posted one battalion in Staroye Kalikino, just north of the road, and Tchaikovsky's battalion in Novoye Kalikino directly blocking the Kalinin–Torzhok highway. Another battalion was in reserve in the vicinity of Rylovo, some 5 kilometers (3 miles) to the rear.

One platoon of Tchaikovsky's battalion, led by Lieutenant Ivan Kandaurov, set up an outpost just southeast of Novoye Kalikino, with its riflemen disposed in ambush positions on both sides of the highway. Kandaurov had telephone wire stretched across the highway, and waited. Events were not long in developing, first in the form of a column of German troops in trucks, led by a pair of motorcycles with sidecars. A soldier in the sidecar was playing a harmonica when the vehicle struck the wire, which rudely dumped its crew on the highway. As the brakes of the column squealed, the Germans jumped down into a hail of machinegun fire and grenades from both sides of the road.

Forced to back down the road towards Kalinin, the Germans summoned reinforcements, including tanks and more infantry in armored carriers. In the meantime, Tchaikovsky sent a battery of 249th Antitank Battalion to reinforce Kandaurov's platoon and the fight escalated. The fighting lasted all day, and, although Kandaurov was wounded three times and finally carried off the battlefield unconscious, the Germans were unable to either recapture the village or clear the road.[169] At the same time, the 2nd Battalion of 900th *Lehr* Brigade (II/Lehr) was recalled from the area of Marino and sent against Kalikino from the northwest. It too failed to break into the village and was thrown back.

At the same time as the fighting around Kalikino raged, another regiment of 133rd Rifle Division attacked towards the junction of the rail line and the Torzhok road, but was turned back by *Kampfgruppe Westhofen*. Colonel Westhofen was the commander of 1st *Schutzen* Regiment, and was controlling the truck-borne second battalions of 1st and 113th *Schutzen* Regiments. They had come up from Staritsa and were manning defensive positions in the west end of Kalinin. Meanwhile 1st Panzer Division command decided to pull I/*Lehr* Battalion back from Marino to protect Mednoye, as there was only a company and a half of Germans currently holding the town.[170]

On October 18th, 1941, the Red Army's counterstroke in the Kalinin region began to gather momentum. XXXXI Corps grasped the situation quickly; by 0800 hours Kirchner and Röttiger recorded that their spearhead was cut off, 36th Motorized Division had taken serious losses and was under heavy attack from the southeast, and, although the Soviet force that had crossed the Volga near Brody/Akishevo seemed to be weaker than it had appeared the previous evening, it was certainly too strong for the elements from Staritsa that had been sent to contain it, and the Staritsa–Kalinin road was under fire.

The weather continued to be cool, with scattered snow showers in places. The low overcast and snow flurries may have contributed to the inability of German air reconnaissance to produce useful results. VIII *Fliegerkorps*'s von Richthofen flew in to the headquarters of Panzer Group 3 again, and brought the bad news that the scheduled ammunition resupply for Kalinin would be delayed. 'Ammunition for XXXXI Corps can not be brought into Kalinin by the *Luftwaffe*, because the ammunition from Warsaw to Smolensk did not arrive on time packed for air transport. The ammunition supply will be postponed to 19 October.' He also emphasized that the *Luftwaffe's* major concentration for the day would be attacking 29th Army elements on both sides of the Volga in the area of Brody/Akishevo.[171]

XXXXI Corps' woes did not end with the cutting off of its spearhead. 36th Motorized Division, having received an armored kick in the pants the previous day from Lesovoi's 21st Tank Brigade, had its hands full defending Kalinin, and could offer no help to the embattled 1st Panzer Division. Overnight the division had been hammered by Soviet artillery fire, and the dawn had seen repeated attacks by Soviet bombers, although it was claimed that German flak downed a number of these planes. At 1400 hours disquieting news came in from Weiss's *Schlachtfliegers*, who reported seeing 'strong tank forces in front of the northern edge of the city.' In fact, there were no Soviet tanks north of the city at all, except for 8th Tank Brigade near Likhoslavl, 36 kilometers (22 miles) northwest of the city. With the phantom 30-kilometer (18-mile) motorized column that they had spotted south of the city the previous day, General Gollnick would probably have been better off if he hadn't asked for Weiss's help with reconnaissance. Troops of 118th Motorized Infantry Regiment were ordered to prepare to reinforce the northern edge of the city, along with a platoon of 5cm antitank guns, which were stationed at Kalinin railroad station ready to respond to threats from north or south of the city.[172]

The attack was not long in coming. 5th Rifle Division had spent the previous day taking on replacements and reorganizing, while 21st Tank Brigade had spent the morning getting itself back together, refueling and supplying ammunition to its remaining tanks. They resumed their attack, striking at the southeast of Kalinin. 87th Motorized Infantry Regiment reported seeing German artillery knock out six tanks with direct fire outside of Greblevo, 5 kilometers (3 miles) southeast of Kalinin, just south of the rail line. Ten minutes later Weiss's *Schlachtflieger* group telephoned to say, 'We're being attacked!' The airmen reported Soviet tanks and motorized infantry were threatening the airfield. A company of 118th Infantry, the antitank gun platoon at the rail station, and the assault gun battery were all dispatched to the airfield. The division felt that if there were only tanks, the combination of the forces sent and the antiaircraft guns around the field could handle the situation. If infantry accompanied the tanks then the situation was seen as much more dangerous.[173]

The attack was reported as having been repulsed by 1550 hours: the Hs-123s had sortied and claimed to have killed one tank, after which the others had fallen back. 36th Motorized Division had been battered again, however. 87th Regiment reported that its 37mm antitank guns were 'worthless' against the enemy tanks (indicating they were the surviving T-34s from Agibalov's battalion). The *Schlachtflieger*, however, had been very helpful, in one case attacking a German battalion HQ that had been overrun by enemy tanks. The regiment reported that it had lost a third of its remaining vehicles from the enemy attack. A gap in the division front facing south had allowed the Soviets through, and, despite orders to do so, neither the 87th nor 118th Regiment could spare the troops to plug it. 36th Artillery Regiment, the division's artillery, reported that it had destroyed eight Soviet tanks so far, 'four by Nebelwerfer, two by 9th Battery/36th Regt, one by 611th Artillery Battalion, one by 2nd Battery/36th Regt. Our own losses, one medium howitzer and an "entire" Nebelwerfer battery. . .'[174] That would make its losses one 15cm howitzer and four six-barreled rocket launchers.

Good news did arrive for the division in late afternoon, in the form of the commander of the advanced detachment of 129th Infantry Division. He reported that his battalion, consisting of three very understrength bicycle companies, would be arriving soon at the Kalinin railroad station. On his march north he had encountered no Soviet forces on the Lotoshino road, but had seen many smashed German vehicles, including an entire workshop company of 36th Division. The battalion, which had no supporting antitank guns or light artillery, would operate under the control of Gollnick's division until the rest of 129th Infantry reached Kalinin.

But the division's troubles were not over. After dark, at 1930 hours, it was reported that 'The Russians are into the artillery positions.' Another company of 118th Regiment was shifted over to try to cover the gap (one company had already been sent there), and engineers were ordered to place mines to prevent Soviet tanks from getting into the city.[175]

Overhead the Soviet air force attempted to carry out Stalin's demand that the Volga bridges be destroyed. 42nd Long Range Bomber Regiment sent in three aircraft to hit German troops concentrated near the bridges. The planes were not detected until on their bombing run, and they got through the hasty antiaircraft fire, but then were set upon by eight Bf-109 fighters. Two of the bombers were set on fire, but the pilots dove to the deck and were able to extinguish the flames. The commander's aircraft, attacked by four fighters, had the machinegun in its dorsal turret put out of action. Transferring the gun from the belly position to the dorsal turret, the gunner was able to down one fighter that had pressed his attack to within 70 meters, probably thinking the turret was out of action. Two gunners died, but the aircraft got home, albeit somewhat damaged.[176]

The bridges themselves were assigned to 81st Long Range Bomber Division. The two regiments of the division, 420th and 421st Long Range Bomber Regiments, were equipped with a rather unusual mix of aircraft. The TB-7 (also better known as the Pe-8) four-engined bomber was used to bomb the bridges from high altitude. Although they were fired on by the German antiaircraft, the bombers all escaped unscathed; unfortunately so did the bridges.

The other unusual aircraft used in these strikes was the Yer-2. This was a twin-engined bomber, in which protection had been sacrificed for long range. At 1245 hours, two Yer-2s were dispatched. Arriving over the target unexpectedly, they dropped four 250-kilogram and two 100-kilogram bombs, but failed to hit the target. Withdrawing from the strike, both planes were intercepted and shot down in flames by patrolling Messerschmidts. One gunner died, the rest of the crews made their way back to Soviet lines, claiming to have shot down one German fighter. At 1507 hours another three aircraft were sent, but suffered the same fate as the earlier pair. Survivors also claimed a German fighter downed. One of the bombers ditched in the Moscow Sea, where the plane remained afloat long enough for the crew to be rescued. With their objective still unhit, yet another pair of Yer-2s was dispatched at 1624 hours. The weather had deteriorated, which helped the bombers approach using cloud cover for protection. Neither aircraft hit the target, despite dropping through the clouds to within 15–20 meters of the Gorbatov Bridge. Although one of the aircraft was intercepted by a solitary fighter on the way home, both aircraft returned home unscathed. The bridges remained undamaged.[177]

The Germans had one thing working in their favor. While 900th *Lehr* Brigade and the bulk of 1st Panzer Division were cut off by the attack of 133rd Rifle Division, the encircled forces were under no substantial pressure from north, northwest, southwest or south yet. Vatutin's command had been transferred to the control of Yushkevich's 31st Army, but Yushkevich had not established communications with these forces, and as yet they were not bringing their substantial weight to bear. 183rd Rifle Division had some forward elements in contact with the *Lehr* Brigade at Marino, but the Germans reported the pressure as 'light.' 185th Rifle Division, with over 12,000 men, had not as yet reached positions to attack Mednoye, and Yegorov's 8th Tank Regiment was still licking its wounds near Likhoslavl.

Rotmistrov's account is vague about events on this date and Yegorov's memoirs speak only about the rest and refitting of 8th Tank Brigade. This was urgently necessary because the brigade's tank regiment had lost both of its tank battalion commanders, the commander of its heavy tank company had been wounded, and a number of platoon leaders had been killed in the earlier fighting. The regiment was down to a handful of tanks. As replacements, Rotmistrov's brigade had received additional tanks (some no doubt from its own workshops), two new battalion commanders and a whole new company of KV tanks under Lieutenant N.I. Lyashenko, all of which needed time to integrate into the force.[178]

In addition to the lack of action against Mednoye from the north, the four rifle divisions of Maslennikov's 29th Army were also not able to attack at the appointed time, primarily because they had not yet reached their attack positions. Colonel Tsarkoz's 243rd Rifle Division had the longest march, from opposite Staritsa northward through Dary and across the T'ma River to strike at Mednoye from the south. To its right, Colonel Zabaluev's 252nd Rifle Division advanced towards Novinki on the T'ma, aiming to strike at Poddubki, on the Kalinin–Torzhok road 6 kilometers (3 miles) east of Mednoye. Major General Bezerin's 119th Rifle Division moved northward along the left bank of the Volga, striking for Gorodnya, 4 kilometers (2 miles) southwest of Kalikino, while Major General Melnikov's 246th Rifle Division, minus its 914th Regiment, followed the 119th.[179]

Meanwhile, on the eastern bank of the Volga, 246th Division's 914th Rifle Regiment was giving XXXXI Motorized Corps no end of trouble. It had already seized Redkino, just west of the Staritsa–Kalinin road, 46 kilometers (28 miles) south-southwest of Kalinin, cutting one of the two German supply routes northward into the city. At 0500 hours, Röttiger recorded that, 'The impression of the enemy this morning [referring to enemy units that crossed from the east bank of the Volga during the previous night] is that, in contrast to the appreciation last night, it is the action of at most a small regimental group.'

At the same time, Röttiger's report expresses continuing concern for the security of Staritsa. Weak forces were all that could be spared to try to contain the bridgehead at Brody and Akishevo, where 914th Rifle Regiment had crossed the Volga. The fighting here lasted all day, prompting a German report at 2030 hours, 'The enemy strength, both at Brod [Brody] and along the Volga, has been too great for the advanced detachments of 14th Motorized Division and 86th Infantry Division [detached from *Gruppe Metz* at Staritsa] to be withdrawn from combat.' 6th Infantry Division, which had begun arriving at Staritsa at 1700 hours, just after sundown, was ordered to send a regiment to clear up the bridgehead over the Volga. The rest of the division was to cross the river and proceed north and northeast along the left bank of the Volga to prevent further Soviet threats against the Staritsa–Kalinin road by snipping them off from the west side of the river.[180]

But the left flank was not Röttiger's only concern. The realization that an enemy tank brigade had suddenly appeared from his right rear southeast of Kalinin and inflicted serious damage on 36th Motorized Division's rear elements was beginning to sink in, and the implications were sobering. German staff officers asked themselves 'What might appear next from this direction?' Another report partially answered this question, to the effect that:

> The enemy column reported yesterday south of Negotino [directly south of Kalinin] can not be found by ground reconnaissance. Because of the unexpected appearance of this enemy, and the continuing attacks from the southeastern direction, it is clear that in the deep eastern flank of the Corps there are enemy forces so strong that sooner or later they must make an attempt to cut the Corps' supply line.[181]

In fact, there were no such forces; to the southeast, only 58th Tank Division was north of Klin, with no tanks and few infantry left to its name, and a reserve rifle regiment was standing guard over the causeway over the Moscow Sea.[182] The Germans, however, did not know this. What they did know was that enemy forces were becoming active in the area west of Volokolamsk, threatening XXXXI Corps' supply line through Lotoshino, where neither Reinhardt's Panzer Group 3 nor von Bock's Army Group Center had been expecting to find Soviet troops. Prisoners claimed that they were part of the Moscow Fortified Zone, but in fact they were Rokossovsky's newly reforming 16th Army. The forces described as 'blowing up bridges and laying mines in the area' were almost certainly some of Lev Dovator's 'cossack girls' from 50th and 53rd Cavalry Divisions. This new threat caused the Panzer Group to order 129th Infantry Division to divert one regiment group to protect the group's right flank, before joining the rest of the division in its march on Kalinin to relieve Gollnick's 36th Motorized.[183]

Also at 0800 hours, corps noted that the road was cut between Kalinin and the mass of 1st Panzer Division; General Kruger's panzer division would have to go back toward Kalinin with part of its forces to clear the road to its rear. Major General Stephan Rittau's 129th Division was urged forward to relieve 36th Motorized Division of the burden of securing Kalinin, an ironic change from the Panzer Group's previous desire for 9th Army to take its infantry divisions and get off the roads that were supplying XXXXI Corps. It was noted that 36th Motorized had suffered 'marked losses, especially in vehicles,' and that the corps was having difficulties due to a lack of ammunition of all calibers.

Röttiger's first interim report of the day showed a little less alarm than the entries in the day book would lead one to expect. It noted that the Germans' drive against Torzhok had reached 'Parjino' (Marino), and that the enemy was attacking the thrust from its northern and southern flanks. It also noted that the enemy had pushed between 1st Panzer's spearhead and Kalinin and cut the road in the vicinity of Kalikino, and there was no contact with the encircled forces. The enemy had counterattacked against Kalinin with tanks and been repulsed, losing twelve tanks in the process. It also refers to the mysterious 30-kilometer-long enemy column approaching Negotino from the southeast and warns to expect repeated attacks from this direction.

In fact during the morning the battered remnants of Lesovoi's 21st Tank Brigade were falling back to the east, trying to regroup under heavy German air attacks and link up with 30th Army. In the process the brigade lost its chief of staff, and a number of other officers and men were killed by the incessant bombing.[184]

The Germans' supply situation, however, could not be described as anything but grim.

Fuel (expressed as percentage of a 'fill' for all vehicles)

1st Panzer Division	10%
36th Motorized Division	5%

Ammunition (percentage of one unit of fire)

	1st Panzer	36th Motorized
infantry wpns	50%	50%
lt inf guns	5%	31%
hvy inf guns	25%	27%
10.5cm howitzers	5%	16%
15cm howitzers	0%	26%
tank guns	10–40%	–
mortars	20–40%	20–40%
antitank guns	10%	no report[185]

XXXXI Motorized Corps' evening report was less optimistic than the morning's. It noted that the corps could not continue the attack towards Torzhok due to ammunition and fuel shortages and because the enemy was 'pushing himself between the spearheads and Kalinin.' It announced that the Soviet bridgehead across the Volga at Akishevo had grown to a kilometer and a half deep and had only been attacked beginning at 1430 hours by the 'rapidly arriving' forces of Major General Friedrich Fürst's 14th Motorized Division (its motorcycle battalion), and the advance detachment of Lieutenant General Joachim Witthöft's 86th Infantry Division. 9th Army, having its own concerns, had ordered the advance detachment from 26th Infantry Division to move back to Staritsa, from where it was to return to its own division. Attacks on Kalinin itself from the north-west (elements of 133rd Rifle Division) and the southeast (elements of 5th Rifle Division) had been beaten off.

Meanwhile General Auleb's 6th Infantry Division had been transferred back to the corps, and was ordered to first eliminate the bridgehead formed by 246th Rifle Division's 914th Regiment, and then to cross the river's western bank at Staritsa and move northeastward along the Volga to the T'ma River. Detached elements of 26th Infantry Division and 14th Motorized Division's 14th

Reconnaissance and 54th Motorcycle Battalions were to revert to their own divisions when relieved by 6th Infantry. Until the situation was cleared up, *Kampfgruppe Metz*, consisting of the advance detachments of 26th, 86th and 162nd Divisions, II Battalion, 59th Artillery Regiment, and 3rd Battery, 611th Artillery Battalion, was to operate under 6th Infantry Division's control.[186]

All in all, the Germans didn't have much to celebrate. Their spearhead, which had suffered significant losses, was nearly out of fuel and ammunition, and was cut off from the corps' main forces in Kalinin and to the southwest. There was an enemy regiment across one of their supply lines at Redkino, and they had taken an unexpected and powerful blow from the rear. Therefore, they had reason to fear attacks against both of their very vulnerable and nearly unprotected flanks. Their one functioning supply line, the Lotoshino road, had been temporarily cut by 21st Tank Brigade's attack, and was now very weakly defended and under pressure from enemy cavalry.

Due to the threats to their flanks and right rear, there was a steady drain of forces, desperately needed to relieve the endangered 1st Panzer Division, to deal with the real and fancied threats to the flanks and supply lines. The situation was very dangerous, and would seem to have suggested that the Panzer Group needed to clarify the situation, bring up additional forces, relieve and resupply their forward units, and determine whether or not any further advance was feasible or advisable.

The fact that Reinhardt did no such thing speaks volumes about the Germans' assessment of the Red Army's capabilities. The situation looked far better from the Panzer Group's headquarters than it did further forward, and back at Army Group Center things looked even more promising. Rather than worrying about the precarious situation of Kirchner's corps, higher headquarters had their attention focused in the distance. Just after noon, the operations officer (Ia) of 9th Army informed the Panzer Group's commander that his new objective was Bzhetsk, 134 kilometers (83 miles) north-northeast of Kalinin. Why Bzhetsk? Instead of reaching towards Army Group North's faltering offensive on the Torzhok–Vyshniy Volochek–Bologoye road, this would put the Panzer Group on a course to take a much deeper stab behind the Soviet forces facing Army Group North's 16th Army. The operations officer was told that it was Panzer Group 3's intention to tackle both objectives, pushing XXXXI Corps up the Torzhok road towards Vyshniy Volochek, while LVI Corps would take care of Bzhetsk. During the day further discussions would ensue until a new plan was issued by evening.

It's not that Reinhardt was unaware of the problems his two corps faced. By 1230 hours he had been told that 1st Panzer was cut in two on the Torzhok road and that enemy forces had crossed the Volga and were interdicting the Staritsa–Kalinin road. Increasingly as the day progressed the Panzer Group commander's attention became focused away from Torzhok and towards Bzhetsk. At 1400 it was opined that 9th Army could deal with Torzhok on its own, as its

VI Corps seemed to be advancing north against weak opposition. Despite the near exhaustion of fuel and ammunition in XXXXI Corps, priority was to be given to getting fuel to LVI Corps so that it could advance to Kalinin and then on to Bzhetsk.[187]

Interestingly, German radio intelligence intercepted a Soviet message indicating that the Red Army command believed Kalinin to be only weakly held by German parachute troops. Soviet assessments of German strength issued this day paint a very different picture, identifying the 1st Panzer and 36th Motorized Divisions, as well as 6th Panzer Division (which had only one motorcycle battalion in the city at this point). It seems most likely that the intelligence data came from at least four days before. Given the fluid nature of the situation, with headquarters shifting forward, and the other indications that German intelligence was less than omniscient, this is not too astonishing. It fit nicely with the German perception of their opponents as being generally incompetent.

Of more concern to Panzer Group 3 was the supply situation. Army Group Center could deliver no more than 200 cubic meters of fuel a day to Vyazma for use by Reinhardt's forces. He had hopes that it could be moved from Vyazma to Sychevka by rail after October 18th, but this turned out to be a very optimistic assessment. What was clearly understood was that this was enough for the needs of one panzer division, not three, plus two motorized divisions and various attached supporting units. It would suffice for immediate needs, but would not be enough to support a major advance such as was being discussed. Army Group Center made it clear that, 'The Army Group cannot give Panzer Group 3 any relief with the fuel supply, since it is focused on Moscow. Forces of Panzer Groups 2 and 4 must not go short.'[188]

By evening it was decided, and Reinhardt issued Order # 26 to Panzer Group 3. If the group's Order # 25 had seemed a bit on the optimistic side, reading # 26 gives one the impression that its author was totally out of touch with the situation or, at the least, thought that enemy resistance was a thing of the past.

Reinhardt's Order # 25, issued four days previously, called for the group's two mobile corps to conduct a double blow against Torzhok. Specifically, Kirchner's XXXXI Motorized Corps was to attack northwestward from Kalinin, which it had just reached, seize Torzhok, and then drive on to Vyshniy Volochek and Bologoye to block off all retreat routes of Soviet forces to the east. At the same time, Schaal's LVI Motorized Corps was to strike northward toward Torzhok from Staritsa, and when this was achieved, then turn to the west and northwest to protect the left flank of Kirchner's corps and act as an inner encirclement ring around the rears of Soviet 22nd and 29th Armies. In so doing, LVI Corps would move across the lines of communication of XXXXI Corps.

Now, in Order # 26, Reinhardt planned something considerably different. Kirchner's XXXXI Corps was to continue its drive on Torzhok, with 1st Panzer and 36th Motorized Divisions, along with 900th *Lehr* Brigade, while 6th Infantry

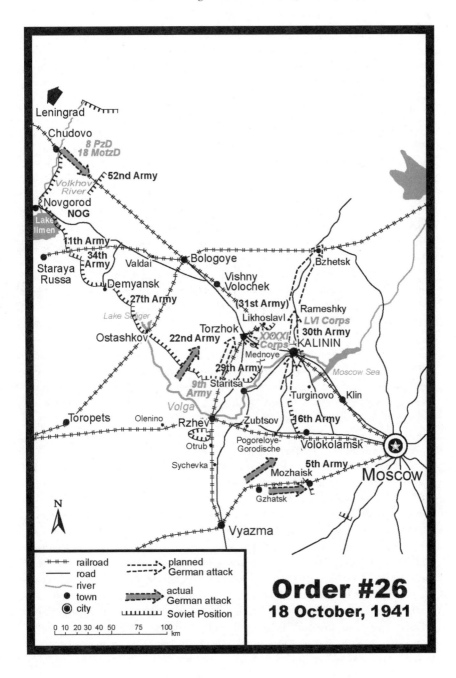

Leningrad
Chudovo
8 PzD
18 MotzD
Volkhov River
52nd Army
Novgorod
NOG
Lake Ilmen
11th Army
34th Army
Staraya Russa
Valdai
Bologoye
Bzhetsk
Vishny Volochek
Demyansk
27th Army
31st Army
Rameshky
LVI Corps
Likhoslavl
30th Army
Lake Seliger
Torzhok
XXXXI Corps
KALININ
Ostashkov
22nd Army
Mednoye
29th Army
Moscow Sea
9th Army
Staritsa
Turginovo
Klin
Volga
Toropets
Olenino
Rzhev
Zubtsov
16th Army
Otrub
Pogoreloye-Gorodische
Volokolamsk
Sychevka
Mozhaisk
5th Army
Moscow
Gzhatsk
N
Vyazma

railroad	planned German attack
road	
river	actual German attack
town	
city	Soviet Position

0 10 20 30 40 50   75   100 km

Order #26
18 October, 1941

Division would secure the corps' left flank and 129th Infantry would relieve the 36th Motorized Division in Kalinin. Although 6th Panzer Division was also attached to Kirchner's corps, it was to mass in Kalinin and was to be used only with Reinhardt's specific permission. Eventually it was intended to transfer back to LVI Corps and follow its advance north.

Meanwhile, instead of moving to the west of XXXXI Corps and attacking across the Volga at Staritsa toward Torzhok, Schaal's LVI Corps was to attack northward through Kalinin toward Bzhetsk, with its 7th Panzer and 14th Motorized Divisions leading its thrust. This would place Schaal's corps to the right, or east, of Kirchner's. Once LVI Corps captured Bzhetsk, they were to defend it facing toward the west (toward Torzhok).

Reinhardt's new order failed to specify exactly what the point of this maneuver was supposed to be. Bologoye lies 113 kilometers (70 miles) northwest of Kalinin, and Bzhetsk 113 kilometers north-north-east of it. Between the two cities are 129 kilometers (80 miles) of forested ground. How this thrust was to link up with Army Group North's push towards Bologoye, assuming it could even be done given the fuel situation, the intensifying Red Army resistance, and the dismal terrain, was not explained. Reinhardt's intention was to take a wider route to encircle the Soviet forces to the north, but it made the previous wildly ambitious plan look conservative by comparison.

The final paragraph in Order # 26 is particularly striking. Paragraph 6 reads, 'The entire available supply of fuel must, in the first instance, go to LVI Corps until the advance on Bzhetsk is accomplished, and to XXXXI Corps only so far as provision is urgently required.' Since XXXXI Motorized Corps was nearly entirely out of fuel at this point, this clearly meant that there was no intention to advance on Torzhok at all. In fact, LVI Corps was unable to even reach Kalinin by the end of October, let alone Bzhetsk.[189]

This strange order raises many unanswered questions. The impetus for the operation was clearly coming from the top, from Hitler, *OKW*, and to some extent *OKH* and Army Group Center. Panzer Group 3 states in its records that it looked more favorably on a drive on Bzhetsk than the Torzhok thrust. Clearly from Army Group up there was little understanding of the severity of the fuel shortages, or the stiffening enemy resistance and counterattacks. But Reinhardt's headquarters was well aware that there was insufficient fuel and ammunition supplies to just maintain XXXXI Corps in its vulnerable position, and little prospect of amassing the over 1,200 cubic meters of fuel needed in Kalinin to get LVI Corps to Bzhetsk. So why did they accept the plan, and issue it as orders? It is clear that the threat posed by the Red Army was discounted, and that Reinhardt had complete confidence that XXXXI Corps could break its spearhead out and possibly continue toward Torzhok, although there was real concern about the threat to the corps supply lines from east and west. There is no basis for drawing conclusions about Reinhardt's state of mind, but it seems just possible that he was perfectly aware that Bzhetsk was out of reach, and that he issued Order # 26 with the clear understanding that it would fail, and its failure would allow him to redirect the Panzer Group in the direction that he wanted to advance in the first place: towards Moscow. At this remove, there is no way to tell. If the plan was serious, however, all that can be said of it is that it was laughably out of touch with reality, although his troops would not be among those doing the laughing.

In fact, at about noon on October 18th, the forces of 36th Motorized Division, reinforced by some tanks probably from 101st Panzer Battalion, did conduct a probe up the Bzhetsk road. However, 256th Rifle Division's 937th Regiment successfully repulsed this attack with well-placed artillery fire.

If the soaring ambition of Reinhardt's order was 'other-worldly,' the report Konev dispatched to the *Stavka* the same day represents fantasy of a different sort. In this report, his first as commander of Kalinin Front, Konev produced a four-paragraph document, which described the situation in detail, including the locations of friendly and, in some cases, enemy units, and explained what his troops accomplished. If one thing about the report is striking, it is that most of the information in it was simply not true. Instead of stating, 'This unit was ordered to do this, but no report has been received to confirm its position,' he reported that his Front's forces *had* reached the locations he had ordered them to reach, even though they had done nothing of the kind.

One can only conclude that, although he lacked reliable communications with his subordinate units, he felt comfortable simply *assuming* each subordinate had done as ordered. It is unlikely that Konev realized the information he sent to the *Stavka* was at best sheer *samogon* ('moonshine'). This casual approach to communications was not the first instance in which Konev reported things as they should be, rather than how they actually were. On October 5th, for example, scarcely three days after the forces of Hoth's Panzer Group had penetrated his lines and were well on their way to surrounding the bulk of his Western Front, he had assured the *Stavka* that the situation was 'normal' and there was nothing important to report. Fortunately for Konev, this time the results were not as catastrophic.

Konev's report, 'A Military Report from the Commander of the Forces of Kalinin Front to the Chief of the General Staff of the Red Army and the Commander of the Forces of Western Front on the Beginning of the Offensive by the Forces of the Front in the Kalinin, Volga River, and Moscow Sea Region,' was issued at 2300 hours on October 18th, 1941. The report noted that prisoner interrogations and documents taken from dead Germans revealed that his forces in the Kalinin region were facing 6th Panzer and 1st and 36th Motorized Divisions (*sic*), and there was an enemy infantry division concentrating in the Lotoshino region. In fact, the 'infantry division' turned out to be one regiment of 129th Infantry Division, which was skirmishing with some of Dovator's cavalrymen.

Interestingly enough, this action was taking place well outside of the area of operations of Konev's Front. The report also noted that, northwest of Rzhev, the enemy had forced the Volga River and was pushing back 22nd Army's 220th and 250th Rifle Divisions. Konev also reported that the enemy air force was very active in the good weather (*sic*) and was both bombing and strafing Soviet troops and also flying air cover against the Red Air Force.

After relating these facts, Konev departed from reality by asserting 174th and 243rd Rifle Divisions had already crossed over to the Volga River's right (eastern) bank '*at Staritsa*, without support,' (author's italics) and that 119th, 246th and 252nd Rifle Divisions had crossed the Volga at Akishevo by the morning of October 18th and were facing a division and a half of Germans. As indicated above, all of this information was erroneous, since none of these forces, except for 246th Rifle Division's 914th Regiment, were across the river, and there had been no attempt to cross at Staritsa at all, much less a successful one. The 914th Regiment was fighting off two battalions of Germans in the vicinity of Redkino.

Further, Konev reported that 183rd and 185th Rifle and 46th and 54th Cavalry Divisions of Vatutin's group were 'marching on Torzhok,' when in fact 183rd Rifle Division had passed Torzhok and its lead elements were engaging the enemy at Marino, and the 185th was detraining north of Likhoslavl. Nor did Konev even bother to mention Rotmistrov's 8th Tank Brigade, which represented fully half of his Front's tank forces.

On the positive side of the ledger, Konev correctly reported 133rd and 256th Rifle Divisions as engaged in bitter fighting against the 'outskirts' of Kalinin, with the 256th fighting for the unnamed heights northeast of the city. However, he incorrectly claimed that the 133rd had seized the area of the Gorbatov Bridge. Since he was present in the area of 133rd Rifle Division, his error is not explicable and may have been a case of self-promoting hyperbole. The Front commander concluded his report by commenting, 'The fighting has established the weakness of our screening fighter aviation. Enemy aviation is still active most of the time with impunity.'[190]

Thus, October 18th ended with both contending commanders exhibiting clear evidence that they were out of touch with the combat situation. This hardly boded well for the morrow. On balance, however, despite the very weak command and control over their forces, the Soviets had a far clearer idea of how the battle was actually developing. Furthermore, if their plans were ambitious, at least they were more realistic than those of their opponents. The fact was, the Germans were in an exceedingly perilous position but did not seem to grasp this. As a result, their only real grounds for hope lay in the imminent arrival of 6th and 129th Infantry Divisions with others following, whose appearance on the battlefield could potentially shift the balance of forces back in favor of the woefully overextended XXXXI Motorized Corps.

October 19th

The weather began to change on October 19th as a warming trend set in during the day. Temperatures rose to 3° C (38° F), morning fog and snow flurries gave way by late afternoon to rain showers. XXXXI Corps complained that bad weather had prevented the *Luftwaffe* from providing either air support or resupply, but at the same time commented on lively Soviet air activity, and claimed that German flak had brought down no fewer than sixteen Soviet aircraft. The Soviets, on the other hand, reported repeated German air strikes, including one that wounded the commander of Rotmistrov's tank regiment, Major A.V. Yegorov. It would seem that in the limited visibility produced by fog, snow, clouds and rain, each side was only able to see opposing aircraft, not their own.

At 0500 hours that day, XXXXI Corps' combat diary records that elements of 6th Infantry Division had successfully driven off the Soviet 914th Rifle Regiment, which had crossed the Volga in the Brody and Akishevo area, to the northeast. By 1700 hours they would report that the enemy bridgehead had been driven in 'with ease.' Although this should have cleared the Staritsa–Kalinin supply road, and 36th Motorized Division recorded at 0830 that an armored car patrol from its reconnaissance battalion had explored the road to Lotoshino for 30 kilometers (18.6 miles) and found it clear, nonetheless Röttiger described the situation in and around Kalinin as being so 'disorderly' that no supply by road or air was possible. Ammunition had to be tightly rationed.[191]

By 0800 hours things were looking even worse. At this point the corps declared the situation of 1st Panzer Division to be 'critical' and noted the enemy was still holding firm to Novoye Kalikino. As a result, it stated, the vanguard of XXXXI Corps, 900th *Lehr* Motorized Brigade, would have to abandon its bridgehead at 'Parjino' (Marino). By noontime, Kalikino was still reported to be in enemy hands. Colonel Multan's 418th Rifle Regiment of General Shvetsov's 133rd Division – tired though it might be – clung to the Kalinin–Torzhok road like a bulldog and would not let go, no matter what the Germans threw at it.[192]

At Marino, General Komissarov's 183rd Rifle Division and *Kombrig* Ryzhkov's Separate Motorized Rifle Brigade were putting steady pressure on 900th *Lehr*. By evening, the decision came to abandon the German's deepest penetration towards Torzhok, and to assemble the brigade in the area of Gorodnya, 28 kilometers (17 miles) to the southeast, and south of the Torzhok road.

At Mednoye, it is a little hard to determine exactly what happened on October 19th. While many of the German and Soviet records have somewhat different accounts of parts of the battles around Kalinin, in general they are recognizable as descriptions of the same events. But at Mednoye, they part company radically. According to Yegorov's account, taking advantage of a blanket of fog over the Tvertsa River at dawn that reduced visibility to 400 meters, 1319th Rifle Regiment of Lieutenant Colonel Vindushev's 185th Rifle Division, fighting alongside Yegorov's refitted tank regiment, emerged from the woods north of the town and fell on the surprised Germans defending the town. The fighting was fierce and despite the foul weather the *Luftwaffe* managed to make an appearance, bombing the town and wounding Yegorov. Nonetheless, by 1400 hours Mednoye was cleared of Germans and 500 Red Army men who had been taken prisoner by the Germans were released.[193]

Vatutin's orders to 185th Rifle Division, however, paint a somewhat different picture:

> 185th Rifle Division and 8th Tank Brigade will forced march by dawn 19.10 to get to the area of Likhoslavl, Ilinskoye, Ivantsevo, from there make a rapid strike on Mednoye, the objective, working closely with 183rd Rifle Division, to destroy the enemy west of Mednoye not allowing him to withdraw from the attack of 183rd Rifle Division to the east. Going further, building on the success, by the close of the day take Poddubki.[194]

From the concentration area south of Likhoslavl to Mednoye is 19 kilometers (12 miles), making a dawn attack by 185th Rifle Division fairly unlikely. Late morning would have been the very earliest that Vindushev's division could have reached the objective, and probably later.

But the records of 1st Panzer Division cast an entirely different light on the situation. The division's records are the poorest of any of those German documents consulted on this project (records from Panzer Group 3, XXXXI Corps, 36th Motorized Division, and 6th Panzer Division). Unlike most of the other unit diaries (*kriegstagbuchen*), which consist mostly of notes giving the time of events all day long, those of 1st Panzer look like they were only written at the end of the day, and they are sloppy and incomplete. Nonetheless, it is hard to reconcile Yegorov's account with: 'Also on the evening of 19 October, the division does not want to give up Mjednoje [Mednoye] yet, since the enemy is not active there, and reconnaissance reports the area 5–8 km around as free of the enemy.'[195]

Then there is the question of what was happening on the Torzhok road southeast of Mednoye. According to the 1st Panzer's records, *Kampfgruppe von Heydebrand* (consisting of the two *schutzen* battalions mounted in halftracks, *I/1 SR* and *I/113 SR*, what was left of Panzer Regiment 1, Panzer Artillery Regiment 73, and the *K.1* motorcycle battalion, although the latter was apparently deployed southwest of Mednoye, covering the flank of 900th *Lehr* at Marino) had tried to fight its way out of the pocket through Kalikino in the early morning. Multan's men were well dug in by this time, and the attack failed. 'The attack is very expensive. The forces are not sufficient to dislodge the strong enemy.' Kalinin Front reported that as a result of this attack's failure, the Soviets captured eighteen light machineguns, and destroyed three tanks, three 'armored vehicles' (probably halftracks), and eight trucks with crews and fuel. The report also noted that additional captured material was being used by the troops, who doubtless were reluctant to report it all.[196]

According to Katz, another rifle battalion of Shvetsov's 133rd Rifle Division, commanded by Lieutenant V. Maliovichko, moved northwest on the highway, striking German defenses at the town of Poddubki (labeled on some maps as Novyye Mermeriny) from the rear. The battalion captured the town with the help of five of Rotmistrov's tanks and their own divisional antiaircraft platoon (three truck-mounted quadruple Maxim machineguns).[197] If this account is true, it does leave open the question of where exactly did *Kampfgruppe von Heydebrand* go when it was repulsed at Kalikino? If it had retreated up the Torzhok road towards Mednoye, it would have been in position to repulse an attack by one rifle battalion, no matter how low the German supply of ammunition and fuel was. The likely answer is that the Germans were massing their forces *south* of the Torzhok road, aiming to breakout through Malitsa or along the Volga to Cherkasovo.

But the question remains unresolved. It is possible that the Soviet claims to taking Mednoye and Poddubki on this day are mistaken about the date the action occurred. Usually documentary records would be considered more reliable than secondary accounts, such as memoirs and histories written at some remove from the events, even by participants. But the records of both 1st Panzer Division and XXXXI Corps show signs of not only some major inaccuracies, but also possibly deliberate attempts to mislead higher headquarters as to the extent of the fiasco.

If indeed the Germans were concentrating both von Heydebrand's group and 900th *Lehr* south of the Torzhok road for their desperation breakout attempt, at sundown a new threat loomed from yet another direction. Konev reported that General Bezerin's 119th Rifle Division of Maslennikov's 29th Army now begun to reach the battlefield. Forward elements of the division began to reconnoiter the villages of Shiryakovo and Gorodnya on the north bank of the T'ma River, looking for a place to cross the river or build a new bridge where a previously existing one had been destroyed. Once the whole division arrived, its riflemen were to conduct an assault over the T'ma River, to reach the villages of Shiryakovo and Gorodnya, 12–15 kilometers (7–9 miles) west of Kalinin. If they could do so successfully, they would be in position to link up with 133rd Rifle Division's 418th Regiment at Kalikino, completing the encirclement around the bulk of 1st Panzer Division and the *Lehr* Brigade. The problem was that as of 1100 hours (Soviet time) on October 19th, 119th Rifle Division was concentrated in the vicinity of Tredubye, 30 kilometers (20 miles) south of the T'ma River. One regiment acted as the division's forward detachment and it was reported held up at Zaborovye at 1100, only about 16 kilometers (10 miles) from the planned crossing site on the T'ma. The report does not mention *what* was holding it up, but since there were no German units south of the T'ma, it most likely was bad roads and/or the *Luftwaffe*. 252nd Rifle Division had even further to go, from the Vasilyevskoye area 6 kilometers (4 miles) west of Akisheva on the Volga.[198] The southern jaw of the Soviet's accidental pincer movement was closing, but it had some distance to cover before it could close on *Kampfgruppe von Heydebrand*.

At 2000 hours Röttiger noted in XXXXI Corps' KTB that 1st Panzer had made no progress all day, and resupply to the spearhead was nearly impossible. As a result, it would be necessary to bring 900th *Lehr* back from Mednoye. Although the Torzhok–Kalinin road was solidly cut at Kalikino and Malitsa, and elements of 29th Army's 119th and 252nd Rifle Divisions were attempting to get across the T'ma River to link up with 133rd Rifle Division, there existed a narrow corridor into the pocket between the Volga and the Torzhok road.[199]

During the day one of the transport columns of 1st Panzer Division managed to deliver 12 cubic meters of fuel to the ferry site the division had established at Cherbova, 10 kilometers (6 miles) west of Kalinin, just east of the mouth of the T'ma River. Fuel, small arms and heavy howitzer ammunition was ferried over the Volga on rafts and from there trucked through Shiryakovo and on to the nearly surrounded forces.

This was not the only difference between Soviet and German descriptions of the fighting. For example, 256th Rifle Division reported repulsing German attacks northeast of Kalinin, a continued attempt by the motorcycle battalion of 6th Panzer with support from a few tanks of 101st Panzer Battalion (Flame) to push on Bzhetsk. German records, however, contain no mention of any attack *from* Kalinin and instead only discuss attacks *against* the city, 6th Panzer's motorcyclists turning back a company-sized attack at 1030 hours. In this case, it would appear that the German account is the more accurate one. Kalinin Front reported that:

> 256th Rifle Division on 19.10.41 waged battle against the enemy, which was occupying the northeastern parts of Kalinin. During the day's battle the division advanced 4–500 meters. The enemy with up to a battalion of infantry, six to eight heavy machineguns, three mortar batteries and two batteries of light artillery rendered persistent resistance to the offensive by 2nd and 3rd Battalions of 937th Rifle Regiment. Losses – 47 wounded, killed and missing – no report. 1st Battalion of 937th Rifle Regiment was operating directly under the command of 5th Rifle Division.[200]

Not only had 1st Panzer and 900th *Lehr* taken a beating on the Torzhok road, 36th Motorized Division was having a very hard time holding its positions southeast and north of Kalinin as well. The tanks from 21st Tank Brigade that had penetrated the position of 87th Infantry Regiment the previous evening had withdrawn, but the morning looked grim to Gollnick's men. There was almost no artillery ammunition, the 10cm guns were completely out of armor piercing shells, there was very little other antitank ammunition, and anyway most of the division's antitank guns had been smashed up in the previous few days' fighting, mostly by Soviet tanks driving directly over them. Antiaircraft guns had been positioned to replace the squashed antitank guns. Each of the two regiments (the 87th and

General of Panzer Troops Georg-Hans Reinhardt (*right*), commander of XXXXI Motorized Corps until October 7th, 1941, then commander of Panzer Group 3.

Major General Paul Kruger, commander of 1st Panzer Division.

Lieutenant General Friedrich Kirchner, commander of XXXXI Corps as of October 15th, 1941, when Lieutenant General Otto Ottenbacher was wounded.

Major Dr. Hans Eckinger (*hatless in centre*), commander of I Battalion, 113 Schutzen Regiment, 1st Panzer Division. Leader of the division's forward detachment, he was killed at Mednoye, October 17th, 1941.

Colonel General Adolph Strauss, commander of 9th Army.

Lieutenant General Ivan Konev, Deputy Commander of Western Front until October 17th, 1941, then commander of Kalinin Front.

German dead at Gorodnya after the retreat from Marino.

36th Motorized Infantry Division column on the approaches to a stream crossing en route to Kalinin. Note that none of the wheels is sunk in mud.

Tanks of the 1st Panzer Division on the march, fall, 1941.

Second from the right is Major General Vasily Yushkevich, who commanded 22nd Army until October 21st, 1941, then took over 31st Army.

Colonel Pavel Rotmistrov (*right*), commander of 8th Tank Brigade (1942 photo).

Lieutenant General Ivan Maslennikov, commander of 29th Army (postwar photo).

The railroad bridge over the Volga, seen from the Kalinin side, with a German 3.7cm antiaircraft gun in place to defend the bridge. Picture probably from November, 1941.

Soviet light artillery, possibly of 247th Rifle Division, October 10th, 1941.

Major Lukin's T-34–57, knocked out just south of Troyanovo. Note the German transport column heading south.

A Soviet ZIS–30 self-propelled 57mm antitank gun. 21st Tank Brigade had four of these.

Soviet 122mm cannon firing from the woods north of Kalinin harassed the German occupiers day and night.

The Gorbatov bridge, November, 1941.

Staritsa, seen from the western bank of the Volga. Note the remnants of the washed-out pontoon bridge at right. German troops are ferrying over the river.

The Gorbatov bridge after Nazi demolition, January, 1942.

118th) protecting the southern edge of Kalinin was assigned an 8.8cm battery. The division's supply section assured the command that 20 tons of ammunition was supposed to arrive by air and that truck columns were on their way, but so far there was little but reassurances to distribute to the gun crews. Little help was expected from the *Luftwaffe;* Weiss's *Schlachtflieger* was assigned to support 1st Panzer Division's desperate fight that day, and besides, they were very short of fuel and ammunition for the planes.[201] The division was deployed with the motorcycle battalion covering the northern edge of Kalinin, linking up with two battalions of 1st Panzer Division at the northwest end of the city, the reinforced motorcycle battalion of 6th Panzer Division facing 937th Rifle Regiment in the northeast corner of the city east of the Tvertsa River. 87th Motorized Infantry Regiment had the toughest assignment, covering the southeast edge of the city. The regiment had lost all of its own antitank guns and infantry guns in the previous day's fighting, as well as a third of its transport. On its right flank was 118th Motorized Infantry Regiment, covering the southern edge of Kalinin. The southwest was held by the newly arrived three bicycle companies of 129th Infantry Division. Like the motorcyclists of 6th Panzer, they were under the control of 36th Motorized Infantry Division. In reserve in the center of the city was what was left of two companies of the division's reconnaissance battalion, while its squadron of armored cars patrolled the roads to the south. The only good news was brought by these patrols which discovered no Soviets on the roads leading south.[202]

By 1000 hours, the attacks began to come in. First 256th Rifle Division's 937th Rifle Regiment attacked east of the Tvertsa, but was beaten off by the motorcyclists of 6th Panzer Division. The attack was renewed at 1030 hours, but after advancing up to 500 meters, it again stalled. By 1050 the division recorded that the situation was bad on all fronts; thinly held front lines, no reserves, no antitank guns (there were in fact two 5cm AT guns assigned to each of the two motorized infantry regiments), no ammunition, and constant enemy pressure. The division was 'hoping for the arrival of 129th Infantry Division.'[203]

Then at 1130 hours, 5th Rifle Division and 21st Tank Brigade renewed their assault on 87th Motorized Infantry Regiment. The attack came in on both sides of the railway line. The attacks grew heavier and by 1230 had broadened the assault 5 kilometers west of the railroad line. An assault gun was sent to reinforce the front. The attack continued into the afternoon with the Soviets breaking through at 1400 hours along the railroad line towards Bortnikovo where the division's headquarters was located. The attack also threatened the airfield in the division's sector; the *Luftwaffe* was alerted and began immediately sending planes to strike at the surging Soviet attack, reported as of regimental strength with tank support. One company of 118th Motorized Infantry Regiment was alerted to defend the airfield, while one bicycle company was detached from 129th Infantry Division's advanced detachment and sent to Bortnikovo to act as a last ditch defense.

A short, hard fight ensued, but after only twenty minutes the Soviets fell back, and by 1435 hours the attack had been driven off. Clearly both 5th Rifle Division and 21st Tank Brigade had suffered serious losses, and despite the weak German defenses, lacked the strength to overcome them. An advanced outpost of one company of 87th Infantry at Volvodino, 4 kilometers (2.5 miles) south of Bortnikovo, defeated an attack by a Soviet rifle company at 1515, and reported taking forty prisoners and knocking out one attacking tank.[204] With evening fast approaching, there was some good news for the Germans. Word arrived that 428th Regiment of 129th Infantry Division was expected the next day, and two battalions of 38th *Flak* Regiment reached Kalinin. Two batteries of 8.8cm guns and twenty-four 2cm light automatic cannon were assigned to reinforce the southern edge of the city, with two batteries of 2cm sent to cover the southwest edge.

There was bad news as well. A truck column bringing badly needed ammunition reported that it had spotted a Soviet tank in position by the bridge at Troyanovo. Although escorted by a few armored cars of 36th Reconnaissance Battalion, the column feared to approach, and requested the division's engineer battalion, with infantry and assault gun support, to be sent to clear this tank away. It was too late with the sky already growing dark, so the column was ordered to laager where it was overnight.

The tank is not hard to identify. It is the late Major Lukin's knocked out T-34-57 number 20, still sitting there since it was disabled on October 17th. It is understandable that after the terrific shock of the tank raid on the German rear no supply column was willing to approach a Soviet tank closely enough to determine if it was still active. The last entry in the division's combat diary records that, 'The moral effect of the tanks on our people is not available.' It is not hard to imagine, though.[205]

Close to sundown General Shvetsov's 133rd Rifle Division struck at northern Kalinin, taking Kiselevo and approaching within 700 meters of the Gorbatov Bridge. German prospects looked very bleak for the next day; the only hope was that 129th Infantry Division was slowly coming to the rescue and maybe, if the weather allowed, there would be some ammunition resupply soon.[206]

While it had become clear to Kirchner and all of his units that XXXXI Corps was in deep trouble, and Reinhardt at Panzer Group 3 was aware that things were not going well, the word seems not to have filtered up to Strauss's 9th Army or to von Bock at Army Group Center. At 1000 hours 9th Army was pushing Reinhardt about his intentions regarding Bzhetsk. Reinhardt was primarily concerned about the supply situation. Although it had been possible to get some ammunition through to Kalinin, it was still very tight, and fuel was still totally inadequate, despite using some Soviet gasoline found at Migalovo airfield. Reinhardt informed 9th Army that, at best, 7th Panzer Division and 14th Motorized Divisions could only contribute a regiment each to any effort on Bzhetsk unless a lot more fuel could be provided. Although there were plenty of promises – to run trains from Vyazma to Sychevka, to allocate twenty transport columns from Guderian's 2nd Panzer Army to support Panzer Group 3 (this latter must have produced cynical smiles from those who were familiar with Heinz Guderian's ferocious defense of any assets under his control) – it all seemed to be something that would happen some time in the future, and the crisis was happening now.

The math was simple. It required 220 cubic meters of fuel to move the depleted 7th Panzer Division 60 kilometers (37 miles) and 100 cubic meters to similarly move the 14th Motorized Division. This represented one fuel 'fill' for these units. 7th Panzer could carry a total of five such fills. 'The Corps therefore needs 320 cubic meters to advance 60 kilometers. In Kalinin the corps would have to have 440 cubic meters just to set out and two fills in Bzhetsk to have a certain freedom of movement.'[207]

The two divisions had their most advanced elements south of Pogoreloye-Gorodishche, more than 80 kilometers (50 miles) south of Kalinin as the crow flies, and of course by road it was further than that. Given the rate at which Panzer Group 3 was getting fuel supplied by Army Group Center, it would seem pretty obvious that Bzhetsk was out of reach, never mind what the Red Army might have to say about such a move. In fact, the fuel columns of 7th Panzer Division were reported to be stuck on the highway between Smolensk and Vyazma, and it was unknown when they might struggle forward to refuel the division. Other supply columns reported delays of up to sixteen hours on the roads south of Zubtsov.[208]

To add to the worries of the Panzer Group, Dovator's Cossacks had brought up a little artillery and were shelling Lotoshino, threatening that supply route. At the same time, according to XXXXI Corps, on the western supply route at least four Soviet heavy batteries were shelling the Staritsa–Kalinin road near 'Jwanisch' (Ivanishchi), 17 kilometers (11 miles) northeast of Staritsa, where the road ran close to the river bank. So both supply roads, though no longer blocked by Soviet forces, were under shell fire. Panzer Group hoped that 9th Army's V Corps (106th and 35th Infantry Divisions) would move to the Lotoshino area and relieve the regiment of 129th Infantry Division there, allowing it to follow the rest of the 129th into Kalinin. V Corps would then be directed to proceed southeastwards, towards Volokolamsk and Moscow, coming under control of 4th Army as they did so. 6th Panzer Division, if it could be refueled, was also to proceed north after 129th Infantry, shoring up the right flank of the panzer group.

The arrival of 129th Division was hoped for on October 20th. It would relieve both regiments of 36th Motorized Infantry holding the southern edge of Kalinin against the assaults by 30th Army, and also relieve the two 'extremely exhausted' battalions of 1st Panzer (*Kampfgruppe Westhofen*) that were holding the western edge of the city against attacks by 133rd Rifle Division. This would allow 36th Motorized to assume the defense of the northern edge of Kalinin, where the division's motorcycle battalion was holding on by its fingernails.[209]

But none of this had penetrated to the level of Army Group Center's headquarters, who contacted Reinhardt at 1930 hours to insist that 'reaching "Wyschni Wolotschek" [Vyshniy Volochek] was important, because the enemy is holding in front of 16th Army. Nevertheless, a reconnaissance in force will be sent towards "Beshezk" [Bzhetsk] . . .' The reference to 16th Army's front, in Army Group North's sector, meant that the northern arm of the grand pincer operation had stalled out, and Panzer Group 3 was expected to rescue it! It seemed to express a blithe unawareness of the fact that not only was XXXXI Corps stalled on the Torzhok road, but was in fact fighting for its life.[210]

At the end of the day, XXXXI Motorized Corps's KTB summed up the day's events. To the southeast of Kalinin, repeated enemy attacks had pierced the lines of 36th Motorized Infantry Division, but been thrown back with losses to the Soviets, although more German trucks had been destroyed in the process. It was also reported that during October 17th and 18th, 36th Motorized Division had destroyed thirty Soviet tanks. Given the losses of 21st Tank Brigade, this figure is very plausible.

Along the Volga to the west, the Soviet bridgehead was reported to have been driven 'into the Volga,' by 6th Infantry Division (although it is noted by Panzer Group 3's KTB that in fact the Soviets here, 914th Rifle Regiment, had retreated towards Kalinin, and had not been destroyed or driven back over the river). 129th Infantry Division was continuing to move up; one battalion serving as an advanced detachment had reached Kalinin, while the rest of the division was between Lotoshino and Staritsa. Further attacks on 36th Motorized Division in Kalinin were expected that night, and, since the motorized infantrymen had received little in the way of ammunition, their position was looking very dangerous indeed.

XXXXI Motorized Corps had suffered serious losses. 1st Panzer was down to fourteen light field howitzers and seven heavy (leaving twenty-one out of the thirty-six pieces it had begun the war with), but some of them were reported as missing by the division on October 12th, making it impossible to determine how many (if any) of the guns had been lost during the most recent fighting. The division's tank strength had declined to thirty-four tanks (eight Pz II, twenty-two Pz III, four Pz IV), or less than a third of the number it had running only seventeen days before. Since nearly all of the guns and tanks were cut off on the Torzhok road, it was not impossible that all of them might be lost. The next day the corps recorded an account of its personnel losses suffered from October 13th–18th. 1st Panzer had suffered 249 casualties, 900th *Lehr* Brigade 210, and 36th Motorized from October 13th–19th had lost 387 men. During the same period, the motorized division had also lost 105 trucks and cars, thirteen tractors, fifteen motorcycles, five field kitchens, one radio van, one light and one heavy howitzer and eight antitank guns, these equipment losses all being between October 17th and 19th (and probably mostly on October 17th). It is very possible that these loss reports were understating the situation, as there is evidence that reports were days behind.

These may seem like tolerable losses compared to the 'book' strength of the units involved, but of course the divisions of XXXXI Corps had been in intense combat since June 22nd, and had received few if any replacements during that time. The infantry divisions of Army Group Center by this time were running at about 50% in their combat battalions and the infantry and tanks of the mobile divisions had had to fight well out in front of the supporting infantry. The fighting south of Leningrad, through very difficult terrain and against well dug-in and determined defenders, had all taken their toll. As a result, it is safe to assume that the mobile divisions of the corps by the beginning of October had no more than 3–3,500 men per division in their *schutzen*, infantry, reconnaissance, engineer and panzer battalions combined. 900th *Lehr* Brigade, with only two battalions, was unlikely to have had more than 800 grenadiers going into the battle, possibly a lot less. Some losses had no doubt been suffered in the initial break-in of Operation Typhoon and while breaking through the fortified line below Sychevka. Almost all the losses would have come from these frontline battalions, and much worse was shortly to come.

This wasn't the only bad news either. With 914th Rifle Regiment of 246th Rifle Division cleared off the Staritsa–Kalinin road, it seemed likely that some supplies could be brought up to Kalinin, but this would not do the isolated battalions in the spearhead up the Torzhok road a lot of good unless the road block at Kalikino and Malitsa could be cleared, and, so far, Colonel Von Heydebrand's group had had no success whatsoever, only suffering more casualties in the attempts to break out.[211]

The battered panzer group set its objectives for the next day as:

- XXXXI Corps: Continue to fight to free the roads for 1st Panzer Division into Kalinin. Get 6th Infantry Division across the Volga and advance in a northern direction
- LVI Corps: Further regrouping 14th Motorized Division south of Pogoreloye-Gorodishche, refuel and regroup 7th Panzer Division in the area around Pogoreloye-Gorodishche

As can be seen, there is no mention of any drive on Torzhok or Bzhetsk in these plans, whatever 9th Army or Army Group Center might be demanding.[212]

October 20th

The character of the battle had now decisively changed and so had the weather. Rain began to fall, presaging the warming trend that would settle in across the entire front during the last third of October and early November. XXXXI Corps noted that the roads had become 'morasses.' Panzer Group 3 described them as 'groundless' and 'almost impassable.' Combined with the desperately low stocks of fuel, it meant that – for the Germans at least – the opportunity for major maneuver was over. Of course, the roads were the same on the Soviet side of the lines and neither side would have an easy time bringing up supplies. All maneuver would be very difficult for everyone until the roads dried out or froze.

Although their movement was slowed, the Soviets managed to score a small victory early in the morning. At 0320 hours *Kampfgruppe von Heydebrand* reported that it was under heavy attack from the southwest (while the enemy were identified as two regiments of 246th Rifle Division, they were more likely from 252nd or 119th Rifle Divisions). 1st Motorcycle Battalion of 1st Panzer Division (*K.1*) came under attack from north and south, and suffered 'substantial loss' in vehicles and men. The Soviets were reported pushing in on Mednoye from the north (185th Rifle Division with support from 8th Tank Brigade) and from the south (243rd Rifle Division and the Separate Motorized Rifle Brigade). The jaws of the Red pincers closed, cutting off 900th *Lehr* Brigade. Colonel Walther Krause's brigade had been pulling back from Marino, and now found itself further isolated. The brigade was ordered to abandon Mednoye and fight its way out between the Torzhok road and the T'ma River. With minimal fuel and ammunition, it was 'do or die' time. Plans for von Heydebrand to break out to Kalinin that morning had to be delayed, and all efforts turned to a desperate defense against attacks from the north, west, and south.

By 0800 hours the *Lehr* Brigade was reported to have taken Novinki, 8 kilometers (5 miles) southeast of Mednoye as the crow flies, but closer to 11 (7 miles) by the muddy secondary roads the brigade had to use, in heavy fighting against the vanguard 924th Rifle Regiment of 252nd Rifle Division trying to establish a bridgehead over the T'ma. Gnilitsy, 7 kilometers (4 miles) southeast of Mednoye, was taken by *Lehr* at 1105 hours. It was hoped that by early afternoon it would be possible to link up with Von Heydebrand, and, then together, to breakout back to Kalinin. Instead, pushing east from Gnilitsy, the panzers of 1st Panzer Regiment that were attached to 900th *Lehr* were the only force to reach von Heydebrand's command, fighting their way through the advanced elements of 119th Rifle Division around Shiryakovo. It was reported that von Heydebrand's men had taken too heavy losses to continue the attack although they were able to fight through to Cherkasovo, a mere 3 kilometers (2 miles) west of Kalinin on the bank of the Volga. The German spearhead, representing the bulk of the combat forces of the once mighty 1st Panzer Division, reported that due to heavy losses in men and equipment the *Kampfgruppe* had no further ability to attack, and would need to rest before it could break out.[213]

At the cost of heavy losses, in men and vehicles, the spearhead of XXXXI Corps had managed to drag itself to within striking distance of such refuge as Kalinin offered. Maslennikov's move to the north had been too slow to successfully trap von Heydebrand's group and Krause's brigade. All that remained between the Germans and the relative safety of the city were elements of 133rd Rifle Division. This division had dug in deeply at Kalikino and Malitsa, and had been attacking

Kalinin from the north, northwest and west at the same time. The German wounded were being evacuated across the Volga at Cherkasovo, but there were no Ju-52s that could fly them to hospitals in the rear in the 'wretched weather' once they had reached Migalovo airfield just south of the river.[214]

Due to the near total lack of fuel, 1st Panzer decided that all vehicles except tanks should be blown up if they could not be got away. Things were so bleak by 1100 hours that Röttiger was speculating that it might be necessary to disband both 1st Panzer and 36th Motorized Divisions due to their losses, especially in equipment, since their *combined* combat effectiveness was that of one weak motorized division.[215]

Further south, the Germans had a little good news. To relieve the threat to the corps' left flank, Lieutenant General Helge Auleb's 6th Infantry Division, once it had cleaned up the Soviet bridgehead over the Volga opposite Brody, was to cross the Volga to the river's west bank and then drive up that left bank of the river until it reached the outskirts of Kalinin. This would prevent any more Soviet efforts to cross the river, and would at the same time aid von Heydebrand's group by attacking the rear of the Soviet forces menacing it from the south.

Even more encouraging, the commander of 129th Infantry Division, Major General Stephan Rittau, arrived at XXXXI Corps' headquarters at 1000 hours, and promised to have two of his regiments up to Kalinin by afternoon, although the third regiment hadn't yet reached Lotoshino. Reportedly, it was delayed by having to pass through 6th Panzer Division's position and was not expected to reach Kalinin until October 23rd. This was very good news, though it is possible that after repeated promises of the imminent arrival of 6th Panzer Division that never seemed to quite happen, XXXXI Corps was a little slower to believe in reinforcements until they actually showed up. This skepticism was justified; only Rittau's leading regiment, 428th Infantry, reached Kalinin that evening. Its III Battalion was assigned to relieve the two weak battalions of 1st Panzer that were defending the western edge of Kalinin against furious attacks by 133rd Rifle Division; meanwhile the other two battalions were to relieve 36th Motorized Division, allowing it to regroup to hold the line on the north edge of Kalinin, likewise under attack from 133rd Rifle Division.

36th Motorized Division had a nervous day. In the morning there had been attacks in company-strength on the motorcycle battalion on the north edge of the city and on the advanced detachment of 6th Panzer Division holding the northeast corner of the city. At 0700 hours another attack hit the exhausted 87th Motorized Infantry Regiment on the southeast edge of the city but it too was repulsed. Later in the morning the division's motorcyclists reported the enemy digging in at Kiselevo, barely a kilometer north of the city and the Gorbatov Bridge. Artillery fire continued to hammer Kalinin, mostly from the north. 5th Rifle Division, with tank support from the dwindling ranks of 21st Tank Brigade, struck again at 87th Motorized Infantry Regiment at 1600 hours. Again they broke into the German rear, losing five of the six or seven tanks that had breached the German lines. A group that the Germans estimated at twenty-five to thirty men held on to a position along the railway within a kilometer of the German division headquarters in Bortnikovo.[216]

Northeast of Kalinin, General Goryachev's 256th Rifle Division had been holding on to the outskirts of the city with only one understrength rifle regiment. At some point, probably by October 20th, the remnants of the division's 934th Regiment were marched around from the west to the northeast of the city to rejoin the division. They were not the only part of the division to rejoin. Before dawn of the 20th, a group of fifteen men, with sooty faces and burnt and torn uniforms, made their way across the Tvertsa River to rejoin their division. They were the survivors of 937th Regiment's 2nd Battalion's 4th Company, led by Lieutenant Bukshenko, who had been cut off in the city, holding a few buildings near the bridge over the Tvertsa, since October 17th. When their fire alerted the Germans to their presence on the 18th, an artillery piece had been rolled up for direct fire on their strongpoint. When the building caught fire, Bukshenko ordered his men to make their way to the neighboring house. On the night of 19th/20th, they decided to pull back out of the city, carrying their two wounded with them.

The fighting continued on this front, and during the day the commander of 937th Regiment, Major Mikhail Trofimovitch Khryukin, was wounded in the leg and the regimental commissar, Chekmarev, had his helmet knocked off by a shell splinter. That night the regiment received reinforcements, including a new commander, Major E.G. Kolkov.[217]

After three days of intense but uncoordinated fighting, Kalinin Front finally seemed to have a clear picture of its situation, and at 2030 hours, issued its orders for the next day. The intention was clear in the order's heading, which read, 'Orders from the Commander of the Forces of Kalinin Front to the Commanders of 29th, 31st, 30th and 22nd Armies on Preparations of Forces for the Attack and Destruction of the Kalinin Group of the Enemy.'

In the order, Konev began by pointing out that the German offensive from Kalinin to Torzhok had been repulsed with heavy losses. It was noted in passing that the enemy was bringing up reinforcements from the south since an infantry division had been identified in the Pogoreloye-Gorodishche area (the 129th). Konev's intention was to hold off the German 9th Army with 22nd Army on his right wing, while 'large forces will encircle and destroy the group of enemy in the area of Kalinin, and, as a result, to seize the city of Kalinin by 21.10, without allowing the enemy to regroup his offensive towards the southeast, towards Moscow. The offensive is to begin at 1100 hours on 21 October.' As it turned out, although this goal was beyond the reach of Kalinin Front's slender resources, Konev's plan dictated the shape of the last part of the battle for Kalinin. Whereas Maslennikov's decision to change his 29th Army's axis of attack from east across the Volga to northeast along the west bank had resulted in an attempted 'small solution' against *Kampfgruppe von Heydebrand* and 900th *Lehr* Brigade between Kalinin and Marino, Konev's intent, like Zhukov's before him, was to seek a 'large solution' against all of XXXXI Motorized Corps, cutting both German supply roads south of Kalinin, linking Khomenko's 30th Army up with Maslennikov's 29th Army in the region just south of Kalinin, and then attacking the city from all points of the compass.

Lieutenant General Nikolai Vatutin had been supposed to turn over the command of his operational group – 8th Tank Brigade, 183rd and 185th Rifle Divisions, 46th and 54th Cavalry Divisions and 46th Motorcycle Regiment – to 31st Army on October 18th. Since that army was not in position to actually take charge of these units, Vatutin had remained on the field, issuing clear and crisp orders to his units through October 20th. Although there is ample evidence that Vatutin, at his headquarters in the area of Torzhok, had good communications (by telephone) with Konev's headquarters in Bzhetsk, these seem to have broken down on the 20th, possibly because both headquarters were in motion.

At any rate, Vatutin issued his last orders to his troops (although interestingly the orders lacked their usual order number and the time they were issued, a striking exception to previous practice, a possible indication that they were in fact never actually sent to the units). They directed 185th Rifle Division with support from 8th Tank Brigade to finish off the enemy forces that had advanced to Mednoye (*KG von Heydebrand*) and then, with the rest of the group, to move off to the southwest, to 'concentrate' on a broad front from Struzhnya, 17 kilometers (10 miles) south of Marino, to Semenovskoye, 5 kilometers (3 miles) south of Mednoye, to Vasilevskoye, 20 kilometers (12 miles) south of Struzhnya. They were then to cross the Volga at Akishevo and Putilovo and subsequently to drive east to Turginovo at the western tip of the Moscow Sea, 38 kilometers (24 miles) south-southwest of Kalinin and 48 kilometers (30 miles) east of their projected crossing point![218] Whether because these orders were never issued, or because Konev's orders superceded them, this attempt to carry out Konev's original intent, as enunciated at least five days previously, was never carried out. Instead the operational group was dispersed, with only 46th Cavalry Division and the remnants of 8th Tank Brigade being given offensive assignments.

While this offensive played out, General Vostrukhov's 22nd Army was to continue with its previous task: the thankless job of containing 9th Army's offensive. This they had been doing for more than a week, counterattacking where they could, but slowly and steadily being pushed back to the north and northeast, falling back 32 kilometers (20 miles) over a period of eight days.

Maslennikov's 29th Army had had its right flank transferred to 22nd Army, and now consisted of 174th, 252nd, 243rd, and 246th Rifle Divisions and 46th Cavalry Division. By Konev's orders it was to both defend the Front's right flank in the area of Staritsa and Akishevo with 174th and 252nd Divisions, and more importantly, put 243rd and 246th Divisions over the Volga, this time closer to

Kalinin, and with the cavalry reaching deep into the enemy's rear in the direction of Turginovo. The attack was to cross the river at two widely separated points – at Izbrizhye, 25 kilometers (15 miles) southwest of Kalinin, and just west of the Migalovo airfield, 13 kilometers (8 miles) west of the city – and to seize Nekrasovo and Danilovskoye on the Staritsa–Kalinin road, 20 and 14 kilometers (12 and 9 miles) south-southwest of Kalinin, respectively. It was planned that these forces would then move east and northeast to link up with 30th Army's 21st Tank Brigade in the Negotino region, 9 kilometers (5 miles) south of Kalinin. In addition, Maslennikov was to hold one rifle division at Vysokoye, 80 kilometers (50 miles) west of Kalinin, behind the Front's right wing. (This division was not designated, and would require one more division than Maslennikov had at this point.) It would not be in position to support the attack over the Volga, and was instead to be deployed to help prevent an enemy attack towards Torzhok from the southwest. Maslennikov's army was not expected to take part in the assault on Kalinin; instead, it was to serve as the anvil, not the hammer, and to choke off reinforcements and supplies from the city, while 31st and 30th Armies destroyed XXXXI Motorized Corps and cleared the city itself.[219]

A rare snapshot of the condition of 29th Army is provided in a report it issued on October 20th, with one copy being sent to the headquarters of Western Front (not Kalinin Front, in action now for three days and supposedly in control of 29th Army). It reported that 119th, 243rd, 246th and 252nd Rifle Divisions were in 'quite satisfactory condition. The total fighting strength is about 60% (for each).' 250th Rifle Division, on the other hand, had only about 1,000 bayonets, collected in part from the many stragglers roaming the army's rear area. Its fighting ability was rated 'low.' Similarly, 220th Rifle Division, with two regiments of about 1,000 men each, along with a thirteen-gun artillery regiment, was considered not stable. 174th Rifle Division, fighting against the advancing 206th Infantry Division near Staritsa, while only totaling about 1,500 men, was considered to be satisfactory in terms of fighting capability. The Separate Motorized Rifle Brigade was also considered satisfactory, but was down to only 300 men. The army's units had from one quarter to one basic ammunition load, while its rations were being provided from local resources. It was finally reported, with winter coming on, that while its summer uniforms and gear were satisfactory, 'winter equipment is not.' The report was signed by the army's chief of staff, Major General Sharapov, and the commissar of the staff, Senior Battalion Commissar Chepurny.[220]

Yushkevich's 31st Army was now assigned 119th and 133rd Rifle Divisions, Rotmistrov's 8th Tank Brigade, and Ryzhkov's Separate Motorized Rifle Brigade, which were to strike at Kalinin from the northwest and north with the objective of linking up with 30th Army by the end of October 21st northwest and south of the outskirts of Kalinin.

Khomenko's 30th Army, now reinforced with 185th Rifle Division, which was to march east above Kalinin, was to attack the city's defenses from the northeast, south and southeast and also prevent any Germans from escaping to the south and southeast. Konev placed in his own reserve 183rd Rifle and 54th Cavalry Divisions and ordered them to the area halfway between Staritsa and Torzhok to back up 22nd Army and 29th Army's right wing.

An optimistic order was given to the Front's VVS, which at this point still consisted of only about forty aircraft from Northwestern Front's air arm, to provide fighter cover over Kalinin and the approaches to it from north and south and to protect friendly forces in Torzhok and Polomenitsy (on the T'ma River, 28 kilometers [17 miles] southeast of Torzhok) region and over the Torzhok and Bzhetsk highways.[221]

At day's end on October 20th, XXXXI Corps recorded its daily KTB entry and also a report on the fighting since the beginning of Operation Typhoon, eighteen days ago. The day's report noted continued Soviet attacks on Kalinin from the north and southeast, both of which were beaten back, but not before an attack with tank support from the southeast broke through German lines and required a local counterattack to contain. Northwest of the city, *Kampfgruppe von Heydebrand* was forced to fall back on Gorodnya by evening after failing to break through the enemy's defenses at Kalikino and Malitsa. The corps continued to report 900th *Lehr* Brigade was still clinging to its defenses around Mednoye and it claimed the brigade was not even in contact with the enemy, but 'A withdrawal could become necessary for supply reasons, if the advance on Torzhok is not possible in the foreseeable future.' Panzer Group 3 seemed to have been better informed than XXXXI Corps, and reported that Mednoye had been abandoned by Krause's *Lehr* Brigade.[222]

At the same time, XXXXI Corps recorded that 6th Infantry Division had disposed of the enemy bridgehead by Brody, although 'the escape of some of the enemy on the eastern bank in a northeast direction must be assumed.' This was a correct assumption: the 914th Rifle Regiment had not been destroyed but was instead making its way northeastward along the bank of the Volga. Given what happened in the next two days, it seems very likely this regiment was resupplied and was able to evacuate its wounded across the Volga once they broke contact with 6th Infantry Division.

Röttiger's longer report on the first eighteen days of Operation Typhoon began by proclaiming how the corps had, 'without a complaint,' advanced 425 kilometers (265 miles). Given that, from October 17th through the 20th XXXXI Corps had not advanced at all, an average rate of advance of over 27 kilometers (16 miles) a day was nothing to sniff at, considering that it had included breaking through the initial Soviet defenses, then the belt of fortifications at Sychevka, then the fighting for Kalinin, and finally the struggle with Rotmistrov's brigade for the Torzhok road. It does put the constant complaints about the miserable roads in perspective too.

After listing the seven stages of the fighting, Röttiger then spent the rest of the report discussing the difficulties the corps had been having:

1. Bad roads and fuel shortages that forced the divisions to leave their field bakeries behind, and a loss of trucks from lack of spare parts.
2. Losses in men and equipment that had been 'within limits' until reaching Kalinin, at which point things had gotten far more costly because the enemy was so strong.
3. A terrible situation regarding fuel supply because it was taking six days for supply columns to travel to the logistics dumps and return.
4. Similar problems with ammunition, somewhat alleviated by the *Luftwaffe*'s resupply efforts, but a shortage of tank ammunition had made it very difficult to repel tank attacks and had led to breakthroughs and losses of equipment.
5. Trouble keeping the corps rear free of enemy, due to lack of adequate forces, allowing the enemy to get behind the leading divisions and cut their supply lines.
6. Such heavy losses that 'Many companies sank to a combat strength of twenty-five to thirty men,' the combined strength of 1st Panzer and 36th Motorized Divisions was no more than that of a weak mixed division, and 3,780 tons worth of trucks [roughly 1,500 trucks!] had been lost and a priority on equipment replacements would be needed to allow the corps to be 'moderately capable.'
7. Continuous fighting that had left the corps in need of several days' rest to recover from exhaustion.

Röttiger concluded his report by stating the corps desperately needed the infantry divisions of 9th Army to come up and relieve it, and by predicting that, unless supply bases could be brought forward, 'future actions will be only intermittent.' To illustrate the corps' lamentable supply status, Röttiger concluded by quoting his 'uncomplaining' troops, who had taken to posting signs along the roads asking, 'Who will trade 10 liters of spirit for 1 loaf of bread?'[223]

Clearly, there was not going to be any German drive to Torzhok, much less Bzhetsk, even if LVI Motorized Corps could be brought up to Kalinin. Indeed, if 129th and 161st Infantry Divisions could not hurry their arrival, XXXXI Motorized Corps was going to be very hard pressed to hold on to Kalinin or even survive Konev's planned encirclement.

Panzer Group 3's assessment of the situation was no more cheerful. At 1130 hours it had recorded that Army Group Center was promising either twenty truck companies (*Grosstransportraum*) or ten companies with trailers would be soon forthcoming; all the panzer group had to do was tell them when the trucks were needed and what route to send them over. Reinhardt's staff calculated that under the best conditions, if the trucks began their journey on October 21st, and if 2,000 cubic meters of fuel were actually made available, the earliest that LVI Corps could be expected in Kalinin would be October 27th (later in the day this was recalculated to an earliest expected arrival time for the corps as November 1st). 9th Army had passed the word to Reinhardt that his group would not be expected to do more than reconnoiter once they had reached Bzhetsk, but,

> Practically, however, that means the start of [sending] a corps, because it is impossible to send weaker forces 200 kilometers [125 miles] out. After reaching Beshezk a blocking line must be established to the west and perhaps to the east also. A simultaneous advance to Wyschni Wolotschek is not possible.[224]

At day's end, things looked gloomier yet from Reinhardt's perspective. The forces on the Torzhok road were still cut off, and the city was under attack from the southeast, west, and northeast, while artillery fire was falling on the city itself. Losses were heavy, 'average battalion strength only 100-200 men . . . Four Russian divisions are seeking to retake Kalinin, so in Kalinin every man is needed.' The panzer group demanded that the advanced detachment of 162nd Infantry Division be sent from Staritsa, and the rest of the division as soon as possible. The objectives for the panzer group were then set for the next day:

> Defense of Kalinin; an advance from Kalinin to Torzhok is provisionally not to be considered. For supply reasons first the areas west of Kalinin between the road and the Volga need to be recovered. During the entire day resources must be inserted into the situation at Kalinin and the oppressive conditions there ended.

How even this was to be accomplished was not spelled out. The road conditions were noted succinctly as 'indescribable.'[225]

October 21st

The rain began to let up on the 21st, turning to scattered showers. The unplanned battle of the Torzhok road was coming to a close, more with a whimper than a bang. Both sides spent part of the day regrouping, a slow and painful business on muddy roads, in an incoherent situation.

General Konev, finally managing to establish communications with his armies, attempted to realize his plan for the battle: to get 29th Army to strike across the Volga to cut off Kalinin from the south, while 31st and 30th Armies took Kalinin and destroyed its defenders. The problem was that 119th, 252nd and 243rd Rifle Divisions of 29th Army were splayed out on the muddy dirt roads from just north of Staritsa to the crossings on the T'ma River and their leading regiments were tangled up in a tough fight against the elements of 1st Panzer Division and 900th *Lehr* Brigade that were trying to claw their way back to the relative safety of the Kalinin perimeter. It was one thing to order a 180° turn, a completely different thing to attempt it in a situation of miserable roads, weak communications, and under enemy air strikes.

At the same time, 31st Army was just getting control of its newly assigned units, while 30th Army – whose constant attacks on Kalinin from the southeast had pinned and bled 36th Motorized Division, preventing it from coming to the aid of 1st Panzer – had finally been forced by exhaustion and heavy losses to call off its attacks to regroup and take on yet more replacements.

General Reinhardt had his own problems. While some of *Kampfgruppe von Heydebrand* had managed to extract themselves from the pocket, and the pocket itself was now within 3 kilometers (2 miles) of the relative safety of Kalinin, it was not yet possible to bring any of the vehicles out. The rearguard, 900th *Lehr*, was still under heavy attack from the north, south, and west. Only flights of Ju-87 *Stukas* shuttling from the Migalovo airport were holding the pursuers at bay.

While Army Group Center continued to enquire how soon the offensive could be resumed against Torzhok–Vyshniy Volochek and Bzhetsk, Panzer Group 3 was concerned with rescuing its spearhead from the debacle on the Torzhok road, holding on to and resupplying Kalinin, and attempting to bring up LVI Motorized Corps at long last.

The first attack of the day fell on the motorcycle battalion of 36th Motorized Division, holding the northern edge of the city covering the Gorbatov Bridge. 133rd Rifle Division's left wing drove south at 0730 hours (German time), and the Germans were not sure they could hold. By 0810 hours, the situation was deemed critical, and a platoon of 2nd Reconnaissance Squadron from the division's reconnaissance battalion was sent to help. No artillery support was available, and an urgent call went out to Weiss's *Schlachtflieger* for support. By 0945 the attack had ground to a halt, with two key churches on the northern edge of Kalinin in Soviet hands. At the same time there came disquieting reports from a company of the advanced detachment of 129th Infantry Division, still subordinate to Gollnick's motorized division, that it had encountered Soviet troops (probably a patrol) in Danilovskoye, southwest of Kalinin on the Staritsa–Kalinin road.

At 1030 hours, the attack resumed, stronger than ever. A composite artillery battalion, consisting of one 10.5cm howitzer battery of the division's own artillery and a 10cm battery of 611th Artillery Battalion, was on route from Staritsa and was promised to the motorcyclists for support by 1100 hours. Air support was temporarily suspended due to low clouds. Soviet artillery fire was said to be 'very annoying.'

By 1645 hours in the late afternoon, the Germans gained the upper hand and forced the exhausted 133rd Division to fall back north a short distance, giving the Germans control of the two churches again. But there they came under heavy fire from 937th Rifle Regiment on the far side of the river and the artillery of 256th Rifle Division. The easternmost church was blown up as the Germans retreated back to positions just north of the Volga.[226] Shvetsov's division had paid a stiff price, losing eighty dead and 320 wounded during October 20th and 21st.[227]

Southeast of the city, the attacks of Khomenko's 30th Army finally died away. This was good timing from the Germans' point of view. 87th Motorized Regiment of 36th Motorized Division had taken the brunt of the attacks, reporting it had 'repulsed seventeen attacks, including eight severe attacks with tanks' since October 14th. The front had been repeatedly penetrated, and the regimental head-quarters directly threatened. The respite was welcome, and by 1430 hours, the regiment was relieved by two battalions of 418th Infantry Regiment of 129th Infantry Division. Since the infantrymen brought no antitank guns with them, 87th Motorized was required to leave such antitank batteries as it still had, along with the assault guns that had been attached, to reinforce the infantrymen.[228]

Lieutenant Colonel Telkov's 5th Rifle Division had entered the battle with fewer than 2,000 men on October 12th, and had lost 525 men by the 19th in the fighting for the city and thereafter. Yet, somehow Telkov's riflemen managed from the 14th through the 21st to keep up a series of daily attacks that badly shook their opponents, the men of General Gollnick's 36th Motorized Division. The 5th was supported by what was left of Lesovoi's 21st Tank Brigade, whose losses continued to mount with every attack. How was it possible for two such weak formations to continue to launch what its opponents perceived to be powerful attacks? While no direct evidence has been discovered, it is pretty clear that, begin-ning no later than the 17th, they had received a significant number of replacements. On October 22nd the Germans would describe the forces attacking Kalinin from the southeast as, 'four strong regiments with 1,000 men in each.'[229] This was clearly 5th Rifle Division, reinforced by the 'Separate' or 'Special' Rifle Regiment.[230] The numbers may represent hyperbole, or just an enthusiastic over-estimate, but clearly, if the 5th had not received replacements, it is unlikely that it could have continued to conduct strong attacks. Except for the battered 21st Tank Brigade, it was the only Soviet unit to the southeast of the city.

One puzzling feature of this part of the battle is Khomenko's repeated unsuc-cessful attacks in the same sector, roughly 5 kilometers (3 miles) wide, between the Volga and the Volokolamsk–Kalinin road. Had Lesovoi's tankers been sent west, against one of the Germans' two critical supply lines, they would have faced little opposition, and could have done more of the same sort of damage they had meted out on October 17th. It would have been a better job for the thinly armored but fast BT tanks and the T-60s.

The sacrifices of 30th Army, though severe, were not entirely in vain, however. Although they failed to overwhelm the defenders of Kalinin and liberate the city, they definitely inflicted terrible punishment on the motorized infantry facing them, and more importantly, they pinned half of XXXXI Motorized Corps in place, preventing it from assisting 1st Panzer Division in its bloody struggle to escape the trap on the Torzhok road.

North of the city, not only had Shvetsov's 133rd Rifle Division hammered at the Gorbatov bridge and continued to hold on to Kalikino–Malitsa with its right flank, but it also struck at the western and northwestern edge of Kalinin, seizing the vital juncture of the railroad and Torzhok highway just north of Doroshika Station. If this could not be cleared, it would be nearly impossible for von Heydebrand's and Kruger's men to get their vehicles and artillery out of the trap. It was already too late for at least twenty-four tanks, which were reported knocked out.[231]

The breakout attempt was postponed until late in the day, and then put off until the following day. The troops were too tired, the enemy attacks too persistent, and fuel and ammunition too scarce for anything else. Röttiger reported that, 'separated elements of 1st Panzer Division rejoined on foot' – a statement open to interpretation. It probably signifies that small groups of *schutzen* were able to filter out of the pocket, because 1st Panzer Division reported at 1715 hours that while III Battalion of 129th Infantry Division's 418th Regiment managed to retake the road/rail junction, Krause's *Lehr* Brigade, just south of Malitsa, was still not in touch with von Heydebrand's group and there was serious concern about the condition of the troops and whether it would be possible to bring them out of the pocket on October 22nd without large material losses. To make this breakout possible, 5 cubic meters of fuel and a quantity of ammunition were scheduled to be ferried over the Volga at Cherkasovo, from Migalovo, where a fuel dump was established. Panzer Group 3 recorded that it was questionable whether it would be possible to extract the tanks and vehicles of the broken spearhead. Some 260 wounded were waiting to be ferried over the Volga to the vicinity of the Migalovo airfield. Attempts by the engineers of XXXXI Corps to build a pontoon bridge over the Volga were thwarted by the rising water in the river. The breakout attempt was going to have to wait until October 22nd.[232]

Konev's critical blow was intended to come from Maslennikov's 29th Army, which was to cross the Volga to cut off Kalinin from any hope of supply or reinforcement. This time they were to cross at Izbrizhye, 32 kilometers (20 miles) upstream from Kalinin, and by the mouth of the T'ma River, only 11.5 kilometers (7 miles) upstream. This would involve extracting the army from its combat with the retreating Germans on the Torzhok road, and countermarching them south again over the same few muddy roads. 119th Rifle Division, which had reported that it was fighting on the approaches to the railroad bridge over the Volga, but turned out to have not yet managed to get all of its units across the T'ma and was instead fighting in the Gorodnya–Shiryakovo area, was transferred to 31st Army. Sort of. In fact, in Kalinin Front's Operational Summary, the division is listed as part of 31st Army and also of 29th Army. It is included in the orders for 29th Army to regroup overnight and cross the Volga on October 22nd and in the orders for 31st Army directing it to take the northwestern and southern portions of Kalinin along with that army's 133rd Rifle Division, 8th Tank Brigade, and the Separate

Motorized Rifle Brigade.[233] Similarly, 252nd Rifle Division, which was reported crossing the T'ma at 0400 hours and fighting against enemy tanks at Novinki at noon, is both listed as part of 29th Army in one entry, and omitted in another entry. (This is not just a typo, because subsequently 252nd Rifle Division was attached to 31st Army and took part in attacks against Kalinin from the west, while 119th Rifle Division shifted south and crossed the Volga to support 246th Rifle.)[234]

Further south, 6th Infantry Division continued to cross the Volga above Staritsa. The bridge over the Volga at Staritsa itself apparently was unusable, and the division was crossing a few kilometers downstream.[235] Four battalions had crossed by 0800 hours and by 1045 hours XXXXI Corps declared that the division's fight to establish its bridgehead was over. By 1900 hours, well after sundown, the bulk of the division was over the Volga and consolidating its bridgehead against what it reported were 'weak defenses.' Panzer Group 3 wanted the division to push northeast, clearing the western bank of the Volga and driving into the rear of the Soviets that were attacking the trapped forces of 1st Panzer Division on the Torzhok road. There continued to be conflict, however, with 9th Army, who wanted the division to push north against Torzhok and Mednoye. Because the rest of 9th Army was making rough work of driving 174th Rifle Division of 29th Army and the weak divisions of 22nd Army north, Lieutenant General Helge Auleb's 6th Infantry Division was reluctant to make any moves north or northeast. Instead it elected to hold its position until Major General Walther Weiss's 26th Infantry, then fighting on the west bank of the Volga just north of Staritsa against 174th Rifle Division, could make enough progress to protect 6th Division's left flank.

German figures paint a grim picture. Between October 13th and 18th, as we have seen, 1st Panzer and 900th *Lehr* lost 112 men killed, 324 wounded, and twenty-one missing, for a total of 457 casualties. 1st Panzer alone, between October 19th and 20th, lost an additional 501 men! Although no loss figures for 900th *Lehr* are provided for this period, they were equally substantial. This is not surprising, since the two formations were badly outnumbered, nearly surrounded, and fighting without the benefit of much artillery support, very short on fuel and ammunition, with limited if any air support, and no effective way to evacuate casualties or damaged equipment. Remember, it was *before* this date that Röttiger had speculated that 1st Panzer and 36th Motorized Divisions might have to be disbanded and combined into one weak motorized division.

The Soviets also claimed to have inflicted substantial losses on the Germans on the Torzhok road:

> By 21 October, 8th Tank Brigade, the Separate Motorized Rifle Brigade, 185th and 133rd Rifle Divisions and also three divisions of 29th Army [the 119th, 252nd, and 243rd] had inflicted a serious defeat on the enemy group in the area of Marino–Mednoye. A significant part of this group was

exterminated. So, for example, just in the woods near Gorodnya village our armies destroyed over 500 enemy soldiers and officers, some tens of motor vehicles, twenty tanks and over 200 motorcycles were captured. Only for elements of the enemy group was it possible to break through to Kalinin.[236]

Just before sundown, Kirchner spoke to Reinhardt, insisting that XXXXI Corps be given several days to reorganize and asserting that any resumption of the offensive to the northwest was not possible at this time. Kirchner urged the panzer group commander to use 6th Panzer, 'as soon as it was available', to clean up the situation along the Lotoshino road, which was the 'only useful supply road' for the corps, and, if 6th Panzer was not available, to use the 7th.

For the next day, the corps planned for 6th Infantry Division to attack to the northeast, enlarging its bridgehead, and to then stop. 129th Infantry and 36th Motorized Divisions were to relieve 1st Panzer Division of responsibility for defending Kalinin and it was hoped that a regiment of Major General Heinrich Recke's 161st Infantry Division would arrive and that the division would be able to take over the defenses of Kalinin by October 23rd.[237]

Migalovo airfield was in some ways the center of the German defense of Kalinin. The airfield was a base for Stuka dive-bombers supporting 1st Panzer Division in its fight for the Torzhok road and of Bf-109 fighters that patrolled the air over the city, preying on the Soviet bombers trying to hit the Volga bridges. It was the landing point for Ju-52 transports bringing in vitally needed fuel, ammunition, and replacements, and evacuating wounded. From here German logistics units delivered fuel and ammunition to frontline units, including a substantial store of Soviet gasoline captured when the field was seized on October 14th. Just west of the landing grounds, 1st Panzer Division had parked its supply, maintenance, medical, other rear service elements, and a lot of trucks in the village of Oparino. The village was garrisoned not only by soldiers of the division trains, but also by elements of a company from 129th Infantry Division's Reconnaissance Battalion, and by 37th Antitank Battalion of 1st Panzer Division. The sector had been quiet until October 21st.

Several patrols from the forces defending Oparino brought in reports of Soviet troops encountered at Danilovskoye. By 1015 hours, 36th Motorized Division (to which the reconnaissance battalion of 129th Infantry was subordinate at that point) noted, 'Leader of the Advance Detachment, 129th Infantry Division reports concerning the situation in the southwest, that weak enemy forces are in "Krasnoje".' Later on at 1400 hours it reported again that 'Krasnoje (northwest of Aparina) is occupied by the enemy. Fifteen prisoners were taken who stated that three battalions have crossed the Volga with the mission to retake Kalinin.' 'Aparina' is clearly Oparino, and 'Krasnoje' is also clearly Krasnovo, which is just west of the Migalovo airfield.[238]

These prisoners were from 246th Rifle Division's 914th Regiment that had crossed the Volga on October 17th and cut the Staritsa–Kalinin road for two days before being driven off to the northwest by the German 6th Infantry Division, now reappearing on the scene. It had not, contrary to German reports, been 'driven into the Volga.' Instead it had made its way along the eastern bank of the river, where the river winds away from the road, and presumably had managed to resupply. During the night of October 20th/21st, it emerged from the woods and captured the village of Motavino, just over 6 kilometers (4 miles) west of the Migalovo airfield. Continuing to push east, it then took Krasnovo, placing Soviet troops less than 5 kilometers (3 miles) from the vital airfield.[239]

Konev took the opportunity offered by the day's delay to reorganize his forces further, considerably improving their command and control situation:

22nd Army would receive 220th and 250th Rifle Divisions from 29th Army's right wing, which were occupying positions extending from Selizharovo eastward to Kholokholnya, and would prevent an enemy break-through to Torzhok from the direction of Selizharovo or Rzhev.

29th Army, now consisting of 119th, 243rd, 246th, and 174th Rifle Divisions and 46th Cavalry Division, was to regroup its forces during the night, and on October 22nd to attack across the Volga, now in the area of Putilovo and the mouth of the T'ma River, and advance towards Danilovskoye. By the end of October 23rd, the army was to have seized Danilovskoye and Nekrasovo, cut the escape [and supply] routes of the enemy in Kalinin, and linked up with 30th Army's forces around Negotino. One rifle division [the 174th] was to take up a position at Lipiga, on the west side of the Volga, to protect the army's right flank, while the cavalry were to break into the enemy rear and strike for Pokrovskoye, on the Volokolamsk–Kalinin road 24 kilometers [15 miles] to the southeast.

30th Army, with 5th, 185th and 256th Rifle Divisions and 21st Tank Brigade, was to attack Kalinin from the northeast, east and south and, by the end of October 23rd, to clear the northeastern and southern sectors of the city, while preventing any enemy from retreating to the south.

31st Army, operating between 29th and 30th Armies, with 133rd and 252nd Rifle Divisions, 8th Tank Brigade and the Separate Motorized Rifle Brigade, was to attack Kalinin from the northwest from the area of Kalikino and Malitsa and, while cooperating with 30th Army, clear the northeastern and southern parts of the city and prevent any enemy retreat to the south or southeast.

The Front Reserve was to consist of 183rd Rifle Division in the Medukhovo region, 15 kilometers [9 miles] southeast of Torzhok, and 54th Cavalry Division in the Polomenitsy region [on the south bank of the T'ma River, 29 kilometers west of the Volga] as before.[240]

This plan was somewhat more realistic than the previous plan, principally in that Konev did not expect his forces to annihilate the whole of XXXXI Corps in a single day. However, careful examination of the forces to be used reveals that the operation was indeed being conducted on a shoestring. Konev was proposing to storm the city with four and two-thirds rifle divisions (the 5th, 133rd, 185th, and 252nd, plus two-thirds of the 256th: the 5th was very weak, the 133rd and 252nd moderately strong, and the 185th was full strength, but in the event never took part in the attacks) and the remnants of two tank brigades (amounting to no more than two dozen tanks at the most). The Germans, while short of supplies of all kinds, had been improving their defenses since October 15th by digging in derelict tanks, fortifying houses, stringing barbed wire and planting mines. In addition, German infantry was beginning to arrive. Although Konev had clear superiority over the Germans in sheer numbers on October 17th, this advantage was decreasing with every passing day. Just as Soviet attacks on the flanks of XXXXI Corps were diverting German strength away from the fight on the Torzhok road and the defense of the city, the push north by 9th Army towards Torzhok was making Konev divert forces to deal with this threat. One of Vatutin's rifle divisions, the 183rd, and one of his cavalry divisions, the 54th, were shifted to the west to backstop the thin lines of 22nd Army, and 8th Tank Brigade and Separate Motorized Rifle Brigade were pulled back to the area of Mednoye–Mermeriny on the Torzhok road to lick their wounds and provide for a reserve. It would remain to be seen whether his forces had the strength to carry a battle of annihilation to the finish.

Conclusions

The battle for the Torzhok road was nearly over. The grandiose plan to encircle the northern flank of Western Front and the southern flank of Northwestern Front, originating at *OKW* (Hitler's headquarters) and passed dutifully down through *OKH* to Army Group Center and Panzer Group 3, was now in ruins. So was XXXXI Motorized Corps. *Kampfgruppe von Heydebrand* and 900th *Lehr* Brigade would manage to extract their survivors, and some of their vehicles and artillery, during the next 24 hours, but 1st Panzer Division could in no way be considered an offensive force of any value. Beginning the attack with possibly as many as seventy-nine tanks, by the end of the third week in October it was down to about ten, with possibly as few as six tanks still running. The *Lehr* Brigade was equally decimated. It was only due to totally inadequate Soviet communications that any of the German spearhead survived to fight another day. Despite the lack of coordination between Vatutin's group, Maslennikov's 29th Army, and Konev, the German attack had been first delayed and bled by the sacrifice of 8th Tank Brigade, and then assailed from all sides by 133rd, 183rd, 185th, 119th, 243rd and 252nd Rifle Divisions and the Separate Motorized Rifle Brigade. While the Germans on the Torzhok road were fighting for their lives, 36th Motorized Division was unable to give it any help at all. This was due to the heroic efforts of 30th Army, which despite the fact that it had only four weak rifle regiments and one very aggressive tank brigade attacking, kept the German motorized troops pinned down and fighting for their very survival on the edge of the city.

There was no longer any question of grand sweeps to Torzhok, Vyshniy Volochek, Bologoye or Bzhetsk. The initiative had been seized by the Red Army. It had been done clumsily and it had, of course, paid for it in blood. But for the final phase of the battle, General Konev would be calling the tune.

Chapter 8

The Battle for Kalinin City, October 22nd–24th

October 22nd

At this point, the only German offensive effort in the Kalinin region was 9th Army's continued grinding north towards Torzhok from the southwest and south. But it was a slow, heartbreaking fight, with 22nd Army giving ground only grudgingly and frequently launching small counterattacks. General Strauss's 9th Army was weak and poorly supplied, and although Kalinin Front's reports would claim that they were supported by sixty or seventy panzers, in fact there were no German tanks west of the Volga anymore.[241]

The rain let up for the day, allowing the *Luftwaffe* to once again dominate the skies, but as for XXXXI Motorized Corps, while its mission was still to advance, it was only concerned with survival and holding on to Kalinin.

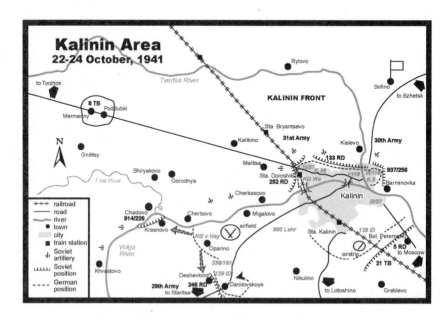

Konev was finally in position to deliver his *coup de grace* to the Germans in Kalinin. Four factors, however, were working against him: German reinforcements, the steadily improving German defenses around the city, the attrition suffered by his forces, and the increasing German pressure against his right flank.

For one thing, time had slipped by and what might have been possible on October 17th, before the arrival of 129th Infantry Division and the approach of 161st Infantry, might not be possible now, five days later. The Germans had also had time to dig in, something they could do even if they were short on fuel and ammunition, and they had not been idle.

German losses had been nearly catastrophic but the Soviets had also lost heavily and the divisions sent in to assault Kalinin were mostly well worn down. Although replacements (in the form of march-battalions and companies) had been brought forward to rebuild some of the units, they had little depth to absorb further losses. Finally, with the German 6th Infantry Division across the Volga, and 9th Army continuing to push north towards Torzhok on its left, Konev was forced to keep an eye over his right shoulder and, instead of being able to concentrate every available division for the storming of Kalinin, he was forced to divert unit after unit to bolster his threatened right flank.

All commanders and commissars of Kalinin Front received an order from Konev, urging them into battle, which ended with the words, 'Warriors of Glory: Boldly storm the enemy! Kalinin has been and will be a Russian city, proudly bearing the name of All-Union *Starosty* M.I. Kalinin!' The word *starosty* denotes a village elder or headman, and referred to Mikhail Kalinin's image as the wily old peasant of the revolution, rather than his formal (and largely symbolic) title of President of the USSR. The orders also demanded close attention to good cooperation between the various combat arms. Since both tank brigades were pretty much spent forces at this point, and air–ground coordination between the Red Army and Red Air Force (VVS, DBA, and PVO) was nearly nonexistent in 1941, this amounted to little more than a statement of good intentions.[242] Nonetheless, the orders showed a little more sober assessment of the situation facing Kalinin Front. Realizing that all of his forces were not ready to begin the offensive, he gave them until the next day to get into position, with the offensive scheduled to kick off at 0800 hours on October 23rd.

Konev's intention was to strike a powerful blow from the west with 29th Army to cut off the Germans in Kalinin, while concentric attacks from the west, northwest, north, northeast and southeast crushed the defenders in the city. This is not what happened.

One of the forces that had been available, Operational Group Vatutin, had been dispersed. Its 185th Rifle Division was marching east to join 30th Army; 183rd Rifle Division had been pulled to the west to backstop 22nd Army's thin lines, along with 54th Cavalry Division. 8th Tank Brigade and 46th Motorcycle Regiment had been fought out, and while survivors of the latter were still fighting as part of 133rd Rifle Division, the rest of the brigade was pulled back into reserve to refit. 46th Cavalry Division was to transfer to 29th Army to support the Volga crossing. Khomenko's 30th Army was simply fought out. 5th Rifle Division, weak to begin with, had battered itself bloody in repeated attacks on 36th Motorized Division, as had 21st Tank Brigade. 937th Regiment of 256th Rifle Division was as worn down as the rest of the army. There were simply no strong or fresh units to throw into the attack, so just as the concentric offensive was about to begin, 30th Army had little left to contribute to it.

Maslennikov's army had originally been ordered to put four rifle divisions over the Volga, a formidable force, assuming they could be supplied and supported. But now there were no longer four divisions to carry out the mission. 174th Rifle Division had been transferred to 22nd Army, and in any case had already been diverted, first fighting the elements of 26th Infantry Division of 9th Army fighting their way north towards Staritsa, and now making a quick redeployment north to help contain the bridgehead of 6th Infantry Division that threatened its rear. 29th Army's 243rd Rifle Division likewise was not able to take part in the Volga crossing because it too was diverted to contain 6th Infantry Division's bridgehead, which posed a threat to any crossing of the Volga. One more division, 252nd Rifle, was handed over to Yushkevich's 31st Army, and was attacking Kalinin from the west, fighting for the road/rail crossing.

This left Maslennikov only 246th and 119th Rifle Divisions to conduct the river crossing and seal off Kalinin from the south. The 119th was still engaged with the withdrawing *Kampfgruppe von Heydebrand*, and when it managed to disengage it would face regrouping south over muddy secondary roads. 246th Rifle Division had put one regiment, 914th Rifle, over the Volga since October 17th. This regiment had been forced north by a regiment of 6th Infantry Division and had marched along the east bank of the Volga to the wooded area west of Kalinin where the river curved east to pass through the city. 915th Rifle Regiment marched to Khvastovo, a tiny village on the Volga 10 kilometers (6 miles) west of Danilovskoye. The crossing was unopposed, but slowed by the fact that there were only two pontoons and small number of boats available at the crossing site. The regiment, under air attack as soon as the sun came up, took all day to get across, finishing by 2000 hours, at which point the division's artillery regiment began crossing. The third regiment of the division, the 908th, had assumed defensive positions facing south, from Chapayevka to Zaborovye, a distance of 10 kilometers. So instead of four divisions, this initial crossing of the Volga was conducted by a single regiment.[243] Later that night 29th Cavalry Regiment was ordered to cross and reinforce the effort. Kalinin Front's Operations Summary, issued at 0800 hours on October 22nd, mentions that 46th Cavalry Division was to assemble well to the south and cross the Volga at Akishevo, but makes no mention of the fact that the German 6th Infantry Division had crossed the river at this spot, and had a substantial bridgehead established there. Some insight into how clear a picture Konev had of the situation can be deduced by the fact that the same document reports that the Front's communications had been knocked out that morning, except to Khomenko's 30th Army. The rest could be contacted only by radio.[244]

Although the big offensive was scheduled for the next day, the fighting didn't slack off much. The first attack of the morning came from 119th Rifle Division that hit the battalion of 129th Infantry Division's 418th Regiment just north of the Volga in the western edge of Kalinin. The attack was successfully beaten back but just south of the Volga an ugly situation began to develop for the Germans. Major A.P. Krutikhin's 914th Rifle Regiment of 246th Rifle Division had crossed the Volga on October 17th at Akishevo and for two days had contested the Staritsa–Kalinin road in the area of Redkino. They had been driven off by a regiment of 6th Infantry Division and had retreated to the north, hugging the east bank of the Volga and staying out of the way of the stream of German reinforcements and supplies moving on the road. Having reached the point where the Volga turned east to Kalinin on October 21st, the next morning they stormed the village of Krasnovo at dawn. Lacking any artillery support, the attack had been bloody; the battalion leading the attack reported being reduced to 50% strength.

At this point Krutikhin was joined by Major Rozov to coordinate artillery support for his regiment. Krutikhin was ordered to continue his attack to the east, taking Ryabeevo and Oparino. Although Rozov indicated that he was unable to get his battery commanders (who in the Red Army acted as forward observers for their batteries) into position to observe targets due to intense German machinegun and mortar fire, at 1020 hours Panzer Group 3's headquarters received a call for help from *Fliegerkorps VIII* at Migalovo airfield, reporting that they were under artillery fire. No immediate response could be provided, as 1st Panzer Division's artillery, just escaped from the pocket, was unable to help. Later counter battery fire was provided and the guns temporarily silenced, but four planes had been damaged. Soviet shelling also forced the supply section of 1st Panzer to evacuate the fuel distribution point they had at the airfield. Later in the afternoon they were able to load 2 cubic meters of captured fuel on to the division's 10th Supply Column.[245]

There was plenty of Soviet artillery in the area. Maslennikov's 29th Army had 644th Corps Artillery Regiment, 432nd and 510th Howitzer Regiments in support of Krutikhin's regiment, while 119th Rifle Division, which had lost its 510th Howitzer Regiment two days earlier when it was stripped out and made an RVGK reserve artillery unit, still had its artillery adjustment platoon, and had been reinforced by three independent 122mm howitzer batteries. 133rd Rifle Division likewise had its 511th Howitzer Regiment, and its own artillery adjustment platoon. Consequently references to the galling Soviet artillery fire run through German reports like a red thread. The withdrawing elements of 900th *Lehr* and of *Kampfgruppe von Heydebrand* got a full dose of it, as did 36th Motorized Division's units defending the northern edge of the city.

During the rest of the morning, Soviet attacks continued against the western and northern edges of Kalinin, as the remnants of von Heydebrand's group made their way out of the pocket. Some of the surviving motorcycles of 1st Panzer's *K.1* Battalion were ferried across the Volga on rubber rafts, but the few remaining tanks of 1st Panzer Regiment, along with the artillery, armored halftracks, artillery tractors and trucks, had to get out over the railroad bridge. How this was done exactly is somewhat of a mystery. On the available maps, while it is possible to move along the Volga's north bank over secondary roads through Shiryakovo, Dmitrovskoye and Cherkasovo, the road does not continue along the river's bank, but turns sharply north to Malitsa. No German or Soviet account reports that the Germans ever took Malitsa from 133rd Rifle Division. In aerial photographs taken later during the war by the *Luftwaffe*, it is possible to trace a small road east along the river bank, but there is no indication of a way across the stream that empties into the Volga between Cherkasovo and the railroad bridge. At any rate, there are clear indications that a few tanks, and most of the artillery, were successfully extracted. It is possible that they moved cross country to bypass Malitsa to the south.

There is an enormous lack of clarity in the German records concerning exactly what got out of the pocket, how, and when. There is some indication that there was some deliberate obfuscation, if not deception, practiced by XXXXI Corps and Panzer Group 3 over the question. As an example, at 1630 hours Army Group Center asked 9th Army to find out 'whether 1st Panzer Division left many vehicles behind. Answer: No, only those which were stuck and in need of repair.' So, does that mean many? Few? What exactly? Does 'stuck' mean out of fuel? Do vehicles destroyed to avoid capture count as 'in need of repair'? There is no way to tell. But the answer to the question from von Bock's headquarters seems remarkably slippery.[246]

The fiercest fighting of the day took place in the west. Elements of 119th Rifle Division pushed the Germans through Dmitrovskoye and Cherkasovo while Colonel A.A. Zabulev's 252nd Rifle Division struck at the high ground around the railroad/road crossing just west of Kalinin. The defense of the western side of Kalinin was conducted by *Kampfgruppe Westhofen*, consisting of two very weak battalions of *schutzen* (II/1, II/113) with no more than 200 men left in each, plus one battalion of 129th Infantry Division's 418th Regiment, and the survivors of Colonel Walther Krause's 900th *Lehr* Brigade. With the Germans chased out of Dmitrovskoye and Cherkasovo, this put the Soviets just across the Volga from Migalovo airfield. Aggressively forward basing their air support had paid big dividends for the Germans, who had assumed that they needed to push their air units forward to be able to provide support for their rapidly advancing spearheads. Now that the spearhead was shattered, and moving in reverse, the disadvantages of this policy were about to be demonstrated.

The battered survivors of 1st Panzer Division received replacements: 160 men had by this time been flown in from the 81st Field Replacement Battalion at Vitebsk. But losses had been 'very high,' both in the Panzer Division and in the

Lehr Brigade. The personnel department of 1st Panzer (IIa) reported that since October 13th, when the fighting began in Kalinin, the division had lost fifty-eight officers and 950 NCOs and enlisted men. The losses in the last few days had been exceptionally heavy. Röttiger demanded documentation for this, and understandably so, as if one counts the daily totals submitted by IIa/1st Panzer Division, one gets a sum that is 30% less than the one cited above. This is probably due to the difficulties the division experienced getting accurate information out of the pocket and with the return of von Heydebrand, the truth was beginning to sink home. The division urgently needed relief.[247]

By evening at 1700 hours, 36th Motorized Division recorded that it had been requested by XXXXI Corps to move 118th Motorized Infantry Regiment's two battalions over to relieve 1st Panzer Division's defenders on the western edge of the city. General Gollnick declined, saying he could not guarantee the defenses of the northern edge of Kalinin without the regiment, and pointing out that he only had two battalions of each of his regiments available (failing to mention his badly battered motorcycle battalion, still in the line north of the Gorbatov Bridge, and the reinforced motorcycle battalion of 6th Panzer Division, holding off 256th Rifle Division's 937th Rifle Regiment in the northeast corner of the city). The other two battalions of Gollnick's division were not available because 'II/87 is dismounted in the rear, and II/118 is dispersed and dismounted, one company is with Corps . . .' (presumably providing security for XXXXI Corps headquarters). It was finally agreed that Gollnick's men would edge over to their left and assume the defense of 500 meters more of 1st Panzer Division's front, but the defense of the railroad/road crossing would remain the responsibility of 1st Panzer. The situation regarding artillery ammunition had improved, but it was not possible to reply to the Soviet artillery pummeling the town from the north, nor was it possible to shell the enemy movements detected opposite the division; such shells as were available had to be saved for 'extreme emergencies.'[248]

The two regiments of Major General Stephan Rittau's 129th Infantry Division were deployed covering the southeast edge of the city. German air reconnaissance detected a large buildup of Soviet forces to the southeast of Kalinin and the Germans expected an attack from this quarter, but by sundown it had still not materialized.[249]

36th Motorized Division handed over the southern sector of Kalinin to 129th Infantry Division, whose second regiment arrived in the early hours of the morning. The 36th, along with the advanced detachment of 6th Panzer Division, then took over the task of securing the northern and eastern edges of the city, with the survivors of 1st Panzer Division's *Kampfgruppe Westhofen* and 900th *Lehr* Brigade covering the northwest and western defenses, holding on just east of Malitsa.

Just west of Migalovo airfield, Soviet attacks continued. Although an artillery preparation was conducted, 'the effect was disappointing.' According to Rozov, the Germans had an excellent system of fires, thus, when the decimated regiment went over to the attack, it was almost instantly repulsed. Reconnaissance soon reported that the enemy was reinforcing his defenses with tanks and armored carriers, elements of 1st Panzer Division's *Kampfgruppe von Heydebrand*.[250]

By 1000 hours German air reconnaissance was reporting to XXXXI Motorized Corps that 'small enemy groups are continuing to cross the Volga west of Danilowskoje [Danilovskoye].' To parry this threat, Kirchner ordered 1st Panzer and 36th Motorized to each send forty trucks to the area of Redkino, there to load up 336th Regiment of 161st Infantry Division and truck it forward to where it could deal with the Soviet bridgehead west of Danilovskoye. The regiment was supposed to be in its assigned position by the afternoon of October 23rd. Meanwhile, elements of 129th Infantry Division were also to attack the enemy from the north in an attempt to push them back over the Volga.[251]

October 23rd

On paper at least, both sides continued to pursue their offensive objectives. Panzer Group 3 were still talking about striking towards Torzhok and Bzhetsk, and began to discuss the possibility of a 'limited operation' in an entirely new direction, to clear the right flank of the group by driving 30th Army from the area between Kalinin, the Volga, Turginovo and the Moscow Sea. Konev's order for the 'warriors of glory to storm Kalinin by the end of the day' remained in force. But in fact, October 23rd seemed to bring a comprehension on both sides of the front lines that there was insufficient strength available to accomplish their stated goals. In both Soviet and German records the day's reports and diaries are full of discussions of the losses taken so far during the battle, and the losses inflicted on the foe.

The reasons the German offensive plans had to be shelved we have already seen. This should have been the day that the concentric attack on Kalinin by the Red Army finally came off. The reasons it didn't are interesting. The concentration that the *Stavka* had organized, sending nine rifle divisions, two cavalry divisions and three brigades converging on the city from all sides, had been disrupted just when it finally seemed on the verge of having a good chance of taking the city. Several factors contributed to the dispersal of these forces, so that instead of nine divisions and three brigades into the attack, the 23rd saw serious attacks by only 31st Army's 252nd and 133rd Rifle Divisions from the west and north, minor probes by the exhausted 256th and 5th Rifle Divisions of 30th Army, while 29th Army's 119th and two regiments of 246th Rifle Divisions attacked from the southwest. Both tank brigades and the Separate Motorized Rifle Brigade had already been burned out in combat. But what had become of the other rifle divisions, the 183rd and 185th, that had been sent by Northwestern Front, and Maslennikov's 174th, 243rd, and the cavalry? Most of the answer lay to the west of Kalinin.

Strauss's 9th Army was no powerhouse at this point. It had gone into Operation Typhoon with seventeen worn down infantry divisions (though three had initially been under the control of Panzer Group 3). It had the lowest priority for fuel, ammunition and supplies of any of the armies of Army Group Center, and was assigned the position on the army group's left flank. It had taken Rzhev in a tough fight and had pushed north from there, but slowly and tentatively. It had also been shedding divisions and corps – its V Corps, under General of Infantry Richard Ruoff, had been operating to the south of Panzer Group 3 and was intended to come under 4th Army, where it battled Rokossovsky's 16th Army around Volokolamsk. Panzer Group 3, after initially politely asking 9th Army to move west and get off the roads that the panzer group wanted to use exclusively, had then begged 9th Army to send infantry divisions to help the beleaguered XXXXI Corps in Kalinin. This had disposed of 129th Infantry Division and was also to absorb the 161st.

9th Army was thus reduced to eleven divisions, and although Soviet accounts repeatedly assert that Strauss had the support of sixty to seventy tanks, in fact he had none at all. To make matters worse, parts of several divisions had to be detached on various tasks. Two battalions were at Staritsa, constituting Group Metz, while others had to be separated from their parent divisions to contain the three rifle divisions southwest of Rzhev. Most of the army's units were drawing supply from the road that ran through Rzhev over a single bridge. Strauss issued orders on the morning of October 23rd urging his infantry 'to advance under all circumstances as long as the weather permits, even if neither fuel nor food supplies but only ammunition can be provided. The *Luftwaffe* will attempt to replace our own artillery where possible.'[252] This has a certain note of uncertainty to it, but in fact 9th Army was able to continue to advance for one basic reason.

As weak as it was, its opponents in 22nd Army, now under Major General V.I. Vostrukhov, was even weaker. The Soviets had some divisions of from 1,500 to as low as 500 men in the line. Attempts were made to bolster some of the weaker ones by rounding up stragglers in the rear where there were large numbers of men wandering around after losing their units during the initial German breakthrough, but of course this expedient did not produce strong cohesive units.

The result of Strauss's push north was to put increasing pressure on Konev's right flank, which might collapse and allow the Germans to get into Torzhok from the south rather than the southwest. After October 21st this threat began to weigh more and more heavily on Konev's mind, and he reacted by shifting 183rd Rifle Division and the Separate Motorized Rifle Brigade to backstop 22nd Army. He also rationalized his army boundaries by transferring 174th, 220th and 250th Rifle Divisions from 29th to 22nd Army. This put all the divisions facing 9th Army's push from the south under one command, although it added little to Vostrukhov's strength.

When 6th Infantry Division crossed the Volga River at Akishevo and built up a bridgehead on the west side of the Volga, this made the situation far worse from Konev's point of view. It threatened to split 22nd Army off from the 29th and allow the Germans to outflank and possibly envelop 22nd Army west of Staritsa. It forced Vostrukhov to pull the tough (though weak) 174th Rifle Division back north to avoid encirclement and in the process removed the Soviet threat to Staritsa completely. It also caused Konev to shift 243rd Rifle Division, a regiment of the 246th, and both cavalry divisions to meet the threat under the command of 29th Army. The upshot of all this was that Maslennikov's decisive strike across the Volga to cut off Kalinin from the south was reduced to less than two divisions.

The decision to shift weight to meet 9th Army's push north was understandable. It is harder to entirely grasp what Konev was thinking regarding 185th Rifle Division, however. The 185th was a huge division compared to many others. Some divisions went into the battle with no more than 1,000–1,500 men. On October 12th 185th Rifle Division reported that it had 12,046 men total in the division, with nine battalions, and 6,393 of the men were combat infantry with 196 machineguns, seventeen mortars, a single antitank gun, and thirty-two artillery pieces.[253] The division, initially part of Operational Group Vatutin, had been relatively slow to get into action but had applied pressure on Mednoye from the north, and helped push the Germans off the Torzhok road. It was then transferred east, officially to 30th Army, to reinforce the army's attack on Kalinin.

The division, commanded by Lieutenant Colonel Konstantin Nikolayevich Vindushev, was sorely needed. The commander of 30th Army reported that of the six regiments (three of 5th Rifle Division, two of 256th Rifle Division and the Special Rifle Regiment), some numbered no more than 2–300 men each.[254] Even assuming Vindushev's men had suffered some casualties in the fighting for Mednoye, its addition would at least triple Khomenko's existing strength and allow the attacks on Kalinin from the northeast and southeast to be dramatically stepped up. But in General Khomenko's report for the day, while he lists his other assets and reports on their strengths and activities, there is no mention of 185th Rifle Division. It does show up, however, in Kalinin Front records, and the way it is reported makes it fairly clear that the division is being treated as a Front asset, not part of Khomenko's 30th Army. The orders issued to the division are the clearest indication that Konev had decided to hedge his bets, and was in fact no longer committed to the attempt to take Kalinin. The division was ordered to 'establish a defensive line by the morning of October 24th' with positions 12–20 kilometers (7.5–12 miles) northeast of Kalinin, straddling the road to Bzhetsk.[255]

It is hard to see why this division was withheld from the assault on Kalinin if Konev was still determined to retake the city. There was no offensive punch left in 30th Army; in fact it was clear to Khomenko that if the enemy, who were reinforcing their numbers in Kalinin, had any offensive intentions, the most likely direction of an assault would be right over his army. His center was protected by three company strongpoints, located 9, 19, and 22 kilometers (5.5, 11, and 13 miles) south and southeast of Kalinin, while south of that there were no more than three patrols of Dovator's 53rd Cavalry Division, scheduled to be relieved on October 24th by a battalion of 120th Motorized Rifle Regiment from 107th Motorized Rifle Division.[256]

It is not clear whether Khomenko predicted an enemy attack on his army through exceptionally good intelligence, or just by consulting his own fears and looking at the map and his unit's strength returns, but he was right on the mark. That very day at 1030 hours Reinhardt and Kirchner began discussions of a

local operation southeast of Kalinin with 129th Infantry Division frontally [northwest] and 6th Panzer Division flanking from the right [south] and when 86th Infantry comes up from the west to penetrate to the reservoir [Moscow Sea]. Seizing the reservoir crossing by 6th Panzer Division from the south would be best, before the end of the week, but the elements of 6th Panzer Division needed will not be able to arrive [by then].

At 1230 the discussion was referred to 9th Army, proposing the employment of paratroopers, 'on the road and railroad embankments over the reservoir . . .'[257]

But Konev did not commit his most powerful reserve to protect 30th Army's extremely weak left flank, but instead positioned it to block any drive towards Bzhetsk. It is possible that he had learned of German intentions to strike north, though they had made little effort in this direction, nor had any forces appeared to carry out such an attack. There is no indication of directions from the *Stavka* to cover this direction; in fact there don't seem to have been any orders from Moscow to Konev for several days, and those that had come earlier had always included admonitions to make sure to protect the northeastern approaches to the capital.

Whatever the reasoning behind this decision, it had the effect of denying the tattered 30th Army the strength to pose a real threat to the Germans in Kalinin. It was going to be up to Yushkevich's 31st Army if Kalinin was going to to be recaptured and the enemy 'Kalinin Group' destroyed.

The weather continued to be warmer, with clouds and intermittent rain, which hampered – but did not stop – German air activity. Air resupply continued, German fighters continued to patrol the skies over the city, and repeated ground support missions hammered the attacking Soviets and their supply columns. Particularly effective were the Hs-123 Henschels of Hauptman Otto Weiss's Second *Gruppe Schlacht/Lehr Geschwader* Two (II.(S)/LG 2). These sturdy biplanes were the predecessor of the Ju-87 Stuka, and Weiss's *Schlacht* ('ground attack') group was the only *Luftwaffe* unit still flying them. Armed with two machineguns (or some-times two 20mm cannon) and up to 950 pounds of bombs, these radial-engined aircraft were capable of very effective low-level attacks. They were so popular with the ground troops that their commander, who became the first *Schlachtflieger* to receive the Oak Leaves to his Iron Cross, was known to the soldiers of XXXXI Corps as 'The Lion of Kalinin.' 36th Motorized Division, which received a lot of support from the *Schlachtflieger,* described the cooperation they got in repulsing attacks in the afternoon by 133rd and 256th Rifle Divisions as, especially good support from the *Schlachtflieger*. It is extraordinary that liaison is good since the *Schlachtflieger* are working from 1:300,000 maps and therefore it is especially difficult to designate the targets. Displaying arrows, etc. on the ground proved itself to be certain, but there is no absolute remedy. The best would be direct communications with the ground.

This was not possible with the Henschels, which lacked radios. For all the appreciation Weiss received from the German ground troops, his own men were not as enthusiastic. For his harsh and demanding command style, his men labeled him 'Weiss the Butcher.'[258]

Northwest of the city, General Goryachev's 256th Rifle Division renewed its attacks on the Kalinin suburbs, fighting against 6th Panzer Division's reinforced motorcycle battalion and one battalion of 36th Motorized Division, but with only meager results.[259] The Germans were now well dug in, with disabled tanks dragged into hull-down positions to act as pillboxes. Even though artillery ammunition continued to be in short supply,[260] the superb tactical use of the German machineguns and mortars, well dug-in along the edge of the built-up area of Kalinin, proved just adequate to fend off attack after attack. Since the 256th had only one very worn down regiment to commit to the attack, it could not gain any significant ground.

As XXXXI Corps was now pressed into the city itself, it seemed to regain its balance and to begin counterpunching. West of the city, a morning counterattack by elements of 1st Panzer Division and a battalion of 129th Infantry retook the crucial road/railroad crossing and established a defense perimeter a short distance west and northwest of the city's edge. This was challenged again in the evening when an attack by 252nd Rifle Division was beaten back after closing to within 40 meters of the German front line.

General Shvetsov's division probed the German defenses all along the northern edge of the city overnight, but did not renew its attacks until evening. At 1600 36th Motorized Division reported that it came under heavy attack that was only turned back with assistance from the *Schlachtflieger*. South of the city 30th Army spent the day apparently licking its wounds and regrouping its forces, but not rising again to face the German machinegun and mortar fire. This allowed 129th Infantry Division facing them to send troops west to combat 29th Army's attack on Danilovskoye. The Germans did, however, continue to keep a nervous eye on what they believed to be a build-up to their southeast. Just as Khomenko was reporting an exaggerated picture of the German forces on his front, German intelligence likewise was reporting threatening information to the southeast and the north. Southeast of the city they correctly identified 21st Tank Brigade, but described its shattered motorized rifle battalion as 21st Rifle Brigade, and claimed both were working under the control of 14th Rifle Division. This was unlikely, because 14th Rifle Division fought the whole war north of the Arctic Circle, in front of Murmansk on the Finnish border. Air reconnaissance at 1500 hours reported an enemy motorized column with tanks proceeding south on the 'Ramyesky–Kalinin road,' which is to say from the Bzhetsk direction. What it was the fliers saw through the clouds and trees is hard to say, because there was no Soviet motorized column, with or without tanks, in the area.[261]

During October 23rd, 119th Rifle Division spent the day getting across the Volga at Chapayevka and securing Putilovo, where there was a better crossing site, a kilometer southwest of Chapayevka. 915th Regiment of 246th Rifle Division was across at Khvastovo, 4 kilometers (2.5 miles) north of Chapayevka, and expanding its bridgehead, but it was not able to come to the assistance of its sister-regiment facing the Germans west of Migalovo airfield. This meant that Major Krutikhin's battered 914th Rifle Regiment, of 246th Division, was on its own. It was attacked on the afternoon of October 23rd by 'several battalions' of infantry, supported by two tanks and some armored carriers (elements of 1st Panzer Division's *Kampfgruppe von Heydebrand*). Striking 2nd Battalion defending on the regiment's right wing, the Germans broke into the Soviet positions, producing wholesale panic. One group of *schutzen* pursued and attacked into Krasnovo, where the regimental headquarters was located. Major Krutikhin led the personnel of the HQ in a counterattack, and, with help from another rifle battalion, destroyed part of the German force and drove off the rest. But the regiment was clearly shaken, and was left clinging to a shallow bridgehead on the edge of the Volga's right (east) bank.[262]

German planning for future operations remained in flux. In the morning Reinhardt's headquarters was discussing having XXXXI Corps use 161st Infantry Division as soon as it arrived in Kalinin, to defend the east side of the city, while 9th Army's XXVII Corps could take over the western part of the city, 'then the mobile units would be free for an advance on Torzhok.'[263] Later in the afternoon there was discussion of getting 9th Army to push 110th Infantry Division north along the Volga (to do the job previously envisaged for 6th Infantry Division), and amassing large quantities of fuel and ammunition in the city to support the attack to Bzhetsk by LVI Corps. Like other discussions of massive infusions of fuel and supplies, the discussion has an other-worldly air to it. Nothing of the kind had happened to date, despite discussions, and in fact nothing of the kind was possible. There was some good news; a store of flour and several bakeries had been discovered in Kalinin, and for the moment at least the shortage of food was somewhat eased.

On both sides of the line, casualties and claims of casualties inflicted on the enemy were being added up. It was not a pretty picture. Panzer Group 3 totaled up the losses in XXXXI Corps during the last two days:
- 1st Panzer Division – 870
- 900th *Lehr* Brigade – 283
- 36th Motorized Division – 708

Both Kirchner and Reinhardt stressed the need to relieve the three units and the personnel department of 1st Panzer Division produced a plan to reorganize the division, calling for cutting the number of *schutzen* battalions from five to two, and reducing the panzer regiment to a battalion. The division implemented a similar plan on November 1st.[264]

Two of Konev's armies gave reports on their losses and the damage they had inflicted on the enemy. Yushkevich's 31st Army claimed to have killed 250 Germans and destroyed three trucks between October 13th and 22nd. They claimed to have captured:

- 2 antitank guns
- 13 submachine guns
- 18 light machineguns
- 4 antiaircraft machineguns
- 5 tanks
- 1 75mm gun
- 14 mortars
- 4 antiaircraft guns
- 12 trucks

This had cost the army 580 casualties, two 76mm guns and one machinegun.

The dating of this reporting period is pretty strange because 31st Army basically comprised a headquarters and a few rear support units until October 17th, and even then it was not in control of any of its subordinate divisions until October 21st. None of the divisions constituting 31st Army had been in action until October 17th.[265]

30th Army reported the following losses for the fighting since October 16th:

- 1,350 men
- 27 tanks
- 7 antitank guns
- 4 76mm guns
- 9 machineguns

They claimed to have destroyed or killed:

- 500 officers and men
- 34 'guns'
- 38 tanks
- 170 trucks
- 15 light trucks
- 2 radio vans

- 70 motorcycles
- 12 fuel tanker trucks
- 28 mortars

In addition they reported capturing:

- 14 prisoners
- 4 antitank guns (knocked out)
- 3 submachine guns
- 6 light machineguns
- 11 motorcycles

The claim of thirty-eight tanks is difficult to believe, given that the army had only been facing the small 101st Panzer Battalion (F) and the two assault gun batteries supporting 36th Motorized Division. All the other numbers seem very credible, except that the number of tanks lost by 21st Tank Brigade seems to be the same as the losses for October 17th alone, and the brigade was heavily engaged for four days after that. It is also likely that the number of captured submachine guns is lower than the reality, as troops were more likely to keep these useful trophies, rather than reporting them and risking having to turn them in.[266]

October 24th

It turned a bit warmer overnight, and the intermittent clouds on October 24th dropped a little rain on the combatants. Soviet artillery fire continued to fall on Kalinin and the airfield overnight. Constant German references to this fire testified not only to the effectiveness of the Soviet fire but also gave indirect evidence of the amount of ammunition they seemed to have available and were willing to expend.

Despite the overcast, both the German and Soviet air forces were quite active. A German reconnaissance sortie along the Volga west of the city at 1430 hours spotted a pontoon bridge across the river, and dive-bombers were sent. The bridge was destroyed before dark but XXXXI Corps reported that evening that the enemy was expected to restore the bridge overnight (which, according to Panzer Group 3, they did) and that the Soviet efforts to cut the Staritsa road would likely continue.[267]

The Soviet air forces began the war divided into five separate services. Front and Army aviation consisted of fighters, light bombers, and ground attack aircraft assigned directly to Fronts and armies. The Red Navy had its own air arm, and another organization, the *DBA* (*Dalny Bombardirovshchik Aviatisya* – Long-range Bomber Aviation) controlled all Soviet long-range bombers. Finally all Soviet air defense forces, including interceptors, but also antiaircraft guns, barrage balloons, searchlights and air early warning networks, were part of the *PVO*

(*Protivo-Vozdushnya Oborona* – Home Air Defense) organization. Some of the best Soviet fighter pilots were concentrated in the *PVO*, particularly in 6th PVO Corps that protected Moscow. Under the pressure of war and the disastrous fighting in the summer and fall of 1941 (the Soviets suffered a ratio of loss in air to air fighting of 8–1 against the *Luftwaffe's* superior aircraft, far better trained and experienced pilots, and well developed tactics), many of the prewar doctrines had been forced to change. During October, 6th PVO Corps was committed to support the armies defending Moscow and Kalinin, and conducted not only interceptions and combat air patrols but also direct support for the Red Army and attacks on German-occupied airfields. The airfield at Migalovo was subject to not only Soviet artillery fire and the threat of direct attack by 246th Rifle Division but also strikes from the air.

Parts of four regiments of 6th *PVO* Corps were chosen for the attack. The fighters of 208th Fighter Regiment of Major S. Kibirin and part of 95th Fighter Regiment (both equipped with Pe-3 heavy fighters), a total of twenty-seven twin-engined fighters, were assigned to conduct the attack while the MiG-3-equipped 27th and 28th Fighter Regiments were to provide cover for them. The attackers were greeted by heavy antiaircraft fire which brought down five of the attackers, including Kibirin's machine and Lieutenant A. Krutilin's aircraft, which crashed on the airfield itself. In return, the Soviets claimed to have destroyed thirty aircraft on the ground, and one Bf-109 was shot down while trying to take off to repel the attack. While the claim for aircraft destroyed on the ground is undoubtedly a gross over-claim, nonetheless it was yet another reminder to the Germans of the continuing threats to *Luftwaffe* aircraft based at the airfield.[268]

The fighting around Kalinin that day took place on three fronts. On the outskirts of the city itself, attacks by 30th and 31st Armies from the west, north-west, northeast and southeast continued. Only the attacks by the relatively fresh 252nd Rifle Division from the west and the indomitable 133rd Division, attacking from the north, had much success. The 252nd (identified by 1st Panzer Division as '257th Rifle Division') attacked in late morning towards the road/railroad crossing northwest of Kalinin, and was repulsed by *Kampfgruppe Westhofen*. The headquarters of 1st Panzer Division, which had been established on the northwest edge of the city, was spotted by the Soviets who brought it under heavy artillery fire. 'We have now been shot out of the division combat headquarters for good,' reported the panzer division's personnel department.[269] The headquarters was forced to fall back 500 meters into the city along the rail line. General Shvetsov's 133rd Rifle Division, which had now been in bitter combat for eight days straight, also succeeded in breaking into the northern edge of the city, advancing some 500 meters and seizing some buildings, only to be driven back by a counterattack by 36th Motorized Division after four hours of hard fighting. North of the city the Germans detected five Soviet batteries and two rocket launchers but because of a shortage of artillery ammunition, could not strike back with artillery and instead summoned the *Luftwaffe*, which conducted strikes on the suspected positions.[270]

256th Rifle Division, attacking from the northeast, managed to reach Barminovka, less than one kilometer east of the city on the Volga, but was forced to break off its attacks and reverted to the defensive, digging in on the edge of the city.[271] 5th Rifle Division and 21st Tank Brigade also broke off their attacks from the southeast, although 5th Rifle Division had reported a 1-kilometer advance by its left wing. This latter report was unconfirmed, and Kalinin Front asked for clarification.[272]

Some of the heaviest fighting occurred west and southwest of Kalinin. 29th Army continued to expand its bridgehead across the Volga. It took all day, but by 1900 hours 119th Rifle Division had all of its infantry across the river and its artillery was being rafted across. A dawn attack by 246th Division's 915th Regiment, which had crossed the previous day, drove through Talutino and into Danilovskoye in house-to-house fighting, only to be beaten back out of the town by a counterattack made by two battalions of 161st Infantry Division's 336th Regiment and some elements of 129th Infantry Division with tank support from the few remaining tanks of 1st Panzer Division. 915th Rifle Regiment also sent elements through the woods east of Khvastovo and attacked Deveshkino (just west of Danilovskoye) where they ran into the German 620th Heavy Artillery Battalion. This battle came to hand-to-hand combat but the Soviets were driven back into the woods. That night a renewed Soviet attack by 915th Rifle Regiment retook both villages.[273]

Although the Germans were well aware that Soviet forces had crossed the Volga, apparently they underestimated the strength of the thrust. Therefore, the attack on Danilovskoye from the southwest caught them by surprise. XXXXI Corps' records insist that the morning attack was repulsed by 0800 hours, primarily by accurate fire from 620th Heavy Artillery Battalion. Röttiger raged about this situation, noting that this was just what the corps had anticipated, and blaming it on 9th Army for having failed to use 6th Infantry Division to clear the western bank of the river by advancing northeast towards Kalinin. Writing after the war, Röttiger reiterated this point, while insisting that 9th Army failed to comprehend the situation and therefore dispatched 6th Infantry Division to the north, towards Torzhok, instead of northeast to assist XXXXI Motorized Corps.[274]

The Soviets were not the only ones attacking west and south of the city, however. Southwest of Kalinin, Major Krutikhin's weary 914th Rifle Regiment at Krasnovo was hit hard, and, after three hours' fighting, Krutikhin's riflemen were forced to abandon the town and withdraw to Motavino, another village 1.5 kilometers to the west. During this fighting the chief of staff of 246th Rifle Division's artillery regiment, Major Kortikov, was mortally wounded. Lieutenant Rozov, who had retreated with the headquarters of 914th Regiment, was then reassigned to the 915th, where he helped direct the short barrage that preceded the storming of Danilovskoye.[275]

The third arena for this struggle was west of the Volga. According to German sources, on October 24th the advance by VI Army Corps, to which 6th Infantry Division had now been added, was stalled due to reportedly 'wretched weather.' Röttiger spoke to the commander of VI Corps, General of Engineers Otto-Wilhelm Forster, at 1430 hours, insisting that the enemy in front of the infantry were retreating to the north. Indeed they were. 9th Army recorded that the enemy in front of 26th Infantry Division fighting just north of Staritsa were reported to be 'making off to the north,' and the division was going in pursuit. This was 174th Rifle Division, which was finding itself in an impossible position, pressed from the south by 26th Infantry Division and with 6th Infantry Division across the river north of it and pushing northwest, threatening the Soviets with encirclement. They were pulled back, briefly, into 29th Army's reserve. Three hours later, at 1600 hours, 9th Army passed the word to Panzer Group 3's headquarters that the Soviets were pulling out north of Staritsa. Forster, however, maintained that the corps' attack could start only if the weather improved. In addition, he wanted help with the operation from XXXXI Corps' 161st Infantry Division, two-thirds of which was at Staritsa, while the leading regiment was engaging the Soviets in the Danilovskoye area.[276] On the other hand, Soviet accounts report no lessening of German pressure, and that the German 9th Army attacked with VI and XXIII Army Corps against 22nd Army and the right wing of 29th Army, forcing the former to fall back in places to the northern bank of the T'ma River.[277]

Further west other elements of 9th Army continued to push 22nd Army north. With several German divisions with air support pushing from the southwest against Lukovnikovo, 46 kilometers (28 miles) west southwest of Kalinin, 22nd Army began preparing a set of fall-back positions 30 kilometers (18 miles) north of the village, and sent the Separate Motorized Rifle Brigade to cover part of this line. The Germans were described as advancing in small groups with support from aviation, artillery and mortar fire, attacking the skeletal 186th, 179th and 250th Rifle Divisions on 22nd Army's right center. Kalinin Front cited unconfirmed reports that the enemy had seized Oreshki, 14 kilometers (8 miles) northwest of Lukovnikovo. The right wing of 29th Army, consisting of 243rd and 183rd Rifle Divisions and 54th Cavalry Division, took up positions on the north bank of the T'ma River from Kunganovo to Nesterovo on the Volga, a distance of some 29 kilometers (17 miles). Just as the T'ma had proved an obstacle for Maslennikov's strike force when it moved north across the river to strike *Kampfgruppe von Heydebrand* from the south, now Konev hoped to use the river as a barrier to 9th Army's push to the north.[278]

Chapter 9

Revised Plans

At 1000 hours on October 24th, an important telephone conversation took place between *OKW* and General Reinhardt, the commander of Panzer Group 3. The subject of discussion was the panzer group's capabilities and its capacity for conducting further operations.[279] An hour later, at 1100 hours, the commanders of Panzer Group 3 and XXXXI and LVI Motorized Corps conferred. Early on during the discussion Reinhardt issued instructions for the continuation of operations. Astonishingly, in light of the events of the past ten days, the panzer group was to stay on the offensive.

During these discussions, Reinhardt warned that the operations would take place in bad weather, and the troops would have to adjust to that reality, stating:

> For the time being, the greatest difficulty is the establishment of a secure base of supply. For this the panzer group will establish a strongpoint in Kalinin. The time to set this up is computed as _____ [left blank in the original] days, so the beginning of operations is to be commenced from that point.[280]

Reinhardt then went on to discuss the specific objectives assigned to his panzer group's two mobile corps. General Schaal's LVI Motorized Corps was to 'prevent the enemy in front of 16th Army [of Army Group North] from retreating and to destroy them. As the first part of this task the corps was to reach Ramjeschki [Ramyeshki – 51 kilometers (31 miles) north of Kalinin] and the rail junction at "Beshek" [Bzhetsk – 113 kilometers (70 miles) north of Kalinin]. To secure the flanks and route of advance, two infantry divisions would be assigned to the corps.' Finally, at some point, XXXXI Corps would be pulled in to reinforce the offensive.

The initial mission Reinhardt assigned to Kirchner's badly battered XXXXI Corps was to secure the area around Kalinin by 'clearing and smashing' the enemy there. The priority was to hold the city, and once that was secure, to initiate an operation to the southeast, to relieve the pressure from 30th Army on the panzer group's right flank. It was stressed that the operation was not time sensitive, and it would be fine if it could be initiated when LVI Corps finally reached Kalinin and was ready to jump off towards Bzhetsk. It was hoped that with the help of 1,800 tons of trucking from Army Group Center, sufficient supplies could be

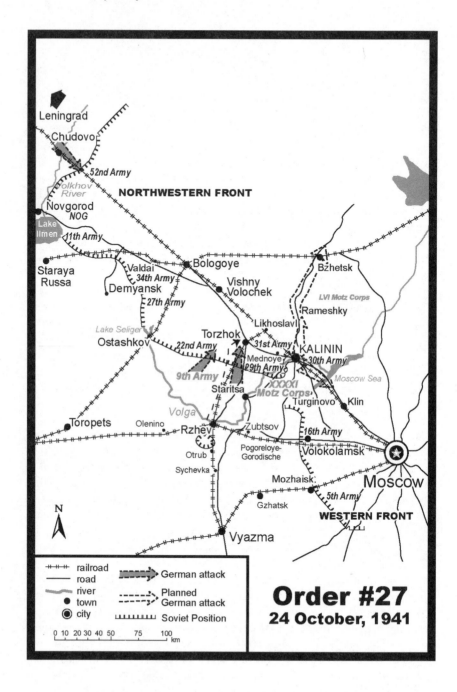

Leningrad
Chudovo
52nd Army
Volkhov River
NORTHWESTERN FRONT
Novgorod
NOG
Lake Ilmen
11th Army
Staraya Russa
Valdai
34th Army
Demyansk
Bologoye
Vishny Volochek
27th Army
Lake Seliger
Ostashkov
22nd Army
Torzhok
Likhoslavl
31st Army
KALININ
30th Army
Mednoye
29th Army
9th Army
Staritsa
XXXXI Motz Corps
Bzhetsk
LVI Motz Corps
Rameshky
Moscow Sea
Turginovo
Klin
Toropets
Olenino
Rzhev
Zubtsov
Volga
Pogoreloye-Gorodische
16th Army
Volokolamsk
Otrub
Sychevka
Mozhaisk
Moscow
5th Army
Gzhatsk
WESTERN FRONT
N
Vyazma

	railroad
	road
	river
●	town
◎	city

→→→	German attack
- - -→	Planned German attack
⊔⊔⊔⊔	Soviet Position

Order #27
24 October, 1941

0 10 20 30 40 50   75   100 km

amassed in the city to support LVI Corps' drive north. Optimistically, this operation was tentatively scheduled to commence on November 2nd, assuming the transport and supplies could be brought up in time.[281]

Reinhardt pointed out that, south of Kalinin, 9th Army's V Corps was moving eastward towards the important road junction at Klin. Further, 86th Infantry Division, which was moving northward by way of Sychevka and would come under XXXXI Corps' control, was to orient itself toward the southeast, with the objective of seizing and securing crossing sites over the Moscow Sea (reservoir). Reinhardt recommended using a 'well coordinated *kampfgruppe*' instead of relying on mass to perform this mission. Paratroops had been requested to support this operation.

While LVI Motorized Corps went off to Bzhetsk in the north, and XXXXI Motorized Corps pushed southeast towards the Moscow Sea, Strauss's 9th Army was going to likewise disperse, with its XXVII Army Corps moving to Kalinin to take over the defense of the city, VI and XXIII Army Corps pushing the Soviet 22nd Army's force northward towards Torzhok, and V Army Corps moving eastward to cover the panzer group's right flank. Reinhardt concluded the meeting by returning again to the subject of supply, stating: 'It is clear that substantial difficulties will continue to arise.' The troops had to prepare themselves for this reality; therefore, they were fully aware that a 'full draw' was not possible.

This meant they had to become extraordinarily frugal with both ammunition and fuel and food supplies. Furthermore, he added, 'they had to cope with the fact that the attack had to be continued on foot, if the road situation and the bad weather did not permit another way.' He went on to demand that all conceivable means of transport must be seized, and supplies moved forward in Russian *panje* wagons (one-horsed carts) and, if there was no other way, by the halftracked prime movers of the artillery. Since road construction troops requested from the army had not been forthcoming, the troops had to help themselves.

At this point, Kirchner rose to point out that the proposed operation would not allow his 'burnt out' divisions to be pulled out and refitted, because one division (the understrength 129th Infantry) could not hold Kalinin by itself. Accordingly, he requested that the elements of 6th Panzer Division (its advance detachment currently supporting 36th Motorized Division's defense of northern and eastern Kalinin) not be released from this duty.

Following the discussion, Reinhardt issued Panzer Group 3's Order # 27. This document spelled out the same objectives and orders covered in the discussion, but with a few more details. If Order # 25 was ambitious and Order # 26 woefully over-optimistic, then Order # 27 carried this wishful thinking to new heights. It correctly assessed that the enemy was trying to build new fortified strategic defenses extending from the front west of Moscow northward to the Volga River and Ostashkov, while at the same time attempting to recapture Kalinin. In concluded that, 'As previously, all signs point to the enemy intention to defend Moscow.' One could not quarrel with that.

The panzer group's objectives were to hold Kalinin until relieved by 9th Army's XXVII Army Corps, to 'clean up the situation to the southeast of Kalinin,' and to attack northward from Kalinin through Ramyeshki to Bzhetsk, 'in order to prevent the enemy facing the inner flanks of Army Groups Center and North from escaping by blocking the railroad and road in the Bzhetsk–Kalinin region.'

129th and 161st Infantry Divisions were specifically to be used by XXXXI Motorized Corps only for the defense of Kalinin rather than the attack to the southeast, and would then be turned over to LVI Motorized Corps for the subsequent attack to the north. Kirchner's corps was to expect relief by 9th Army's XXVII Corps no earlier than October 29th and the arrival of LVI Corps (with 7th Panzer and 14th Motorized Division) by October 26th (a wildly optimistic prediction).[282]

The orders to Kirchner, which read, 'Insofar as possible, attack the enemy southeast of Kalinin' and 'clear the area between the reservoir and Kalinin, if possible,' sound distinctly tentative. Once again the order referred to a request for paratroop assistance to assist in the seizure of the long causeways over the Moscow Sea (currently defended by 20th Reserve Rifle Regiment, which numbered only '400 bayonets') and admonished the corps to seize the objective with a surprise attack.[283]

LVI Motorized Corps' attack northward from Kalinin was to be led by the corps' attached 129th and 161st Infantry Divisions, which were to open the way for 7th Panzer and 14th Motorized Divisions and, thereafter, follow them to secure the corps' supply line and Ramyeshki. Once committed to action, the two mobile divisions were to capture Bzhetsk and the key rail junction 30 kilometers (18 miles) to the east at Sonkovo. The panzer group expected LVI Corps to report the start time for the offensive within the next two days.

Order # 27 concluded by stating:

> I ask the generals commanding the troops to act so that everything works out, despite the great difficulties with weather, roads and supplies, so that the ordered operations quickly break through and bring a victorious conclusion to this year. Any improvisation which contributes to the overcoming of the continuing obstacles is correct.
>
> [signed] Reinhardt.[284]

The yawning gap between the expectations Reinhardt expressed in this order and the grim realities the panzer group faced leaves one wondering whether its author was out of touch with the real situation or whether the order was meant to be taken seriously at all. In fact, there would be no advance from Kalinin to Bzhetsk, no successful drive on Torzhok by 9th Army, and no grand encirclement of the Soviet armies facing the inner flanks of Army Groups North and Center.

Konev had no reserves besides 185th Rifle Division, and no prospect of any reinforcements coming. Consequently, his plans remained unchanged. His right flank, 22nd Army and part of 29th, would continue to resist 9th Army's push north, while his left would 'continue to destroy the Kalinin Group of the enemy.'[285] All he could do to reinforce his attack on the city was to commit 257th Rifle Regiment of 185th Division to reinforce 5th Rifle Division's depleted numbers. But it would not be enough. Just as Reinhardt's and *OKW's* plans for a massive encirclement were to soon fade away and be forgotten, so would Konev's plans to liberate Kalinin have to be deferred for another two months. Hard fighting would continue, but no dramatic changes in the situation would happen until the middle of November, when the Germans would give up on any further attacks to the north or northwest from Kalinin, and turn their eyes towards Moscow, while the Soviets would be forced to accept the fact that they lacked the strength to retake Kalinin for the present, and go over to the defensive.

Chapter 10

Aftermath, October 25th–Early November

Fighting and Planning

Despite Reinhardt's and Konev's optimistic expectations, the fighting in the Kalinin region slowly wound down on all three fronts. West of the Volga, 9th Army's forces continued to try to reach Torzhok, southwest of Kalinin part of Maslennikov's 29th Army fought a bitter battle for possession of the Danilovskoye–Staritsa road against 129th and 161st Infantry Divisions, and at Kalinin Yushkevich's 31st and Khomenko's 30th Armies launched several more attacks against the Germans' defenses, but with ever-diminishing strength and little hope for success.

As it attempted to advance northward west of the Volga, 9th Army faced the same serious supply problems that had hamstrung XXXXI Motorized Corps. Just as Konev had no choice but to shift forces to his right wing to contain Strauss's advance, Strauss was forced to shift forces to *his* right wing to assist Kirchner at Kalinin and to cover the southeastern flank of the panzer group at Lotoshino. Although 9th Army continued to exert pressure on the Soviet defenses west of Kalinin, and force 22nd Army and Maslennikov's right wing to pull back across the T'ma River, the Germans could go no further and the front stabilized along the T'ma.

During this fighting, Rotmistrov's 8th Tank Brigade, which had been refitting at Mednoye until October 27th, was finally reunited with its motorized rifle battalion and committed along this front. Fighting alongside Ryzhkov's Separate Motorized Rifle Brigade and 54th Cavalry Division, Rotmistrov's *tankists* helped to bring 9th Army's offensive to a halt on the T'ma River, well short of its objective of Torzhok.

Over Shulgino, 8 kilometers (5 miles) south of Danilovskoye, where 1st Panzer Division's supply echelon was headquartered, another *Fieseler Storch* liaison plane came to grief at the hands of Soviet fighters. Again, a high ranking officer of the *Luftwaffe* was aboard. Lieutenant Colonel Bues, air liaison officer (*KoLuft*) to Panzer Group 3, was badly wounded and his pilot was killed.[286]

Also on October 27th, Army Group North finally realized that its forces east of the Volkhov River were far too weak to continue the drive on Tikhvin to the northeast and the push towards Bologoye to the southeast at the same time. Therefore, after Hitler rejected a request from Field Marshal von Leeb of Army

Group North to goad Panzer Group 3 into renewing its offensive toward Bologoye, von Leeb had no choice. He withdrew 8th Panzer and 18th Motorized Divisions from Malaya Vishera, where they had been inching forward against stiffening resistance through awful terrain to try to reach Bologoye, and instead dispatched them northeast towards Tikhvin. Like Strauss and Reinhardt, von Leeb's army group was attempting to conduct an offensive deep into terrible terrain in deteriorating weather against a pugnacious opponent who was counterattacking on several fronts. Army Group North was at the limits of its strength, weak and overstretched, and with critical shortages of fuel, ammunition, and air assets. It focused on a less ambitious effort, taking Tikhvin and cutting Leningrad's last lifeline. They would ultimately succeed, only to be soon driven out again by desperate Soviet counterattacks.[287]

South of Rzhev in 9th Army's rear, three rifle divisions of 30th Army had been bypassed by the rapid German advance and encircled by the German 6th and 106th Infantry Divisions since October 12th. Because 9th Army was stretched to the limit, it lacked the strength necessary to mop up this pocket. Consequently the three divisions (162nd, 242nd and 251st Rifle) were surrounded by a thin line of detachments from various divisions of 9th Army. On October 27th, after fighting in isolation for fifteen days, these divisions attacked northward and successfully fought their way through the thin German lines to reach 29th Army before the end of the month. In addition to embarrassing the Germans, this escape caused considerable confusion and damage in the 9th Army's rear echelons. All three divisions had suffered heavily and in early December the Soviets disbanded 162nd and 242nd Divisions to provide fillers for other divisions. The 251st, although it had no more than 2,000 men left by the end of the year, was eventually rebuilt and fought on to the end of the war.

South of Kalinin, in the Danilovskoye region, bitter fighting raged on for days, during which the town repeatedly changed hands. On October 26th Kalinin Front reported to the *Stavka* that 119th and 246th Rifle Divisions had destroyed eight enemy tanks, three tankettes (almost certainly machinegun-armed Pz Is), two armored cars and eighty-six trucks, and had captured another thirty vehicles with fuel and equipment, five guns, six light and two heavy machineguns and counted over 300 enemy dead on the field. The next day 246th Rifle Division claimed it had inflicted over 350 casualties on the Germans, along with twenty-six trucks, five cars and two tanks.[288] However, the following day forces of the German 161st Infantry Division, reinforced by elements of 1st Panzer Division and a battalion from 14th Motorized Division, launched a determined attack on Soviet defenses that forced 246th and 119th Rifle Divisions and 46th Cavalry Division to gradually withdraw toward the Volga. Faced with this reality, on October 30th Maslennikov authorized all three divisions to withdraw back across the Volga to the river's western bank. Maslennikov had no choice but to report to Konev:

During the six days of active offensive operations, 246th Rifle Division, reinforced by one regiment of 243rd Rifle Division and one dismounted regiment of 46th Cavalry Division, the expected success was not achieved. Four times Danilovskoye was in our grasp, but we could not hold it . . . In reserve we had only 150–170 bayonets.[289]

Once back across the Volga these forces took up defenses facing southwest and participated in the defense against the German 9th Army's advance.[290]

Just as 29th Army was forced to give up its attempts to cut off Kalinin from the south, so too 30th Army soon had to abandon its attempts to storm the city from the northeast and southeast. General Khomenko, the commander of 30th Army, submitted a report to NKVD head Lavrenti Beria (and seems to have also reported the same information to Konev) which expressed acute concern about the weakness of his center and left (southern) wing and assessed that the enemy seemed to be preparing for a new offensive. This assessment prompted Khomenko to reach the following conclusions regarding future operations:

1. The army is weak, with some regiments having as few as 300 men, and is short on officers. This makes it exceedingly difficult to both advance and to cover the frontage assigned to the army.
2. The enemy has up to six infantry regiments, one to two tank regiments and two artillery regiments, including 129th Infantry Division, facing 30th Army.[291] The enemy is temporarily on the defensive in Kalinin, but is preparing a new offensive.
3. The imminent enemy attack (according to a report that required verification) is designed to surround the Soviet Kalinin Group and then strike at Moscow.
4. The most likely axis [direction] of the enemy attack is from Kalinin towards Klin.
5. The greatest threat to the army is an enemy offensive along the Turginovo and Zavidovo axis or toward Klin.

This report clearly indicates Khomenko was no longer thinking in terms of clearing the Germans out of Kalinin any time soon. His army's 256th and 5th Rifle Divisions were badly worn down and 21st Tank Brigade was decimated, on October 20th reporting thirty-four tanks still running, including eight T-34s, four BT-2s, five BT-5s, six BT-7s, two T-26s and nine T-60s, as well as three ZIS-30 self-propelled guns.[292]

Konev, in his report to the *Stavka*, recounted the weakness of his Front, and complained that:

There are no free reserves in the composition of the Front for the completion of the mission. Sub-units have suffered heavy losses. There is a large deficiency of ammunition. Therefore, I please raise the question to the *Stavka* of the Supreme Command about the inclusion in the composition of the Front of 82nd Motorized Rifle Division, stationing it in the area of Zagorska.[293]

This was a forlorn hope. The powerful 82nd Motorized Rifle Division, which had arrived full strength from the Far East in the third week in October, had been immediately committed to 5th Army defending the Warsaw–Moscow highway east of Mozhaisk. There was no chance that the *Stavka* was going to weaken the most direct route to Moscow in order to strengthen the Kalinin Front.

By the end of the month every army in Kalinin Front had gone over to the defensive. There would be a few limited attacks launched in November but a full fledged attempt to liberate the city would have to wait until after the Soviet counter-offensive started in the first week in December.

As previously noted, although the Soviets halted their infantry attacks on Kalinin, they continued to shell the city, the roads leading into it, and the airfields through which the Germans were bringing in supplies. Because the shelling inflicted heavy losses on the *Luftwaffe*, it was forced to evacuate all of its units from the Kalinin area by month's end. Conversely, at the same time, the *Stavka* managed to find some air units with which to reinforce Kalinin Front: specifically, 10th and 193rd Fighter Aviation Regiments (seventeen MiG-3s in the 10th and nineteen LaGG-3s in the 193rd), and 132nd Bomber Aviation Regiment, equipped with thirteen new Pe-2 bombers.[294] Konev's Kalinin Front was further reinforced on October 28th by the belated arrival of 10th Army headquarters, which was assigned to form the basis for Konev's headquarters. With his new headquarters, Konev finally had adequate communications with which he could control his four armies effectively.

Postscript: The Calm after the Storm

By early November the fighting in the Kalinin area died down, primarily due to the mutual exhaustion of the opposing sides. The deteriorating weather, in particular the continuing intermittent mixture of rain and snow, reduced the muddy roads to the point that maneuver and resupply were extremely difficult for both sides.

Konev's forces had paid a terrible price to stop the offensives by 9th Army and Panzer Group 3 but in the process the Germans had also suffered heavily. General Kruger's 1st Panzer, which had begun the war against the USSR with 145 tanks, and had gone into Operation Typhoon in early October with 109 tanks, was reduced to nine tanks in working order by the third week in October.[295] After two weeks of frenetic repair work, the division was able to report forty-eight tanks in running order by November 4th, but this number was reached only by adding the 101st Panzer Battalion (flame) to the division, giving it a total armored strength of fifteen Pz IIs, seven Pz II (flame), twenty-two Pz IIIs and four Pz IVs – in other words, twenty-six medium tanks.[296] The division was reorganized radically at the end of October. It now consisted of:

- Division Headquarters – 81st Signal Battalion with one company each of radios and telephones, an armored car platoon with two armored cars (the remnants of the disbanded reconnaissance battalion)
- 1st Panzer Regiment, with 101st Panzer Battalion (F) – reorganized with a single battalion of two companies with thirty running tanks total (eighteen more were subsequently repaired)
    Battalion Headquarters – two command tanks, three Pz IIs
    3rd Company – six Pz IIs, fourteen Pz IIIs
    4th Company – three Pz IIIs, four Pz IVs
- *Schutzen* Brigade –
    one halftracked battalion (*I/113*) with two rifle companies and one heavy weapons company with eight 8cm mortars and eleven machineguns
    702nd Heavy Infantry Gun Company with two self-propelled 15cm infantry guns and two towed 15cm infantry guns (702nd Infantry Gun Company began the war with six self-propelled guns)
    one motorcycle battalion of three companies (one of them from the reconnaissance battalion which was disbanded)
    one company of the 37th Antitank Battalion (2nd) with four 5cm and four 3.7cm antitank guns and two *PzJg I* self-propelled 4.7cm antitank guns taken from 900th *Lehr* Brigade
    one platoon of three 2cm antiaircraft guns
- 1st *Schutzen* Regiment
    2nd Battalion, 1st Regiment (*II/1*) of three companies and a heavy weapons company with three 8cm mortars and eight machineguns
    2nd Battalion, 113th Regiment (*II/113*) with three companies and a heavy weapons company with five 8cm mortars and eight machineguns
    Third Company, 37th Antitank Battalion with five 5cm and three 3.7cm antitank guns
- Panzer Engineer Battalion with two companies in trucks plus one platoon in halftracks
- 83rd Antiaircraft Battalion with one 'combined' company of seven 8.8cm guns (the division began the war with three of these guns), a company with nine 2cm antiaircraft guns and one company with five 2cm guns.
- 73rd Panzer Artillery Regiment with two light battalions each of two batteries of four 10.5cm howitzers and one medium battalion of two batteries of four 10.5cm cannon.[297]

In fact, 1st Panzer Division was neither rebuilt nor did it take part in any major German operation until the late fall of 1943, when it reappeared built up to over-strength and committed to the fighting west of Kiev in late November of the year.[298] 36th Motorized Division was also reorganized, consolidating some units, but no details are available in the documents the authors examined. Surprisingly, 900th *Lehr* Brigade, though it had taken a battering in the summer north of Yartsevo and had gone through the meat grinder on the Torzhok road, nonetheless by November 1st the organization of the brigade remained nearly intact. The motorized infantry battalion still had all of its medium machineguns and 8cm mortars, though from its original six 3.7cm and two 5cm antitank guns only two 3.7cm guns remained and all the infantry guns were gone. The armored *schutzen* battalion still had two companies in halftracks and one on motorcycles, though its weapons company was missing all of its infantry guns and antitank guns. The antitank battalion had twenty-two 3.7cm antitank guns in two companies, indicating an attachment of six guns, probably from those that had been part of the infantry and *schutzen* battalions, and all of its surviving *PzJg I* self-propelled antitank guns were gone; transferred to 1st Panzer Division. The artillery battalion had all twelve of its 10.5cm howitzers. There is no information available showing how many troops remained in the unit.

The 9th Army's and Panzer Group 3's infantry divisions fared no better. Both 161st and 129th Infantry Divisions had been badly battered in the fighting during the summer, particularly the former. Khomenko refers to 129th Infantry as 'not a full fledged combat unit' when it appears in front of his army.

All the losses of these two divisions were not taken at Kalinin, but 161st Infantry Division, which had borne most of the brunt of the fighting for Danilovskoye, suffered 1,466 casualties, including 319 missing, between October 25th and 28th. It reported on November 2nd that it was reorganizing in the following manner: each of the division's three infantry regiments would disband one battalion. The battalions of one regiment would have two infantry companies of 70 men each, while its machinegun company would have 85–90 men, and the battalions of the other two regiments would have three 70-man infantry companies apiece and a machinegun company of 85–90 men.[299] This meant that the division decreased from an original strength of thirty-six infantry and machinegun companies down to twenty-two, and those were at half strength! Although the division suffered serious losses during the heavy fighting around Smolensk in August rather than at Kalinin in October, its condition is a good indication of the damage the Red Army inflicted on the *Wehrmacht* by mid-October. And this was *before* the really cold weather of December and its attendant frostbite casualties.

129th Infantry Division was reorganized so that each of its three infantry regiments was reduced from three to two battalions each, the reconnaissance battalion was reduced to a squadron (company), the antitank battalion similarly was reduced to one company, and the artillery regiment was reduced to one light battalion and one medium battalion with two instead of three batteries each.[300]

In addition to these deficiencies in its units' strengths, Panzer Group 3 was still unable to concentrate LVI Motorized Corps in the Kalinin area due to the persistent shortage of fuel. The corps remained widely dispersed. On November 2nd, much of 6th Panzer Division and 7th Panzer's panzer regiment and artillery were still in the Gzhatsk region, the bulk of 14th Motorized Division was at Pogoreloye-Gorodishche, while much of the rest of the division was just north of Staritsa, and other smaller elements of 6th and 7th Panzer Divisions were strung out in a long, thin security line extending from just south of Kalinin southeastward to Lotoshino, where they faced Dovator's cavalry.

The Soviets, of course, had suffered heavily in the fighting also. 119th Rifle Division of 29th Army, which had participated in the bloody fighting against the withdrawal of XXXXI Corps' spearhead in the Gorodnya area and then crossed the Volga to participate in the fighting for Danilovskoye, was nearly bled dry. Its regiments were reported on October 28th as having no more than 150–120 men each. The stalwart 133rd Rifle Division, from October 24th to the 28th, reported losing 404 men killed and missing and another 844 men wounded.[301]

Eventually in mid-November the panzer group concentrated most of its forces south of the Moscow Sea (although no paratroops were ever forthcoming) and launched an offensive that first pushed 30th Army's 5th Rifle Division back northeast over the Volga, cleared up the Soviet threat to the Lotoshino road and southeast Kalinin, and then drove south of the Moscow Sea to seize Klin, just 80 kilometers (50 miles) northwest of Moscow. In the following three weeks the remaining units of Panzer Groups 3 and 4 attacked southeastward, pushing through 30th Army's thinly manned left (southern) wing and forcing back Rokossovsky's 16th Army, then defending the northwestern and western approaches to Klin and Moscow, step by step. During this fighting, 1st Panzer Division managed to push a small *kampfgruppe* eastward across the Moscow–Volga canal north of Moscow, while other forces reached so close to Moscow from the north that they claimed that they were able to see the Kremlin's towers in the distance.

But they got no further. On December 5th, with Stalin's permission, General Zhukov unleashed 1st Shock Army, the first of ten new reserve armies that the Soviets had been assembling behind Moscow to defend the Soviet capital. The front had been fed the minimum of reinforcements necessary to prevent its collapse and no more. The reserves had been hoarded for the day when the Germans exhausted their offensive strength and committed their last reserve. Now the time had come. Western Front's limited counterattack succeeded, and then grew, first into a counterstroke and finally, into full-fledged counter-offensive. In intense fighting in the bitter cold of winter, Western Front's armies, soon joined by those of Konev's Kalinin Front, drove Army Group Center's forces away from the Soviet capital and to the edge of destruction.

During the struggle along the approaches to Moscow from mid-November through December 5th, the front that had stabilized from the Ostashkov region eastward through Kalinin hung like a balcony over the northern flank of Army Group Center. When Western Front's counterattacks in the Moscow region proved successful on December 5th, the armies of Konev's Kalinin Front were committed to the offensive. After ten days of bitter fighting, on December 16th, the forces of Kalinin Front's 31st Army succeeded in forcing the Germans to abandon the city and conduct a fighting withdrawal in the ice and snow. As these counterattacks expanded into a full-scale offensive, the threat posed by the over-hanging balcony preserved in the fighting in October developed into a nearly deadly threat to Army Group Center's left flank and entire left wing. As a result, by mid-December 1941, instead of Konev's Kalinin Front, it was Army Group Center and its 9th Army and Panzer Group 3 which faced looming disaster.

Chapter 11

Conclusions

The most striking feature of the Battle of Kalinin is that, to date, historians writing from both the German and Soviet perspectives have almost completely ignored its significance. Histories based primarily on German sources have viewed the battle as a sideshow to the Battle of Moscow, a neat triumph of German tactical daring and courage, but little else.[302] German memoirists, and those who relied on their accounts, maintained that the city was seized by a small force (whose strength is usually much understated) and then held successfully against daunting odds. This treatment of the battle barely if ever mentions German plans to capture Torzhok, much less to conduct an even grander encirclement of all Soviet forces north of Ostashkov and in the Valdai Hills. If discussed at all, both gambits are perceived simply as errors on the part of 9th Army's commander, General Strauss. The fact that the Germans succeeded in holding on to the city caps their triumph and ends the story so far as these historians tell it.[303]

The German view overlooks the reason that Panzer Group 3 conducted its thrust northward to Kalinin in the first place: to fulfill the grand plan of encircling and destroying seven Soviet armies (Western Front's 22nd and 29th, and Northwestern Front's 27th, 34th, and 11th, plus 52nd Army and the Novgorod Operational Group under direct control of the *Stavka*) east of Lake Ilmen and in the Valdai Hills. This concept was entirely consistent with Hitler's views of Operation Barbarossa, as outlined in the December 5th, 1940 planning conference, where he insisted that it was necessary to 'liquidate all large Red Army forces on Army Group Center's flanks before proceeding to Moscow.'[304] Like his strike into the rear of Southwestern Front in September, the drive to Kalinin in October was a logical consequence of the idea of clearing the flanks of the eastward thrust to Moscow. The concept, of Panzer Group 3 serving as the southern pincer and part of Army Group North's XXXIX Motorized Corps providing the northern one, originated before Operation Typhoon actually kicked off.[305]

This ambitious plan was decisively defeated, and, in the process, half of Panzer Group 3 was burnt out before the final drive on Moscow. Moreover, German Army Group Center had proved unable to clear the Soviet forces from its northern flank. While this did not seem important in October and November 1941, it certainly would by January 1942, by which time it posed a deadly threat to the army group's existence. Soviet forces striking southwest from Ostashkov penetrated nearly to Yartsevo, the German start line for Operation Typhoon.[306]

170

In many ways the Battle of Kalinin was a microcosm or fractal of the larger mosaic of Operation Barbarossa, and, indeed, of the entire first period of what the Soviets called 'The Great Patriotic War.' From the German side, at the lowest tactical level there was almost always a combination of sound doctrine, good training, experience and confidence, while at the top, at the operational and strategic levels, there was a wildly unrealistic optimism, based on unfounded assumptions of enemy inferiority and willful disregard of the constraints of time, distance, and logistics. Pushing a pencil across a map to draw a big circle around your opponent's armies is much easier than actually providing the fuel, ammunition and food to sustain the forces represented by the point of the moving pencil. And, like the German assumptions undergirding all of Plan Barbarossa, the underlying assumption of the offensive toward Kalinin, Torzhok, Bologoye, and indeed Moscow, was that, faced by 'Blitzkrieg' tactics and operational maneuvers, the Red Army would inevitably collapse.

In fairness to German planners, we have to admit we have the advantage of hindsight over them. We *know* how the Battle of Moscow ended; they had no such knowledge. In point of fact, all of Operation Barbarossa turned out far more difficult than anticipated. The Red Army, instead of being destroyed in the first three weeks of the war, fought back tenaciously, and counterattacked again and again. Despite the immense losses suffered by the Soviets, somehow they continued to resist against all odds and expectations.

Consequently, when Operation Typhoon began, the relatively easy penetration of Western Front's defenses and the ensuing encirclement of the Soviet armies standing in front of Moscow gave the Germans, from the simplest foot soldier to the Führer himself, a sense of euphoric relief. Now, finally, it was done, the 'Russians' were defeated, Moscow was about to fall like a ripe plum, and perhaps the entire war would all be over before Christmas. This was the German mindset on the eve of the Battle of Kalinin.

The official story, repeated constantly by German memoirists and historians who followed their lead, was that only the intervention of 'General Mud', and, later, 'General Winter', prevented German forces from seizing Stalin's capital. This has been repeated so often that it is pretty much accepted, without careful examination, as conventional wisdom.[307]

It did indeed rain a lot at the end of October, which brought the German advance to a halt and it was mid-November before the ground froze sufficiently to support much cross-country vehicular movement and made the roads more useable. However, the whole 'General Mud' concept actually glosses over the crucial period between October 7th, when the panzer pincers snapped shut around Western and Reserve Fronts, and the very end of the month when the rains came every day. There were days in mid-October when it rained and the roads that were heavily trafficked became 'indescribable.' But there were also more than a few days during this period when it was quite possible to maneuver. A closer look at the movements of various units, from the race by Rotmistrov's 8th Tank Brigade to block the Germans from erupting out of Kalinin, to Dr. Eckinger's rush into the city, to the daring raid by Lesovoi's 21st Tank Brigade, clearly demonstrate that all maneuver was *not* prevented by muddy roads. The fact is that there was something else that stopped the Germans from reaching Moscow in mid-October.

Viewed in a far wider context, the German advance toward Moscow in October and November 1941 was probably the most dramatic moment in the Second World War. It took place at a time when the Red Army had no major reserves available in the region to form a continuous front and halt the German drive. However, as the German drive to seize Moscow developed, large Soviet forces were on their way from the Far East and Central Asia, and others were hastily being raised, trained, and minimally equipped. By early December ten armies were assembling in reserve behind the Soviet capital, just waiting for the moment when Army Group Center's advance ran out of steam and had committed its last reserves. In the meantime, a handful of Red Army rifle and cavalry divisions, tank brigades, artillery regiments and schools, and militia units, and the like were all that barred the way to Moscow.

Speculation about things that did not happen is pointless, but if Hitler was going to win the war, he had to destroy the Soviet Union and its Red Army. The best chance he had to do that was in October and November 1941. While there was no guarantee that taking Moscow would have accomplished this goal, it is hard to imagine how it could have been done without the fall of the Soviet capital.

All along the line, from Tula in the south to Kalinin in the north, the Germans pushed forwards after encircling and destroying most of Western and Reserve Fronts' armies and splintering Bryansk Front. Although the Germans had to leave most of their infantry and some of their mobile forces to contain and reduce these large pockets, they assumed they had sufficient strength in panzer and motorized infantry divisions to complete the advance on Moscow and capture it. This turned out to be a fatally flawed assumption.

Along virtually every major axis leading into the Soviet capital, they found determined defenders blocking the road, defenders who refused to roll over and play dead. Not only did Zhukov and the *Stavka* stitch together a thin line in front of the Germans that decisively delayed them but they also inflicted such casualties on the German spearheads that they rendered them incapable of taking the last steps to their final objective.

The losses XXXXI Motorized Corps suffered in and around Kalinin were echoed along every axis of the German advance. XXXX Motorized Corps, which was trying to push its way through the historic Borodino battlefield of 1812 to capture Mozhaisk on the direct highway to Moscow, suffered such casualties that its subordinate SS '*Das Reich*' Motorized Division had to disband one of its three regiments to bring the other two up to the strength of reinforced battalions, while 10th Panzer Division lost half its tanks in a week of bitter fighting against one reinforced Soviet rifle division.[308] A similar fate befell Guderian's Second Panzer Army as it strove to conquer Tula and cut its way behind Moscow from the south, as well as XXXXVI Motorized Corps, which tried in vain to destroy Rokossovsky's 16th Army along the Volokolamsk axis.

In the final analysis these losses, coupled with those suffered in the two months of deadly fighting around Smolensk, the impossibility of adequately supplying its forces, *and* the deteriorating roads, combined to force Army Group Center to call a halt for a few weeks to regroup and resupply its forces before it could resume the drive on Moscow in mid-November. The forces that finally struggled forward against similarly worn down defenders during the last three weeks of Operation Typhoon had been gutted by the time they reached their furthest penetrations, and were set up for the Soviet riposte that began on December 5th.

Like Army Group North's setback at Tikhvin in the north during early November and Army Group South's defeat at Rostov in late November and early December, the events at Kalinin in late October should have given Army Group Center and the German Army's *OKH* and Hitler's *OKW* some hint of what was to come in December. The attacks against Panzer Group 3's XXXXI Motorized Corps launched by Vatutin's Operational Group, the raid by Lesovoi's 21st Tank Brigade, and, finally, the attempted counterstroke by Konev's Kalinin Front foreshadowed the blows that soon followed at Tikhvin and Rostov, and then in December in front of Moscow.

The German High Command, however, failed to take the hint. As Paul Simon put it, 'A man hears what he wants to hear and disregards the rest.' The euphoria of October 7th, when Army Group Center's pincers closed around Western and Reserve Fronts' armies at Vyazma, continued through October 24th, despite the near destruction of 1st Panzer Division. It is famously said that, 'while amateurs discuss tactics, professionals discuss logistics.' Given the truth of this statement, reading Reinhardt's orders to his forces leaves one amazed. This man was a seasoned and thoroughly professional soldier, and yet the logistical nightmare his forces faced seemed a minor inconvenience to him.

When on October 16th Kirchner complained bitterly about his relative weakness, and his opponent's strength (which was real enough, but not yet really known to Kirchner), Reinhardt, without arguing with Kirchner's assessment, urged him on anyway, saying, 'It must be attempted.' He made a gamble, staking his spearhead that speed and German tactical competence would triumph over distance, logistics, the bad roads and weather, and the Red Army. Although abundantly aware that he could not supply his divisions with fuel, ammunition, or even adequate food, Panzer Group 3's commander nonetheless assigned them deep objectives, requiring them to advance over poor roads, in bad weather, and through terrain that was a succession of woods, swamps, and lakes. Simply advising his troops to make use of 'any improvisations' necessary to bring supplies forward, and requiring his panzer group to struggle forward on foot, made sense only if his enemy had given up the ghost, and he was conducting a pursuit.

This is fundamental to understanding the Battle of Kalinin. The Germans assessed the situation and concluded that they were involved in a pursuit against a beaten enemy. This sort of situation required audacity, risk taking, and speed. The enemy was believed to have no significant reserves, so the security of the forces conducting the pursuit was of less significance. Serious resistance was not expected, and even when it came, on October 15th and 17th, it was seen as a temporary phenomenon. The failure to discuss the potential enemy resistance is striking in Reinhardt's operational orders. The only obstacles that were discussed were the shortage of fuel and the condition of the roads.

Making matters even more absurd, Reinhardt issued further orders to advance on Bzhetsk at a time when enemy forces were vigorously attacking his panzer group's position from at least three sides and had already decimated his spearhead division and rendered one of his two motorized corps *hors de combat*. Rather than abandon the vision of a huge encirclement, the orders he issued were to continue as before. It seemed that the German commanders could not come to grips with the fact that the Red Army was not on the verge of collapse. Five weeks later the scales would drop from their eyes, but by then it would be too late for many of their troops.

The Soviet assessment of the situation was very different from the German one. Despite the chaotic conditions, very weak communications, and limited ability to gather intelligence, the *Stavka* determined that the situation was essentially a meeting engagement, and acted accordingly. They threw everything they could spare in the direction of the key point: the city of Kalinin. Their intention was offensive from the very beginning. Their assessment was fundamentally correct, and even though they lacked the ability to coordinate their forces, or even to establish clear command relations, they succeeded in demolishing the ambitious German plan.

The Soviet response to the disaster of the first week in October was also characteristic of the way the Red Army fought the first period of the Great Patriotic War. With the front broken and the bulk of their forces encircled, the *Stavka* was none the wiser for three crucial days. When the truth finally reached the Kremlin, the reaction was immediate: to scrape up every resource possible and throw it in the enemy's way to slow him down while reserves could be brought up from the depth of the country. Stalin's most determined and pugnacious commander, Georgi Zhukov, was brought south from besieged Leningrad to take control of the fight in front of Moscow. Communications and intelligence were both very weak, so the Red Army's reaction to German moves was often slow, and poorly coordinated. However, an examination of the Battle of Kalinin shows that while unclear as to exactly what the Germans were intending to do, and well behind events at first, the Soviets ultimately understood the situation better than the Germans did, and took appropriate action.

The *Stavka* reacted to 1st Panzer Division's thrust to Staritsa by ordering forces from Western Front's right wing, reserves from Northwestern Front, and what little it could afford from its own resources (one tank brigade, two motorcycle regiments, and an understrength reserve rifle regiment) thrown towards the city to block the German advance, and then to attack, drive it back or to cut it off and destroy it.

Unlike their opponents, the Soviets were not hampered by any illusions that their enemies were on the verge of giving up. As a result, while unable to bring all their forces into action together, they did succeed in concentrating sufficient force at the key points and then inflicting a stinging defeat on Kirchner's motorized corps. This guaranteed the failure of the grandiose German plans for the encirclement of the Soviet forces in the Valdai Hills.

The Soviet concept of operations for the battle was aggressive from the beginning. While 5th and 256th Rifle Divisions were sent to Kalinin with the intention of defending the city and stopping the German drive (in their understrength condition, even this was more than they could do), the two tank brigades, Vatutin's Operational Group, 133rd Rifle Division, and Maslennikov's shock group were all committed with the idea of counterattacking the enemy and destroying him. Konev was sent to control the battle with totally inadequate communications means and was neither capable of coordinating the efforts of the three armies fighting for Kalinin nor even at times getting a clear picture of where they were or what they were doing.[309] Given these shortcomings and the fundamental weakness of his forces, it is not too surprising that it proved beyond the capability of Kalinin Front to succeed in destroying its opponents and retaking the city. Nonetheless, by aggressively taking the fight to the enemy instead of passively awaiting his blows, the Red Army was able to seize the initiative from the *Wehrmacht* and force the Germans to react to one crisis after another.

The fact that the Soviets undertook a serious offensive *in mid-October* has been overlooked by historians. On every other axis of the German advance on Moscow the Germans faced only limited counterattacks by battalions or tank brigades. The fighting on these roads was characterized by German attacks by divisions and corps against outnumbered Soviet defenders. The fighting was fierce, but the Germans kept the initiative everywhere. Only at Kalinin was there a Red Army attack not by battalions and brigades but by armies.

The fact that this has not received much examination by military historians is curious. German and German-influenced historians of course have little interest in highlighting a bloody German failure at this stage of the fighting. The failure of Soviet, Russian, and other historians to examine it in the detail it deserves can only be explained by the fact that the events directly in front of Moscow, and at Tikhvin and Rostov, have attracted so much focus that most other parts of the long front have simply escaped notice.

One other factor warrants comment. The Red Army had one overlooked advantage that the Germans lacked. Soviet historians, particularly the 'popular' ones, speak of the 'mass heroism' that saved Moscow from the enemy. Anyone familiar with Soviet writing on the war is familiar with the amount of hyperbole that is so often encountered in most combat accounts. There is in fact no country whose popular histories do not glorify their own forces and their heroism; the Soviets just tended to do it more crudely and formulaically than some. Few historians anywhere spend much time recounting the instances when their own troops panicked, withdrew before inferior forces, or failed in costly attacks because the enemy was just too strong or because of bad planning or bad leadership.

In this case, however, while obviously not a complete picture of the performance of Soviet troops, there is something here that should *not* be overlooked. Across the entire front, the troops of the Red Army, workers' militia, and NKVD showed remarkable courage and determination in the face of seemingly insurmountable odds. When this is acknowledged, some historians attribute it all to Russian nationalism and a refusal to allow the Germans into the heart of 'Holy Mother Russia.'[310] This no doubt played a part, as did anger against the invaders who were laying waste to the country and whose brutal and murderous treatment of the civilian population and prisoners was well known among the Soviet troops.

But among many Red Army soldiers there was also another force at play. For many of them, there was also a feeling that whatever its shortcomings, Soviet socialism was something that was *theirs*, that was building up *their* country and giving it a chance at a better life, and they were willing, if necessary, to die to stop those who came to destroy it.[311]

Examples of this 'mass heroism' are not hard to find in the fight for Kalinin. The Germans noted that, as was the case in many other Russian cities, the civilian population of Kalinin vigorously participated in its defense on October 13th and 14th. This civilian support was not limited to the defense of the city; 133rd Rifle Division's bold strike to cut off 1st Panzer Division at Kalikino and Malitsa was aided by civilians who scouted the way and pointed out German positions and headquarters. 256th Rifle Division, fighting for the northeastern corner of Kalinin, similarly benefited from civilians who risked their lives to spy on the Germans and provide food and help to the Soviet fighters.

The determination and courage of the tank crews of 8th and 21st Tank Brigades were remarkable. It cannot be said that either brigade was handled brilliantly tactically, although the lack of radios and the lack of experience of the 21st meant that once committed into action control was largely lost and the companies and platoons fought independently. Despite this both units fought with exceptional courage and determination. One T-34, hit and immobilized in Mednoye, fought on despite German calls for the 'Russians' to surrender. When their ammunition ran out, they responded to renewed calls to come out with their hands up by singing *The International*, even while the Germans piled brushwood under the tank and set it afire. The bravery of the crews of 21st Tank Brigade, both those who fought their way into the city, and others who fought their way out of captivity with only their hands, speaks loudly of their dedication.

The same can be said for the soldiers of 133rd Rifle Division, a pre-war Siberian division that retained all of its subunits, including a howitzer regiment and a field artillery regiment, antitank and reconnaissance battalions, etc.[312] It entered combat after a twelve-hour forced march through rain and mud, crossed a small river by improvised means and the next day cut off 1st Panzer Division, beating back every effort to break into its positions for the next four days, and then participated in repeated attacks that penetrated into the edge of the city.

Similarly, 5th Rifle Division, which joined the battle with barely 2,000 men, was driven out of the city in heavy fighting with mechanized forces and flamethrowing tanks, only to come back with repeated counterattacks that again had to be beaten back in hand-to-hand fighting. Any commander assuming that men and women like these were on the edge of collapse was a commander who was leading his soldiers into disaster.

When all is said and done, the fighting along the Kalinin axis represented in microcosm the mosaic of the battle for Moscow as a whole. As such, it proved that an accumulation of 'small cuts' inflicted by far less skilled but highly motivated opponents can indeed humble the most powerful, confident, renowned, and arrogant invaders.

Acknowledgments

The authors would like to acknowledge the help of our friends who generously gave their assistance in our research and understanding of the battle. To Colonel David Glantz, US Army (Ret), who suggested this article in the first place and would not take no for an answer, and who provided an unending source of inspiration and encouragement; to Don Haugen, whose maps add a lot of clarity to the text; to Paul Bessemer and Dr. Bruce Gudmundsson, who helped with the translation; to Bob Mackenzie, web researcher extraordinary; to Colonel Eric Walters, USMC (Ret) for assistance and encouragement above and beyond any imaginable call; to Lt. Colonel Gary Rhay, US Army (Ret), and Matthew Hallinan, who provided useful and thoughtful criticism; and to Tamara and Kathleen for putting up with their partners' obsession all these years. Thank you. None of the above, however, has any responsibility for any errors or for the conclusions, which are ours alone.

Notes

1. Röttiger, Hans, 'XXXXI Panzer Corps during the Battle of Moscow in 1941 as a Component of Panzer Group 3,' in Newton, Steve (ed.), *German Battle Tactics on the Eastern Front, 1941–1945* (Atglen, PA: Schiffer Publishing Ltd, 1994), p. 27. Röttiger served as XXXXI Motorized Corps' Chief of Staff at Kalinin. Hereafter cited as Röttiger and page reference. In fact the Germans did not use the term 'Panzer Corps' until 1942; at the time of the battle for Kalinin they used 'Motorized Corps,' and sometimes just 'Corps.'

2. Zolotarev, V.A., *Russkii Arkhiv: Velikaia Otechestvennaia 15 (4/1) (Moskovskoi bitve)'* ('Russian Archives: Great Patriotic (War): Volume 15 (4/1), the Battle of Moscow'), Moscow: TERRA, 1997: Document 1: 'Directive of the Commander of Army Group Center on the Preparations for Operation "Taifun".' Hereafter cited as Zolotarev and document.

3. Frequently in German documents and popular histories mention is made of highways or high roads, usually leading to Moscow. Western readers, especially in the US, should realize that these are not modern highways, but in fact two-lane macadam/asphalt roads more similar to a secondary county road in the USA than a modern intercity highway. They were, however, virtually the only hard-surface roads in the Soviet Union, and so need to be identified in comparison to the dirt tracks that comprised most of the roads.

4. Zolotarev, Document 1.

5. Bock, F. von, *Ya stoyal u vorot Moskvy* ('I stood at the gates of Moscow'), Russian translation of *Zwischen Pflicht und Verweigerung: das Kriegstagebuch* ('Between Duty and Refusal: The War Diary'), Moscow: Yauza, Eksmo, 2006 (original German: Munich, Berlin: Herbig, 1995), entry for October 7th. Hereafter cited as von Bock and entry date.

6. Zolotarev, Document 11: 'Directive of OKH to the Commander of Army Group Center on the Direction of 3rd Panzer Group.'

7. Zolotarev, Document 13: 'Directive from the Commander of Army Group Center to the Commander of 9th Army on the Offensive in the Kalinin Direction.'

8. HGp Nord, Ia, Kriegstagebuch Nr. 4, NARA Microfilm Roll T311/53, first frame 7065390, entries for October 2nd–5th, 1941. Hereafter cited as KTB Nord and date of entry.

9. KTB Nord, entries for October 6th–8th.

10.   ...rev, Document 16: 'Order from Commander Army Group Center on ...ontinuation of Operations in the Moscow Direction.'

1...   ...tarev, Document 76: 'Directive of the STAVKA VGK to Commanders ...lorthwestern and Western Front, Deputy Commander of Forces of the ...stern Front Colonel General I.S. Konev on the Establishment of Kalinin ...ont.'

        Boevye deystviya Sovetskikh voisk no Kalininskom napravlenii v 1941 godu (s 0 oktyabrya 1941 g. po 7 yanvarya 1942 g.), ('The combat operations of Soviet Forces along the Kalinin axis during 1941 (from October 10th to January 7th 1942)), in *Sbornik voenno–istoricheskikh materialov Velikoi Otechestvennoi voiny, Vypusk 7* ('Collection of military-historical materials of the Great Patriotic War, Issue 7'), Moscow: Voenizdat, 1952), pp. 6-7. Hereafter cited as Vypusk 7 and page reference.

...   The Soviet census of 1939 provides the number 216,131, as reported on the University of Toronto website, http://www.chass.utoronto.ca/datalib/codebooks/utm/ussr_1939.htm.

14.   *Kriegstagebuch PzGr 3, AOK 3, 1 Sep–31 Oct 41* ('Panzer Group 3 Operations Officer War Diary for 1 Sep to 31 Oct 1941'), 15415/35, NARA Microfilm roll T313/23, first frame (7496190), October 13th, 1300 hrs. Hereafter cited as KTB PzGp 3 and date. Kirchner had been commander of 1st Panzer Division, but was wounded in the Luga River bridgehead in mid-July. Apparently he was accompanying the division in a supernumerary capacity while recovering, and was assigned to command the corps when Ottenbacher was wounded. Interestingly, there are no references at all to the loss of Ottenbacher, or the temporary assignment of Kirchner in the KTB of XXXXI Corps. On October 27th Lieutenant General Walther Model, previously commander of 3rd Panzer Division, arrived to take over XXXXI Corps as a permanent assignment.

15.   'Der Vorstoss auf Kalinin,' Anlagenband IVb zum Kriegstagebuch, XXXXI Armee Korps (Motz), Oct 15-Nov 20, 1941, NARA, Microfilm roll T314/980, item number 18741/10, starting frame 850. Hereafter cited as Anlagen XXXXI Corps and date. Although the only reference to it is dated November 8th, it provides the battalion's tank strength as of November 1st as two Pz III, six Pz II, and five Pz II (F) flame tanks, with another thirty-three tanks, including twenty Pz II (F), under repair. The battalion took part in the fight for Kalinin, but its strength going into the fight, and its subsequent losses, are not known.

16.   Anlagen XXXXI Corps, October 12th, 1941.

17.   Glantz, David M. (ed.), *The Initial Period of War on the Eastern Front* (London: Frank Cass, 1991), p. 129. Contains a diagram and discussion by Colonel Rolf O.G. Stoves of 1st Panzer Division. Hereafter cited as *Initial Period of War*. Cf Thomas L. Jentz, *Panzer Truppen*, Volume 1 (Atglen, PA:

Schiffer Military History, 1996), vol. 1, p. 206. Hereafter cited as Jentz, *Panzer Truppen*. This cites eleven Pz I and only twenty Pz IV at the start of Operation Barbarossa. On p. 192 of the same book, Jentz gives slightly different starting figures. Stoves also notes that 1st Panzer Division had a habit of acquiring every armored halftrack assigned to it or carelessly left unguarded, and this persisted throughout the war.

18. Lexicon-der-Wehrmacht at website http://www.lexikon-der-wehrmacht .de/Gliederungen/Infantriedivisionen/36ID.htm.

19. *Anlagen IVb, Generalkommando XXXXI, A.K. Ia Tagesmeldung, October 12th, 1941,* 6.) 36th Motorized Division was missing its entire 15cm howitzer battalion and three 10.5cm howitzers; 6th Infantry Division was missing one 10.5cm howitzer; 1st Panzer didn't submit a report, but was probably short a few guns; 620th Heavy Artillery Battalion was missing two 15cm guns, 611th Artillery Battalion was short three 10.5cm guns; II/59 Artillery Regiment was missing five 15cm howitzers; and I/51 Nebelwerfer Regiment lacked one battery of four launchers.

20. Röttiger, pp. 17, 26, and 28.

21. Vypusk 7, p. 12.

22. Most of the following data on Soviet units and their histories is from Charles Sharp, *The Soviet Order of Battle in WWII* (George F. Nafziger, 1995), volume I: *The Deadly Beginning (Tank, Mechanized, and Motorized Divisions and Tank Brigades formed before 1942)*; volume V: *Red Sabers (Soviet Cavalry Corps, Divisions, and Independent Brigades, 1941–45)*; volume VIII: *Red Legions (Soviet Rifle Divisions formed before June 1941)*; and volume IX: *Red Tide (Soviet Rifle Divisions formed from June to December 1941)*. The information on 21st Tank Brigade and Separate Motorized Rifle Brigade's tank strength is from the website http://www.armchairgeneral.com/ rkkaww2/battles/moscow/wftankstaff.htm#Oct16 (hereafter cited as Combat Path 21 TB), as well as Fes'kov, V.I., Kalashnikov, K.A. and Golikov, V.I. *Krasnaya Armiya v pobedakh I porazheniyakh 1941–1945 gg.* ('The Red Army in Victory and Defeat 1941–1945'), Tomsk: Izdatel'stvo Tomskogo Universiteta, 2003 (hereafter cited as Fes'kov, Kalashnikov & Golikov).

23. Collective authors, *Vnutrennie Voiska n Velikoi Otechestvennoi Voinie 1941–45 gg.* ('Internal Troops in the Great Patriotic War 1941–45'), Moscow: Yurizdat, 1975, p. 545. These NKVD divisions were numbered as regular Red Army rifle divisions from 243 to 266 with gaps, and were used to form the bulk of 29th, 30th, and 31st Armies in July 1941.

24. *Donesenie o chislennom I boevom sostave 31 Armii po sostoyaniyu na 20.09.1941 g.*, TsAMO, F. 219, op. 679, D. 28 ('Report on the Size and Combat Strength of 31st Army on September 20th, 1941'), as found at http://podvig-naroda.mil.ru/ Hereafter cited as 31 Army Strength, September 20th.

25. Lopukhovsky, Lev, *Viazemskaia katastrofe 41–go goda* ('The Vyazma tragedy of 1941'), Moscow: Iauza Eksmo, 2006. Hereafter cited as *Katastrofa*.
26. Maistrovsky, M. Ya. (ed.), *Na pravom flange Moskovskoye bitvy* ('On the Right Flank of the Battle of Moscow'), Tver: Mosk. Rabochii, 1991. This is a collection of excerpts from memoirs concerning the battle for Kalinin. Hereafter cited as *Na Pravom Flange* with reference to the particular memoirs quoted, in this case I.S. Konev, *Vospominanya.*
27. *Na Pravom Flange*, C. Fugleman, *Vsem Smertyam Nazlo*; also Ivanov, P. and Rigel'man, S., *Yarche Legend* ('Bright Legend' – a history of 21st Tank Brigade in 1941), Mosk. Rabochii, 1983; *Kommandovanie Korpusnogo i Divizionogo zvena Sovetskikh Vooruzhennykh Sil perioda velikoi otechestvennoi voiny* ('Commanders of Corps and Division Units in the Soviet Armed Forces during the period of the Great Patriotic War'), Moscow: Izdat. Military Academy M.V. Frunze, 1964; Pokrovskii et al., *Perechen' No. 7: Upravlenii brigad vsekh rodov voisk vkhodivshikh v sostav desitvuyushchei armii v gody velikoi otechestvennoi voiny 1941–1945 gg.* ('List # 7: HQ of brigades of all branches of forces in the active army during the period of the Great Patriotic War 1941–1945'), Moscow: Voennoe Izdatdel'stvo Ministertva Oborony Soiuza SSR, 1956 (General Staff document originally classified SECRET); Kolomiets, M., *Tanki v bitve za Moskvu* ('Tanks in the Battle of Moscow'), Moscow: Eksmo, 2009; Kolomiets, M., *T-34. Pervaia polnaia Entsiklopediia* ('T-34. First Complete Encyclopedia'), Moscow: Eksmo, 2009; website rkka.ru/tby021. Sources for motorcycle regiments: Pokrovskii et al. *Perechen' No. 14: Tankovykh, Samokhodno-Artilleriiskikh I mototsikletniykh polkov, vkhodivshikh v sostav desitvuyushchei armii v gody velikoi otechestvennoi voiny 1941–1945 gg.* ('List # 14: Tank, Self-Propelled Artillery, and Motorcycle Regiments in the composition of the forces of the active army during the Great Patriotic War 1941–1945], Moscow: Voennoe Izdatdel'stvo Ministertva Oborony Soiuza SSR, 1960 (General Staff document originally classified SECRET); Website: mechcorps. rkka.ru; *Spravochnik: Otdel'nyi mototsiklet-nyii polk 1941 g.* (Separate Motorcycle Regiment 1941).

There is considerable confusion regarding the command of 21st Tank Brigade in Soviet sources. In at least one source, Colonel Boris Mikhailovich Skvortsov is listed as commander of the 21st from October 9th to November 5th, 1941. But on a different page of the same source, he is also listed as commander of 61st Tank Division in the Red Banner Far Eastern Front, facing the Japanese in Manchuria, from March 11th, 1941 to June 11th, 1942. It appears that while Skvortsov may have been officially designated commander of the newly forming tank brigade, he never in fact came west to command it, and Lieutenant Colonel Lesovoi in fact commanded the brigade at the battle of Kalinin, as indicated by Muriev in his *Proval Operatsii Taifun* ('Defeat of Operation "Typhoon"'), 1966.

28. *Na Pravom Flange*, P.A. Rotmistrov, *V boi idut tankisti*, A.V. Yegorov, *Poedinok*; also Armstrong, Richard N., *Red Army Tank Commanders, The Armored Guards*, Atglen, PA: Schiffer Military/Aviation History, 1994 (mostly drawn from Rotmistrov's two memoirs), pp. 316–19 (hereafter cited as Armstrong).

29. Vypusk 7, p. 16.

30. Seaton, Colonel Albert, *The Battle of Moscow*, New York: PEI paperback, 1980, p. 105. Hereafter cited as Seaton.

31. Anlagen IVb, Generalkommando XXXXI AK Ia, Order # 29/41, October 9th, 1941, 2230 hrs 'Corps Order for the Attack on Sztaritza.'

32. Anlagen XXXXI Corps, October 9th, 1941; *XXXXI Mot Korpsbefehl 29/41 09.10.41 2230 uhr.*

33. Anlagen IVb, Generalkommando XXXXI AK Ia, Order # 29/41, October 9th, 1941, 2230 hrs 'Corps Order for the Attack on Sztaritza.'

34. Vypusk 7, p. 12.

35. 31 Army Strength, September 20th.

36. KTB XXXXI Corps, October 10th, 1700 hrs.

37. Ibid, 1900 hrs.

38. Zhukov, G., *The Memoirs of Marshal Zhukov*, New York: Delacorte Press, 1971, p. 328. Hereafter cited as Zhukov.

39. Bergstrom, Christer, and Migalovo, Andrey. *Black Cross/Red Star, Air War on the Eastern Front*, volume I, *Operation Barbarossa, 1941*, Pacifica, CA: Pacifica Military History, 2000, p. 196. Hereafter cited as BC/RS. The *Luftwaffe* or German Air Force was organized into a number of *Luftflotten*, roughly equivalent to a numbered US Army Air Force. Each *Luftflotte* was usually made up of two *Fliegerkorps*. The *Fliegerkorps* in turn was composed of several *Geschwader*, the basic tactical unit of the *Luftwaffe*, with a paper strength of from 132 to 172 aircraft, depending on the type. A *Geschwader* was identified by a letter code, for branch of service (*J* for fighters, *Z* for long-range fighters, *Sch* for ground-attack, and *K* for bombers), so *JG3* would be *Jagdgeschwader 3* or 3rd Fighter Squadron. The *Geschwader* was made up of *gruppen* or groups, each composed of three or four twelve-plane *Staffeln*. The *gruppen* were designated with Roman numerals, so *II./JG 3* would be the second group of 3rd Fighter *Geschwader*. The *staffeln* were designated with Arabic numerals, so *1.II/JG 3* would be the first *staffel*, second *gruppe*, 3rd Fighter *Geschwader*. All German air units were well understrength by October, 1941.

40. Röttiger, p. 23: 'The extent of the enemy's air activity against the Corps spearheads surpassed everything so far experienced in Russia. . . . VIII Air Corps was able to bring only little relief, since the airfields for its fighter units were, of necessity, still far behind the lines.' On the other hand, on October 9th Röttiger wrote in the corps daily report, '10) Enemy air activity during the day was weak, during the evening increasing bombing activity.' *Anlagen*

IVb, German and Soviet accounts of the battle indicate significant air activity by both sides, but with the German effort far surpassing the Soviet.

41. KTB PzGp 3, October 11th, 1535, 1630 hrs. The *'Gigant'*, or Me-321 glider, was a monster, 28.15 meters long (92' 4"), with a 55 meter (180' 5") wingspan, and could deliver 23 long tons of cargo.

42. This points to a problem the Germans encountered throughout the Kalinin battle: a lack of adequate maps. Until the Germans captured a complete map set when they overran the headquarters of 2nd Shock Army in 1942, they were operating with inadequate and inaccurate 1:300,000 scale maps. There are regular references in their reports to confusion as to the location or existence of roads and bridges. At the end of the operation, Panzer Group 3 blamed a substantial part of its supply difficulties on its inadequate map resources: KTB PzGp 3, October 23rd, 0635 hrs.

43. KTB PzGp 3, October 11th, 1425, 1930, and 2120 hrs.

44. KTB XXXXI Corps, October 11th.

45. Vypusk 7, pp. 12–14.

46. *Na Pravom Flange,* I.S. Konev, *Vospominaniya.*

47. *Na Provom Flange*, Kalininskaya Oboronitelinyaya Operatsiya.

48. *Na Pravom Flange*, map: *Polozhenie Voisk v raiyon Kalinina no 14 Oktyabrya 1941 g.* Also from a report from General Khomenko to People's Commissar of Internal Affairs Lavrenti Beria, dated October 24th, describing the course of the battle and the actions of 30th Army from October 10th–23rd, taken from *Lubyanka in the Days of the Battle for Moscow,* Moscow: Belfry Publishing House, 2002 (hereafter cited as Khomenko).

49. Zolotarev, Document 68, 'Report of the Military Soviet of Western Front to the High Command and Chief of the General Staff of the Red Army on the Enemy Offensive in the Kalinin Direction and Actions for the defense of Kalinin,' October 12th, 1941, signed Zhukov (commander), Sokolovsky (Chief of Staff), Bulganin (Commissar). Reference: TsAMO, F. 208, op. 2511, D. 1029, lL. 61, Podlinnik.

50. Combat Path 21 TB.

51. KTB PzGp 3, October 12th, 0131 hrs.

52. KTB XXXXI Corps, October 12th; also Stoves, Rolf O.G., *Die 1. Panzer-Division, 1935–1945,* Eggolsheim: Dorfler Publishing, 2006, p. 114 (hereafter cited as Stoves). The original book of the same title, a far more detailed version with less pictures and text in German only, will be cited as Stoves 1. Panzer-Division.

53. KTB XXXXI Corps, October 12th.

54. Seaton, p. 106 is typical.

55. KTB XXXXI Corps, October 12th.

56. Ibid;also Anlagen IVb, Generalkommando XXXXI. A.K. Ia Tagesmeldung, 12.10.41.

57. BC/RS, p. 196.
58. Ushakov, S.F., *Vo Imya Pobedy: Ocherki* ('For the Victory: Sketches'), Moscow: DOSAAF, 1987. Episodes from October 1941, 'First Sortie of the 42nd Long Range Bomber Regiment' from the 'All Aces' website http://www.allaces.ru/ (hereafter cited as Sketches).
59. KTB XXXXI Corps, October 13th, 0900 hrs.
60. Ibid; also *Na Pravom Flange, Kalininskaya Oboronitelinyaya Operatsiya*.
61. KTB XXXXI Corps, October 13th, 1700 hrs.
62. KTB XXXXI Corps, October 13th; Glantz, D.M., Atlas of the Battle of Moscow, The Defensive Phase: 1 October–5 December, 1941, Carlisle, PA: self-published, 1997, p. 29 (hereafter cited as Atlas); Zolotarev, 'Operational Summary [by the] Staff of Western Front of the Locations and Military Activities of the Forces of the Front,' # 0350/219, dated October 14th, 1941, 2000 hrs. This document, signed by Front Chief of Staff Sokolovsky, Chief of Operations Malandin, and Military Commissar Kazbintsev, is woefully inaccurate and behind events by at least 24 hours.
63. *Na Pravom Flange*, A.F. Semenov, *V Nebe Nad Volgoi*; also BC/RS, p. 198.
64. KTB PzGp 3, October 13th, 1600 hrs. There are many contradictory reports on this incident and its consequences. In a report submitted to Lavrenti Beria, head of the NKVD on October 24th, General Khomenko claimed that his 30th Army had killed Ottenbacher. Radio Moscow broadcast this news, causing the German Propaganda Ministry to put out a press release that appeared in the *Montreal Gazette* of October 28th, 1941, stating that Ottenbacher's plane was forced down behind German lines and the general received minor injuries. More confusing is the question of who took over XXXXI Motorized Corps. In a footnote to Röttiger's postwar account of the battle, Newton states that it was General Walther Model who took over the corps, which in fact he did at the end of October. This is also reported in Samuel W. Mitcham and Gene Mueller's book, *Hitler's Commanders: Officers of the Wehrmacht, the Luftwaffe, the Kriegsmarine and the Waffen SS* (Cooper Square Publishers, 1992). Kirchner had been wounded in July, and most sources state that General Kruger took over 1st Panzer Division at that time and continued to command it until December 31st, 1943 – see http://www.lexikon-der-wehrmacht.de/Gliederungen/Panzerdivisionen /Gliederung.htm. It is possible that while recovering from his wound Kirchner was accompanying the division in a supernumerary status, or he could have resumed command. In any case, Model arrived at the end of the month to replace him, and no record shows Kirchner in command of the corps for more than a day, which is quite unusual. He may have commanded up until the end of the month, or may have had the temporary command title, while Röttiger ran the corps.

65. KTB XXXXI Corps, October 13th, 1945 hrs.

66. KTB PzGp 3, October 13th, 2100 hrs.

67. KTB PzGp 3, October 13th, 1941, at 2334 hrs, headed 'Overheard Transmission.'

68. *Na Pravom Flange*, P.A. Rotmistrov, *V boi idut tankisti*; P.A. Rotmistrov, *Stal'naya gvardiya, Moscow, Voenizdat*, 1984, pp. 73–4 as quoted in Armstrong, pp. 316–17; and *Na Pravom Flange*, A.V. Yegorov, *Poedinok*. Yegorov was the commander of the tank regiment of Rotmistrov's brigade.

69. *Na Pravom Flange*, I.S. Konev, *Vospominanya*, and N.B. Ivushkin, *Za Kazhdy Dom*. 930th Rifle Regiment, or at least two battalions of it, had been detached to support 178th Rifle Division in 22nd Army. *Na Pravom Flange*, in a chapter discussing the Soviet liberation of Kalinin in the winter of 1941/42, shows a map with 256th Rifle Division still having only 934th and 937th Rifle Regiments in evidence, and it is dated December 2nd, 1941.

70. KTB XXXXI Corps, October 14th.

71. Atlas, p. 31.

72. KTB 36 MotzD, October 14th.

73. KTB XXXXI Corps, October 14th.

74. Afanasiev, N.I. et al. *Dorogami Ispytanii I Pobed* ('Roads of Trials and Triumph: History of 31st Army'), Moscow: Voenizdat, 1986, p. 12.

75. *Na Pravom Flange, Kalininskoye Operatsionoye Napravlenie V Planakh Nemetsko-Fashistskogo*; KTB XXXXI Corps, October 14th; Haupt, Werner, *Die Schlachten der Heeresgruppe Mitte 1941–1944: Aus der Sicht der Divisionen* ('The Battles of Army Group Center 1941–1944: from the view of the divisions'), Friedberg, FRG: Podzun-Pallas-Verlag, 1983, p. 95 (hereafter cited as Haupt).

76. Haupt, p. 95.

77. Ibid; also KTB XXXXI Corps, October 14th; *Na Pravom Flange, Kalininskoye Operatsionoye Napravlenie V Planakh Nemetsko-Fashistskogo*.

78. KTB XXXXI Corps, October 14th.

79. Haupt, p. 95.

80. KTB XXXXI Corps, October 14th; KTB PzGp 3, October 14th, characterized the losses at 1100 hrs as 'substantial'.

81. KTB 36 MotzD, October 14th, 1500 hrs. These had to be attacks by Il-2 *Shturmoviks*, the only Soviet 'bombers' with significant armor.

82. KTB XXXXI Corps, October 14th.

83. Ibid.

84. *Na Pravom Flange*, K.I. Sushan, *Perviye Zalpi*.

85. *Na Pravom Flange*, P.A. Rotmistrov, *V boi idut tankisti*; also Rotmistrov, *Stal'naya gvardiya*, pp. 73–4, as quoted in Armstrong, pp. 316–17; and *Na Pravom Flange*, A.V. Yegorov, *Poedinok*.

86. Bergstrom, Christer, *Barbarossa – The Air Battle July–December, 1941*, Hersham, UK: Ian Allen Publishing, 2007. Hereafter cited as Barbarossa-Air.
87. *Na Pravom Flange*, C. Fugleman, *Vsem Smertyam Nazlo*.
88. KTB PzGp 3, October 11th–14th, various entries.
89. Anlagen IVb, Generalkommando XXXXI, A.K., October 14th.
90. Glantz, David M., *The Battle for Leningrad, 1941–1944*, Lawrence, KS: University Press of Kansas, 2002, pp. 95–9 (hereafter Battle for Leningrad); *'Svedeniya o boevom I chislennom sostav 52 armii na 20.10.41–30.10.41 g.'* ('Information concerning military and numerical composition of 52nd Army from October 20th to 30th, 1941'), TsAMO, F. 221, op. 1351, D. 175, from website: http://podvignaroda.mil.ru/ Note, the two sources give slightly different information on the order of battle of 52nd Army.
91. Anlagen IVb, 3.PzGp Behfel 25, October 14th 1941.
92. Anlagen IVb, 3.PzGp Behfel 25, October 14th 1941, para 3) 3.Pz Gp.
93. Seaton, p. 105.
94. KTB PzGp 3, October 14th, 2100 hrs.
95. KTB PzGp 3, October 14th, 1330 hrs.
96. Vypusk 7, p. 14.
97. *Na Pravom Flange*, I.S. Konev, *Vospominaniya*.
98. KTB PzGp 3, October 15th, 0535 hrs.
99. KTB PzGp 3, October 15th, 0700 hrs, discussing the implementation of Order # 25, officially issued to the group's subordinate units at that time.
100. *Na Pravom Flange*, P.A. Rotmistrov, *V boi idut tankisti*, A.V. Yegorov, *Poedinok*.
101. *Na Pravom Flange*, N.B. Ivushkin, *Za Kazhdy Dom*; also KTB XXXXI Corps, October 15th. The push against 256th Rifle Division came from the motorcycle battalion of 36th Motorized Division, probably supported by elements of 101st Flame Panzer Battalion.
102. KTB XXXXI Corps, October 15th; also Anlagen IVb, Generalkommando XXXXI, A.K., October 15th; KTB PzGp 3, October 15th, 2000 hrs.
103. Vypusk 7, p. 15.
104. *Ia, Kriegstagebuch 7 20 Sep–12 Apr 1942, 1 Pz Div* ('Operations Officer War Diary # 7 for 1st Panzer Division covering 20 September, 1941 to 12 April, 1942'), NARA Document number 24293/1, Microfilm reel T315/26, starting at frame 351, October 15th, 1250 hrs. (Hereafter cited as KTB 1 PzD.)
105. *Na Pravom Flange*, A.V. Yegorov, *Poedinok*, P.A. Rotmistrov, *V boi idut tankisti, Kalininskaya Oboronitelinyyaya Operatsiya*.
106. KTB 1 PzD, October 15th. This represents little advance from where the division stood in the morning, and, while vague about specifics (usually an

indication that there wasn't much good news to cheer about), is not inconsistent with Rotmistrov's and Yegorov's versions of events.

107. Combat Path 21 TB.
108. *Katastrofa*, p. 192.
109. *Na Pravom Flange*, C. Fugleman, *Vsem Smertyam Nazlo*. All three Red Army commanders in this encounter – Dovator, Lesovoi and Klynfeld – were of Jewish background: a regular nightmare for the German *übermensch*.
110. *Boevoi prikaz 29 Armii: general-leitenant Maslennikov 15.10.1941* ('Military Combat Order of 29th Army: Lieutenant General Maslennikov, October 15th, 1941'), TsAMO, F. 208, op. 2511, D. 62, from website http://podvignaroda.mil.ru
111. KTB PzGp 3, October 15th, 2000 hrs.
112. Anlagen IVb, XXXXI AK Behfel 31/41, October 16th 1941.
113. Erickson, John, *The Road to Stalingrad*, New York: Harper and Row, 1975, p. 220.
114. Anlagen IVb, XXXXI AK Behfel 31/41, October 16th 1941.
115. Barbarossa-Air, p. 105; BC/RS, p. 234. In the latter source the date given for the transfer is October 21st, but in KTB PzGr 3, October 16th, 1240 hrs, it clearly indicates that fighters had arrived at Kalinin that day, and, as the events of the next day would show, Stuka and ground-attack aircraft were operating from Kalinin airfields on October 16th.
116. *Na Pravom Flange, Kalininskaya Oboronitelinyaya Operatsiya*.
117. Ibid.
118. KTB XXXXI Corps, October 16th, 0800 hrs.
119. KTB PzGr 3, October 16th.
120. *Na Pravom Flange*, A.V. Yegorov, *Poedinok*, P.A. Rotmistrov, *V boi idut tankisti, Kalininskaya Oboronitelinyaya Operatsiya*.
121. *Na Pravom Flange*, , I.S. Konev, *Vospominaniya*.
122. *Na Pravom Flange*, Col. G.S. Katz, *Tri Dnya V Oktyabr*. Katz was editor of 133rd Rifle Division's newspaper.
123. *Na Pravom Flange*, M.N. Rozov, *V Polkakh Ostavalosi Po 150 Shtikov*. Colonel Rozov was a battalion commander in 777th Artillery Regiment, 246th Rifle Division.
124. *Na Pravom Flange, Kalininskaya Oboronitelinyaya Operatsiya*; Vypusk 7, p. 14. Initial orders from the *Stavka* had called for three rifle divisions to be sent from Northwest Front. In the event, two were sent (183rd, 185th), along with two cavalry divisions (46th, 54th), 8th Tank Brigade and 46th Motorcycle Regiment.
125. Zolotarev, Document 74: 'Directive of the *Stavka* VGK to the Commander of the Forces of Northwestern Front on Mission of the Forces of the Front in the region of Kalinin,' # 003038, dated October 16th, 1941, 2300 hrs.
126. Zolotarev, Document 73: 'Directive of the *Stavka* of the VGK to

Commanders of Western and Northwestern Fronts on use of Forces of Northwestern Front in the region of Kalinin under Commanders of Forces of Western Front,' # 003037, dated October 16th, 1941, 1945 hrs.

127. *Na Pravom Flange,* N.B. Ivushkin, *Za Kazhdy Dom*; also Anlagen IVb, XXXXI AK Behfel 31/41, October 16th 1941.

128. KTB PzGp 3, October 16th, 0800 hrs; KTB 36 MotzD, October 16th (no time given, but morning report). 36th Motorized Division lists the POW bag as 550, Panzer Group 3 only credits 400.

129. KTB PzGr 3, October 16th, 2340 hrs.

130. Ibid.

131. *Anlagen zum Kriegstagebuch, 'Tagesmeldungen' Pz Gr 3, Ia, Pz AOK 3, 15415/39, 1 Sep–31 Oct 1941,* NARA Microfilm Reel T313/23, first frame 7496852.

132. Ibid.

133. KTB XXXXI Corps, October 16th; Anlagen IVb, XXXXI AK Behfel 31/41, October 16th 1941; also *Anlagen zum Kriegstagebuch, 'Tagesmeldungen' Pz Gr 3, Ia, Pz AOK 3, 15415/39, 1 Sep–31 Oct 1941,* same day.

134. KTB XXXXI Corps, October 16th, 1920 hrs.

135. KTB PzGr 3, October 16th, 1240 hrs.

136. KTB PzGp 3, October 16th, 0800 hrs.

137. Battle for Leningrad, pp. 94–9.

138. *Na Pravom Flange,* C. Fugleman, *Vsem Smertyam Nazlo.*

139. *36th Infantry Division (Motorized) 22768/4, Ia, Kriegstagebuch No. 2, 22 Sep–5 Dec 1941, 17 October, 0930 hrs,* NARA Microfilm Reel T315/898, first frame 346. Hereafter cited as KTB 36 Motz.

140. *Na Pravom Flange,* C. Fugleman, *Vsem Smertyam Nazlo.*

141. KTB 36 Motz, 0930 hrs.

142. *Na Pravom Flange,* C. Fugleman, *Vsem Smertyam Nazlo.*

143. KTB 36 Motz, 1100 hrs.

144. *Na Pravom Flange,* C. Fugleman, *Vsem Smertyam Nazlo*, also *Kalininskaya Oboronitelinyaya Operatsiya*; Combat Path 21 TB. Both Major Lukin and Captain Agibalov had received the Hero of the Soviet Union for their fighting at Khalkin Gol in 1939.

145. Combat Path 21 TB; Vypusk 7, p. 29. Note that Vypusk 7 claims German losses of thirty-eight tanks, seventy guns and mortars, 170 trucks, and up to 500 soldiers and officers. It is hard to imagine how any accurate report could have been made, given the high speed of the attack, and the casualties suffered. On October 19th Anlagen IVb, XXXXI AK Tagesmeldung, October 19th gives a list of equipment lost by just the 36th Motorized Division in the fighting from October 17th to 19th as 105 trucks, thirteen tractors, fifteen motorcycles, five field kitchens, one 10.5cm howitzer, one

15cm howitzer, and eight antitank guns. Kolomiets, *Tanki v bitve za Moskvu*, p. 65 indicates that between October 17th and 19th the brigade suffered the loss of twenty-one T-34s, seven BTs, one T-60, one self-propelled 57mm gun, ninety killed and 154 wounded. On October 21st the brigade reported detailed losses in personnel:

Tank Regiment HQ – 8 officers, 3 NCOs killed or missing

Reconnaissance Platoon – 1 NCO, 4 EM wounded

Brigade HQ – 1 killed, 1 wounded

Rifle/Machinegun Battalion – 15 killed, 143 wounded, 254 missing

Losses from the tank regiment are not listed

In addition, while citing the same losses for the Germans from October 16th–20th, it adds two intriguing details. Of the thirty-eight German tanks destroyed, two are listed as 'medium' tanks, meaning Pz III. That would mean the rest would be Pz II light tanks, or Pz II(F) flamethrower tanks. It is likely that the number of lost tanks is an overestimate, and almost all of them came from 101st Panzer Battalion (F). Of the 170 trucks claimed destroyed, twelve are listed as fuel tankers, a critical loss for the Germans.

146. KTB PzGr 3, October 17th, 1300 hrs.

147. KTB XXXXI Corps, October 17th.

148. KTB XXXXI Corps, October 17th, 18th; Anlagen IVb, XXXXI AK Tagesmeldung, October 21st. Part of the explanation for the discrepancy between the number of destroyed trucks claimed by 21st Tank Brigade and the number listed by 36th Motorized Division is that the Soviet tankers destroyed many trucks from XXXXI Corps rear units, possibly including some from 1st Panzer Division.

149. KTB XXXXI Corps, October 17th; Armstrong pp. 318–19, quoting Rotmistrov, gives the date for the destruction of the brigade HQ as the 17th, not the 16th, also he reports nine KV and T-34 tanks remained in service. Yegorov's figures in *Na Pravom Flange* are less than consistent, citing more tanks in total (still running and under repair) than the total he says they took to the battle. On the other hand, Rotmistrov claims the brigade had T-60 tanks, and the only brigade which had received these at this point was 21st Tank Brigade, so Yegorov's description of the brigade's 2nd Battalion being armed with T-40 and T-38 tanks is more credible.

150. *Na Pravom Flange, Kalininskaya Oboronitelinyaya Operatsiya.* It is worth noting that Rotmistrov subsequently served as a tank army commander under Konev from the summer of 1943 through the spring of 1944 in the Ukraine, before becoming the Chief Marshal of Tank Forces for the Red Army.

151. *Na Pravom Flange*, N.B. Ivushkin, *Za Kazhdy Dom.*

152. Stoves, p. 114. This is a bit on the hyperbolic side. There was only one heavy tank operational in 8th Tank Brigade that day; if the T-34s are counted as heavy, that would make six, still a pretty slender pack. In Stoves' longer book

of the same title, in one paragraph he claims that Eckinger's halftrack was hit by a KV-2's 152mm howitzer, killing Eckinger and wounding the others in the halftrack. Later in the same paragraph he identifies the ambushing tank as a T-34. This seems more likely, since for one thing there were no KV-2s present in the battle, and for another, a 152mm shell would not have left any wounded survivors in the halftrack. The phrase 'fresh Siberian troops' comes up a lot in Stoves' account of the fall and winter of 1941. In this case, there is a grain of truth in it, at least in terms of the Siberians. Both 119th and 133rd Divisions, which shortly attacked the rear of 1st Panzer Division from south and north respectively, were Siberian divisions, but as both had been at the front since mid-summer and both were understrength at this point, the description 'fresh' is a misnomer. Eckinger's death was commented on by both Panzer Group 3's records and by the division personnel department, who called him 'the best soldier in the division.'

153. *Na Pravom Flange*, Col. G.S. Katz, *Tri Dnya V Oktyabr.*
154. *Na Pravom Flange*, P.A. Rotmistrov, *V boi idut tankisti, Kalininskaya Oboronitelinyaya Operatsiya.* The Soviet strength cited seems to be badly underestimated. 133rd Rifle Division was a strong division, and 183rd Rifle Division had over 6,000 men, while 185th Rifle Division had twice that many. Just the two rifle divisions of Vatutin's group amounted to over 18,000 men by themselves.
155. Tank strengths are always a problem. 1st Panzer, which began in June, 1941, with 145 operational tanks, and at the end of September had 111 (Jentz, *Panzer Truppen*, p. 211; *Initial Period of War*, p. 127; Stoves, p. 129), on October 16th was down to seventy-nine (Röttiger, p. 53, footnote citing Burkhardt Muller-Hillebrand, *Das Heer*, p. 205). This number of seventy-nine tanks, almost certainly counting those under repair and including all the tanks in 101st Panzer Battalion (Flame), is also cited in KTB PzGp 3, October 14th, 1330 hrs. On October 18th (Anlagen IVb, XXXXI AK Tagesmeldung, October 18th) there is a rare report on panzer strength, which it gives as eight Pz II, twenty-two Pz III, and four Pz IV, for a total of thirty-four runners. If the footnote in Röttiger is correct, that would suggest a loss of forty-five tanks in two days. While there was intense fighting with 8th Tank Brigade during this period, this does seem high. And 1st Panzer's troubles had only begun.
156. *Na Pravom Flange, Kalininskaya Oboronitelinyaya Operatsiya.*
157. The Germans had their own woes bridging the Volga. When the advanced detachment of 26th Infantry Division attempted to cross the Volga at Staritsa, the captured Soviet pontoon bridge there broke and '70 meters of pontoons swam away.' This would be the bridge that the panzer group had planned to use to send 7th Panzer and 14th Motorized Divisions across the Volga to strike at Torzhok. KTB PzGp 3, October 17th, 1100 hrs.

158. *Na Pravom Flange,* M.N. Rozov, *V Polkakh Ostavalosi Po 150 Shtikov;* KTB PzGp 3, October 17th, 1030 hrs; KTB XXXXI Corps, October 18th, 0500 hrs.

159. Vypusk 7, pp. 16–18; Zolotarev, Document 76: 'Directive of the Stavka VGK to Commanders of Northwestern and Western Front, Deputy Commander of Forces of the Western Front Colonel General I.S. Konev on the Establishment of Kalinin Front,' # 003053, dated October 17th, 1941, 1830 hrs. Reference: TsAMO, F.3, op. 11556, D.3, ll. 139–40, Kopiya; *Na Pravom Flange, Kalininskaya Oboronitelinyaya Operatsiya.*

160. *Na Pravom Flange,* M.N. Rozov, *V Polkakh Ostavalosi Po 150 Shtikov.*

161. *Na Pravom Flange,* I.S. Konev, *Vospominanya; Boevoi prikaz 29 Armii: general-leitenant Maslennikov 15.10.1941* ('Military Combat Order of 29th Army: Lieutenant General Maslennikov, October 15th, 1941'), TsAMO, F. 208, op. 2511, D. 62, from website http://podvignaroda.mil.ru

162. Vypusk 7, p. 21.

163. Note that Konev's first report, which went to Stalin, not Zhukov (his superior officer at the time), was dispatched by U–2 courier plane, not radio. While Maslennikov could reach Beria in Moscow by radio, and Zhukov could in turn reach him, the fact that Konev was not privy to this discussion strongly suggests that Konev did not have any radio or at least none capable of reaching Moscow or Maslennikov.

164. *Na Pravom Flange, Kalininskaya Oboronitelinyaya Operatsiya.* The command and control problem was aggravated by the fact that Major General Vasily Nikitich Dalmatov, an NKVD officer, commanded 31st Army until October 13th, but no commander was assigned to 31st Army between October 13th and 19th, when Major General Vasily Aleksandrovich Yushkevich, a regular Red Army officer who had previously commanded 22nd Army, took over (Afanasiev et al, *Dorogami Isp'tanii I pobed,* p. 269). Major General V.I. Vostrukhov took over 22nd Army. Dalmatov became Deputy Commander of the Moscow Defense Zone, building and controlling rear area security for which his NKVD background suited him.

165. *Boevoe rasporyazhenie 18.10.1941* ('Military Instruction October 18th, 1941'), TsAMO, F. 221, op. 1351, D. 21, from website: http://podvignaroda.mil.ru/ There is some evidence that General Konev had friends in the historical branch of the Red Army, and several studies, some of them done during the war, seem to have been written with an eye to burnishing Konev's reputation and minimizing Vatutin's role in several actions both were involved with, including the Korsun-Shevchenkovsky Operation. Despite his key role in numerous battles, and commanding the most important Front during operations in 1943–early 1944, Vatutin never received a marshal's rank, or the Hero of the Soviet Union. Since Vatutin did not survive the war, he had no opportunity to write memoirs.

166. KTB PzGp 3, October 17th, 1600 hrs.

167. KTB PzGp 3, October 17th, 0940 hrs.

168. *Ia, Kriegstagebuch 16 Sep–30 Nov 1941, 6 Pz Div* ('Operations Officer War Diary for 6th Panzer Division covering 16 Sep to 30 Nov 1941'), NARA Microfilm reel T315/323, frames 235 thru 371, entries for October 10th and October 13th.

169. *Na Pravom Flange*, Col. G.S. Katz, *Tri Dnya V Oktyabr*. Kandaurov survived the battle, and the war, collecting the Order of Lenin for his stand at Kalikino, two Orders of the Red Banner, two Orders of Suvurov, an Order of the Red Star, four more wounds, a concussion, and eventually a lieutenant colonel's rank. Tchaikovsky for his part received a battlefield promotion to captain the next day directly from General Konev.

170. KTB 1 PzD, October 18th (there are no time references in the KTB for this date).

171. KTB PzGp 3, October 18th, 0600, 0930 hrs.

172. KTB 36 MotzD, October 18th, 1400, 1415 hrs.

173. KTB 36 MotzD, October 18th, 1400, 1455 hrs.

174. KTB 36 MotzD, October 18th, 1730 hrs.

175. KTB 36 MotzD, October 18th, 1930 hrs. Despite shifting the two companies of 118th Regiment, 87th Regiment reported at 1920 hrs that the gap was still not closed. The artillery formed hedgehog positions; the infantry were not able to restore the situation overnight. Lesovoi's tankers had lost none of their aggressiveness despite their losses of the previous day.

176. Sketches; the OBD Memorial, TsAMO, F. 58, op. 818883, D. 1655, ll. 16, 17, however, lists both crews as killed or missing from the flight.

177. *Dalny Bombardirovshchik Yer-2* ('Long Range Bomber Yer-2'), in *Aviamaster*, # 2, 1999.

178. *Na Pravom Flange*, A.V. Yegorov, *Poedinok*.

179. Vypusk 7, pp. 21–2; Atlas, p. 39. Interestingly, the German records refer to Marino ('Mar'ino, Maryino') as Parjino throughout. It is possible it represents telephone or radio transmission that was hard to understand, as the Germans were not well equipped with maps of the area

180. KTB XXXXI Corps, October 18th, 0500, 1600, 1700, 2030 hrs.

181. KTB XXXXI Corps, October 18th, 0800 hrs.

182. Ibid.

183. KTB PzGp 3, October 18th, 1905 hrs.

184. Combat Path 21 TB.

185. Anlagen IVb, XXXXI AK Tagesmeldung, October 18th.

186. Ibid.

187. KTB PzGp 3, October 18th, 1230 and 1400 hrs.

188. KTB PzGp 3, October 18th, 1630 hrs.

189. KTB PzGp 3, October 18th, 1630 hrs; Glantz, *Atlas*, pp. 40–5.

190. Zolotarev, Document 79: 'Military Report from the Commander of the Forces of Kalinin Front to the Chief of the General Staff of the Red Army and the Commander of Forces of Western Front on the Beginning of the Offensive by the Forces of Western Front in the Area of Kalinin, Volga River, Moscow Sea,' # 0123, dated October 18th, 1941, 2300 hrs. Reference: TsAMO, F. 213, op. 2002, D. 5, l. 21, Podlinnik.
191. KTB XXXXI Corps, October 19th, 0500, 1700 hrs; KTB 36 MotzD, October 19th, 0830 hrs.
192. KTB XXXXI Corps, October 19th, 0500, 0800, 1200 hrs.
193. *Na Pravom Flange*, A.V. Yegorov, *Poedinok*. There is evidence that all three regiments of 133rd Rifle Division were in action by this time. In Afanasiev et al, *Dorogami Isp'tanii I pobed*, pp. 15–16, there are citations of heroic actions by soldiers of 418th, 521st and 681st Rifle Regiments, all involving combat in the Kalinin area.
194. *Boevoe rasporyazhenie na 02.30, 19.10.1941 g* ('Military Instruction of 0230 hrs, October 19th, 1941'), TsAMO, F. 221, op. 1351, D. 21, from website : http://podvignaroda.mil.ru/ Orders to 185th Rifle Division and 8th Tank Brigade.
195. KTB 1 PzD, October 19th, time unknown. Division headquarters was located in Kalinin, and cut off from the forces on the Torzhok road, but were in radio contact.
196. Ibid; *Opersvodka na 20:00 19.10.1941 g* ('Operational Summary at 2000 hrs, October 19th, 1941'), by Staff of Kalinin Front, Colonel General Konev, TsAMO, F. 208, op. 2511, D. 30, from website: http://podvignaroda.mil .ru/ . Hereafter cited as KF Operational Summary with date.
197. *Na Pravom Flange*, Col. G.S. Katz, *Tri Dnya V Oktyabr, Kalininskaya Oboronitelinyaya Operatsiya*.
198. KF Operational Summary, October 19th; Glantz, *Atlas*, p. 39; Vypusk 7, p. 22; 29th Army Operations Summary # 130, 1100 hrs, October 19th. Each division ordered north by Maslennikov had been reinforced – the 119th had three independent 122mm howitzer batteries and a battery of 873rd Antitank Regiment attached, the 252nd had two battalions of 510th Howitzer Regiment and a battery each of 213th Antitank Battalion and 873rd Antitank Regiment attached, and 644th Corps Artillery Regiment was to follow the division. 243rd Rifle Division, headed for Mednoye, had a battery of 873rd AT Regiment and two more battalions of 510th Howitzer Regiment in support. All were expected to be on or across the T'ma River from 0900 to noon on October 20th.
199. *Abt. Qu., Kriegstagebuch 20 Sep 1941–12 Apr 1942 1 Pz Div* ('Logistics Officer War Diary for 1st Panzer Division covering 20 September, 1941 to 12 April, 1942'), NARA Microfilm reel T315/26, item # 23756, first frame 152, October 19th, 1941. Hereafter cited as KTB 1 PzD Qu and date.

200. *Na Pravom Flange,* N.B. Ivushkin, *Za Kazhdy Dom;* KTB 36 MotzD, October 19th, 1030 hrs.
201. KTB PzGp 3, entries for October 18th–19th.
202. KTB 36 MotzD, October 19th, 0830 to 1150 hrs.
203. KTB 36 MotzD, October 19th, 1050 hrs.
204. KTB 36 MotzD, October 19th, 1515 hrs.
205. KTB 36 MotzD, October 19th, 1830 hrs.
206. KTB 36 MotzD, October 19th, twenty-two entries from 0800 to 1830 hrs.
207. KTB PzGp 3, October 19th, 1400 hrs.
208. KTB PzGp 3, October 19th, 1010 hrs.
209. KTB PzGp 3, October 19th; and KTB XXXXI Corps, October 19th.
210. Ibid, several entries.
211. Anlagen IVb, XXXXI AK Tagesmeldung, October 19th, 20th.
212. KTB PzGp 3, October 19th, 1930 hrs.
213. KTB 1 PzD, October 20th, 1352 hrs.
214. KTB XXXXI Corps, October 20th, 0500, 0800, 1100 hrs.
215. KTB XXXXI Corps, October 20th, 0840, 1700 hrs; KTB 1 PzD, October 20th, 0320, 0800, 1105, 1315, 1352 hrs. The actual discussion in KTB XXXXI Corps at 0940 hrs reads, 'A great difficulty is in preparing to bring back the vehicles of the *Lehr* Brigade when only insignificant fuel supplies can be arranged. However, all vehicles, with the exception of the few tanks, must be blown up, if they have "technical damages" [and] cannot be repaired on the spot.' From questions posed by higher HQs (Army Group Center), it seems apparent that there was considerable deception going on concerning the fate of the vehicles of 900th *Lehr* Brigade and 1st Panzer Division. The quotes around 'technical damages' are in the original. Blowing up damaged vehicles to prevent their capture was one thing, but destroying perfectly good trucks and tractors because they were out of fuel, or bogged down, or worse abandoning them to the enemy intact, was not acceptable to higher headquarters.
216. KTB XXXXI Corps, October 20th, 1000 hrs; KTB 36 MotzD, October 20th, 0515, 0700, 0945, 1030, 1600, 1930, 1940 hrs.
217. *Na Pravom Flange,* N.B. Ivushkin, *Za Kazhdy Dom.*
218. *OG Severo-Zapadnogo fronta; general-leitenant Vatutin, 20 Oktyabr, 1941* ('Military Orders, Operational Group Northwestern Front; Lieutenant General Vatutin, October 20th, 1941'), TsAMO, F. 221, op. 1351, D. 21, from website: http://podvignaroda.mil.ru/.
219. Zolotarev, Document 83, 'Orders from the Commander of Forces of Kalinin Front to the Commanders of 29th, 31st, 30th and 22nd Armies on Preparations of Forces for the Attack and Destruction of the Kalinin Group of the Enemy.' Reference: TsAMO, F. 213, op. 2002, D. 5, ll. 40–1 Podlinnik.

220. *Spravka o sostoyanii soedinenii 29 armii* ('Report on the composition of units of 29th Army'), TsAMO, F. 208, op. 2511, D. 106.
221. Zolotarev, Document 83.
222. Anlagen IVb, XXXXI AK Tagesmeldung, October 20th; KTB PzGp 3, October 20th, 1430 hrs.
223. XXXXI AK Tagesmeldung, October 20th.
224. KTB PzGp 3, October 20th, 1130, 1730 hrs.
225. KTB PzGp 3, October 20th, 2300 hrs.
226. KTB 36 MotzD, October 21st, 0730, 0945, 1030, 1400, 1645, 1730 hrs.
227. Kalinin Front Operational Summary, October 21st, 2000 hrs. Hereafter cited as KFOS.
228. KFOS, 1430 hrs.
229. Anlagen IVb, XXXXI AK Tagesmeldung, October 22nd.
230. This regiment was part of the meager reinforcements Moscow dispatched to the Kalinin battle. It is referred to both as a Separate regiment and a Special regiment. It is never spelled out what sort of unit this was but in the chaotic days of October, 1941, it seems to have been formed from troops culled from military administration units in the Moscow area. It contained approximately 400 'bayonets' and few if any heavy weapons.
231. KTB PzGp 3, October 21st, 1100 hrs.
232. KTB 1 PzD, October 21st, 1715 hrs; KTB PzGp 3, October 21st, 1100, 1230, 1930 hrs.
233. KFOS, October 21st, 2000 hrs; *Kalinin Front Operational Journal*, October 21st, no hour listed (hereafter cited as KFOJ). Vypusk 7, p. 24, also quotes Konev's orders as directing the 29th Army to regroup south during the night of October 20/21, but all of the conflicting directives cited in KFOS and KFOJ say that the march south was to take place during the night of October 21/22, with the attack time set for 1100 hrs on October 22nd.
234. KFOJ, October 21st.
235. The bridge at Staritsa remains one of the mysteries of the battle. Stoves (p. 114) reports the bridge as having been demolished by the Soviets before the Germans took Staritsa, while the records of XXXXI Corps report it as having been captured, its capacity estimated one day at 6 tons and the next as 16, when it was identified as an 'expedient' bridge built by the enemy. A report from Western Front to the *Stavka* also confirms the bridge's capture, attributing it to German paratroopers and later in the same document to reconnaissance troops. Subsequently there are numerous references in the KTB XXXXI Corps and its Anlagen to different engineer units being ordered to repair and strengthen the bridge, or to stop doing so. Nonetheless, when 6th Infantry Division is ordered to cross the Volga from east to west, it does so not at the Staritsa bridge, but by crossing on assault boats and rafts, and it takes some time to get the whole division across in this manner. It

seems likely that the rise in the river on October 17th that washed away the Soviet assault bridges at Brody-Akishevo did substantial damage to the bridge at Staritsa, and it was not yet in service by October 20th.

236. Vypusk 7, p. 22.

237. KTB XXXXI Corps, October 21st, 2000 hrs.

238. KTB 1 PzD, October 21st, 1745 hrs; KTB 36 MotzD, October 21st, 1015, 1400 hrs.

239. *Na Pravom Flange*, M.N. Rozov, *V Polkakh Ostavalosi Po 150 Shtikov*.

240. Vypusk 7, p. 24. Afanasiev et al, *Dorogami Isp'tanii I pobed* (p. 14) has a different take on the organization of 31st Army. It gives the army on October 17th, 119th and 133rd Rifle Divisions and 8th Tank Brigade, and on October 19th, 183rd Rifle Division, 46th and 54th Cavalry Divisions and Separate Motorized Rifle Brigade were added, and 133rd Rifle Division was pulled back into Front reserve. On October 21st 133rd Division was reassigned to the army, and 252nd Rifle Division was added.

241. Vypusk 7, p. 28. It also, more believably, claimed a hundred *Luftwaffe* sorties per day supporting 9th Army.

242. Ibid.

243. KFOJ, October 22nd, p. 9; *Na Pravom Flange*, M.N. Rozov, *V Polkakh Ostavalosi Po 150 Shtikov*.

244. KFOS, October 22nd, points 3 and 7.

245. KTB 1 PzD Qu, October 22nd; KTB 36 MotzD, October 22nd, 0630 hrs; KTB PzGp 3, October 22nd, 1020 hrs; *Na Pravom Flange*, M.N. Rozov, *V Polkakh Ostavalosi Po 150 Shtikov*.

246. KTB PzGp 3, October 22nd, 1630 hrs.

247. KTB 1 PzD IIa, October 22nd. The motorcycle battalion, *K.1*, seems to have been especially hard hit. One company is reported to not only have lost all its motorcycles, but also its clothing, replacements for the latter being found in Kalinin. This suggests something more serious than having their machines stuck in the mud, more like the result of having to swim across the Volga to escape the pocket.

248. KTB 36 MotzD, October 22nd, 0730 hrs.

249. KTB XXXXI Corps October 22nd, 0800, 1300, 1600 hrs; Anlagen IVb, XXXXI AK Tagesmeldung, October 22nd.

250. Vypusk 7, p. 25; *Na Pravom Flange*, M.N. Rozov, *V Polkakh Ostavalosi Po 150 Shtikov*.

251. KTB XXXXI Corps, October 22nd, 1700 hrs.

252. KTB PzGp 3, October 23rd, 0655 hrs.

253. 'Military Composition of Forces of Northwestern Front on 12.10.1941', from Staff of Northwestern Front: Captain Zubtsov, TsAMO, F. 221, op. 1351, D. 177, from website: podvignaroda.mil.ru

254. Lubyanka.

255. KFOJ, October 23rd (quoting from Military Orders # 3, dated 23.10.41). The very size of 185th Rifle Division may have been a hint to why it seemed to have so little influence on the battle. There were very few Soviet divisions in the front line with anything approaching their full authorized *shtat* (TO&E). Most of those were divisions from the Far East, where they had been maintained at full pre-war strength to ward off any potential Japanese offensive. But this was not the case of Vindushev's division. It entered the war as a mechanized division with 90% of its required manpower, but no tanks and nearly no trucks. Its infantrymen had had no time for individual or unit training when the war started. After fighting at Daugavpils, the division was pulled out of the front, converted to a rifle division with the addition of a reserve regiment, and then committed as part of Vatutin's operational group to the battle for Kalinin. It is highly probable that the division, though huge, was completely inexperienced and untrained. This may explain why it had far less impact on the battle than some divisions with a fifth of its numbers.

256. Lubyanka. In addition, 20th Reserve Regiment, with '400 bayonets', was covering the causeways over the Moscow Sea and with four platoons was protecting communications between 5th Rifle Division and 30th Army HQ.

257. KTB PzGp 3, October 23rd, 1030, 1230 hrs. When the attack finally came, it would be mid–November, and involved a strike to the southeast, towards Klin and Moscow, below the Moscow Sea.

258. BC/RS, p. 234; KTB 36 MotzD, October 23rd, 1600 hrs. In German, 'Weise the Butcher' becomes '*Weiss der Fleischer*', a play on the commander's name as well as a comment on his command style. The shelling of the airfield continued through the end of the month. The shortage of heavy artillery ammunition made the Germans rely on the *schlachtflieger* and Stukas to conduct counterbattery efforts. The duel became rather one-sided, and on October 29th Weiss's fliers lost seventeen aircraft to artillery fire while sitting on the ground. The next day was as bad, as eight Bf-109s of II./JG 52 were destroyed on the ground by artillery. That did it for the *Luftwaffe* command, who ordered the field evacuated. The evacuation of the ground crews, who had previously been involved in fighting off ground attacks, was done by very nervous Ju-52 pilots, who abandoned much equipment in their hurry to get off the ground. Several of the transports were damaged, and one suffered a direct hit and was burned out. Forward basing has its disadvantages.

259. *Na Pravom Flange*, N.B. Ivushkin, *Za Kazhdy Dom*.

260. KTB 36 MotzD, October 23rd (no time listed), states that the ammunition was better, but still tight. 80 tons was reported en route but 'stuck in the mud.' It was also noted in the same sentence that the 'Russian bridgehead south of the city' (119th and 246th Rifle Divisions) had the road blocked anyway, and the ammunition could not get through.

261. KTB PzGp 3, October 23rd; KTB XXXXI Corps, October 23rd, 1500 hrs.
262. *Na Pravom Flange*, M.N. Rozov, *V Polkakh Ostavalosi Po 150 Shtikov*. According to the daily report of XXXXI Corps for October 23rd, part of 129th Infantry Division and 336th Regiment of 161st Infantry Division attacked the enemy northeast of Kasanskoye and 'destroyed him.' Kasanskoye has not been found on any map in the author's possession, but is in the area of Krasnovo. Given the events of the next day, the authenticity of this report is somewhat dubious.
263. KTB PzGp 3, October 23rd, 1030 hrs.
264. KTB PzGp 3, October 23rd, 1635 hrs; KTB 1 PzD IIa, October 23rd.
265. KFOS, October 23rd, 0800 hrs.
266. Ibid.
267. Anlagen IVb, XXXXI AK Tagesmeldung, October 24th; KTB PzGp 3, October 24th, 1650 hrs.
268. *Neizvestnaya Bitva v Nebe Moskva 1941-1942 – Oboronitelnyi Period* ('Unknown Battles in the Skies of Moscow 1941–1942 – The Defensive Period'), Moscow, Izdat Tekhnika-Molodezhy, 1999.
269. KTB 1 PzD IIa, October 24th.
270. KTB 36 MotzD, October 24th, 1300, 1700 hrs; PzGp 3 Anlagen zum KTB 'Tagesmeldung' Ia, 2400 hrs. Based on POW statements, XXXXI Corps expected a coordinated night attack from the north, east and west on Kalinin. It never materialized.
271. *Na Pravom Flange*, N.B. Ivushkin, *Za Kazhdy Dom*; KFOS # 9, October 25th, 3, 4. Kalinin Front reports that all of the attacks on the city were stopped by 'strong enemy defenses, artillery, and air support.' Note that the Operational Summaries of Kalinin Front were one or two days behind in reporting events. Thus summaries # 9, issued at 0800 hrs, and # 10, issued at 2000 hrs, on October 25th reported on events of the previous day.
272. *Opersvodka na 20:00 24.10.1941 g.* ('Operational Summary at 2000 hrs, October 25th, 1941'), paragraph 5 by Staff of Kalinin Front, Colonel General Konev, from website: http://podvignaroda.mil.ru/
273. *Na Provom Flange*, M.N. Rozov, *V Polkakh Ostavalosi Po 150 Shtikov*; KTB 1 PzD, October 24th, 1150 hrs.
274. KTB XXXXI Corps, October 24th, 0800 hrs; Anlagen IVb, XXXXI AK Tagesmeldung, October 24th.
275. *Na Pravom Flange*, M.N. Rozov, *V Polkakh Ostavalosi Po 150 Shtikov*.
276. Anlagen IVb, XXXXI AK Tagesmeldung, October 24th.
277. Vypusk 7, pp. 26–8.
278. KFOS # 10, October 25th, 2000 hrs.
279. KTB XXXXI Corps, October 24th, 1000 hrs.
280. Anlagen IVb, XXXXI AK, October 24th, 'Report of Meeting with 3rd Panzer Group.'

281. Ibid; KTB PzGp 3, October 24th, 1030 hrs.
282. Ibid, both.
283. Lubyanka.
284. Anlagen IVb, XXXXI AK, October 24th.
285. Zolotarev, Document 120: 'Report of the Commander of Forces of Kalinin Front to the Chief of Staff of the Red Army on the Course of the Battles in the region of Kalinin with the Kalinin group of the enemy,' October 26th, 1941, 1830 hrs.
286. KTB PzGp 3, October 25th, 1530 hrs.
287. KTB Nord, entries for October 2nd–6th.
288. Zolotarev, Document 120: 'Report of the Commander of Forces of Kalinin Front to the Chief of Staff of the Red Army on the Course of the Battles in the region of Kalinin with the Kalinin group of the enemy,' October 26th, 1941, 1830 hrs.
289. *Na Pravom Flange*, M.N. Rozov, *V Polkakh Ostavalosi Po 150 Shtikov*.
290. Ibid.
291. This includes everything in Kalinin, including units facing 29th and 31st Armies. Actually *facing* 30th Army were about a regiment of the weak 129th Infantry Division and the motorcycle battalion of 6th Panzer Division – four battalions and 101st Panzer Battalion (Flame) and about a regiment of artillery.
292. Khomenko; also *Na Pravom Flange*, N.B. Ivushkin, *Za Kazhdy Dom*, indicates that 256th Rifle Division went over to the defensive by October 24/25 after managing to seize a few buildings at the northeast edge of the city. The division then worked hard installing barbed wire and minefields to cover the complex of trenches and bunkers that they dug on the edge of the city; see also Fes'kov, Kalashnikov & Golikov, p. 254.
293. Zolotarev, Document 120: 'Report of the Commander of Forces of Kalinin Front to the Chief of Staff of the Red Army on the Course of the Battles in the region of Kalinin with the Kalinin group of the enemy,' October 26th, 1941, 1830 hrs.
294. Anishchenkov, P.S. and Shurinov, V.E., *Tret'ya Vozdushnaya* (Third Air) (Voenizdat, Moscow, 1984), pp. 4 and 5. These units became active on October 27th, and between then and the end of the month the fighters flew forty-eight fighter missions, twenty-one ground-attack missions, and three bombing missions. They had twenty-four air battles with German aircraft during this period. The bombers flew eighteen missions; twelve of them ground-attack missions and six reconnaissance missions. On November 15th the Front was reinforced with 5th Fighter Regiment of twenty LaGG-3s and 569th Assault Regiment with twenty Il-2 *Shturmoviks*.
295. Jentz, *Panzer Truppen*, p. 211; Newton, Steven, *Hitler's Commander: Field*

Marshal Walther Model: Hitler's Favorite General, New York: Da Capo Press, 2005, p. 152.

296. Anlagen IVb, XXXXI AK Tagesmeldung, November 4th.
297. KTB 1 PzD, October 31st, 1941. The total lack of 7.5cm infantry guns or light antitank guns in the battalion heavy weapons companies is striking, as is the dramatic reduction in the strength of the division. The extra 8.8cm antiaircraft guns and 10.5cm cannon are also curious. It is not explained in the documents but it seems likely that the former were temporarily attached from one of the *Flak* battalions in Kalinin, and the latter might have been from 611th Artillery Battalion. This battalion only reported the loss of one gun during the raid of 21st Tank Brigade on October 17th, but it is conceivable that more guns were lost, and the leftovers were attached to 1st Panzer Division.
298. Stoves, R., *Die Gepanzerten und Motorisierten Deutschen Grossverbaende 1935–1945*, Friedberg, FRG: Podzun-Pallas Verlag, 1986, pp. 11–15.
299. Anlagen IVb, XXXXI AK Tagesmeldung, November 2nd.
300. KTB PzGp 3, October 29th, report from XXXXI Corps to Panzer Group.
301. *Zhurnal boev'kh deistvii Kalininskogo fronta 10.1941 g* ('Journal of Military Activities of Kalinin Front, October, 1941'), pp. 22–3.
302. Seaton, pp. 106–7; Ziemke, E. and Bauer, M. *Moscow to Stalingrad*, New York: Military Heritage Press, 1988, pp. 37, 40; Haupt, pp. 106–7; Kurowski, Franz, *Panzergrenadier Aces*, Mechanicsburg: Stackpole Books, 2010), pp. 99–100. Both Haupt and Kurowski give some attention to the fighting in Kalinin, and the blow to morale caused by the death of Major Eckinger, without ever discussing the reason for his being at Mednoye, nor the plight of 1st Panzer Division.
303. Newton, *German Battle Tactics on the Eastern Front, 1941–1945*, p. 88; Stoves, p. 114; von Luck, Hans, *Panzer Commander*, New York: Dell Publishing, 1989, pp. 75–6.
304. Private correspondence with Colonel David Glantz, February 22nd, 2010.
305. Zolotarev, Document 5: 'Directive from Commander of Army Group Center on the Offensive' (# 1620/41, dated October 26th, 1941). Reference: TsAMO, F. 500, op. 12462, D. 114, ll. 55–8.
306. Ziemke and Bauer, *Moscow to Stalingrad*, pp. 146–9.
307. Everyone talks about the weather . . . In the KTB of XXXXI Corps there are daily reports on the weather, but usually limited to two words – 'Cold, cloudy.' Panzer Group 3's KTB also has daily comments which tend to be longer, but not infrequently differ from those of XXXXI Corps, despite the fact that the two headquarters were not more than 15–20 km apart. 6th Panzer Division's KTB lists the temperature, sometimes for both day and night, as well as brief weather commentary. 1st Panzer Division only rarely mentioned the weather in its records, 36th Motorized Division never did.

Soviet comments on the weather can be found in a few of the Kalinin Front reports, and in some of the memoir literature there are comments on the weather. From these it is possible to get a general picture as follows: from October 9th through 14th it was cold, from –8° to 1° C. Everyone agrees there was a lot of snow on October 15th, and it was still cold the next day. After that the reports are less in agreement, but the 17th was warmer, with road conditions deteriorating, it got cold again on October 18th, then on the 19th through the 21st it rained, clearing up some on the 21st. The 22nd through 25th saw warm weather, with possibly some rain, but also some improvement in the roads, only to have the rain return on the 26th. After this the roads were pretty impassable. All in all the roads were useable to some degree on all but the 19th–23rd, four days out of fourteen.

308. KTB 10 Panzer Division, NARA Microfilm roll T315/566, October 19th; KTB SS Das Reich, NARA Microfilm roll T354/121, October 19th.

309. It remains one of the mysteries of the battle why it took so long for 10th Army HQ to reach the battlefield to provide Konev with an actual headquarters apparatus, and particularly why 31st Army HQ, already in the area, was not used for this purpose.

310. One of the most widely publicized and heroic efforts in the defense of Moscow was conducted by General Panfilov's 316th Rifle Division, freshly raised in Kazakhstan. A third of the officers and soldiers of the division, and its commander, were Kazakhs, who can hardly be described as Russian nationalists. There was a sense, however, that Moscow was the capital of *their* country, and that they would do whatever they had to keep the Germans from taking it.

311. Roger R. Reese, *Why Stalin's Soldiers Fought: the Red Army's Military Effectiveness in World War II*, Lawrence, KS: University Press of Kansas, 2011, pp. 135, 307. While the formulaic repetition by Soviet authors that the Communist Party was the architect of victory, and that the widespread support for all aspects of Soviet socialism was the primary motivator of the Red Army, is not credible, to dismiss this as not being part of the picture, and to argue that the Red Army only fought for fear of a bullet in the back or for love of 'Holy Mother Russia' is to defy logic. An army so opposed to its own government and social system as some writers, including German memoirists, Western Cold Warriors, and some Russian accounts would have us believe, has never in history stood up to the repeated severe shocks that the German armed forces administered to the USSR in 1941. It has never happened, and if knee-jerk anti-Communism is discarded, it is not hard to see why this is so.

312. Most of the pre-war divisions lost their howitzer regiments and reconnaissance battalions during the summer and fall of 1941. Divisions that retained all their artillery, antitank, reconnaissance and other units, like the full

strength 32nd and 78th Rifle Divisions from the Far East, came as a rude shock to the Germans in October. For the specific dates when most divisions lost their howitzer regiments and other sub-units, see Grylev et al. *Perechen' No. 5: o vvedenii v deistvie polozheniya o poryadke otneseniya ob'edineniya, soedinenii, chastei, korablei, uchrezhdenii i zavedenii sovetskikh vooruzhennykh sil k sostavu deistvuyushchei armii v gody velikoi otchestvennoi voiny 1941–1945 gg.* ('List # 5: Introduction to the active positions and order of reference of elements of the sub-units, units, formations, vessels, establishments and institutions of the Soviet armed forces in the composition of the active army during the Great Patriotic War 1941–1945'), Moscow: Voennoe Izdatdel'stvo Ministertva Oborony Soiuza SSR, 1970 (*General Staff document formerly classified SECRET*).

Bibliography

Abbreviations

NARA – National Archives and Records Administration (US). In all cases used here, specifically the facility in College Park, MD that houses the captured German Records collection

TsAMO – Central Archives of the Ministry of Defense (Russian Federation)

Primary Sources

German

Listed in order from army group to army or panzer group, corps and division numerically within each level of command.

'HGp Mitte [Army Group Center], KTB, Anlagen und Tagesmeldungen' [Appendices and Daily Reports to the War Diary] 26974/17, NARA Roll T311/289

'HGp Nord [Army Group North], Ia, Kriegstagebuch Nr. 4' [Operations Officer War Diary # 4] 22927, NARA Roll T311/53

'Pz Gr 3, Ia Kriegstagebuch Pz AOK 3, 1 Sep–31 Oct 41' [Panzer Group 3 Operations Officer War Diary for 1 Sep to 31 Oct 1941] 15415/35, NARA Roll T313/23

'Anlagen zum Kriegstagebuch, "Tagesmeldungen" Pz Gr 3, Ia, 1 Sep–31 Oct 1941' [Appendices and Daily Reports to the Operational War Diary of Panzer Group 3, 1 Sep to 31 Oct 1941] Pz AOK 3, 15415/39 NARA Roll T313/23

'Ia, Kriegstagebuch XXXXI Korps' [Operational War Diary of XXXXI Corps] 18741/1, NARA Roll T314/979

'Anlagenband IVa zum Kriegstagebuch' XXXXI Korps [Appendices Volume IVa to War Diary of XXXXI Corps] Oct 2–9, 1941, 18741/9, NARA Roll T314/980

'Anlagenband IVb zum Kriegstagebuch,' XXXXI Korps [Appendices Volume IVa to War Diary of XXXXI Corps] Oct 15–Nov 20, 1941, 18741/10, NARA Roll T314/980

'Ia, Kriegstagebuch 7 20 Sep 1941–12 Apr 1942 1 Pz Div' [Operations Officer War Diary Number 7 for 1st Panzer Division covering 20 Sep 1941 to 12 Apr 1942] 1. Pz Div 24293/1. NARA Roll T315/26

'Ia, Anlagen A zum Kriegstagebuch 7. Kriegsgliederung der unterst. Verbande' [Operations Appendix A to War Diary # 7, Combat Organization of Subordinate Units] 1. Pz Div 22022/3, NARA Roll T315/22

'IIa, Tatigskeitsbericht zum Kriegstagebuch 7, 1 Pz Div 20 Sep 1941–5 Apr 1942' [Personnel Staff Officer Progress Report to War Diary # 7, 1st Panzer Division 20 Sep 41–5 Apr 42] 1. Pz Div 22022/2 NARA Roll T315/22

'Ia, Kriegstagebuch 16 Sep–30 Nov 1941 6 Pz Div' [Operations Officer War Diary for 6th Panzer Division covering 16 Sep–30 Nov 1941] 6. Pz Div 25448/3. NARA Roll T315/323

'Ia, Kriegstagebuch No. 2, 36th Inf Div (Mot), 22 Sep–5 Dec 41 36th Inf Div (Mot)' [Operations Officer War Diary # 2 for 36th Motorized Infantry Division (covering) 22 Sep–5 Dec 1941] 22768/4, NARA Roll T315/898

Bock, Fedor von. *Ya stoyal u vorot Moskvy* ('I stood at the gates of Moscow'), Russian translation of *Zwischen Pflicht und Verweigerung: das Kriegstagebuch* ('Between Duty and Refusal: The War Diary'), Moscow: Yauza, Eksmo, 2006 (original German: Munich, Berlin: Herbig, 1995)

Stoves, Rolf O.G. *1. Panzer Division 1935–1945: Chronik einer der drei Stamm-Divisonen der deutschen Panzerwaffe* ('1st Panzer Division: A Chronicle of one of the three original divisions of the German armored forces'), Bad Nauheim, FRG Verlag Hans-Henning Podzun. [This was written by a veteran officer of 1st Panzer Division, and is as close to an 'official history' of the division as has been published anywhere]

Stoves, Rolf O.G. *1. Panzer Division 1935–1945: Aufstellung, Bewaffnung, Einsätze, Männer* ('1st Panzer Division 1935–1945: Founding, Arming, Missions, Personnel'), Dörfler, Zeitgeschichte. [This is a short and picture-heavy version of the previous book, including partial English translation of the German]

Trevor-Roper, H.R. *Blitzkrieg to Defeat: Hitler's War Directives 1939–1945*, New York: Holt, Rinehart & Winston, 1964. [Translated copies, with commentary, of all of Hitler's Directives during the war]

Soviet (Russian)

(no author listed) *Lubyanka v dni bitvy za Moskva* ('The Lubyanka in the Days of the Battle of Moscow'), Moscow: Belfry, 2002. [Contains declassified documents regarding the Internal Security forces in the Battle of Moscow, including the NKVD-based Red Army units in 29th, 30th and 31st Armies]

Boevoi sostav Sovetskoi armii, chast' 1 (iiun'–dekabr' 1941 goda) ('The combat composition of the Soviet Army, part 1 (June–December 1941)'), Moscow: Voenno-istoricheskii otdel', Voenno-nauchnoe Upravlenie General'nogo Shtaba (Military-Historical Department, Military-Scientific Directorate of the General Staff), 1963. [A complete listing of all the combat units in the Red Army at the first of every month throughout the war, with controlling headquarters. Absolutely indispensable source for reconstructing basic Soviet orders of battle]

Grylev et al. *Perechen' No. 5: o vvedenii v deistvie polozheniya o poryadke otneseniya ob'edineniya, soedinenii, chastei, korablei, uchrezhdenii i zavedenii sovetskikh vooruzhennykh sil k sostavu deistvuyushchei armii v gody velikoi otchestvennoi voiny 1941–1945 gg.* ('List # 5: Introduction to the active positions and order of reference of elements of the sub-units, units, formations, vessels, establishments and institutions of the Soviet armed forces in the composition of the active army during the Great Patriotic War 1941–1945'), Moscow: Voennoe Izdatdel'stvo Ministertva Oborony Soiuza SSR, 1970. [General Staff document formerly classified SECRET]

Kommandovanie Korpusnogo i Divizionogo zvena Sovetskikh Vooruzhennykh Sil perioda velikoi otechestvennoi voiny ('Commanders of Corps and Division Units in the Soviet Armed Forces during the period of the Great Patriotic War'), Moscow: Izdat. Military Academy M.V. Frunze, 1964

Pokrovskii et al. *Perechen' No. 7: Upravlenii brigad vsekh rodov voisk vkhodivshikh v sostav desitvuyushchei armii v gody velikoi otechestvennoi voiny 1941–1945 gg.* ('List # 7: HQ of brigades of all branches of forces in the active army during the period of the Great Patriotic War 1941–1945'), Moscow: Voennoe Izdatdel'stvo Ministertva Oborony Soiuza SSR, 1956. [General Staff document originally classified SECRET]

Pokrovskii et al. *Perechen' No. 14: Tankovykh, Samokhodno-Artilleriiskikh I mototsikletniykh polkov, vkhodivshikh v sostav desitvuyushchei armii v gody velikoi otechestvennoi voiny 1941–1945 gg.* ('List No. 14: Tank, Self-Propelled Artillery, and Motorcycle Regiments in the composition of the forces of the active army during the Great Patriotic War 1941–1945], Moscow: Voennoe Izdatdel'stvo Ministertva Oborony Soiuza SSR, 1960. [General Staff document originally classified SECRET]

Sbornik voenno-istoricheskikh materialov Velikoi Otechestvennoi voiny, vypusk 7 ('Collection of military-historical materials of the Great Patriotic War, issue 7'), Moscow: Voennoe Izdatdel'stvo Ministertva Oborony Soiuza SSR, 1952. [Contains documents on the Battle of Moscow, including captured German directives and orders]

Zolotarev, V.A. (ed.) *Russkii Arkhiv: Velikaia Otechestvennaia T.15 (4/1) (Moskovskoi bitve)* ('Russian Archives: Great Patriotic (War): Volume 15 (4/1), the Battle of Moscow'), Moscow: TERRA, 1997. [Contains copies of Front and Army directives and orders throughout the Battle of Moscow, including the documents establishing Kalinin Front]

Secondary Sources

Books

(no author listed) *Neizvestnaya Bitva v Nebe Moskva 1941–1942 – Oboronitelnyi Period* ('Unknown Battles in the Skies of Moscow 1941–1942 – The Defensive Period'), Moscow: Izdat Tekhnika-Molodezhy, 1999

Collective authors. *Vnutrennie Voiska n Velikoi Otechestvennoi Voinie 1941–45 gg.* ('Internal Troops in the Great Patriotic War 1941–45'), Moscow: Yurizdat, 1975. [Collected documents on the forces of the NKVD and Border Guards throughout the war]

Afanasiev, N.I. et al. *Dorogami Ispytanii I Pobed* ('Roads of Trials and Triumph: History of 31st Army'), Moscow: Voennoe Izdatdel'stvo Ministertva Oborony Soiuza SSR, 1986

Anishchenkov, P.S. and V.E. Shurinov. *Tret'ya Vozdushnaya* ('Third Air'), Moscow: Voennoe Izdatdel'stvo Ministertva Oborony Soiuza SSR, 1984

Armstrong, Richard N., *Red Army Tank Commanders, The Armored Guards*, Atglen, PA: Schiffer Military/Aviation History, 1994

Baryatinskii, Mikhail. *Sovietskie Tankov'e Asy* ('Soviet Tank Aces'), Moscow: Yauza Eksmo, 2008

Bergstrom, Christer, and Migalovo, Andrey. *Black Cross/Red Star, Air War on the Eastern Front, Volume I, Operation Barbarossa, 1941*, Pacifica, CA: Pacifica Military History, 2000

Bergstrom, Christer. *Barbarossa – The Air Battle July–December, 1941*, Hersham, UK: Ian Allen Publishing, 2007. [More detailed than Bergstrom and Migalovo's first volume, making great use of German and Soviet pilot and unit reports to 'unravel' the results of the air battles]

Erickson, John. *The Road to Stalingrad*, New York: Harper & Row, 1975

Fes'kov, V.I., Kalashnikov, K.A. and Golikov, V.I. *Krasnaya Armiya v pobedakh I porazheniyakh 1941–1945 gg.* ('The Red Army in Victory and Defeat 1941–1945'), Tomsk: Izdatel'stvo Tomskogo Universiteta, 2003

Glantz, David M. *The Battle for Leningrad, 1941–1944*, Lawrence, KS: University Press of Kansas, 2002

—— *The Initial Period of War on the Eastern Front*, London: Frank Cass, 1991

Gunston, Bill. *Aircraft of the Soviet Union*, London: Osprey, 1983

—— *The Osprey Encyclopedia of Russian Aircraft*, London: Osprey, 1995. [Gunston's two encyclopedia-sized books are invaluable as one-stop references on the Soviet aircraft of World War Two, especially rare and relatively obscure types like the Yer-2 used over Kalinin]

Haupt, Werner. *Die Schlachten der Heeresgruppe Mitte 1941–1944: Aus der Sicht der Divisionen* ('The Battles of Army Group Center 1941–1944: from the view of the divisions'), Friedberg, FRG: Podzun-Pallas-Verlag, 1983. [Includes the basic German account of the taking of Kalinin compiled from the divisional and personal records of the participants on the German side]

Jentz, Thomas L. *Panzer Truppen: The Complete Guide to the Creation & Employment of Germany's Tank Force, 1933–1942,* Volume 1, Atglen, PA: Schiffer Military History, 1996

Kolomiets, Maksim. *Tanki v bitve za Moskvu* ('Tanks in the Battle of Moscow'), Moscow: Eksmo, 2009. [Covers the Soviet tank and motorized brigades and divisions from the beginning of 'Typhoon' through the beginning of the Moscow Counteroffensive in December, 1941]

—— *T-34. Pervaia polnaia Entsiklopediia* ('T-34. First Complete Encyclopedia'), Moscow: Eksmo, 2009. [Includes the record of the building and fielding of the T-34-57 tanks which were unique to 21st Tank Brigade at Kalinin]

Kornyukhin, G.V. *Vozdushchnaya Voina nad SSSR 1941* ('Air Battles over the USSR 1941'), Moscow: Veche, 2008

Kurowski, Franz, *Panzergrenadier Aces,* Mechanicsburg: Stackpole Books, 2010. [Discusses Lt. Feig, of Eckinger's group, who captured the Gorbatov Bridge and was subsequently wounded and evacuated over the Volga at Cherkasovo]

Lopukhovsky, Lev. *Viazemskaia katastrofe 41–go goda* ('The Vyazma tragedy of 1941'), Moscow: Iauza Eksmo, 2006

Maistrovsky, M. Ya. (ed.) *Na pravom flange Moskovskoye bitvy* ('On the Right Flank of the Battle of Moscow'), Tver: Mosk. Rabochii, 1991. [A collection of memoirs and essays by Soviet/Russian participants in the fighting at Kalinin in 1941, from all levels from Konev down to individual civilians and soldiers]

Mitcham, Samuel W., and Mueller, Gene, *Hitler's Commanders, Officers of the Wehrmacht, the Luftwaffe, the Kriegsmarine and the Waffen SS,* New York: Cooper Square Publishers, 1992

Moshchanskii, I.V. *Ot Tragedii Vyaz'my do Pobedy pod Moskvoi* ('From the Vyazma Tragedy to the Victory at Moscow'), Moscow: Veche, 2008

Muriev, D.Z., *Proval Operatsii 'Taifun'* ('Defeat of Operation "Typhoon"'), Moscow: Voennoe Izdatel'stvo Ministertva Oborony Soiuza SSR, 1966

Newton, Steve (ed.) *German Battle Tactics on the Eastern Front, 1941–1945,* Atglen, PA: Schiffer Publishing Ltd, 1994. [Includes Rottinger's postwar account of the Kalinin battle from his perspective as XXXXI Corps' chief of staff]

—— *Hitler's Commander: Field Marshal Walther Model: Hitler's Favorite General,* New York: Da Capo Press, 2005

Piekalkiewicz, Janusz, *Moscow: 1941 The Frozen Offensive,* Novato, CA: Presidio, 1985

Reese, Roger R., *Why Stalin's Soldiers Fought: the Red Army's Military Effectiveness in World War II,* Lawrence, KS: University Press of Kansas, 2011

Rotmistrov, Pavel A. *Stal'naya gvardiya* ('Steel Guards'), Moscow: Voennoe Izdatel'stvo Ministertva Oborony Soiuza SSR, 1984

Seaton, Colonel Albert. *The Battle of Moscow*, New York: PEI paperback, 1980
——— *The Russo-German War 1941–45*, Novato, CA: Presidio, 1990
Sharp, Charles C. *The Soviet Order of Battle in WWII, Volume I 'The Deadly Beginning'* (The Tank, Mechanized, and Motorized Divisions and the Tank Brigades formed before 1942), West Chester, OH: George F. Nafziger, 1995
——— *The Soviet Order of Battle in WWII, Volume V 'Red Sabers'* (Soviet Cavalry Corps, Divisions, and Independent Brigades, 1941–45), West Chester, OH: George F. Nafziger, 1995
——— *The Soviet Order of Battle in WWII, Volume VIII 'Red Legions'* (Soviet Rifle Divisions formed before June, 1941), West Chester, OH: George F. Nafziger, 1995
——— *The Soviet Order of Battle in WWII, Volume IX 'Red Tide'* (Soviet Rifle Divisions formed from June to December, 1941), West Chester, OH: George F. Nafziger, 1995
Stoves, Rolf. *Die Gepanzerten und Motorisierten Deutschen Grossverbaende 1935–1945* (The Armored and Motorized German Large Formations 1935–1945), Friedberg, FRG: Podzun-Pallas Verlag, 1986
Ushakov, S.F. *Vo Imya Pobedy: Ocherki* ('For the Victory: Sketches'), Moscow: DOSAAF, 1987
Zhukov, G. *The Memoirs of Marshal Zhukov*, New York: Delacorte Press, 1971
Ziemke, E. and Bauer, M. *Moscow to Stalingrad*, New York: Military Heritage Press, 1988

Websites:

http://allaces.ru/
– A site full of accounts by and about military pilots from all nations in World War Two.

http://rkkaww2.armchairgeneral.com/
– This site is a wonderful place to start any research into the Soviet forces in the Great Patriotic War in English: aside from a great collection of extracted archive materials and maps, the forum is full of knowledgeable people to help find answers.

http://www.lexikon-der-wehrmacht.de/
– This site was our first checkpoint on German Army data: everything from unit organization and history to biographies of commanders, a great 'first stop' for the researcher interested in the Wehrmacht.

http://militaria.lib.ru/
– A marvelous library of military history, general history, and memoir material, both Russian and translated from other languages. Many of our references came from this site, and in other cases it was actually easier to simply open the book on this site than to dig it out of a personal library!

http://ilpilot.narod.ru/
– Another site full of information on the air forces during the war.
http://www.podvignaroda.mil.ru/
– This is the new 'Mother Lode' for researchers. The Russian Ministry of Defense, through this site, is making available literally thousands of documents from the Central Archives. This book could not have been written without the material now available from this site. Among other things, the Operational Summaries and Combat Journals of the Soviet units involved are here, as well as a host of the Orders, Directives, and Reports from the commands involved. Best of all, these are not transcriptions, but photocopies of the original documents, so that marginal notes and complete signature blocks are also visible – which sometimes reveal as much as the content of the document!
http://www.rkka.ru/
– Another excellent compilation of extracted archive material on the Red Army.
http://www.soldat.ru/
– A mixed collection of material, but it includes downloads of the *Perecheny* and the *Boevoi Sostav* – indispensable original sources for establishing unit histories and 'combat paths' of Soviet units during the war.
http://www.tankfront.ru/
– A mass of data on every armored or mechanized unit of almost every army in World War Two, complete with references to sources.
http://tashv.narod.ru/
– Includes downloads of the *Sborniks* ('Collections of Materials') compiled by the Soviet General Staff; another mass of original source material on Soviet operations.
http://www.wwii-photos-maps.com/
– Has copies of *Luftwaffe* aerial photos of the Kalinin area taken in September–October 1941, among a great deal of other material. A great source for making the maps 'come alive' with what the terrain actually looked like at the time of the battle.

Appendix 1

German Order of Battle

In the Kalinin Area, October 10th–24th, 1941

NOTE: *What follows is the formal 'Order of Battle' from the Wehrmacht-wide Returns of October 10th, 1941. However, the German Army normally fought in 'Kampfgruppen' (Battle Groups) tailored to the tactical situation. The most common Kampfgruppen in 1941 were built around Infantry Regiments or Reconnaissance Battalions in the Infantry Divisions, and the Schützen Regiments and Brigades or the Motorcycle Battalions and Reconnaissance Battalions in the Panzer Divisions. See the text for specifics of the actual combat organization, which could change almost daily and rarely reflected the precise 'paper' organization of the unit.*

This list excludes all signal, supply, survey, weather, decontamination, traffic, police, blocking, replacement, propaganda and observation units.

All German forces were under Army Group Center throughout the battle.

9th Army (Colonel General Adolf Strauss)
  847th Heavy Artillery Battalion (15cm howitzers)
  860th Heavy Artillery Battalion (only one battery of 21cm mortars)
  [NOTE: The German 21cm 'Morser' was in fact a slightly shorter-barreled howitzer]
  4th Battery, 55th Antiaircraft Battalion (3.7cm and 2cm light antiaircraft)
  7th, 145th, 210th Bridge Construction Battalions
  17th Senior Construction Staff
  34th , 42nd Construction Troops Commands
  18th, 22nd, 57th, 79th, 91st, 208th, 321st, 408th Construction Battalions
  532nd Road Construction Battalion
V Corps (General of the Infantry Richard Ruoff)
  5th Infantry Division (Major General Karl Allmendinger)
    14th, 56th, 75th Infantry Regiments
    5th Artillery Regiment
    I Bn, 41st Artillery Regiment (Heavy)
    5th Pioneer, Reconnaissance, Antitank, Signal Battalions
  35th Infantry Division (General of the Infantry Walter Fischer von Weikersthal)
    34th, 109th, 111th Infantry Regiments

35th Artillery Regiment
I Bn, 71st Artillery Regiment (Heavy)
35th Pioneer, Reconnaissance, Antitank Battalions
<u>106th Infantry Division</u> (General of the Infantry Ernst Dehner)
 239th, 240th, 241st Infantry Regiments
 107th Artillery Regiment
 106th Pioneer, Reconnaissance, Antitank Battalions
22nd, 136th Artillery Commands
627th Artillery Regimental Staff
842nd Light Artillery Regiment (10cm howitzers)
II Bn, 38th Artillery Regiment (15cm howitzers)
II Bn, 44th Artillery Regiment (15cm howitzers)
1st Nebelwerfer Regiment Staff
III, V *Nebelwerfer* Battalions (15cm *Nebelwerfer-41*)
Staff and 1st Company, 103rd Survey Battalion
Pioneer Regiment Staff for Special Purposes 'Behrisch'
745th, 754th Pioneer Battalions
54th Bridge Construction Battalion
2 Bridging Columns 'B'
154th, 214th Construction Battalions
<u>VI Corps</u> (General of Pioneers Otto-Wilhelm Förster)
 <u>26th Infantry Division</u> (Lieutenant General Walter Weiss)
  39th, 77th, 78th Infantry Regiments
  26th Artillery Regiment
  I Bn, 62nd Artillery Regiment (Heavy)
  26th Pioneer, Reconnaissance, Antitank Battalions
 <u>110th Infantry Division</u> (Lieutenant General Ernst Seifert)
  252nd, 254th, 255th Infantry Regiments
  120th Artillery Regiment
  110th Pioneer, Reconnaissance, Antitank Battalions
 126th Artillery Command
 677th Artillery Regiment Staff
 IV Bn, 109th Artillery Regiment (15cm howitzers)
 848th Heavy Artillery Battalion (15cm howitzers)
 6th/47th Antiaircraft Battalion (3.7cm, 2cm antiaircraft guns)
 517th Pioneer Regiment Staff
 632nd, 743rd Pioneer Battalions
 2 Bridging Columns 'B'
 135th, 320th Construction Battalions
<u>VIII Corps</u> (Colonel General Walter Heitz)
 <u>8th Infantry Division</u> (Major General Gustav Höhne)
  28th, 38th, 84th Infantry Regiments

8th Artillery Regiment
I Bn, 44th Artillery Regiment (Heavy)
8th Pioneer, Reconnaissance, Antitank, Signal Battalions
28th Infantry Division (Lieutenant General Johann Sinnhuber)
7th, 49th, 83rd Infantry Regiments
28th Artillery Regiment
I Bn, 64th Artillery Regiment (Heavy)
28th Pioneer, Reconnaissance, Antitank Battalions
87th Infantry Division (Lieutenant General Bogislav von Studnitz)
173rd, 185th, 187th Infantry Regiments
187th Artillery Regiment
187th Pioneer, Reconnaissance, Antitank Battalions
189th Assault Gun Battalion (StuG III assault guns)
561st Antitank Battalion (3.7cm guns)
5th/48th Antiaircraft Battalion (3.7cm, 2cm antiaircraft guns)
3rd/66th Antiaircraft Battalion (3.7cm, 2cm antiaircraft guns)
103rd, 130th, 145th Artillery Commands
613th Artillery Regiment Staff
II Bn, 55th Artillery Regiment (15cm howitzers)
II Bn, 57th Artillery Regiment (10cm cannon)
808th Heavy Artillery Battalion (21cm mortars)
III Bn, 213th Artillery Regiment (10cm howitzers)
517th Pioneer Regiment Staff
746th Pioneer Battalion
3 Bridging Columns 'B'
137th Construction Battalion
XXIII Corps (General of the Infantry Albrecht Schubert)
102nd Infantry Division (Lieutenant General John Ansat)
232nd, 233rd, 235th Infantry Regiments
104th Artillery Regiment
102nd Pioneer, Reconnaissance, Antitank Battalions
206th Infantry Division (Lieutenant General Hugo Höfl)
301st, 312th, 413th Infantry Regiments
206th Artillery Regiment
206th Pioneer, Reconnaissance, Antitank Battalions
251st Infantry Division (Lieutenant General Karl Burdach)
451st, 459th, 471st Infantry Regiments
251st Artillery Regiment
251st Pioneer, Reconnaissance, Antitank Battalions
256th Infantry Division (Lieutenant General Gerhard Kauffmann)
456th, 476th, 481st Infantry Regiments
256th Artillery Regiment

256th Pioneer, Reconnaissance, Antitank Battalions
184th Assault Gun Battalion
607th Antiaircraft Battalion (3.7cm, 2cm antiaircraft guns)
271st Army Antiaircraft Battalion (8.8cm antiaircraft guns)
18th and 122nd Artillery Commands
II Bn, 62nd Artillery Regiment (10cm cannon)
634th Heavy Artillery Battalion (10cm cannon)
II Bn, 39th Artillery Regiment (15cm howitzers)
816th Heavy Artillery Battalion (21cm mortars)
Pioneer Regiment Staff for Special Purpose von Burger
742nd Pioneer Battalion
2 Bridging Columns 'B'
2 Bridging Columns 'T'
104th Construction Command
44th, 123rd Construction Battalions
XXVII Corps (General of the Infantry Alfred Wäger)
  86th Infantry Division (General of the Infantry Joachim Witthöft)
    167th, 184th, 216th Infantry Regiments
    186th Artillery Regiment
    186th Pioneer, Reconnaissance, Antitank Battalions
  162nd Infantry Division (Lieutenant General Hermann Franke)
    303rd, 314th, 329th Infantry Regiments
    326th Artillery Regiment
    326th Pioneer, Reconnaissance, Antitank Battalions
  273rd Army Antiaircraft Battalion (3.7cm, 2cm antiaircraft guns)
  69th Artillery Regiment Staff
  859th Heavy Artillery Battalion (21cm mortars)
  161st Infantry Division (Lieutenant General Heinrich Recke)
    336th, 364th, 371st Infantry Regiments
    241st Artillery Regiment
    241st Pioneer, Reconnaissance, Antitank Battalions
  255th Infantry Division (General of the Infantry Wilhelm Wetzel)
    455th, 465th, 475th Infantry Regiments
    255th Artillery Regiment
    255th Pioneer, Reconnaissance, Antitank Battalions
  SS Cavalry Brigade (Standartenfuhrer Fegelein)
    1st, 2nd SS Cavalry Regiments
    SS Motorcycle-Reconnaissance Battalion (three squadrons)
    SS Artillery Regiment (two batteries)
    [NOTE: During October this brigade was being reinforced with:
    SS Pioneer Company
    SS Antiaircraft Battery]

Panzer Group 3 (Colonel General Georg-Hans Reinhardt)
[NOTE: Panzer Group 3 was under 9th Army HQ until October 13th, and after that date alternated between 9th Army and control by Army Group Center]
XXXXI Corps (Motorized) Lieutenant General Otto Ottenbacher until October 13th, then General of Panzer Troops Friedrich Kirchner. General of Panzer Troops Walter Model was supposed to take over the Corps, but he did not arrive until the end of October and according to some German documents did not actually take over until November 15th)
  1st Panzer Division (Lieutenant General Walter Krüger)
    1st Panzer Regiment (two battalions)
    1st *Schützen* Brigade
        1st, 113th *Schützen* Regiments (two battalions each)
        702nd Heavy Infantry Gun Company
        1st Motorcycle Battalion
      73rd Artillery Regiment (Motorized)
      4th Reconnaissance Battalion
      37th Pioneer, Antitank Battalions
  36th Infantry Division (Motorized) (Lieutenant General Hans Gollnick)
    87th, 118th Infantry Regiments (Motorized)
    36th Motorcycle Battalion
    36th Artillery Regiment (Motorized)
    36th Pioneer, Reconnaissance, Antitank Battalions
  900th *Lehr* Brigade (Colonel Walter Krause)
    900th Infantry Regiment (Motorized) (two battalions)
    900th Antitank, Artillery, Signal Battalions
    900th Pioneer Company
    901st Assault Gun Battery (6 StuG III)
  6th Infantry Division (Lieutenant General Helge Auleb)
    18th, 37th, 58th Infantry Regiments
    6th Artillery Regiment
    I Bn, 42nd Artillery Regiment
    6th Pioneer, Reconnaissance, Antitank Battalions
  101st Flamethrower Panzer Battalion *[attached to 1st Panzer Division]*
  600th Assault Gun Battalion Staff
  660th, 665th Assault Gun Batteries (StuG III assault guns)
  605th Antiaircraft Battalion (3.7cm, 2cm antiaircraft guns)
  I Bn, 46th Antiaircraft Battalion (3.7cm, 2cm antiaircraft guns)
  30th Artillery Command
  803rd Artillery Regiment Staff
  611th Heavy Artillery Battalion (10cm cannon)
  II Bn, 59th Artillery Regiment (15cm howitzers)
  620th Heavy Artillery Battalion (15cm cannon)

III Bn, 51st *Nebelwerfer* Regiment (15cm *Neberlwerfer-41*)
628th Pioneer Regiment Staff
52nd Pioneer Battalion
4 Bridging Columns 'B'
506th Light Bicycle Road Construction Battalion
LVI Corps (Motorized) (General of Panzer Troops Ferdinand Schaal)
  6th Panzer Division (Lieutenant General Franz Landgraf)
    11th Panzer Regiment (two battalions)
      65th Panzer Battalion (used as a third battalion by the Panzer Regiment)
    6th *Schützen* Brigade
      4th, 114th *Schützen* Regiments (two battalions each)
      6th Motorcycle Battalion
    76th Artillery Regiment (Motorized)
    57th Pioneer, Reconnaissance Battalions
    41st Antitank Battalion
  7th Panzer Division (General of Panzer Troops Hans Freiherr von Funck)
    25th Panzer Regiment (three battalions)
    7th *Schützen* Brigade
      6th, 7th *Schützen* Regiments (two battalions each)
      705th Heavy Infantry Gun Company
      7th Motorcycle Battalion
    78th Artillery Regiment (Motorized)
    37th Reconnaissance Battalion
    42nd Antitank Battalion
    58th Pioneer Battalion
  14th Infantry Division (Motorized) (Lieutenant General Friedrich Fürst)
    11th, 53rd Infantry Regiments (Motorized)
    54th Motorcycle Battalion
    14th Artillery Regiment (Motorized)
    14th Pioneer, Reconnaissance, Antitank Battalions
  129th Infantry Division (Lieutenant General Stephen Rittau)
    427th, 428th, 430th Infantry Regiments
    129th Artillery Regiment
    129th Pioneer, Reconnaissance, Antitank Battalions
  210th Assault Gun Battalion
  125th Artillery Command
  783rd Artillery Regiment Staff
  151st Artillery Battalion (10cm cannon)
  II Bn 51st Artillery Regiment (10cm cannon, 15cm howitzers)
  733rd Heavy Artillery Battalion (21cm mortars)
  51st *Nebelwerfer* Regiment (– III Bn) (15cm *Nebelwerfer-41*)
  643rd Antitank Battalion (self-propelled 4.7cm guns)

678th Pioneer Regiment Staff
630th Pioneer Battalion
218th Construction Battalion
3 Bridging Columns 'B'
10th Construction Troop Command
548th Bridge Construction Battalion
80th Construction Battalion
1/3 of 905th Assault Boat Command

Appendix 2

Soviet Order of Battle

In the Kalinin Area, October 10th–24th, 1941

NOTE: *At the beginning of October the Germans had broken through Western Front in several places with Panzer Groups 3 and 4, and by October 7th the Vyazma encirclement had been closed. On October 10 th, although still listed in the official order of battle, several Soviet Army HQs had virtually ceased to function or had completely lost touch with their units. Likewise, several large formations were out of contact with any higher HQ or in the process of being overrun by rapidly moving German motorized Kampfgruppen. Consequently, this OB has numerous notes and qualifications in it, because the usual 'chain of command' did not always apply in the situation in which the Soviet units found themselves.*

This list excludes all signal, medical, chemical defense, transport, bakery, veterinary, field post, state bank and ration transport units.

All Soviet forces were under Western Front on October 10th. On October 17th they came under Kalinin Front, an HQ formed from Western Front's 'Kalinin Group' and the HQ of 10th Army moved up from behind Southwestern Front.

22nd Army (Major General Vasily Aleksandrovich Yushkevich)

[NOTE: When Yushkevich took over 31st Army in late October, 22nd Army was temporarily commanded by the Deputy Army Commander, Major General Vladimir Ivanovich Vostrukhov]

<u>5th Rifle Division</u> (Colonel Anisim Illaryonovich Svetlyakov)

[NOTE: Actually at Chernizdor in the Moscow Military District. Just assigned to Western Front's 22nd Army on October 10th, but immediately thereafter assigned to the Front Reserves, put on trains, and deposited in Kalinin where it eventually came under 30th Army HQ]

142nd, 190th, 336th Rifle Regiments

27th Artillery Regiment

61st Antitank Battalion, 324th Antiaircraft Battalion

28th Reconnaissance Company

54th Sapper Battalion

<u>110th Rifle Division</u> (Colonel Stepan Trofimovich Gladyshev)

[NOTE: Formed from 4th Moscow Militia Division on September 26th; on October 10th reported a total strength of 6000 officers and men]

1287th, 1289th, 1291st Rifle Regiments
971st Artillery Regiment
200th Antitank Battalion, 695th Antiaircraft Battalion
470th Reconnaissance Company, 463rd Sapper Battalion
133rd Rifle Division (Major General Vasily Ivanovich Shvetsov)
[NOTE: Like 5th Rifle Division, the 133rd was first ordered south to rebuild Western Front before Moscow, but was diverted to reinforce Konev's 'Kalinin Group' and ended up detraining northeast of Kalinin. Fought directly under Kalinin Front command until assigned to 31st Army]
418th, 521st, 681st Rifle Regiments (1 battalion per regiment)
400th Artillery Regiment, 511th Howitzer Regiment
122nd Training Battalion, 249th Antitank Battalion
290th Antiaircraft Battalion, 169th Reconnaissance Battalion
269th Sapper Battalion
174th Rifle Division (Colonel Pavel Fedorovich Ilyinikh)
[NOTE: Assigned to 29th Army by October 12th]
494th, 508th, 628th Rifle Regiments
598th Light Artillery Regiment
179th Antitank Battalion, 453rd Antiaircraft Battalion
197th Reconnaissance Company
178th Sapper Battalion
179th Rifle Division (Brigade Commander Nikolai Ivanovich Konchits)
[NOTE: Originally formed as a 'Lithuanian National' Division in 1940]
215th, 234th, 259th Rifle Regiments
619th Artillery Regiment
13th Antitank Battalion, 137th Antiaircraft Battalion
505th Sapper Battalion
186th Rifle Division (Colonel Anton Petrovich Pilipenko)
[NOTE: On September 3rd reported only 2778 men and 38 vehicles left in the division]
238th, 290th, 298th Rifle Regiments
327th Artillery Regiment
227th Antitank Battalion, 264th Antiaircraft Battalion
107th Reconnaissance Company, 255th Sapper Battalion
249th Rifle Division (Major General German Fedorovich Tarasov)
917th, 921st, 925th Rifle Regiments
792nd Artillery Regiment
307th Antitank Battalion, 526th Antiaircraft Battalion
328th Reconnaissance Company, 417th Sapper Battalion
256th Rifle Division (Major General Sergei Georgievich Goryachev)
[NOTE: Although never officially reassigned, 930th Rifle Regiment spent the battle attached to 179th Rifle Division in 22nd Army]

(930th), 934th, 937th Rifle Regiments
531st Light Artillery Regiment
334th Reconnaissance Company, 422nd Sapper Battalion
43rd, 336th Corps Artillery Regiments (152mm howitzers)
56th Corps Artillery Regiment (152mm cannon, 152mm howitzers)
390th Corps Artillery Regiment (122mmm and 152mm howitzers)
[NOTE: Originally the divisional howitzer regiment of 17th Rifle Division]
545th Corps Artillery Regiment (122mm cannon, 152mm howitzers)
301st, 360th RVGK Howitzer Regiments (152mm howitzers)
11th Separate Mortar Battalion (120mm mortars)
183rd, 397th Separate Antiaircraft Battalions (37mm, 76mm antiaircraft guns)
113th, 114th, 115th Motorized Engineer Battalions
Added by October 14th:
22nd, 39th Separate Engineer Battalions
Added in late October:
251st Separate Sapper Battalion
29th Army (Lieutenant General Ivan Ivanovich Maslennikov)
  178th Rifle Division (Lieutenant Colonel Aleksandr Petrovich Kvashnin)
    386th, 693rd, 709th Rifle Regiments
    332nd Artillery Regiment
    178th Antiaircraft Battalion *[disbanded Oct 15th, 1941]*
    139th Reconnaissance Battalion, 211th Sapper Battalion
  243rd Rifle Division (Colonel Yakov Gavrilovich Tsarkoz)
    906th, 910th, 912th Rifle Regiments
    775th Artillery Regiment
    324th Reconnaissance Company, 413th Sapper Battalion
  246th Rifle Division (Major General Ivan Ivanovich Melnikov)
    *[NOTE: On October 12th, this unit reported 6613 officers and men on hand, with
    114 machineguns, three mortars, two antitank guns, and ten artillery pieces total]*
    908th, 914th, 915th Rifle Regiments
    777th Artillery Regiment, 305th Antitank Battalion
    326th Reconnaissance Company, 415th Sapper Battalion
  250th Rifle Division (Colonel Pavel Afinogenovich Stepanenko)
    *[NOTE: This division was reported as having no more than 250 men left 'in line'
    by the second half of October]*
    918th, 922nd, 926th Rifle Regiments
    790th Artillery Regiment, 778th Howitzer Regiment
    527th Antiaircraft Battalion
    329th Reconnaissance Company, 418th Sapper Battalion
  252nd Rifle Division (Colonel Aleksandr Alekseyevich Zabaluev)
    924th, 928th, 932nd Rifle Regiment
    277th Artillery Regiment, 270th Howitzer Regiment

332nd Reconnaissance Company, 420th Sapper Battalion

Separate Motorized Rifle Brigade (*Kombrig* A.N. Ryzhov)
1st, 2nd Motorized Rifle Regiments
2nd Artillery Regiment

[*NOTE: According to the new organization of October 9th, this unit was adding a tank battalion and an antiaircraft battalion. It reported the tank battalion with thirty-two tanks on hand by October 16th]*

115th Reserve Rifle Regiment
13th Border Guards Unit (Regiment)
18th Border Guards Unit (Regiment)

[*NOTE: Border Guards were supposed to provide 'rear area' security for the Red Army, but in the rapid German advances of 1941 they were often pulled into front line combat and acted as regular rifle troops]*

29th Separate Cavalry Regiment
644th Corps Artillery Regiment (122mm cannon, 152mm howitzers)
432nd RVGK Howitzer Regiment (122mm, 152mm howitzers)

[*NOTE: This was the divisional howitzer regiment of 178th Rifle Division, which had been 'stripped out' of the division on 14 September]*

873rd Antitank Regiment (85mm guns)
213th Separate Antitank Battalion (45mm guns)

[*NOTE: This was the divisional antitank battalion of 178th Rifle Division, which had been 'stripped out' of the division in late September]*

71st, 72nd, 267th Separate Engineer Battalion
63rd Pontoon Bridge Battalion

30th Army (Major General Vasily Afanasyevich Khomenko)

[*NOTE: Technically, the very weak 107th Motorized Rifle Division was assigned to 30th Army on October 10th, but it was physically located well south of the Kalinin area, and Western Front quickly reassigned it to their own Front Reserves. It was not released back to the area just south of Kalinin until the end of October.*

As can be seen below, 30th Army's divisions had been surrounded and were not really under the army's control on October 10th. The Army HQ took control of the units fighting in Kalinin after October 14th, but they were virtually all units new to the army.]

162nd Rifle Division (Colonel Nikolai Fedorovich Kolkunov)

[*NOTE: On October 10th this division was in a 'pocket' which 9th (German) Army never quite managed to wipe out. It broke out of encirclement late in October, but was too badly depleted to be rebuilt, and the division was officially disbanded in early December]*

501st, 627th, 720th Rifle Regiments
605th Light Artillery Regiment, 634th Howitzer Regiment
141st Antitank Battalion, 473rd Antiaircraft Battalion
241st Reconnaissance Battalion, 187th Sapper Battalion

<u>242nd Rifle Division</u> (Major General Kirill Alekseyevich Kovalenko)
[NOTE: On October 10th was in the same pocket with 162nd Rifle Division. This unit reported only 700—800 men on hand in two groups on October 10th. It was never rebuilt after escaping from encirclement, and was officially disbanded in mid-December]
   897th, 900th, 903rd Rifle Regiments
   769th Artillery Regiment, 772nd Howitzer Regiment
   300th Antitank Battalion, 519th Antiaircraft Battalion
   321st Reconnaissance Battalion, 410th Sapper Battalion

<u>251st Rifle Division</u> (Colonel Vladimir Filippovich Stenin)
[NOTE: On October 10th was in the same pocket with 162nd Rifle Division. This unit reported a total of 772 men on hand on October 10th. Of the three encircled divisions, this is the only one which survived without being completely reformed. It ended the war with the honorific title 251st Vitebskaya Order of the Red Banner, Order of Suvorov Rifle Division]
   919th, 923rd, 927th Rifle Regiments
   789th Artillery Regiment
   331st Reconnaissance Company, 419th Sapper Battalion
871st Antitank Regiment (85mm guns)
1 battery of M-13 rocket launchers (no designation given)
12th Separate Mortar Battalion
122nd Separate Engineer Battalion
51st Pontoon Bridge Battalion
263rd, 499th Separate Sapper Battalions
Added by October 14th:
1st Bn, 14th Guard Mortar Regiment (BM-13 rocket launchers)
Added by November 1st:
133rd Separate Engineer Battalion

31st Army (Major General Vasily Nikitich Dolmatov)
[NOTE: On October 10th this HQ had virtually ceased to function, and it was placed into Western Front reserve on October 12th to regroup in the area of Torzhok. It was 'reactivated' on October 19th and officially took control of the units of Operational Group Vatutin and other units north of Kalinin on October 20th, under command of Major General Vasily Aleksandrovich Yushkevich]

   <u>119th Rifle Division</u> (Major General Aleksandr Dmitrievich Berezin)
   [NOTE: Actually operating under 29th Army HQ; 510th Howitzer Regiment was 'stripped out' and added to 29th Army as a separate army support unit on October 20th]
      920th Rifle Regiment (from 247th Rifle Division on October 6th, 1941)
      421st, 634th Rifle Regiments
      349th Light Artillery Regiment, 510th Howitzer Regiment
      216th Antitank Battalion, 257th Antiaircraft Battalion

143rd Reconnaissance Company

224th Sapper Battalion

<u>126th Rifle Division</u> (Colonel Yefim Vasilyevich Bedin)

[NOTE: On September 3rd the division had only 4309 officers and men, and had not been rebuilt. By October 12th it was officially under 29th Army, but was disbanded in early December]

366th, 539th, 550th Rifle Regiments

358th Light Artillery Regiment, 501st Howitzer Regiment

265th Antitank Battalion, 240th Antiaircraft Battalion

198th Reconnaissance Battalion, 175th Sapper Battalion

<u>220th Rifle Division</u> (Major General Nikifor Gordeyevich Khoruzhenko)

[NOTE: Under 29th Army by October 11th]

376th, 653rd, 673rd Rifle Regiments

660th Artillery Regiment

46th Antitank Battalion

489th Reconnaissance Company, 381st Sapper Battalion

<u>247th Rifle Division</u> (Colonel Sergei Pavlovich Tarasov)

[NOTE: This division was destroyed on October 10th–13th: it was the bulk of the troops retreating up the Staritsa–Kalinin road that 1st Panzer Division ran over on those days, and it was never rebuilt. It was officially 'deleted from the order of battle' on October 14th and the remnants added to 250th Rifle Division. A new 247th Rifle Division was formed from the remnants of the division staff and the Separate Motorized Brigade in December]

909th, 916th Rifle Regiments

[NOTE: 920th Rifle Regiment of this division had been separated and added to 119th Rifle Division on October 6th]

778th Artillery Regiment

306th Antitank Battalion, 525th Antiaircraft Battalion

327th Reconnaissance Battalion, 416th Sapper Battalion

392nd Corps Artillery Regiment (152mm howitzers)

542nd Corps Artillery Regiment (152mm howitzers)

537th Motorized Engineer Battalion

Kalinin Area, not under Army command:

16th Border Guard Detachment

[NOTE: fought under the control of 30th Army and after October 14th, under 8th Tank Brigade]

84th NKVD Regiment for Railroad Security

[NOTE: Actually in charge of militia and security troops in Kalinin; came under control of 30th Army]

Northwestern Front Junior Officers' Course

[NOTE: Officially placed under 30th Army on October 13th]

Reinforcements: October 10th–24th

Operational Group Vatutin (Lieutenant General Nikolai Fedorovich Vatutin)
*[Arriving from Northwestern Front starting October 15th; most units became part of
31st Army on October 20th]*

  8th Tank Brigade (Colonel Pavel Alekseyevich Rotmistrov)
  *[NOTE: On October 12th, this unit reported 1735 officers and men, eighteen
  mortars, six antitank guns, eight 76m field guns, forty-five tanks, sixteen armored
  cars on hand]*
    8th Tank Regiment (two battalions)
    8th Motorized Rifle Battalion
  46th Cavalry Division (Colonel V.S. Sokolov)
  *[NOTE: On October 12th, this unit reported a total of 1859 officers and men on
  hand]*
    57th, 59th, 61st Cavalry Regiments
    53rd Horse Artillery Battalion, 53rd Artillery Park
  54th Cavalry Division (Colonel I.S. Esaulov)
  *[NOTE: On October 12th, this unit reported a total of 1308 officers and men on
  hand]*
    83rd, 89th, 119th Cavalry Regiments
    58th Horse Artillery Battalion, 58th Artillery Park
  46th Motorcycle Regiment
  *[NOTE: On October 12th, this unit reported a total of fourteen armored cars (three
  unserviceable), seventeen mortars and five antitank guns on hand; no manpower
  report]*
  183rd Rifle Division (Major General Konstantin Vasilyevich Komissarov)
  *[NOTE: On October 12th, this unit reported 7898 officers and men, 232 machine-
  guns, twelve mortars, no antitank guns, and fifteen artillery pieces on hand]*
    227th, 285th, 295th Rifle Regiments
    623rd Artillery Regiment
    18th Antitank Battalion, 22nd Reconnaissance Company
    304th Sapper Battalion
  185th Rifle Division (Lieutenant Colonel Konstantin Nikolayevich Vindushev)
  *[NOTE: On October 12th, this unit reported 12,046 officers and men, 196 machine-
  guns, seventeen mortars, one antitank gun, and thirty-two artillery pieces on hand]*
    257th, 280th, 1319th Rifle Regiments
    695th Artillery Regiment
    58th Reconnaissance Battalion, 340th Sapper Battalion
  698th Antitank Regiment (76mm guns)
  1 battalion of BM-13 rocket launchers (no numerical designation)
Arriving from Moscow area on October 15th–16th: later added to 30th Army HQ
Separate Special Regiment *(formed from schools in the Moscow area, strength given
  as 400 'bayonets')*

20th Reserve Rifle Regiment (*a replacement/training unit from the Moscow District*)
Arriving from Moscow area on October 15th: officially under 30th Army HQ same day

21st Tank Brigade (Lieutenant Colonel Andrei Levovich Lesovoi)
[NOTE: Officially, Colonel Boris Mikhailovich Skvortsov was listed as the brigade commander, but he was also listed as the commander of 61st Tank Division in the Far East, and Lesovoi is listed by 30th Army documents as the commander 'on the spot' when the brigade went into action. On October 10th, the brigade had sixty-one tanks and four ZIS-30 self-propelled 57mm antitank guns on hand]

    21st Tank Regiment (two battalions)
    21st Motorized Rifle Battalion

2nd Motorcycle Regiment
11th Motorcycle Regiment

Appendix 3

German Directives, Orders and Reports

Hitler Directive # 35 (*Operation 'Taifun'*)

The Führer and Supreme Commander Führer Headquarters,
Of the Armed Forces 6 September 1941
    10 copies
Directive No. 35

Combined with the progressive encirclement of the Leningrad area, the initial success against enemy forces in the area between the flanks of Army Groups South and Center have provided favorable conditions for a decisive operation against the Timoshenko Army Group which is attacking on the Central Front. This Army Group must be defeated and annihilated in the limited time which remains before the onset of winter weather. For this purpose it is necessary to concentrate all the forces of the Army and Air Force which can be spared on the flanks and which can be brought up in time.

On the basis of the report of the Commander-in-Chief Army, I issue the following orders for the preparation and execution of these operations:

1. On the Southern sector of the front the aim is the annihilation of the enemy forces in the triangle Kremenchug–Kiev–Konotop by the forces of Army Group South which are advancing northward across the Dnieper, acting in conjunction with the attack by the southern flank of Army Group Center. As soon as the completion of this task allows, those formations of 2nd and 6th Armies and of Panzer Group 2, which have become free, will be reformed for the new operation.

Beginning about 10 September at latest, the motorized forces of Army Group South, reinforced by infantry divisions and supported at the main point of attack by 4th Air Fleet, will make a surprise movement from the bridgehead secured by 17th Army northwestwards on and beyond Lubny. At the same time 17th Army is to gain ground in the direction of Poltava and Kharkov.

The offensive against the Crimea from the lower Dnieper will continue, with support from 4th Air Fleet; so will – so far as available forces permit – the offensive from the Dnepropetrovsk bridgehead. An advance by motorized forces south of the lower Dnieper towards Melitopol would be of substantial advantage for the mission of 11th Army.

On the *Central front*, the operation against the Timoshenko Army Group will be planned so that the attack can be begun at the earliest possible moment (end of

September) with the aim of destroying the enemy forces located in the area east of Smolensk by a pincer movement in the general direction of Vyazma, with strong *concentrations* of armor on the flanks.

For this purpose mobile focal points are to be established with motorized units as follows:

On the southern flank (probably in the area southeast of Roslavl, the direction of the thrust being northeast), from the available forces of Army Group Center and 5th and 2nd Panzer Divisions, which will be released for this purpose.

In the 9th Army sector (the thrust being probably towards Bjeloj), by bringing the strongest possible forces from the area of Army Group North.

Only when Army Group Timoshenko has been defeated in these highly coordinated and closely encircling operations of annihilation will our central Army be able to begin the advance on Moscow with its right flank on the Oka and its left on the Upper Volga.

The *Air Force* will support the offensive with 2nd Air Fleet, which will be reinforced at the appropriate time, especially from the northeast area. It will concentrate on the flanks and will employ the bulk of its dive-bomber units (VIII Air Corps) in support of the motorized forces on both flanks.

2. On the *Northeastern Front*, in conjunction with the Finnish Corps attacking on the Karelian peninsula, we must (after the capture of Schlusselburg) so surround the enemy forces fighting in the Leningrad area that by 15 September at the latest substantial units of the motorized forces and of 1st Air Fleet, especially VIII Air Corps, will be available for service on the Central Front. Before this, efforts will be made to encircle Leningrad more closely, in particular in the east, and should weather permit, a large-scale air attack on Leningrad will be carried out. It is particularly important in this connection to destroy the water supply.

In order to assist the Finnish advance beyond the fortifications along the old Russo-Finnish frontier, as well as to narrow the battle area and eliminate enemy air bases, forces of Army Group North will move north across the Neva sector as soon as possible.

With Finnish cooperation, the Bay of Kronstadt will be so completely closed by mine laying and artillery that enemy forces will be unable to escape into the Baltic to Hango and the Baltic Islands.

As soon as the necessary forces can be made available, the battle area around Leningrad is to be covered to the eastward and on the lower Volkhov. The link-up with the Karelian Army on the Svir will only take place when the destruction of the enemy around Leningrad is assured.

3. As regards *further operations* it is intended that the offensive towards Moscow by Army Group Center should be covered by a flank guard composed of available motorized forces in the Army Group South sector and advancing in a general northeasterly direction, and that forces from Army Group North should be moved

forward on both sides of Lake Ilmen to cover the northern flank and to maintain contact with the Finnish Karelian Army.

4. Any saving of time and consequent advance of the timetable will be to the advantage of the whole operation and its preparation.

Signed: Adolf Hitler

Reference: Trevor-Roper, H.R. *Blitzkrieg to Defeat*, pp. 96–8.

Comments: *This is the basic 'Führer Directive' that ordered the attack towards Moscow by Army Group Center. Note that the flanks of the Army Group are to be covered in this advance (and on to Moscow) by Army Groups North and South, and there is no mention at all of any Army Group Center attacks to the north or south – only an encirclement battle against 'Army Group Timoshenko' (the Soviet Western, Bryansk and Reserve Fronts) followed by an advance due east on Moscow.*

Directive of the Commander of Army Group Center on the Preparations for Operation 'Taifun'

No. 1300/41 Top Secret   16 September 1941

Directive for New Operations

1. After receiving replacements the Army Group will go on the offensive at the beginning of October.

2. 4th and 9th Armies will have Panzer Groups 4 and 3 subordinated, which at the time of the attack must be strengthened with one infantry corps each, so that they are ready with strong assault groups of motorized, tank and infantry units to accomplish a breakthrough of the enemy defenses on both sides of the road Roslavl, Moscow and to the north of the highway and destroy the connections between the inner flanks of the enemy forces. For this purpose they will be, while oriented to the east and depending on the situation, prepared to turn against the general line Vyazma, Drogobush or from both sides of Vyazma. 9th Army should use every opportunity to break through the wooded area to the northern flank of the army and advance troops in the direction of Rzhev.

[The third and fourth paragraphs cover operations of 2nd Army and Panzer Group 2]

5. The right flank of 16th Army will defend the line of lakes Ostashkov, Lake Ilmen, Volkhov.

[The sixth through eighth paragraphs cover the southern boundaries of the Army Group and the internal boundaries between 4th Army, Panzer Group 4, and Panzer Group 2]

9. Boundaries:

e) Between Army Group Center (9th Army) and Army Group North (16th Army): Gorki (20km northwest of Veliki Luki), Lake Nagovye, Lake Volga, Torzhok (all points are considered north of the Army Group area).

Reference: *TsAMO, F. 500, op. 12462, D. 114, ll. 12–18, 23–6, translated from the German*
Comments: *This is the 'implementing directive' from Army Group Center regarding the attack towards Moscow. What is fascinating is that the future initial objective of Panzer Group 3's thrust, Torzhok, is specifically indicated as being outside of the Army Group boundaries. In fact, this order makes no mention of any operation other than a classic encirclement battle in the Vyazma area – even the specifics of a further advance on Moscow are not mentioned, nor any advances other than due east.*

Directive of OKH to the Commander of Army Group Center on the Direction of Panzer Group 3

No. 1569/41 Secret   8 October 1941 2310 hrs

According to just received instructions from the High Command of the Armed Forces (*OKW*), the Führer instructs that (Panzer) Group Hoth [*Panzer Group 3*] at Vyazma and to the north of it should be released as soon as possible by parts of (Panzer) Group Hoepner [*Panzer Group 4*] and directed in a general northern direction, so that in cooperation between the northern flank of 9th Army with southern flank of 16th Army it will be possible to destroy the opponent in the area between Belyi and Ostashkov.

The High Command asks to be informed on the actions of Army Group Centre in regard to this order.

OKH, General Staff, Operations Section
No. 1569/41 Secret

Reference: *TsAMO, F. 500, op. 12462, D. 114, l. 66, translated from the German*
Comments: *Here is the first official indication that the German High Command is going to unravel the advance on Moscow. The Vyazma encirclement was just closed the day before, and it can be assumed that the trapped Soviet armies around Vyazma will be destroyed in the near future. Faced with this success, the High Command of the Army (OKH) is going to take Panzer Group 3 and send it to the area east of Ostashkov behind the front facing Army Group North's 16th Army and almost directly away from Moscow.*

Directive from the Commander of Army Group Center to the Commander of 9th Army on the Offensive in the Kalinin Direction

No. 1895/41 Top Secret   10 October 1941 1030 hrs

9th Army will subordinate to Panzer Group 3 one infantry corps of at least two infantry divisions for use in the assault towards Kalinin and Staritsa.

Second, occupy points Zubtsov and Rzhev as soon as possible (and) advance units to occupy the area of Staritsa.

The central mass of the infantry forces of 9th Army to implement the offensive will echelon to the northern flank of the army, adhering to the right flank roads leading to Moscow and the left flank through Staritsa towards the southwest bank of the Volga (southeast of Kalinin).

To complete the destruction of the opponent surrounded west of Vyazma, one division should be stationed in the area of the town to process prisoners and stragglers of the enemy.

Boundary line between 9th and 4th Armies (after the conclusion of the Vyazma battle): highway to Vyazma (Vyazma itself belongs to 9th Army); highway Vyazma–Gzhatsk, post road Gzhatsk–Moscow (to 9th Army). Panzer Group 4 received priority on highways (within 9th Army).

Army Group Center Operations Section
No. 1895/41 Top Secret

Reference: *TsAMO, F. 500, op. 12462, D. 114, l. 71, translated from the German*
Comments: *This directive firmly orients 9th Army to the north, both as a flank guard for the Army Group and as part of the advance against the Soviet forces opposite Army Group North. It is also a tacit admission that the original concept of Army Group Center's flanks being covered by Army Group North is not going to happen, so Army Group Center has to watch its own flanks with its own forces. The direct advance on Moscow will now be reduced to 4th Army and Panzer Groups (Armies) 2 and 3, with almost half of Army Group Center's infantry in 9th and 2nd Armies operating only to the flanks.*

Panzer Group 3 Operations Brief (dated October 11th, 1941)

The difficulties of the vehicle status and fuel supply for the fast troops are known to the higher command. Without regard to these difficulties, the operations have to be quickly brought to a conclusion, even if the objectives are reached only with parts of the units and they have to drive the vehicles to the limit of their operational life.

All units will have to be creative to offset the low fuel supplies and overcome the condition of the vehicles even while in combat.

They are therefore already leaving behind all dispensable staffs and units and taking all their serviceable vehicles and halftracks and leaving the units in special camps or prepared special rear areas.

Tank, rifle, pioneer and signal troops are to be classified together so that units set up with the commandeered vehicles are separated from the less useful. It must be done soon; if the situation does not change, from the divisions only brigades or reinforced regiments will remain operational.

The strength of the Supply Troops must be given special attention and to take care of that, the troops must remain healthy. Paying for horse-drawn local vehicles may be expedient (also for combat elements).

LVI and XXXXI Corps will give the necessary instructions for decommissioning and reorganizing within their areas.

Signed: Reinhardt

Reference: *'Anlagen' to the KtB of XXXXI Motorized Corps, NARA T314/980*
Comments: *This is an extraordinary document. The German forces have not even reached Kalinin, the heavy fall rains have not yet started, and already Panzer Group 3 command admits that most elements of the Corps will have to be dismounted and left behind for lack of supplies! The phrase 'from the divisions only brigades or reinforced regiments will remain operational' means that the German Command believes that they are only involved in a pursuit operation from here forward, and that no heavy combat is to be expected that might require full divisional assets. That expectation will not survive the next week.*

Order from the Commander of Army Group Center to the Commander of 9th Army on the Shift of Panzer Group 3 to the Command of Army Group Center and its Objectives

No. 1937/41 Top Secret   12 October 1941

Panzer Group 3, occupying Kalinin, holding Zubtsov and Staritsa, will perhaps later advance forces to Torzhok.

Panzer Group 3 needs to conduct reconnaissance on Kalinin through Rameshki and from Torzhok towards Vyshniy Volochek and Ostashkov.

The Panzer Group is to prevent, if possible, the withdrawal to the east, both the enemy retreating under pressure from the inner flanks of Army Group Center and Army Group North, as well as parts of the enemy still resisting.

Panzer Group 3 with the attached 129th and 6th Infantry Divisions, as of 0600 hrs 13.10 will be directly under the Army Group. Supply will continue through 9th Army.

Army Group Center
Operations Section
No. 1937/412 Top Secret

Reference: *TsAMO, F. 500, op. 12462, D. 114, l. 76, translated from the German*
Comments: *This order from the Army Group not only cuts the subordination of the panzer group to 9th Army, it also directs Panzer Group 3 firmly to the north: Vyshniy Volochek and Ostashkov are east of the Valdai, well to the rear of the Soviet Northwestern Front and far, far north of the original boundaries established for Army Group Center's operations. The order is also a bit premature, because as of October 12th, Panzer Group 3 does not occupy Kalinin – it is still approaching the city, and will be fighting to take and then hold it for the rest of the month.*

Order from Commander Army Group Center on the Continuation of Operations in the Moscow Direction

No. 1960/41 Top Secret   14 October 1941

1. The enemy in front of the Army Group is defeated. The remains are retreating everywhere, counterattacking in places. The Army Group is pursuing the enemy.

[The second and third paragraphs cover operations of 4th Army, Panzer Groups 2 and 4]

4. 9th Army and Panzer Group 3 should not allow the withdrawal of enemy forces facing the northern flank of 9th Army and the southern flank of 16th Army, cooperating with 16th Army for this purpose and further – to destroy the enemy.

Panzer Group 3 for this purpose, while keeping Kalinin, will reach the Torzhok area as soon as possible and advance without delay to Vyshniy Volochek in order to prevent the main forces of the enemy across the Tvertsa (river) from crossing the upper reaches of the Msta river to the east. It should increase reconnaissance towards Kashin, Bezhetsk, Pestovo. It must also hold the line Kalinin, Staritsa and south until the arrival of 9th Army units.

9th Army, in cooperation with the right wing of Panzer Group 3, will destroy the enemy in the area of Staritsa, Rzhev, Zubtsov which still resists on the front of VI and XXIII Army Corps, and then the left wing will rotate through Lukovnikovo to the north. The main direction of further advances – to Vyshniy Volochek. The right flank of the army should as soon as possible move to occupy Kalinin and relieve there elements of Panzer Group 3. With further progress to the north the army should move north of the Volga Reservoir to cover his flank from the east.

Army Group North will have as its task to tie down forces on the front of the southern flank of 16th Army by its pursuit of the enemy. The center of 16th Army has the task to pin down the enemy on both sides of Lake Ilmen and immediately operate to prevent possible attempts to organize the withdrawal of units.

Addendum (Appendix) 1 to Order of Army Group Center Operations Section No. 1960/41 Top Secret of 14 October 1941

4.) 9th Army:

V, VI, XXIII, XXVII Corps HQ

26th, 35th, 106th, 110th, 161st, 162nd, 206th, 251st, 256th Infantry Divisions

255th Infantry Division detached to cover the rear of the army

5th, 28th, 102nd Infantry Divisions awaiting individual orders for transportation (from Smolensk)

86th Infantry Division – in Army Group reserve going to 9th Army

5.) Panzer Group 3:

XXXXI and LVI Motorized Corps HQ

1st, 6th, 7th Panzer Divisions

14th, 36th Motorized Divisions, 900th Motorized Brigade

6th, 129th Infantry Divisions

Reference: *TsAMO, F. 500, op. 12462, D. 114, ll. 77–85, translated from the German*

Comments: *With this Operations Order, Panzer Group 3 and 9th Army are both firmly oriented to the north, to cooperate with Army Group North in the destruction of*

Soviet Northwestern Front and Soviet Western Front's 22nd and 29th Armies. One third of Army Group Center's armor and infantry are now directed away from Moscow in a major diversion of resources from that objective.

Panzer Group 3 Order Number 25
Dated 14 October 1941
Effective 15 October 1941 at 0700 hrs

1.) Enemy see attached Enemy Briefing Number 28. [*Not included with the document in the archives*]

2.) Army Group Center is finishing the battle near Vyazma, is beginning the advance on Moscow and destroying the enemy halted in the area of Valdai–Ostashkov–Rzhev or retreating.

9th Army is advancing with VIII and V Corps on both sides of the Volga reservoir to the northeast, with XXVII Corps towards Kalinin, with VI and XXIII Corps through Rzhev towards Torzhok and will relieve Panzer Group 3 in stages.

Army Group North has started an advance in a southeastern direction to destroy the enemy in the area southeast of Leningrad through an attack to the northeast.

3.) Panzer Group 3, which is directly assigned to Army Group Center, is preventing an escape through the inner flanks of Army Groups Center and North of the enemy or his stopping (and setting up defenses). To this end the Panzer Group will hold Kalinin, Staritsa and Zubtsov and with strong forces advance on Torzhok and prevent the enemy from moving to the north and east by blocking the roads and trails. The Panzer Group is to hold itself ready when relieved by infantry to advance through Vyshniy Volochek to the railroad junction at Bologoye or east in the direction of Yaroslavl.

The advance: XXXXI Corps on the right, LVI Corps on the left.

4.) Tasks:

a.) XXXXI Corps (1st Panzer Division, 6th Panzer Division, 36th Motorized Division, 129th Infantry Division) Hold Kalinin with elements and defend to the north and southeast. With the bulk of the corps move on Torzhok and block to the north and northwest. If possible send elements to Rameshki to deny the enemy roads to the east and north. Combat reconnaissance will be sent to Vyshniy Volochek, in order to interrupt there the roads from the west and north.

b.) LVI Corps (7th Panzer Division, 14th Motorized Division, 6th Infantry Division) will undertake with part of its forces to secure and hold Staritsa and Zubtsov. With the bulk of the corps move through Torzhok and block to the west and southwest. Reconnaissance in the direction of Ostashkov.

c.) 900th Lehr Brigade remains in the service of the panzer group in the area of Kalinin. It can be requisitioned by XXXXI Corps for the defense of Kalinin.

5.) Boundary Lines:

a.) Between 4th Army and 9th Army:

Gzhatsk (9th Army)–Sheyeda Stratilatskaya (9th)–Yaropolets (9th)–along the Lama River–Volga reservoir (4th Army)

b.) <u>Between XXXXI Corps and LVI Corps</u>:

Krasnii Kholm (LVI Corps)–Ulyanovskoye (LVI)–Staritsa (LVI)–road Staritsa, Torzhok (LVI)–Torzhok (XXXXI)–Ostashkov (LVI)

c.) <u>Between Army Groups Center and North</u>

Lake Seliger–Staritsa–southwestern corner of Volga reservoir

6.) The proposal to adapt the unit organization to the vehicle situation and fuel supply situation cannot be acted upon yet. It is not possible to fulfill the pursuit and blocking tasks with complete divisions. Frequent special pursuit operations [*raids*] in the front line with vehicles with small fuel consumption will be sufficient. Not required, limited mobile units are to be left in the rear. The remaining infantry, motorized and *schützen* (motorized infantry) units are to be made mobile with their usual vehicles and the rest left behind with the required security supplied by the corps. Non-required, un-mobile units remain in the area and (under command of) their corps. The billeting areas will be those in the relevant areas provided by the controlling Corps HQ.

7.) <u>The Army Troops</u> remain in the control of the divisions of the corps.

8.) <u>Air Reconnaissance</u>:

a.) <u>Tactical Air Reconnaissance</u> by 2nd (F)/33 [*Luftwaffe unit*] in the area of Volokolamsk–Klin–Kimry–Kashin–railroad junction east of Bzhetsk–Bologoye–Valdai–Ostashkov.

It is to be assessed:

What enemy remains in the area of Torzhok–Vishniy Volochek–Valdai–Selizarovo?

What is on the line Torzhok–Bologoye to the north, east or southeast behind the Volga?

b.) <u>Combat Air Reconnaissance for the Corps</u>: will be forward of the spearheads.

9.) <u>Engineer Service</u>:

a.) LVI Corps will pull its pioneer battalions from the repair of the stretch (of road) Pogoreloye Gorodishche–Mishina–Staritsa (urgently!) and undertake the restoration of the Russian 16-ton expedient (temporary) bridge over the Volga at Staritsa, (and building) ramps as well as the establishment and repair of a road on the west bank of the Volga to the road Staritsa–Torzhok.

b.) The Panzer Group will in the next days send several Army Bridging Columns B-type to Pogorjeloje Gorodishche. Command allocation will follow

c.) <u>Commander of 10th Construction Troops</u> will control the 'Rollbahn 3' after October 16th from Kholm through Sychevka to Zubtsov.

10.) <u>Movement Control</u>

<u>Traffic Regulation</u> is by the corps within their areas, behind the line Vyazma–Sychevka–Rzhev by 9th Army.

Supply traffic for XXXXI Corps must move through the LVI Corps area.

11.) <u>Command and Control</u>:

[The following] are assigned:

6th Panzer Division under XXXXI Corps until it reaches Ramenye

129th Infantry Division under XXXXI Corps until it reaches the railroad line Volokolamsk–Krasnii Kholm

6th Infantry Division under LVI Corps until it reaches Staritsa

LVI Corps will take over the area Staritsa–Zubtsov as of 0800 hrs October 16th.

12.) <u>Signals Organization</u>:

a.) <u>Wire Organization</u>:

<u>Signal Regiment Panzer Group 3</u> will build the group (wire) axis Pogoreloye Gorodishche–Staritsa on the road Staritsa–Torzhok with group stations in Staritsa, Ladino, and later Torzhok. The Panzer Group Signals Regiment No. 3 will run the corps axis of XXXXI Corps on the road Staritsa–Kalinin and build a group station in Kalinin later.

<u>XXXXI Corps</u> will advance its corps axis on the road Staritsa–Kalinin to its combat HQ and later set up on the group net a group station in Kalinin.

<u>LVI Corps</u> Will use the group stations at Pogoreloye Gorodishche and Staritsa, later the group station at Ladino or connect the group axis Staritsa–Torzhok to its combat HQ

<u>900th *Lehr* Brigade</u> will connect to the group station in Kalinin.

b.) <u>XXXXI Corps</u> will set up a radio station in Kalinin for 'domestic' traffic (administration).

13.) <u>Group Combat HQ</u>: at Karabino

Signed: Reinhardt

Reference: *'Anlagen' to the KtB of XXXXI Motorized Corps, NARA T314/980*
Comments: *This is Panzer Group 3's implementation of the Army Group Operations Order of the same date. Most interesting is that up to now LVI Motorized Corps has been operating south and east of XXXXI Corps, so to fulfill the objectives of this order that corps will have to turn almost 180 degrees, move north across the rear area supply lines of XXXXI Corps, and then move with 'the bulk of the corps' north on the same highway Kalinin–Torzhok that XXXXI Corps is using. Not specified is how most of five motorized/armored divisions are going to advance on a single road without the greatest traffic jam in history resulting. A clue is in Paragraph 9, which instructs LVI Corps to use all of its engineer assets to rebuild a bridge at Staritsa so an alternate route to the north can be opened up. The belief by the German command that heavy motorized traffic could somehow use a tiny temporary bridge over the Volga and dirt (mud!) roads north from Staritsa took a long time to die, but in the end none of the panzer or motorized divisions ever used this route.*

Another clue as to future operations is in Paragraph 6, which indicates that 'It is not possible to fulfill the pursuit and blocking tasks with complete divisions' – in other words, the supply and traffic situation will only allow operations by smaller Kampfgruppen and detachments. The expectation that these units will suffice for future combat operations might be justified on this date, when the fighting in Kalinin involved an opponent of mostly militia and very weak rifle troops, but will receive a series of rude shocks in the next 72 hours.

XXXXI (Motorized) Corps Order # 31/41
Dated October 16th, 1941

1.) a) <u>The Enemy</u> in front of Panzer Group 3 and 9th Army has been defeated. The remainder is either conducting local counterattacks around Moscow and to the northeast around Torzhok or retreating.

b) <u>Panzer Group 3</u> in cooperation with 9th Army will prevent a retreat of the enemy forces standing before the north flank of 9th Army and the south flank of 16th Army and destroy them. To do this the panzer group will take the zone around Torzhok and from there immediately move against Vyshniy Volochek in order to prevent the mass of the enemy units from retreating over the Tvertsa and the upper reaches of the Msta [River] to the east.

c) <u>9th Army</u> will move with XXVII Corps to Kalinin, with VI Corps and XXIII Corps through Rzhev to Torzhok and destroy the [enemy] units that Panzer Group 3 breaks up.

<u>LVI Corps</u> will take over the security and blocking of Volga crossings in Staritsa and Zubtsov with elements.

The corps will move with the mass of the corps through Staritsa along the railroad line south of Torzhok and block to the west and southwest.

2.) <u>XXXXI Corps</u> (1st Panzer Division, 6th Panzer Division, 36th Motorized Division, 129th Infantry Division) will hold Kalinin with elements and then block to the north and southeast. The mass of the corps will move on Torzhok and block to the north and northwest, while sending out combat reconnaissance towards Vyshniy Volochek to interrupt there the routes from the west and north.

3.) <u>Objectives for 17 October 1941</u>:

a) <u>1st Panzer Division</u> will attack with the mass of the division towards Torzhok while holding a support position at Mednoye.

The division will as soon as possible pass the securing of Kalinin to 36th Motorized Division and during its advance provide its own security to the west.

The remainder of the forces in the bridgehead at Staritsa (without 2nd Bn 59th Artillery Regiment) will rejoin the division during the course of 17 October.

b) <u>36th Motorized Division</u> will take over the defense of Kalinin and move into the northeast part of the city.

The division will advance to the west corresponding to the action of 1st Panzer Division against forces along the Kalinin–Torzhok road, relieving the security forces of 1st Panzer Division at the earliest. Especially it is important to prevent enemy units from the west from pushing between the Volga and 1st

Panzer Division. Details are to be worked out between the divisions directly.

The 1st Bn 118th Infantry Regiment in the bridgehead at Staritsa will rejoin the division during 17 October.

c) Group Metz will hold the bridgehead at Staritsa and relieve other units of XXXXI Corps as soon as possible during the course of 17 October as the mass of 14th Motorized Division arrives. As soon as the last elements of XXXXI Corps are out of their present assignment [at Staritsa], the Command responsibility will pass from 14th Motorized Division to 6th Infantry Division.

Details will be ordered [in another set of orders] separately.

d) 6th Panzer Division will give the bulk of its fuel supplies to 114th Rifle Regiment (minus 2nd Bn) and on 17 October move it to Kalinin. With the arrival of this reinforced *Kampfgruppe*, the Advance Detachment of 6th Panzer Division will be back under the division's control. The division will take command of all of its elements in Kalinin. Final control of the division in Kalinin will start (by the division HQ) as soon as the arrival of the *Kampfgruppe* of 114th Rifle Regiment in Kalinin is affirmed.

e) 129th Infantry Division will march from the area in and south of Ulyanovskoye through Ashurkovo and reach Kalinin by way of Nesterovo, Grishino, Gnilitsy, Negotino, so that it can take over the defense of Kalinin from 36th Motorized Division by 21.10. 0600 [0600 hrs on October 21st] so that division is available for further use.

A strong Advance Detachment is to be started on the march towards Kalinin right now and upon arrival will come under 36th Motorized Division.

4.) Reconnaissance

Ground and Air Reconnaissance is to assess above all the movements and whereabouts of the enemy in the southeast and north of Kalinin and watch the movements opposite the bridgehead at Staritsa and across the Volga.

5.) Boundary between XXXXI and LVI Corps Krasnii Kholm (LVI)–Ulyanovskoye (LVI)–Staritsa (LVI)–road Staritsa–Torzhok (LVI)–Torzhok (XXXXI)–Ostashkov (LVI).

6.) Artillery

a) II Bn/59th Artillery Regiment is relieved from control of 1st Panzer Division at Staritsa and will come under 30th Artillery Command.

b) 3rd Battery/611th Artillery Regiment will return to control of its parent battalion at the same time II/59th Artillery Regiment changes control.

c) 620th Artillery Battalion will remain with 1st Panzer Division for long range fire in direct support as the Corps Command requires.

d) 665th Assault Gun Battery after refueling in Pogoreloye Gorodishche will move by way of Ulyanovskoye, Lotoshino and the area near Negotino [10 km south of Kalinin]. Battery commander will report to the Combat HQ of 36th Motorized Division when he arrives. Report to the Corps HQ when the battery arrives in Negotino.

7.) <u>Pioneer</u> (Engineers)

a) <u>52nd Pioneer Battalion</u> in place on the supply road and the road Staritsa–Kalinin to repair or reinforce damaged bridges and passages, where necessary.

The battalion will be prepared to use elements (of the battalion) to clear barriers and mines in the Kalinin area.

b) <u>506th Light Bicycle Road Construction Battalion</u> is repairing and maintaining the supply road Staritsa–Kalinin in accordance with the weather and the supply situation of the corps. Once the snow situation no longer requires earth moving, the battalion will take over clearing and operating the road.

c) For all the work make broadest use of prisoners and the civilian population under the supervision of German guards.

d) As a Corps Supply Road, 628th Pioneer Regimental Staff (Motorized) should explore a road from Pogoreloye Gorodishche that leads through Ulyanovskoye and from there to the road Chernav'–Popad'ino bypassing Staritsa to the road Staritsa–Kalinin. Report the result to the Corps HQ.

8.) a) <u>10th FLAK Regimental Staff</u> will undertake with its assigned FLAK units the high and low altitude defense over Kalinin with points of main effort over the Volga bridges and the airfield at Peremerki.

A FLAK battlegroup will be prepared to work with 1st Panzer Division, which can respond to direct requests from 1st Panzer Division [for support]. Details must be worked out directly with 1st Panzer Division.

The units in Staritsa for defense will remain there under control of 6th Infantry Division at their current assignment. They can move to Kalinin and there be used for air defense.

b) <u>605th FLAK Battalion</u> (minus 1 company) remains attached to 36th Motorized Division and in accordance with the ammunition situation [and] in conjunction with 1st Bn 29th FLAK Regiment is to be used for defense of the air over Kalinin and at the disposal of 36th Motorized Division.

9.) <u>Traffic Regulation</u>

<u>The Field Police of XXXXI Corps</u> will undertake with its assigned units the regulation of traffic from Ulyanovskoye to Kalinin (inclusive) with main effort at Ulyanovskoye and Kalinin.

10.) <u>XXXXI Corps Signal Battalion</u> builds and maintains in addition to Panzer Group 3 and neighboring units:

a) <u>Wire</u> to 1st Panzer Division (primary), 36th Motorized Division and Group Metz.

b) <u>Radio</u> to all assigned divisions and Group Metz.

11.) Corps Combat HQ at Bakanova, 18 km southwest of Staritsa

For the General Commanding

Chief of the General Staff [signed] Röttiger

References: *'Anlagen' to the KtB of XXXXI Motorized Corps; NARA T314/980*
Comments: *This is an example of higher headquarters being behind events, even in the very proficient German Army of 1941. The day BEFORE this order was issued, on October 15th, Rotmistrov's tank brigade had driven 1st Panzer Division and 900th Lehr Brigade right back down the Torzhok road to the Volga bridge in Kalinin – not exactly evidence that they 'have been defeated'. Nor, given the rather serious losses to the German vanguard, is it likely that the men of 1st Panzer/900th Lehr would have characterized it as only a 'local counterattack'! The rest of the order will turn out to be equally 'out of touch'. Not only will 36th Motorized not be able to take over the defense of Kalinin, on October 17th it will be fighting off the 21st Tank Brigade raid from the south and asking 1st Panzer Division for help. 6th Panzer Division and LVI Corps will be mired in supply difficulties and most of LVI Corps will, in fact, never move north despite repeated directives to do so.*

Finally, Paragraph 7 (c) is noteworthy, as an example of the casual attitude of the German military in Russia to war crimes: the use of prisoners or enemy civilians for forced labor on military projects is strictly prohibited by the Geneva Conventions. While mild compared to the wholesale slaughter being committed by the Einsatzgruppen behind the front in 1941, it shows graphically the Wehrmacht's explicit complicity in violating the Laws of War while fighting in the Soviet Union.

Panzer Group 3 Order # 26
Dated 18 October 1941, 2200 hrs

1.) <u>Panzer Group 3</u> will move behind the enemy to the east and northeast in the area of Torzhok–Ramushki–Bzhetsk.

2.) <u>Objectives</u>

<u>LVI Corps</u> (7th Panzer Division, 14th Motorized Division) will rapidly move through Lotoshino and Staritsa, Kalinin, Ramushki to the rail and road junction at Bzhetsk and block it to the west. Part [of the corps] will be left in Ramushki to block there. The beginning [of the move] is to be reported to the Panzer Group HQ.

XXXXI Corps (1st Panzer Division, 6th Panzer Division, 36th Motorized Division, 900th Lehr Brigade, 129th Infantry Division, 6th Infantry Division) will first of all hold Kalinin, block the road and railroad east of Torzhok and clear the area of (outside of) Torzhok–(outside of) Staritsa–Kalinin of the enemy. Use the 6th Panzer Division only with permission from the Panzer Group.

3.) <u>Boundaries</u>

a) <u>Between Panzer Group 3 (XXXXI Corps) and 9th Army (VI Corps) from 18 October</u>:

Zubtsov (9th Army)–Staritsa (9th Army)–Troitskoye (Panzer Group 3)–Tvertsa–bend near Petropavlovskoye (Panzer Group 3)–line of the Tvertsa (river) to the north. The main advance road (*Rollbahn*) of the Panzer Group will not move from these boundaries.

b) Between LVI Corps and XXXXI Corps
Falls south of Kalinin–forward of Kalinin–Kalinin (XXXXI Corps)–railroad Kalinin–Vyshniy Volochek (XXXXI Corps).
4. Supply Roads and Traffic Regulation as [previously] ordered.
Traffic regulation in Kalinin from 22 October will be by the Panzer Group.
5.) Signals
Panzer Group Signal Regiment 3 will construct the group (wire) axis behind the foremost elements of LVI Corps from the group center at Kalinin first to Ramushki. Group axis falls [from] Staritsa to Torzhok.
LVI Corps will connect through the group axis.
XXXXI Corps will connect through the group center at Kalinin.
6.) The entire available supply of fuel must in the first instance go to LVI Corps until the advance on Bzhetsk is accomplished, to the XXXXI Corps only so far as provision is urgently required.
[Signed] Reinhardt

Reference*: 'Anlagen' to the KtB of XXXXI Motorized Corps, NARA T314/980*
Comments: *Let's see: as of this date, 1st Panzer Division is surrounded north of Kalinin, 36th Motorized is fighting to hold Kalinin, 6th and 7th Panzer Divisions have enough fuel to move about one battalion each, the Luftwaffe yesterday had to bomb enemy tanks off of their own airfield – situation excellent, we're advancing on Bzhetsk! As noted in the text, this order appears to have been intended mostly for show: based on the actual supply and combat situation on the ground there is no way it could have been carried out. Among other things, if 'the entire available supply of fuel must . . . go to LVI Corps' then XXXXI Corps is not going to move anywhere anytime soon. Even disregarding the enemy (of which the order is utterly silent) supply difficulties make the ordered actions completely impossible.*

Action Memorandum (XXXXI Motorized Corps)
  Dated 20 October 1941 (report on activities for previous eighteen days)
  After eighteen days of battle the status of the corps is as follows:
The troops have without complaint in the course of military operations covered 425 km almost continuously in the attack. The battles during this time were hard and laid immense demands on the leaders and troops. The high points can be described as the following elements of the battle:
  a) Overcoming the swampy areas of Svitskiy and the Vorkolosh area
  b) The fighting south of and around Beli
  c) The attack across the Dnepr
  d) The breakthrough through the fortifications near Sychevka
  e) The battles on the south side of the Volga near Zubtsov and Staritsa
  f) Taking Kalinin and the advance in the Torzhok direction
  g) The defensive fighting in the defense of Kalinin.

During this time there were growing difficulties with supply with the increasing distance from the base. The continuing advance of the corps was only possible by finding and using captured fuel. However, they nevertheless overcame the trafficability of bad roads and tracks and the increasing scarcity of fuel already noticeable in all areas. These were addressed by leaving behind the bakery companies, so that the troops had no daily bread, and the long distances to the (base) camps so far to the rear (around 600 km for the supply depots!) meant that the loss of trucks could not be made good due to lack of spare parts.

The losses in men, weapons and material of all kinds remained within limits until the seizure of Kalinin. With the capture of Kalinin, the enemy was found to be so strong on the ground and in the air that the corps had to use all its forces to form a six-day-long hard ring around the city against attacks from the southeastern, northern, and northwestern directions.

The supply situation was already so stretched to reach Kalinin, that since the taking of the city this condition has intensified from day to day. Due to the remoteness of the panzer group's bases, a regular supply was not feasible. One (supply) column, which left (base) with 28 cubic meters of load capacity, returned six days later with a total of 6 cubic meters of capacity left. It is the same in all other areas, especially for ammunition supplies.

With the able assistance of the Luftwaffe, and as in previous days, the essentials of fuel and a trifle of the missing ammunition was supplied, but often it reached the troops just in time to be fired. Especially in the field of tank ammunition was this deficiency noticeable, so that Russian tanks were often able to break through the defensive front and cause considerable vehicle and equipment losses to the defense.

Due to the lack of forces it was also not possible to clear the entire rear area of scattered enemy groups, so that the enemy pushed himself between the corps and the divisions and further interrupted supplies.

During the defensive fighting in Kalinin the personnel and equipment losses were many times the losses during the initial attack. Many companies sank to a combat strength of 25–30 men as a result.

The combat strength of the corps (without infantry divisions) is at present the equivalent of a mixed motorized division and a weak panzer division. 1st Panzer Division and 36th Motorized Division could combine into a mixed motorized division, while 6th Panzer Division, with fuel supply, is a weak panzer division. To replenish these units it is necessary to put them first on the equipment list and supply 3780 tons of additional transport capacity. If these supplies are provided, the corps' equipment will again be moderately capable.

Due to the physical exhaustion of the combat troops and the condition of the units, they require several days of extraction from combat.

It remains to be seen whether at present the weather, the supply situation and the personnel combat situation of the 'fast units' of the corps will allow their further use with desired results. In this context, the question must be raised whether under the given circumstances the foot-marching infantry divisions do not wait but come forward faster, especially when the corps' strong advance detachments become separated from the mobile divisions for limited tasks.

A long-range operation by the corps however, with the present supply situation, hardly seems likely in the near future since the prerequisites are no longer available.

In any case, further actions will be only intermittent until new construction of supply bases becomes possible and is ordered. An advance bit by bit may result on the basis of the experiences of the last week unless first provision is secured to supply the next leap.

The tense supply status might be hardly better illustrated than through single signs that the troops place along the roads and carry the following inscription: 'Who will trade 10 liters of spirit for 1 loaf of bread?'

Reference: *'Anlagen' to the KtB of XXXXI Motorized Corps, NARA T314/980*
Comments: *The traditional view of the Battle of Moscow from the German side is that they were stopped by the weather, specifically the fall rains and mud. This document does not, to say the least, support that interpretation. Instead, XXXXI Corps ascribes the supply problems to 'the increasing distance from the base' and then describes extraordinary measures that had to be taken just to get to Kalinin and stay there, let alone support additional offensive action in any direction. That the corps was living 'hand to mouth' for ammunition, fuel, and rations after two weeks of 'Operation Typhoon' does not show the 'professional' German Army's logistical planning and capability in a good light. Although not specifically stated, lack of ammunition, especially artillery ammunition, also meant that the heavy firepower could not compensate for low numbers of men in the front lines, and so contributed to the high losses suffered while trying to defend the Kalinin area against counterattacks.*

(XXXXI Corps) Report of Meeting with Panzer Group 3 Dated 0300 hrs, 24 October 1941

At the beginning of the discussion the Operations Officer of the Panzer Group gave the group instructions for the continuation of the operations. In connection with this, the (panzer group) commander made some remarks. He explained that the operations in all circumstances were taking place in bad weather and the troop (units) had to adjust to that. The greatest difficulty for the time being [was] the establishment of secure supplies. For this the panzer group had to establish a strongpoint in Kalinin. The time required to set up this strongpoint is computed on ____ [*left blank in document*] days, so that the beginning of operations is to be counted (from that).

Then the commander discussed the employment of LVI Corps. The task of that corps is to prevent the enemy in front of 16th Army from retreating and destroy them. As the first part of this task the corps must reach Ramushki and the junction at Bzhetsk. To secure the flanks and the route of advance the corps will be assigned two infantry divisions. In the continuation of this operation XXXXI Corps will be pulled in, depending on the release of additional forces, to reinforce the battle. As the next point the commander described the orders to XXXXI Corps. The corps has first the area around Kalinin to clear and to smash the enemy holding there. He is counting on the fact that the enemy forces are not too large, particularly since V Corps is now advancing on Klin. To further this task 86th Infantry Division, which is moving forward by way of Sychevka, is subordinated to the corps. In the extension of this operation it is then the task of the corps, in cooperation with 86th Infantry Division, to take possession of the line Volga–reservoir. The commander imagines the accomplishment of this task in such a way that the mobile forces of the corps take possession of the dam, relying less on mass than on a well coordinated combat team (*Kampfgruppe*). The cooperation of paratroops is requested.

XXVII Corps is moving to Kalinin and will take over the sector to the west so that the forces of XXXXI Corps there can be released.

In the end the commander came back to the subject of supply. It is clear that substantial difficulties will continue to arise. The troops had to be prepared for it, so that they were aware that 'a full draw' was not possible. They had to become extraordinarily frugal both with ammunition and fuel and food supplies. Furthermore the troops had to be accustomed to the fact that the attack had to be continued on foot, if the road situation and the bad weather did not permit any other way. All conceivable auxiliary means had to be seized if supplies could not be transported any other way. If necessary they had to be moved by halftracks and 'panje' wagons. Road construction forces, which had been requested from the Army, had not been supplied so the troops must help themselves. In the following discussion the commander of XXXXI Corps stated that the indicated appointments would not allow the relief of the 'burnt out' divisions, because one division would not be enough to hold the front north of Kalinin. The commander for this reason did not want the elements of 6th Panzer Division released from the defense of Kalinin if it [the situation] should turn out differently. The corps could not itself change those orders.

Reference: '*Anlagen*' *to the KtB of XXXXI Motorized Corps, NARA T314/980*
Comments: *The call to establish a 'strongpoint' in Kalinin returns to a directive issued earlier in the operation. It means that Kalinin will become a collection point for vehicles and weapons for which no fuel or ammunition is available, and operations will continue only with those elements of the divisions that can be supplied with halftracks and farm carts: 'Kampfgruppen' of regimental or battalion size. The expectation that these will be enough to accomplish any of the far-ranging objectives envisioned, after the events of the previous week, approaches clinical delusion on the part of the Panzer Group command.*

Panzer Group 3 Order # 27
Dated 24 October 1941

1.) The enemy is seeking, with forces escaping from XXIII Corps, with parts of Northern Front and with new troops arriving from Moscow, to build a new defense position on the line Moscow–fortification position–Volga river–Ostashkov and to retake Kalinin, in order to guarantee the connection with Northern Front or from the protection of this defense position to retreat to the east. As previously all signs point to the enemy intention to defend Moscow.

The taking of Kalinin was a major success for XXXXI Corps, for the enemy an especially sensitive blow, its defense in spite of the major supply difficulties is owed to the leadership and troops of XXXXI Corps. Also all the supply troops completed special assignments and fully share in the successes.

The intentions of Army Group Centre and 9th Army are unchanged.

V Corps is attacking in the direction of Klin, VI and XXIII Corps towards Torzhok. XXVII Corps (advancing on both sides of the Volga) against the enemy west of Kalinin.

2.) Panzer Group 3 is holding Kalinin until relieved by 9th Army (XXVII Corps) cleaning up the situation to the southeast of Kalinin and attacking through Kalinin to the north, through Ramushki to Bzhetsk, in order to prevent by blocking the railroad and road in the area of Bzhetsk–Kalinin the enemy escaping before the inner flanks of Army Groups Center and North.

3.) Objectives:

a.) XXXXI Corps (1st Panzer Division, 6th Panzer Division, 36th Motorized Division, afterwards 129th and 161st Infantry Divisions, later 86th Infantry Division)

1.) Hold Kalinin until the arrival of XXVII Corps (earliest 29 October)

2.) As far as possible attack the enemy southeast of Kalinin

3.) Clear the area between the reservoir and Kalinin if possible.

4.) Through a surprise attack gain possession of a bridgehead over the reservoir. Paratroops have been requested to assist in seizing the bridgehead.

129th and 161st Infantry Divisions are only for the defense of Kalinin, not for the attack to the southeast. With the arrival of LVI Corps [presumably on October 26th] they will support an attack to the north. LVI Corps desires that they organize the defense front so that on October 26th they can be immediately prepared for their assault tasks.

86th Infantry Division on October 23rd has begun to move from Sychevka against the enemy southeast of Lotoshino and with its arrival in Lotoshino (at earliest 29 October) will come under XXXXI Corps.

The advance detachments of 86th and 162nd Infantry Divisions are to remain in Staritsa until 6th and 26th Infantry Divisions have reached a line north of Staritsa [presumably by October 26th]. Then the detachment of 86th Infantry Division moves to Lotoshino, and the detachment of 162nd Infantry Division to Kalinin.

The start time of the attack against the enemy southeast of Kalinin and its performance is to be reported to Panzer Group 3. After accomplishing this task an advance in a northern direction in cooperation with LVI Corps is planned.

b.) LVI Corps (7th Panzer Division, 14th Motorized Division, 129th and 161st Infantry Divisions) to break through the enemy north of Kalinin using the infantry divisions so that immediately upon arrival of 7th Panzer Division and 14th Motorized Division south of Kalinin and completion of new fuel supply, no later than 2 November, the two divisions can set out for Ramushki through Bzhetsk. Ramushki, Bzhetsk and the railroad junction 30 km east of Bzhetsk are to be blocked. 129th Infantry Division and 161st Infantry Division are to secure the supply line and to relieve the units left in Ramushki and then to block between the strongpoints left by the fast troops.

The start time for the attack against the enemy north of Kalinin and the intended execution will be reported to the Panzer Group by October 26th.

4.) Boundary Lines

a.) Between V Corps and XXXXI Corps:

Yaropolets (V Corps)–line of the Lama–south bank of the Volga–reservoir

b.) Between XXXXI Corps and LVI Corps:

center of Kalinin–Pischtschalkina (LVI Corps)–line of the Orsha to Romanovo–Gorizy (LVI Corps)

c.) Between LVI Corps and XXVII Corps:

Center of Kalinin–Tvertsa river to the junction with the Kava–Kava River–Nikolskoye (XXVII Corps)–railroad to Vyshniy Volochek

d.) Between XXXXI Corps (later XXVII Corps) and VI Corps:

Zubtsov (VI Corps)–Staritsa (VI Corps)–line of the Volga to Brod (VI Corps)–Ivanovskoye (XXXXI Corps)–Marino (VI Corps)

5.) Air Reconnaissance in accordance with Group Order # 25.

6.) Signals Organization in accordance with Group Order # 26.

7.) Command Authority

The panzer group will exercise command over 129th Infantry Division and 161st Infantry Division for LVI Corps at the request of the corps.

During the preparations for the attack LVI Corps can communicate directly with the infantry divisions.

XXXXI Corps is also required to comply with the wishes of LVI Corps for the preparation for the attack right now, as far as ensuring the safe defense of Kalinin.

8.) The corps will report to the panzer group by October 26th which immobile units can be made mobile according to the provisions of Group Order # 26 Paragraph 6.

9.) I ask the generals commanding the troops to act so that everything comes out, despite the great weather, road, and supply difficulties so that the ordered operations quickly break through and bring a victorious decision to this year.

Any improvisation is right, which contributes to the overcoming of the continuing obstacles.

Signed: Reinhardt

[#]

Reference: *'Anlagen' to the KtB of XXXXI Motorized Corps, NARA T314/980*
Comments: *This order is pretty much an admission that the full drive to the north by all of Panzer Group 3 is not going to happen: XXXXI Corps is now directed to the southeast, in the direction of Moscow, which they thought was their objective two weeks earlier. LVI Corps is still supposed to attack north, but none of its divisions have in fact been able to move much for the past two weeks, and to think that the supply situation will suddenly allow them the fuel to become mobile is not realistic. In fact, of course, the German panzers will make no more attacks to the north of Kalinin, no German paratroops will be committed to any operation in this area, and the attack from the north against Moscow won't get started for another two weeks, after the frost starts to harden the ground and some supplies have finally been accumulated.*

Appendix 4

Soviet Directives, Orders and Reports

Report of the Military Soviet of Western Front to the High Command and Chief of the General Staff of the Red Army on the Enemy Offensive in the Kalinin Direction and Actions for the Defense of Kalinin
Dated 12 October 1941

Two tank divisions, one motorized division, and (at least) three infantry divisions from the region of Sychevka, Zubtsov are attacking towards Kalinin. One tank division at 0935 hrs 12 Oct 41 was in the region 25 km southeast of Staritsa.

To defend the northern banks of the Volga, 22nd and 29th Army commanders are to put a regiment of antitank guns on trucks to the region east of Staritsa covering the approach to Kalinin.

Send 174th Rifle Division to Staritsa to cover direction towards Rzhev.

Chief of Garrison of Kalinin ordered from his garrison to cover Boriskovo, Pokrovskoye.

If the enemy breaks into Kalinin, request one rifle division and one tank brigade from the High Command reserve to Western Front at Kalinin.

Signed: Zhukov, Sokolovsky, Bulganin

References: *Russkii Arkhiv 15 (4/1), TERRA, Moscow, 1997, 'Bitva pod Moskvoi sbornik dokumentov' ('Battle of Moscow, collection of documents'), Document # 68, pp. 101–2.*
Comments: *This is the first Soviet document that specifically addresses the defense of Kalinin and the Kalinin area, and it shows some of the problems under which the Soviet command was laboring. 1st Panzer Division will be in Staritsa by the afternoon of October 12th, and on the following day will overrun everything on the road from Staritsa to the outskirts of Kalinin. On the date of this order, the Kalinin garrison consists of a few NKVD police troops, Northwestern Front's junior officers' school, and some militia armed with old Canadian Army rifles. Alone, they do not have the slightest hope of defending the city against 1st Panzer Division. A rifle division and tank brigade arriving after the Germans have entered Kalinin will be much, much too late to do more than try to counterattack and drive them back out: a tall order since the Germans are heading for Kalinin from the southwest and south with most of a corps!*

Report from Western Front to the High Command on Measures for the Defeat of the Enemy Offensive in the Kalinin Direction

[Undated]

On Direct (Wire)

Deliver Immediately

T. (Comrade) Stalin

Reporting our views on destroying the enemy group at Kalinin and preventing its movement on Moscow:

1. On 14 and 15.10 (1941) attack the group with all aviation from the High Command Reserve, aviation of Northwestern Front and units of aviation from the right flank of Western Front.

2. On the same days elements of 5th Rifle Division, units from Khomenko (*translator's Note: 30th Army*), worker's and destruction detachments stubbornly defend the outskirts of the city, not allowing the enemy to capture the city itself.

From the area of Bezborodovo, where today (are) concentrating a motorcycle regiment and a reinforced rifle regiment, on the morning of 14.10 advance in the area of Gorodnya, Mezhevo, and from there launch an attack in the direction of Salygino into the flank of the enemy.

Collect over the next two days a group consisting of four rifle divisions in the area of Staritsa, Gorky, from where three rifle divisions can strike into the rear of the enemy in the overall direction of Ryazanove. One rifle division can cover that group from the south.

In the course of two days send from Northwestern Front 8th Tank Brigade, one rifle division to the area of Mednoye and attack towards the city.

By 14.10 send to the area of Zavidovo a tank brigade from High Command Reserve, from there to attack together with aviation, a motorcycle battalion and a rifle regiment in the direction of Salygino.

Beginning of the Operation: 16.10. Request approval.

Zhukov

Bulganin.

Reference: *Maistrovskii, M. Ya. (ed.), Na pravom flange Moskovskoye bitvy ('On the Right Flank of the Battle of Moscow'), Tver: Mosk. Rabochii, 1991, pp. 15–16*
Comments: *This 'report', actually a message sent directly to Stalin from Zhukov at Western Front HQ, is undated, but from context must have been sent on October 13th. It lays out almost exactly what Konev and the Soviet command will attempt at Kalinin over the next two weeks. Of course, very little will happen exactly as planned, not least because Zhukov and the Western Front staff have underestimated the speed and strength of German forces heading for Kalinin. Otherwise, they could not expect two tank brigades, two rifle regiments and the equivalent of three motorcycle battalions to attack and destroy XXXXI Motorized Corps' two divisions and one brigade, or that on October 14th–15th the outskirts of Kalinin will be defended – that is already happening on October 13th.*

Military Combat Order of 29th Army: Lieutenant General Maslennikov
Dated 13 October 1941

Military Combat Order No. 028 Staff 29th Army (at) Alenino 13.10.41 1530 (hours) Map 500,000

1. Enemy units have reached the front ZUBTSOV, POGORELOYE-GORODISHCHE and are reported moving in the Kalinin direction.

2. 29th Army in accordance with directive from the Military Soviet of the Front is to pull back to the northern bank of the Volga and occupy defenses on a line STARITSA, MOSCOW SEA.

3. On the right 22nd Army is still retreating.

On the left – 30th Army is retreating to a line STARITSA, MOSCOW SEA, which it will defend together with our army.

4. 119th Rifle Division is to immediately retreat through ALENINO, MEDVEDEVO, RZHEV, MANUILOVO, KALEDINO and by the end of the day October 14th concentrate in the area of STARITSA, taking up defense of the west bank of the Volga and south of the STARITSA River.

Boundary to the right – SOROKINO, to the STARITSA River, west of STARITSA.

5. 178th Rifle Division is to retreat through AFANASOVO, MURAVYEVO to the bridge 5 km northwest of RZHEV and GRISHINO. Onward through TIMOFEYEVO, GLEVOVO, PLOTNIKOVO, METININO, KLIMOVO and by the end of the day October 14th concentrate in the area of BELY, NOVOYE, SHAVKOVO, and take up defense to the southwest, south and to the STARITSA river.

6. 220th Rifle Division, subordinated to Group SMIRNOV, will move out of KHOLMIKA to PODDUVYE, moving through POLOZ, KULNEVO, MEDVEDEVO, RZHEV, ALEKSINO, together with the Border Regiment at PODDUVE, and by the end of the day October 14th concentrate in the area of KALEDINO, taking up defense of the west bank of the Volga as far as south of the line NASHCHEKINO, KRUSHCHOVO.

Boundary to the right – MISHINO, NASHCHEKINO, MANUILOVO.

7. 115th Reserve Regiment will take up defense of the line of the west bank of the Volga on the front TROITSKOYE, ISAKOVO. To take up defense by the end of the day October 14th.

8. 250th Rifle Division, subordinating to itself 916th Rifle Regiment, and elements of 247th Rifle Division in the area of the division or along the march route, will retire, conducting battle on the line LEBEDEVO, ALENINO, AFANASOVO, driving from MURAVYEVO to the bridge 5 km northwest of RZHEV to GRISHINO. By the end of the day October 14th concentrate in the area of ZALKOVO, GLEBOVO, PANINO, and take up defense of a front to the west and southeast of a line through LIPUNOVO.

9. 252nd Rifle Division will cover elements of the army crossing the Volga

River, then turn to defense of the line PANINO, TURVAYEVO, left flank on the Volga. Defend in place until the rest of the army has crossed the Volga, not allowing the enemy into RZHEV through ZUBTSOV, OSUGA. By the end of the day October 14*th* withdraw through RZHEV to KLESHNEVO, BEZGACHEVO and, taking control of 115th Reserve Regiment, take up defense of the line TROITSKOYE, ISAKOVO.

10. 174th Rifle Division to cover the retreat of the army, strongly defending the line of the north bank of the Volga from the mouth of the DUNKA River, (including) ZUBTSOV. Defend until end of the day October 15th.

11. Colonel (comrade) Miroshnichenko, taking control of 13th Border Guard Unit and reserve units in RZHEV, will keep order in the rear of the retreating forces.

12. Elements of the army will retreat no faster than 50–70 km per 24 hours.

13. ARTILLERY:

a/ To be allocated as follows:

178th Rifle Division – 3rd Bn, 432nd Howitzer Regiment and a battery of 213th Antitank Battalion

252nd Rifle Division – a battery of 213th Antitank Battalion and a battery of 122mm howitzers from 119th Rifle Division

119th Rifle Division – 432nd Howitzer Regiment minus 3rd Bn and a battery of 873rd Antitank Regiment

250th Rifle Division with its own units.

Antitank Reserve – two batteries of antitank guns [*from 873rd marked in by hand*], one battery of 213th Antitank Battalion and a battery of 76mm guns.

b/ With the divisions observe all readiness to attack enemy infantry and tanks.

c/ Artillery control – march with the divisions, distributed through the columns according to the orders of the divisional artillery commander.

d/ To control artillery fire prepare to focus on the following areas:

178th and 119th Rifle Divisions – POKROVSKOYE, BOROZDINO and the front of the northeast. 252nd Rifle Division to the area of KRUSHCHOVO and the front to the east and southeast. 250th Rifle Division from the area of LIPUNOVO and the front to the south and southwest.

e/ Base for fuel supply up to 1400 hrs October 14th – MEDVEDOVO, to the end of the day October 15th – PANINO/ northeast of RZHEV. Base for ammunition supply to the end of October 14th – MONCHAKOVO and later PANINO.

14. Command Post on October 14th – woods 1 km northeast of RZHEV and later LIPUNOVO.

Commander 29th Army: Lieutenant General Maslennikov

Member of Military Soviet: Division Commissar Gurov

Chief of Staff, 29th Army: Major General Sharapov

Chief of Operations: Lieutenant Colonel Kronik

[*NOTE: Kronik's is the only signature that actually appears on the document*]

Reference: *TsAMO, F. 208, op. 2511, D. 62, from website:* http://podvig-naroda.mil.ru/

Comments: *This is a good example of how even a Soviet command (29th Army) that still has relatively good control over its own forces can be caught short when German forces are 'running loose'. Contrary to Paragraph 3, 30th Army is not 'retreating', it is disintegrating and there are no intact Soviet units south of the Volga River on this date, except for the units defending the city of Kalinin. Staritsa has already fallen to 1st Panzer Division and the Germans are fighting for the outskirts of Kalinin. Luckily for 29th Army, none of the German panzer thrusts is aimed directly at them, and the army and its units will have some 'breathing space' to get a grip on the situation.*

Report of the Chief of Staff of the Red Army to I.V. Stalin on Actions to Counter the Kalinin Group of the Enemy

Dated 13 Oct 41

13 Oct 41 commander of Northwestern Front is ordered to concentrate 8th Tank Brigade and a motorcycle regiment in the region of Torzhok and a rifle division out of his reserves and attack the enemy in the direction of Kalinin.

Signed: Shaposhnikov

Reference: *Russkii Arkhiv 15 (4/1), TERRA, Moscow, 1997, 'Bitva pod Moskvoi sbornik dokumentov' ('Battle of Moscow, collection of documents'), Document 70, p. 103.*

Comments: *On the same day that 29th Army thinks it is going to be defending Staritsa, the Stavka in Moscow is already looking up the road to Kalinin. Following up within hours on Zhukov's initial assessment and letter to Stalin, the Stavka is setting in motion the forces Zhukov requested. Within a short time, reflecting the appreciation of how much more the Germans have in Kalinin area, the forces ordered south from Northwestern Front will more than double.*

Operational Summary by the Staff of Western Front of the Locations and Military Activities of the Forces of the Front

No. 0350/219 dated 14 Oct 41 2000 hrs

22nd Army – enemy on the army's front were active during the day but with no (major) developments.

249th Rifle Division defending the line Bol. Ramenye, Sig [*Seliger*] lake, Volga [river], Selizharovo, B. Kosha

179th Rifle Division and one regiment of 174th Rifle Division defending line of (exclusive) B. Kosha, Povadino, Yeltsy, to the river Ytomlya

186th Rifle Division defending line of (excluding) river Ytomlya, Filatovo, Par [15 km northwest of Rzhev]

256th Rifle Division in region of Kalinin

133rd Rifle Division had elements arriving in region of Vereya. At 1000 hrs 14 Oct on thirteen echelons [trains] [*NOTE: originally said 1600 hrs 13 Oct*] due to all arrive by end of 14 Oct

Army Staff at Tsyatskoye (4 km east of Kuvshinovo)

29th Army – defending left bank of Volga River covering Gubino, Rzhev. 178th and 119th Rifle Divisions, on 14 Oct concentrating in the region west of Staritsa; 220th Rifle Division, north of them, in area of Nov. Rukav, Zalkovo, Shchetinino, Panino (25 km northeast of Rzhev); 252nd Rifle Division on 13 Oct at Dubrovinoya (8 km southwest of Rzhev) and Panino, on 14 Oct to move to north bank of Volga River to defend line of (excluding) Rzhev, Peskovo; 250th Rifle Division early on 14 Oct concentrating in area of Vysokoye, Neverovo, Shavkovo; 243rd Rifle Division on 14 Oct 41 'disengaging' (retreating) from area of Staritsa.

At the end of 13 Oct enemy units had reached line of Monchalovo, Kortovo, Makarovo, to the south and southwest enemy tank columns were in Aleksino (15 km northeast of Zubtsov), infantry were near Lebedevo and Veretino (12 km southwest of Zubtsov)

In the afternoon of 13 Oct enemy parachutists seized the bridge at Staritsa

According to a report from the commander of 252nd Rifle Division units of 6th Tank and 36th Motorized Divisions were operating in a northwestern direction out of the region of Zubtsov.

Staritsa was taken by a reconnaissance group of the enemy on 13 Oct

A motorized rifle brigade has been sent to liquidate the enemy near Staritsa

Army Staff is at Medukhovo.

Signed: Sokolovsky, Malandin, Kazbintsev

[Sokolovsky = Chief of Staff of Front; Malandin = Chief of Operations; Kazbintsev = Military Commissar of the Western Front Staff]

Reference: *Russkii Arkhiv 15 (4/1), TERRA, Moscow, 1997, 'Bitva pod Moskvoi sbornik dokumentov' ('Battle of Moscow, collection of documents'), Document 71, pp. 103–5.*

Comments: *By now the Stavka has a pretty good picture of its own units, so control has been re-established after the panic of the first week of October. However, there is still considerable confusion over exactly what the Germans are doing: note the report (presumably from some subordinate HQ) that the bridge at Staritsa had been seized by German paratroops! The Soviet commands still had some trouble understanding just how fast German motorized troops could move, even after the dreadful experiences since June 22nd. The commander of 252nd Rifle Division has also mis-identified 1st Panzer Division as 6th Panzer Division, and has confused a single Kampfgruppe of 36th Motorized Division at Staritsa as the entire division – both typical mistakes when trying to get a picture of the fluid German operations. The most dangerous point, however, is that the Germans are much further east than reported: 1st Panzer Division, in fact, is already in the center of Kalinin and has seized the Volga bridges there by the time this report was compiled.*

Report of the Military Soviet of Western Front [to] the High Command and Chief of the General Staff of the Red Army on Plans to Destroy Enemy Tank Groups in the Klin, Mozhaisk, and Podolsk Directions
Dated 15 October 1941

As of 16.10 [October 16th] the enemy will have concentrated tank groups in the following directions: 3rd Tank Group 'Hoth' (6th, 20th, 10th, 7th Tank Divisions and 36th, 14th Motorized Divisions) towards Moscow by way of a) Turginovo, Klin; b) Lotoshino, Novopetrovskoye; c) Ruza, Kubinka. 4th Tank Group 'Höppner' (5th, 2nd Tank Divisions, 17th, 3rd Motorized Divisions) from direction of Borovsk and Maloyaroslavets to Podolsk.

To counter the enemy tank groups:

a) 21st Tank Brigade counter advances in direction of Turginovo, Pushkino, Kalinin.

b. 22nd Tank Brigade, an artillery regiment of PTO [antitank], battalion of RS [rocket launchers] from region of Teryaevo, Suvorovo to support by fire counterattacks against the enemy.

c) 20th Tank Brigade and an artillery regiment of PTO, 4th Battalion of RS towards Vasyukovo direction.

d) 9th Tank Brigade and an artillery regiment of PTO, one battalion of RS towards region of Mitenino, Mityaevo and a tank battalion and motorized rifle brigade in area of Yermolino.

Request from the reserve of the High Command antitank artillery regiments and tank units to advance routes at Klin, Novopetrovskoye, Kubinka, Kransaya Pakhra and Podolsk.

Signed: Zhukov, Bulganin, Sokolovsky

Reference: *Russkii Arkhiv 15 (4/1), TERRA, Moscow, 1997, 'Bitva pod Moskvoi sbornik dokumentov' ('Battle of Moscow, collection of documents'), Dcument 72, p. 106.*
Comments: *This is the order that started 21st Tank Brigade on the way to its raid into Kalinin, two days after Zhukov requested such a tank brigade from the High Command reserves. More interesting is that the Soviet intelligence on Panzer Group 3 has both 10th and 20th Panzer Divisions assigned: both are actually in Panzer Group 4 on the direct road to Moscow, well south of Panzer Group 3's operations.*

Military Combat Order of 29th Army: Lieutenant General Maslennikov
Dated Military Combat Order No. 030 Staff 29th Army (at) PASHINA 15.10.41 1130 (hours)

Map 500,000

1. The enemy, advancing his front, penetrated into the Kalinin direction,

forcing the Volga with an infantry division and sixty tanks, seizing SEMEN-OVSKOYE, KOLTSOVO, BAKHMATOVO.

2. 29th Army will concentrate in the areas of STARITSA, AKISHEVO and strike the enemy with two assault groups, penetrating in the Kalinin direction.

Right Group – 174th and 243rd Rifle Divisions and one howitzer regiment

Left Group – 246th, 252nd, and 119th Rifle Divisions, one regiment of Corps artillery and one howitzer regiment

3. On the right – 22nd Army is destroying advance enemy elements in the areas of SEMENOVSKOYE, KOLTSOVO, BAKHMATOVO.

On the left 30th Army is active in the area of KALININ.

4. 243rd Rifle Division with 510th Howitzer Regiment and one battery of 873rd Antitank Regiment will attack to the flank and rear in the STARITSA direction and destroy the advancing enemy.

The division will attack in three echelons guiding on the right on a front of 700–1000 meters.

5. 174th Rifle Division with 360th Howitzer Regiment (minus one battalion), and one battalion of 56th Corps Artillery Regiment and one battalion of 336th Corps Artillery Regiment, will attack together with 243rd Rifle Division towards PUSHKINO in the south to provide (right flank) protection for 243rd Rifle Division's attack.

Division will attack in two echelons.

6. 246th Rifle Division and one battery of 873rd Antitank Regiment and 432nd Howitzer Regiment will attack in the direction of AKISHEVO, RYAZANOVO, attacking the enemy who penetrated into the Kalinin Direction in the flank and rear, destroying them.

Division will advance in three echelons on a front of 700–1000 meters.

7. 252nd Rifle Division with 644th Corps Artillery Regiment and one battery of 213th Antitank Battalion will conform to 246th Rifle Division's attack in the second echelon and exploit its attack towards RYAZANOVO and the south.

8. 119th Rifle Division with three separate 122mm batteries will attack as the third echelon in the direction of AKISHEVO, RYAZANOVO, developing the successes of 243rd and 252nd Rifle Divisions.

9. Motorized Rifle Brigade after arrival of 243rd Rifle Division will be Army reserve in the area of SUKROMLYA, CHERNAVY, ILBINO.

10. ARTILLERY: Be in immediate readiness – during the approach

Duties:

1) Deny the enemy approaches to the south and southeast along the Volga on the line STARITSA, ULITINO, GORKY.

2) Massed fires to support the attack firing at enemy (defense) systems on the south bank of the Volga and in the areas of STARITSA, GORKY.

3) Deny the approach of enemy reserves and counterattacks from the depth (of the defense).

4) Prevent enemy tank attacks, by preparing the entire fire of the artillery on possible lines of advance of tank attacks.

5) Suppress enemy artillery which blocks the advance of the divisions.

11. 250th and 220th Rifle Divisions with their elements will continue to stubbornly defend in accordance with the orders in Military Order No. 029 and prevent the enemy from interfering in the operations.

12. Chief of Engineer Forces for the Army will gather all the army's resources for river crossing and local materials to support river crossing of the Volga River, prepared to ferry two divisions in the area of STARITSA and three divisions up to the line AKISHEVO, GORKY.

Readiness for the (crossing operation) – immediately

Additional (support) crossings – by 1000 hrs 16 October.

13. Start of the Offensive:

1) 243rd and 246th Rifle Divisions concentrate immediately, [be ready] no later than the start of the day 15 October;

2) second and third echelons no later than 1200 hrs 16 October.

14. Military Reports required:

a) On the concentration of the divisions

b) On the start of the offensive

c) During the battle, at least every two hours

d) On the reaching of objectives

15. Army Staff – at PASHINO

Commander 29th Army: Lieutenant General Maslennikov

Member of Military Soviet: Division Commissar Gurov

Chief of Staff, 29th Army: Major General Sharapov

Deputy Chief of Operations: Captain Razdershin

[*NOTE: Razdershin's is the only signature that actually appears on the document*]

Reference: *TsAMO, F. 208, op. 2511, D. 62, from website:* http://podvig-naroda.mil.ru/

Comments: *This is the order starting 29th Army's counterattack across the Volga. Notice that 1st Panzer Division and 900th Brigade in Kalinin are identified as an 'infantry division with sixty tanks' – which is actually a pretty accurate indication of the German strength on the ground, but seriously underestimates their mobility: three of the 'infantry division's' infantry battalions are in halftracks and the rest are motorized in trucks.*

Directive of the STAVKA of the VGK to Commanders of Western and Northwestern Fronts on Use of Forces of Northwestern Front in region of Kalinin under Commanders of Forces of Western Front

No. 003037 dated 1945 hrs 16 October 1941

STAVKA of the High Command orders:

Active forces operating against the enemy in the Kalinin direction will all be under the direction of the commander of Western Front, General of the Army Zhukov.

Signed: Vasilievsky

Reference: *Russkii Arkhiv 15 (4/1), TERRA, Moscow, 1997, 'Bitva pod Moskvoi sbornik dokumentov' ('Battle of Moscow, collection of documents'), Document 73, p. 107.*

Comments: *Kalinin was actually in the rear area of Northwestern Front (The Front junior lieutenants' school was located in the city). This order put the arriving forces from Northwestern Front's Operational Group under Western Front, consolidating the command arrangements in the Kalinin area. Zhukov, in turn, placed his Deputy Commander of Western Front, Konev, in charge in the Kalinin area as the Kalinin Group of Western Front, and on October 17th this command was redesignated as Kalinin Front.*

Military Combat Order of the Kalinin Group of Western Front: Colonel General Konev

Military Combat Order No. 1 Staff Kalinin Group of Western Front 2200 hrs 16 October 1941

Map 100,000

1. The enemy 36th Motorized Division and elements of 6th Tank Division have seized KALININ and are advancing up the road in the direction of TORZHOK.

2. Kalinin Group of Forces/133rd Rifle Division, 256th, 5th, 246th, 252nd, 119th Rifle Divisions, 8th Tank Brigade, 21st Tank Brigade, Separate Regiment/ by the morning of 17 October besiege and exterminate the enemy in the area of KALININ without allowing his advance along the Leningrad highway to TORZHOK or his withdrawal to the south and southwest.

I ORDER:

3. Commander 133rd Rifle Division. With the movement of your division into the area of BRYANTSEVO, KALIKINO all elements active in this direction/ 8th Tank Brigade and 46th Motorcycle Regiment/ I subordinate to you. (Your) Division will occupy the initial positions STAR, KALIKINO, BRYANTSEVO and by 1000 hrs 17 October start an offensive to the western and northwestern parts of KALININ to master the outskirts of the city and having solidly covered the areas of KISELEVO, STAR, DOROSHIKHA to continue the offensive to ZHENTIKOVO to cut the withdrawal route of the enemy to STARITSA.

8th Tank Brigade [will] support the infantry to the outskirts of the city of KALININ for fighting off counterattacks and antitank protection. Do not let the tanks get involved in the street fighting.

To the right of AKISHEVO is the route of 246th Rifle Division, 252nd and 119th Rifle Divisions of 29th Army. From the south towards the city of

KALININ come 5th Rifle Division, 21st Tank Brigade and the Special Regiment under the command of Major General comrade KHOMENKO.

4. 256th Rifle Division. [At] 1000 hrs 17 October will attack in the eastern outskirts of the city of KALININ to take the bridge over the Volga/railroad/ and subsequently into the city of KALININ.

5. Commander 30th Army Major General KHOMENKO/5th Rifle Division and 21st Tank Brigade, Separate Regiment/ will destroy the enemy in the area of SADKOVO and advance into the eastern part of KALININ. Do not allow the enemy to retreat to the south and southeast.

6. Commander 29th Army/246th, 252nd, 119th, 174th, 243rd Rifle Divisions/ [are] to continue the offensive in the direction of RYAZANOVO, POKROVSKOYE, cutting off withdrawal routes to the south.

7. Air Forces of Northwestern Front (VVS NWF)

a/ support 133rd Rifle Division, 256th Rifle Division, 5th Rifle Division and 21st Tank Brigade in the destruction of the enemy in the area of KALININ, not to allow the approach of columns from the south, to close the Moscow highway in the area of GREBLEVO, not to allow the enemy to leave KALININ along the Leningrad highway.

b/ Cover the group of forces in the area of KALIKINO, ZMEYEVO, MEDNOYE.

8. My HQ – ZMEYEVO. Operations Group (staff) – YAMOK

Signed: Deputy Commander of Western Front: Colonel General Konev

Reference: *TsAMO, F. 221, op. 1351, D. 40, from website: http://podvig-naroda.mil.ru/*

Comments: *This is one of the few written orders known to have been issued by Konev while his command was still Kalinin Group of Western Front. Unfortunately, the lack of an organized command structure in the improvised 'Kalinin Group' will seriously hamper implementing this order. For example, 5th Rifle Division will remain tied down in direct fighting for Kalinin city and the Special Regiment will not arrive from the Moscow Military District in time, so 21st Tank Brigade will make an unsupported 'raid' into the German rear instead of a coordinated offensive. Furthermore, Rotmistrov has moved his brigade into action faster than Konev realized: by the time this order was issued 8th Tank Brigade had already been fighting 1st Panzer's tanks for 24 hours, while 133rd Rifle Division was still on the march and not yet engaged. Finally, to expect the uncoordinated and outnumbered Soviet air forces in the area to support the ground attacks, interdict enemy movement, and cover their own forces against Luftwaffe attacks presupposes a Soviet air superiority that is simply imaginary.*

Operational Group Staff Northwestern Front: Colonel Ygolkin Message No. 2

Dated 16 October 1941

SPECIAL IMPORTANCE
Coded
[to] Commander of Forces Northwestern Front
Copies: Chief of Staff of the Red Army, Commanders 22nd, 29th Armies
Military Message No. 02 Operations Group Staff Northwestern Front. [at] V. Volochek

16.10.41 0500 hrs Map 100.000

1. The enemy on 14.10 occupied the western part of KALININ with forces of at least an infantry regiment, fourteen tanks, antitank artillery and mortars /supposedly [from] 36th Motorized Division/. By 1600 hrs 15.10 [they] started an advance up the highway out of KALININ to KALIKINO and the railroad; [we were] not able to repulse this attack. During 15.10 motor-mechanized units of unknown size and number have approached and occupied southwestern area of KALININ.

2. Elements of 29th Army – 174th, 243rd, 246th, 252nd Rifle Divisions – on a line STARITSA, VYSOKOYE, MARTYNOVO on 16.10 are attacking with all elements in the direction of KALININ to envelop the Kalinin Group of the enemy from the southwest. The right flank of the army – 250th and 220th Rifle Divisions – occupy a line along the VOLGA river from the area of GUBINO, ZUBTSOV, MOLOKOVO. Army HQ – PASHINO.

3. Forces of the Operational group of General Vatutin are continuing to follow the general instructions from Northwestern Front to concentrate on the line YESENOVICHI, SHEVELINO, BOROVOYE.

8th Tank Brigade, 46th Motorcycle Regiment, 934th Rifle Regiment, a battalion of RS [*rocket launchers*] and 16th Border Unit at 1600 hrs 15.10 were advancing on the northwestern section of KALININ, fighting off enemy counter-attacks supported by artillery and mortar fire with success and by the end of 15.10 the brigade occupied the line MEZHURKA, MALITSA, DOROSHIKHA, GLAZKOVO.

4. VATUTIN has decided: by the morning of 17.10 complete concentrations: 183rd Rifle Division in the area of ESENOVICHI; 46th Cavalry Division – BORZY,YILBINO, BOGUNOVO; 54th Cavalry Division – SHEVELINO, OSTASHKOVO, PENY; 185th Rifle Division – SVYATSEVO, B. PETROVO, BUDOVO; 698th Antitank Regiment – DIMITREVSKOYE, woods /2 km north of MEDNOYE/;

8th Tank Brigade and attached units on the morning of 16.10 will continue advancing against the northwestern part of KALININ, with the objective of seizing the northern part of KALININ, in cooperation with the left flank units of 29th Army.

Chief of Staff of the Operational Group of Northwestern Front
Colonel /Ygolkin/
Lieutenant Colonel /Abdulayev/

Reference: *TsAMO, F. 221, op. 1351, D. 63, from website:* http://podvig-naroda.mil.ru/
Comments: *This is Vatutin's report on the operations by his Group on October 15th, when 8th Tank Brigade and other units managed to drive the Germans all the way back to the Volga bridges. As a result, Vatutin was contemplating driving right into the city, but in fact on October 16th the Soviet forces will be driven back to the north and suffer serious losses. What is interesting, and a comment on the confused Soviet command climate in the Kalinin area, is that Vatutin is reporting to Northwestern Front when he is supposed to be under Western Front, and Western Front HQ (and General Konev, his supposed boss) is not even getting a copy of this report. As a result, in Western Front's own Combat Journal for October 15–16th, the operations of Vatutin's Operational Group are completely unreported.*

Directive of the *Stavka VGK* to Commanders of Northwestern and Western Front, Deputy Commander of Forces of the Western Front Colonel General I.S. Konev on the Establishment of Kalinin Front

No. 003053 dated 1830 hrs 17 October 1941

To establish control of forces in the direction of Kalinin the STAVKA of the Supreme Command orders:

1. Forces, active and (out of contact) in the Rzhev direction and Kalinin will become part of Kalinin Front which will be directly under the orders of the Stavka of the Supreme Command.

2. The composition of forces of the Kalinin Front will be 22nd, 29th, and 30th Armies of Western Front, 183rd, 185th, and 246th Rifle Divisions, 46th and 54th Cavalry Divisions, 46th Motorcycle Regiment and 8th Tank Brigade of Northwestern Front.

3. Commander of Kalinin Front will be Colonel General Konev. His staff will be from the staff of 10th Army. The Front staff will be established in the region of Bezhetsk.

4. The boundary with Northwestern Front: Poshekhonye–Volodarskh––Ostolopovo station–Akademicheskaya station–Lake Istoshno; Kalinin Front boundary with Western Front: Berendeyevo station–Verbilky station––Reshetnikovo station–KnyazhI Gory station–Sychevka.

5. Mission of the Front – defeat the enemy forces in the Kalinin region and liquidate the penetration between Western and Northwestern Fronts and the enemy threat to encircle Moskva from the north.

In the name of the Stavka of the Supreme Command [signed] I. Stalin, A. Vasilievsky

[NOTE: Handwritten on original document: 'Communicated 18 Oct 41 at 0630 hrs by telephone of comrade Stalin, A. Vasilievskii']

Reference: *Russkii Arkhiv 15 (4/1), TERRA, Moscow, 1997, 'Bitva pod Moskvoi sbornik dokumentov' ('Battle of Moscow, collection of documents'), Document 76, p. 108.*

Comments: *This is the order establishing Kalinin Front, which was supposed to end the 'command confusion' in the Kalinin area. Unfortunately, 10th Army, which is supposed to provide the staff of the Front, is far to the south in Southwestern Front, and will take a week or more to arrive and give Konev and the Front a functioning staff. In the meantime, Soviet command and control in the Kalinin area will continue to be improvised, which is usually a recipe for disaster in 1941.*

Directive of the Kalinin Group: Colonel General Konev

Military Combat Order No. 0122 Staff of Kalinin Group 18.10.41 2030 hrs
Maps 500,000 and 100,000

1. In the area of KALININ the enemy has concentrated one tank, one motor-ized and one infantry division, are trying with an insignificant group to attack towards MEDNOYE and in the south in the direction of TURGINOVO. 133rd Rifle Division made its way from MEDNOYE area [so that the enemy] group is cut off by the successful actions of the infantry. 133rd and 256th Rifle Divisions [are] conducting successful fights to the northwest and northeast and in the suburbs of KALININ.

2. Kalinin Group of Forces is to persistently defend the <u>banks of LAKE SELIGER, the VOLGA river, not allowing a break [out] of the enemy in the TORZHOK direction and to continue an encirclement and destruction of the enemy group in the area of KALININ between the VOLGA river and the MOSCOW SEA.</u> [*NOTE: underlining in red pencil or crayon on original document: not certain when it was added or by whom*]

3. 22nd Army/249th, 179th, 186th, 178th, 250th and 220th Rifle Divisions/ strongly defend the line of LAKE SELIGER, VOLGA river, to STARITSA not allowing the enemy to advance on TORZHOK from the southwest and south.

Boundary on the left, /including/ STARITSA station/including/ SHCHER-BOVO, VYDROPUZHSK, VOZDVIZHENKA.

4. 29th Army /174th, 243rd, 246th, 252nd and 119th Rifle Divisions/ cross the VOLGA river on a front STARITSA, AKISHEVO and continue operations to the right of the SHOSHA river, the main forces to continue to advance in a direc-tion RYAZANOVO, DANILOVSKOE with the objective to destroy the enemy group south of KALININ, not allowing it to withdraw in a southern or south-western direction. One rifle division will advance on the left bank of the VOLGA river towards KALININ.

5. Group of Lieutenant General VATUTIN /183rd and 185th Rifle Divisions, 46th and 54th Cavalry Divisions, 8th Tank Brigade and Motorized Brigade/ <u>to use the headquarters of 31st Army as a staff, forces of the motorized brigade and</u>

<u>8th Tank Brigade to destroy the enemy group broken in the area of MEDNOYE, by 1200 hrs 19.10 to concentrate: 183rd and 185th Rifle Divisions in the area of MARINO, STRUZHNYA, MEDNOYE, TROITSA,</u> [*underlining in red pencil or crayon on original document*] to be in readiness to strike through a ferry at AKISHEVO in the direction of KALININ on in the general direction of TURGINOVO. 46th and 54th Cavalry Divisions [concentrate] in the area of MOSHKY, AKISHEVO, STRUZHNYA in readiness for action in a direction through a ferry at AKISHEVO, LEUSHINO, LOTOSHINO with the objective of erupting into the rear of the enemy.

6. 133rd and 256th Rifle Divisions continue to advance with the objective of destroying the enemy in the area of KALININ and taking the city of KALININ.

7. 30th Army /5th Rifle Division, 21st Tank Brigade, Separate Regiment/ attack from the southeast towards KALININ not allowing the enemy to break [out] to the south and southeast in the direction of TURGINOVO and KLIN.

8. VVS: a/ [is to make] repeated attacks by all aircraft to support the destruction of the enemy group in the area of KALININ, not allowing it to advance to the north or the south from KALININ;

b/ [is to] cover the concentration of Group VATUTIN and [other] groups to the north and east of KALININ.

9. Command Post – SOF'INO/ 7 km north of KALININ/ Staff of the Group setting up in the area of BEZHETSK.

Commander of Forces of Kalinin Group: Colonel General Konev

Reference: *TsAMO, F. 221, op. 1351, D. 40, from website:* http://podvignaroda-.mil.ru/

Comments: *Some 26 hours after Konev was named commander of Kalinin Front, this document was issued from 'Kalinin Group' (of Western Front). Note also that it is signed only by Konev, not his Chief of Staff or Chief of Operations, and Chief Political Officer (Front or Operations Section Commissar) as would be normal. Command confusion indeed! The content of the order, however, is directly in accordance with the Stavka Directive: close off the German penetration to the north, south and east, and retake Kalinin and destroy the German forces there.*

Military Instruction 18 October 1941 from Operations Group Vatutin/staff

SPECIAL IMPORTANCE

[To] Commander 31st Army

Commander 8th Tank Brigade

Copies: Chief of Staff of the Red Army /coded/

I convey to you the orders of Colonel General Konev:

Command of 31st Army to immediately unite in their hands the direction of all troops, operating in the direction of TORZHOK, KALININ to include 8th Tank

Brigade and the garrison of the town of TORZHOK; and subsequently the motor-mechanized brigade of 29th Army, which [is] moving on 18.10 to the area of MEDNOYE and the TVERTSA river.

You must act without delay resolutely and vigorously.

Task of the forces of 31st Army: in cooperation with 29th and 30th Armies – destroy the Kalinin Group of the enemy and take KALININ. Private task [subsidiary task] – during 18.10 eliminate the enemy tanks that broke through, not allowing any to get away.

Immediately contact [your] subunits and comrade KONEV, who can be contacted by telephone: request BEZHETSK, and then MOLOT.

Report to comrade KONEV on the actions [taken] and copy to me three times a day.

Commander of Forces Operations Group Northwestern Front

Lieutenant General N. Vatutin

Military Commissar Operations Group Northwestern Front, Regimental Commissar Kochmarev

Chief of Staff Operations Group Northwestern Front, Colonel Ygolkin

18.10.41

Reference: *TsAMO, F. 221, op. 1351, D. 21, from website: http://podvignaroda-.mil.ru/*

Comments: *In the previously listed Combat Order of 18 October, Konev instructed Group Vatutin's units to use 31st Army Headquarters as a 'staff' (paragraph 5). From this document, it is obvious that 31st Army HQ was out of contact with both Konev's headquarters and the units it was supposed to control. In fact, Vatutin's Operational Group HQ would remain in control of its units until October 20th (see Vatutin's Directive Number 027 dated October 20th, below). Had Konev's instructions been followed to the letter, there would have been a serious 'command vacuum' north of Kalinin after October 18th as 31st Army struggled to find and contact the units, and the combat against 1st Panzer Division and 900th Lehr Brigade on the Kalinin–Torzhok road might have gone very wrong for the Soviet forces.*

Military Report from the Commander of Forces of Kalinin Front to the Chief of the General Staff of the Red Army and the Commander of Forces of Western Front on the Beginning of the Offensive by the Forces of the Front in the Area of Kalinin, Volga River, Moscow Sea

No. 0123 Dated 18 Oct 1941 2300 hrs

Map 1:500,000

1. In the area of Kalinin we have noted prisoners and dead from 6th Tank [*Panzer*] Division, 1st and 36th Motorized Divisions. In the area of Lotoshino established an enemy infantry division concentrating. Northwest of Rzhev the enemy forced the Volga River in the area of Bakhmutovo and attacking in a north-

eastern direction against elements of 220th and 250th Rifle Divisions. [Enemy] Aviation in the course of the good weather day was very active in bombing and ground attack actions and taking opportunities to fly cover against our aviation.

2. Kalinin Front, defending the line of Lake Seliger, Volga River to Staritsa, is continuing the offensive to completely destroy the enemy in the area of Kalinin, Volga River, and Sea of Moscow.

22nd Army is defending line of Lake Seliger, River Volga section to Sytkovo. 186th Rifle Division is pressuring [by] crossing [*swimming, in Russian!*] across in the area of Baumatovo against enemy to the north. 29th Army is defending from Volga River to Staritsa. 174th and 243rd Rifle Divisions are crossing to right bank of the Volga at Staritsa without support. 119th, 246th and 252nd Rifle Divisions crossed at Akishevo by morning 18.10 against one and a half divisions. 183rd, 185th Rifle Divisions, 46th and 54th Cavalry Divisions are making a march to the area of Torzhok. 133rd and 256th Rifle Divisions are leading 30th Army in bitter battles against the outskirts of Kalinin. 256th Rifle Division is busy northeast of the outskirts of the city, fighting over undesignated heights in this area. Units are entrenching, organizing labor and performing reconnaissance. Elements of 133rd Rifle Division seized area of Gorbatov bridge in Batino.

Losses and trophies are not known accurately. Units are experiencing great difficulties with the supply of ammunition and fuel. The combat units are weakly covered by [our] fighter aviation. The more numerous enemy air units act with impunity.

Signed: Konev

Reference: *Russkii Arkhiv 15 (4/1), TERRA, Moscow, 1997, 'Bitva pod Moskvoi sbornik dokumentov' ('Battle of Moscow, collection of documents'), Document 79, pp. 110–11.*

Comments: *In this report, Konev accurately identifies the units in Kalinin, where 6th Panzer Division had a detachment supporting 1st Panzer and 36th Motorized Divisions. His report is not entirely accurate, however: only elements of one rifle division actually got across the Volga. The phrase 'units are entrenching, organizing labor and performing reconnaissance' is a clue that they are not attacking, and that the overall pace of the operations to retake Kalinin is, in fact, slowing down. The last paragraph is one of the few specific Soviet references to supply difficulties, which must have been considerable: among other things, the German seizure of Kalinin had blocked the direct road and rail connection to everything north of Moscow and to Northwestern Front, making supply of 22nd, 29th Armies and Vatutin's Group very difficult. Compare also the comment in the last paragraph about the German aviation acting 'with impunity'. The problem was that the Soviet air effort over Kalinin, while having some successes, was uncoordinated, so that the Soviet ground commanders and units never knew when or where their own aviation would appear. Kalinin Front's own assigned air units would not appear over the battlefield until nearly the end of October, and then were too weak to have much effect.*

Military Order, Staff Operational Group Northwestern Front;
Lieutenant General Vatutin

Dated 18 October 1941

Colonel Rotmistrov

1. The enemy in the area of KALININ has been defeated. In the northern part of the city of KALININ, MALITSA and KALIKINO he is still engaging our troops.

Small groups of the enemy broke into the area of PODDUBKI, MEDNOYE, POLUSTOVO, where they have been cut off from their forces.

YOUR RETREAT IS A CRIME

2. I ORDER:

Immediately, without losing a single hour of time, return to LIKHOSLAVL, where together with elements of 185th Rifle Division quickly attack towards MEDNOYE, destroying the enemy group after breaking through to capture MEDNOYE.

Continue to attack towards KALIKINO and on 20.10.41 enter into KALININ.

3. Along the highway from TORZHOK to MEDNOYE is the detachment [under] comrade LUKYACHENKO. From the south by VOLNTSEVO is the motorized rifle brigade of 29th Army.

4. [I] require you to fully [take control] of yourself. [I] require the most resolute actions and high energy. Enough cowardice.

5. I [will be at] LIKHOSLAVL by 0700 hrs 19.10. Report every two hours.

Commander Operations Group Northwestern Front, Lieutenant General Vatutin

Military Commissar of Operations Group Northwestern Front, Regimental Commissar Kochmarev

18.10.41

[#]

Reference: *TsAMO, F. 221, op. 1351, D. 21, from website: http://podvig-naroda.mil.ru/*

Comments: *This order looks like the end of Rotmistrov's career: he had retreated from battle with his brigade without orders. Regardless of circumstances, that was enough to get a commander shot in 1941. In fact, this was Vatutin giving Rotmistrov another chance, when Konev was calling for his immediate arrest. Basically, Rotmistrov has to get his brigade back into battle As Soon As Possible Or Else. Rotmistrov was lucky to have been given the chance: he would pay back Vatutin in 1943, when his 5th Guards Tank Army would come forward out of Konev's Steppe Front in the Stavka Reserves to support Vatutin's Voronezh Front in the Battle of Kursk.*

Military Combat Order of 29th Army: Lieutenant General Maslennikov

Military Combat Order No. 031 Staff 29th Army [at] STANISHINO 19.10.41 1200 [hours]

Maps 100,000 and 500,000

1. Enemy tank and motorized divisions have taken KALININ and, building on the success in a western direction, parts of the motor/mechanized units have gone on to MARINO. On the roads from the south to KALININ reserves are approaching. [On] the Front MOLOGINO, STARITSA an offensive by up to two infantry divisions is being held by our units. Enemy aviation has been active in the air.

2. To the right – 22nd Army is conducting battle on the front OSTASHKOV, SELIZHAROVO, FROLOVO. Boundary with it: RZHEV, /excluding/ TORZHOK

To the left 256th and 5th Rifle Divisions are conducting battle in the eastern and northeastern parts of KALININ.

From the north from the area of BOIKOVO, VASILYEVSKOYE 133rd Rifle Division is attacking and from LIKHOSLAVL the 185th Rifle Division. From the direction of VYSHNIY VOLOCHEK, ESENOVICHI towards TORZHOK are advancing the 54th Cavalry Division, 183rd Rifle Division and 46th Cavalry Division.

3. 29th Army. The main part of its forces during the day 20.10.41 will concentrate in the area west of KALININ on the north bank of the VOLGA river and attack from the southwest, west and northwest in collaboration with 133rd and 256th Rifle Divisions to seize KALININ, advancing and destroying the retreating enemy.

4. 119th Rifle Division with a battery of 873rd Antitank Regiment and three separate 122mm howitzer batteries will follow the march route LIPIGA, ZABOROVYE, GILNEVO, STEPANKOVO and by 0900 hours 20.10.41 concentrate in the area of SHIRYAKOVO, GORODNYA, KALIKINO and with the seizure of a bridge over the VOLGA river attack the enemy in KALININ from the southwest and west.

When they arrive in the concentration area division HQ – SHIRYAKOVO.

5. 252nd Rifle Division with a battery of 213th Antitank Battalion, 873rd Antitank Regiment, and two battalions of 510th Howitzer Regiment will follow the march route VASILEVSKOYE, ZHIKHAREVO, GORODISHCHE, ZMEYEVO, MIKHEYEVO, NOVINKI, PODDUBKI and concentrate in the area of VETLINO, GLINKI, /excluding/ PODDUBKI by 1000 hours 20.10.41 to develop the success of 119th Rifle Division, after taking a bridge advance into the northwestern part of KALININ and destroy the enemy in KALININ in cooperation with 119th Rifle Division.

Once arriving in concentration area division HQ – GRIBOVO / 3 km northeast of PODDUBKI/.

644th Corps Artillery Regiment will follow the march route of the division and concentrate in the same area by 1200 hours 20.10.41.

6. 243rd Rifle Division with a battery of 873rd Antitank Regiment, two battalions of 510th Howitzer Regiment will follow the march route VASIL'EVSKOE, TREDUV'E, LIPIGA, IVANOVSKOE, ROZHDESTVO, TUTAN' and concentrate in the area VOL'NTSEVO, SEMENOVSKOE, GNILITSA Station.

By 1200 hours 20.10.41. take MEDNOYE, destroying the enemy in the area of MEDNOYE and continuing on, to ensure the basic support of the army group of forces from the west and northwest.

Once in the concentration area the division HQ – SEMENOVSKOYE.

7. 246th Rifle Division without 914th Rifle Regiment, with a battery of 873rd Antitank Regiment, 432nd Howitzer Regiment will follow the march route STANISHINO, TARUTINO, NESTEROVO, KOSHEVO, VERGLEVO, ZMEYEVO and concentrate in the area of GILNEVO, SUKHOI RUCHEI, BORKI and constitute the army reserve.

Concentration by end of day 20.10.41.

Once in the concentration area, division HQ – GOSTILKY.

8. 914th Rifle Regiment with its units on the east bank of the VOLGA river attack on the eastern bank in the direction of KALININ destroying staffs and base [units], signal stations, ferries, with the ultimate goal of seizing a bridge over the VOLGA in KALININ on the road to TORZHOK.

9. Separate Motorized Rifle Brigade will concentrate at MEDUKHOVO and continue covering the ferrying at KRUPSHEVO-OSINKI and SAVINSKOYE, not allowing the enemy to cross the TVERTSA river.

29th Cavalry Regiment, subordinated to the commander of the motorized brigade, will concentrate at OSINKI and push reconnaissance to MARINO.

10. The Group of Forces under Major General Khoruzhenko, consisting of 250th, 220th, and 174th Rifle Divisions and the unit under Major Smetanin /allocating all to the commander and freeing Major Smetanin/ [*NOTE: meaning merge Smetanin's 'ad hoc' unit into the regular units and send him back to his regular job*] with attached artillery stubbornly defend the line BERNOVO, BOGATKOVO, DARY, TSENTUROVO, covering the operations of the army from the south and southwest.

HQ Group of Forces – VANEYEVO.

With special pressure deter the enemy forces from advancing more than 10 km towards the main group of the army, defending on the lines:

1/ IUDKHA, PERESLEGINO, VOZHANKY, PESTOVO, TERPILOVO, HQ – TREDUBYE

2/ CHERNAVY, SIMONKOVO, UPIRVICHI, POLOMENITSY, LIPIGA, NESTEROVO, HQ – IVANOVSKOYE.

3/ GORKY, DMITROVSKOYE, KOSTINO, SUCHI GORKY, GOLKHINO, GILNEVO, HQ – MEDNOYE.

Liaison on the right with 178th Rifle Division.

11. ARTILLERY: On the march be ready to repel attacks by motor-mechanized forces of the enemy. Willingness to open fire – immediately upon their approach. Tasks:

1/ To defeat enemy units and destroy by fire equipment and manpower on the divisions' fronts.

2/ Not to allow enemy tank attacks, to cover by fire any potential direction of attack. Allocate up to 50% of the 76mm divisional guns to fight against tanks.

3/ Not allow the approach of enemy reserves from the depths.

4/ Artillery of 246th Rifle Division support by fire from the left bank the advance of 914th Rifle Regiment.

5/ To fight enemy artillery that opposes the divisions' advance.

12. Chief of Engineer Forces [is] to use army engineer and pontoon units to support 119th and 252nd Rifle Divisions, giving them the necessary forces and support.

13. All units and subunits are to have three days' supply of food, two complete refills of fuel and ammunition in accompanying rear support.

14. On the march, marching order is dispersed, with well-organized antitank and air defense. Upon meeting the enemy act boldly and decisively, destroying his tanks with fire from all arms and with fire bottles. Maintain continuous duplicate communications with the army staff and between units.

15. Army Staff [HQ] as of 1200 hrs 20 October – DUBOROVO.

16. Send reports:

1/ On receiving an order

2/ On reaching the line LAPTEVO, GORODISHCHE, TREDUBYE

3/ On reaching the river T'MA

4/ On reaching the concentration area

Send reports by courier officers and duplicate by radio.

Commander 29th Army: Lieutenant General Maslennikov

Member of Military Soviet: Division Commissar Gurov

Chief of Staff, 29th Army: Major General Sharapov

Chief of Operations: Lieutenant Colonel Kronik

Military Member of the Operations Staff: Senior Politruk Porshakov

[*NOTE: Kronik's and Porshakov's are the only signatures that actually appear on the document*]

Reference: *TsAMO, F. 208, op. 2511, D. 62, from website: http://podvig-naroda.mil.ru/*

Comments: *This order changes 29th Army's 'axis of advance' from one across the Volga into the rear of the German force in Kalinin to one to the east and northeast to cut off 900th Brigade and 1st Panzer Division and break into the city north of the*

Volga. Unfortunately for Soviet hopes, it was just too late, and the combination of miserable roads and bad weather for once will favor the Germans, keeping the 29th Army forces from moving fast enough to finish off 1st Panzer's Group Heydebrandt and 900th Lehr Brigade.

Military Order, Operational group Northwestern Front; Lieutenant General Vatutin

Military Order No. _____ Staff of Operations Group Northwestern Front

20.10.41 ___ hrs ___ minutes

Maps 500,000 and 100,000

[*NOTE: Order number and time information left blank in original*]

1. The enemy, while continuing to retain KALININ with 4th Tank Group /1st, 6th Tank Division, 36th Motorized Division/, reinforced by one infantry division – at the same time has pushed fresh forces out of the city of KALININ and has created a new group of forces in the area of RZHEV, ZUBTSOV, POGORELOE GORODISHCHE. In order to ensure its operation in the area of KALININ the enemy is still retaining small groups of infantry and tanks in the area of PODDUBKI and MEDNOYE, and is attacking on a line SYTNIKI, STARITSA with forces not less than three infantry divisions in the overall direction of TORZHOK.

The enemy air force remains active in the area of KALININ, attacking combat troops and into the rear areas.

2. On the right – 29th Army, [which] crossed the Volga on the front STARITSA, AKISHEVO, most of the forces conducting an offensive in the direction of RYAZANOVO, DANILOVSKOYE.

3. Operations Group Northwestern Front /183rd, 185th Rifle Divisions, Motorized Rifle Brigade, 46th, 54th Cavalry Divisions, 8th Tank Brigade/, destroying with part of its forces the enemy group, which advanced to the area of MEDNOYE, by the morning of 21.10 will finish concentrating most of its forces in the area of VASILEVSKOYE, ZABOROVYE, MALITSA, SEMENOVSKOYE, STRUZHNYA.

The challenge facing the Operations Group of Northwestern Front – cross the river Volga at locations AKISHEVO, PUTILOVO, DMITROVSKOYE, rapidly developing an offensive in the direction: AKISHEVO, YEMELYANOVO, TURGINOVO and through TURGINOVO to control KALININ, in collaboration with 133rd and 256th Rifle Divisions in the city of KALININ to surround the enemy east of the Volga river. In the future, having finished the enemy between the Volga and Shosha rivers, working closely with units of 29th Army and 30th Army, destroy the enemy in this area and not let them retreat south of the Shosha river.

4. 183rd Rifle Division – concentrate by 0600 hrs 21.10 in the area of ZABOROVYE, GUDKOVO, KUMORDINO, and during 21.10 prepare to

ferry over the river Volga through IZBREZHYE and PUTILOVO. The immediate task – by morning of 22.10 cross the Volga river and move though the areas of KRYUCHKOVO, MAKSIMOVSKAYA, BORISKOVO. In the future rapidly reinforce success towards PUSHKINO, TURGINOVO.

5. 185th Rifle Division with 8th Tank Brigade and 57th Pontoon Battalion /minus one company/ – immediate task, during the course of 20.10 destroy the enemy in the areas of PODDUBKI, GORODNYA, MALITSA, KALIKINO, by morning of 21.10 reach the front of the river T'ma, CHERKASOVO, MEZHURKA and establish contact with the 133rd Rifle Division in the area of DOROSHIKHA station. In the future, prepare ferrying sites during 21.10 at the sites SHCHERBOVO, MEZHURKA, cross the Volga and move on the front MIGALOVO, NIKULINO to subsequently take KALININ in cooperation with elements of 133rd and 256th Rifle Divisions.

6. Motorized rifle brigade, concentrate during 20.10 in the area of LIPIGA, KHREPTOVO, IVANOVSKOYE – the immediate challenge during 21.10 reach the Volga river in the area of PUTILOVO, CHAPAYEVO and by the night of 22.10 cross the Volga river, concentrate in the area of POYRADINO, SHULGINO, NEKRASOVO. In the future, rapidly build on the success in the direction of MAKSIMOVSKAYA, IVANTSEVO, PODDUBKI, blocking the retreat of the Kalinin Group of the enemy to the south.

7. 46th Cavalry Division and one company of 57th Pontoon Battalion, concentrate by 1900 hrs 20.10 in the area of VASILYEVSKOYE, IVACHEVO, SREZNEVO, immediate task – move to the Volga river and, during the course of 21.10 prepare 46th and 54th Cavalry Divisions in the area of VOEVODINO BRODY – by the night of 22.10 cross the Volga river and move to the area of BOLDYREVO, MOLKINO, YEMELYANOVO. In the future – working closely with 54th Cavalry Division, rapidly develop success in the direction of KALISTOVO, TURGINOVO into the headquarters and rear of the enemy.

8. 54th Cavalry Division, move by 2400 hrs 21.10 to the western bank of the Volga river in the area of VOEVODINO BRODY, immediate task by morning of 22.10 to cross the Volga river with 46th Cavalry Division and move to the area of PANAFIDINO, then DVORNOVO, KOL'PINO. In the future, in close cooperation with 46th Cavalry Division, develop success in the direction of PIROGOVO, MIKULINO GORODISHCHE, LOTOSHINO into the headquarters and rear services of the enemy.

9. Chief of the Engineer Forces of the Operations Group, prepare the engineer and pontoon units of the group for ferrying troops over the Volga river, getting them the necessary forces and means.

10. In the units and subunits have a three-day supply of food, full (basic load) of ammunition and two fills of fuel/lubricants, accompanying the supply columns with strong cover.

11. On the march move well dispersed, with well organized antitank and

antiaircraft defenses. Meet enemy forces with courage and determination, destroying his tanks with fire from all types of guns and bottles with flammable mixtures. Carefully organize all types of reconnaissance and monitoring. Maintain continuous, duplicate communications with the Group HQ and each other.

12. Group Staff – RAMUSHKY /20 km northeast of TORZHOK/ after 1800 hrs 21.10 Group staff – MEDUKHOVO. VPU after 1800 hrs 21.10 – STAN-ISHINO.

Commander of Forces Operational Group Northwestern Front, Lieutenant General Vatutin

Military Commissar of Operational Group Northwestern Front, Regimental Commissar Kochmarev

Chief of Staff Operational Group Northwestern Front, Colonel Ygolkin

20.10.41

Reference: *TsAMO, F. 221, op. 1351, D. 21, from website: http://podvig-naroda.mil.ru/*

Comments: *In this order, Vatutin and his staff take on responsibility for destroying the enemy north of Kalinin, crossing the Volga, cutting off the entire Kalinin Group, and then, in cooperation with the rifle units around the city, completing the destruction of all the German units in the Kalinin area. A tall order, especially since, as they will again over a year later at Stalingrad, the Soviets have badly underestimated what they are up against. The 'small groups of infantry and tanks in the area of PODDUBKI and MEDNOYE' are in fact, most of 1st Panzer Division and 900th Lehr Brigade, and the remnants of 8th Tank Brigade and the lagging 185th Rifle Division are not about to destroy them in the course of a single day! Likewise, given the problems 29th Army is already experiencing crossing the Volga and keeping units on the opposite bank supplied and operational, further attempts to cut off Kalinin in that direction, although operationally attractive, are risky indeed.*

Directive, Operational Group Northwestern Front; Lieutenant General Vatutin

SPECIAL IMPORTANCE

[to] Commanders 183rd, 185th Rifle Divisions, 46th, 54th Cavalry Divisions, 8th Tank Brigade and

46th Motorcycle Regiment

Copies: *Commander Northwestern Front*

Commander Kalinin Front

[*NOTE: Entire 'Copies' line is handwritten in*]

Staff Operations Group Northwestern Front No. 027 20.10.41 1450 hrs

Map 100,000

In accordance with the *Stavka* Directive No. 003053, 183rd, 185th Rifle Divisions, 46th, 54th Cavalry Divisions, 8th Tank Brigade, 46th Motorcycle

Regiment are removed from the composition of Northwestern Front and become part of the composition of Kalinin Front. Orders for the units will come from the Army HQ of 31st Army.

Staff Army HQ 31 – RAMUSHKY /20 km northeast of TORZHOK/.

Until the rear of 31st Army gets organized, material support and medical and veterinary services for the units mentioned above will be provided by the logistic agencies of Northwestern Front [operating] through the rear area of 31st Army.

Signed: Commander of Forces Operations Group Northwestern Front, Lieutenant General Vatutin

Military Commissar Operations Group Northwestern Front, Regimental Commissar Kochmarev

Chief of Staff Operations Group Northwestern Front, Colonel Ygolkin

Reference: *TsAMO, F. 221, op. 1351, D. 21, from website: http://podvig-naroda.mil.ru/*

Comments: *This order, apparently issued mere hours after the previous ambitious offensive plan, effectively negates that order. With Vatutin's Group HQ giving up control to a 31st Army command which doesn't even have organized rear services and supply, keeping up the pressure on the Germans in Kalinin is going to be very difficult. In fact, this inopportune 'hand off' of command north of Kalinin, coupled with 29th Army's problems moving forces northwards through the mud, gave the Germans just enough time to wiggle out of the trap they were in on the Torzhok road. In the next three days after this order was issued, 1st Panzer and 900th Brigade will make it back to Kalinin, albeit with serious losses that will require reorganization of the entire force by the end of the month.*

Index